INFANT AND CHILD
IN THE CULTURE OF TODAY

THE GUIDANCE OF DEVELOPMENT

BOOKS BY ARNOLD GESELL

THE NORMAL CHILD AND PRIMARY EDUCATION

EXCEPTIONAL CHILDREN AND PUBLIC SCHOOL POLICY

HANDICAPPED CHILDREN IN SCHOOL AND COURT

THE PRE-SCHOOL CHILD FROM THE STANDPOINT OF PUBLIC HYGIENE
AND EDUCATION

THE RETARDED CHILD—HOW TO HELP HIM

THE MENTAL GROWTH OF THE PRE-SCHOOL CHILD

INFANCY AND HUMAN GROWTH

GUIDANCE OF MENTAL GROWTH IN INFANT AND CHILD

AN ATLAS OF INFANT BEHAVIOR (TWO VOLUMES, 3,200 ACTION
PHOTOGRAPHS)

INFANT BEHAVIOR—ITS GENESIS AND GROWTH (with Thompson)

THE PSYCHOLOGY OF EARLY GROWTH (with Thompson)

THE FEEDING BEHAVIOR OF INFANTS—A PEDIATRIC APPROACH TO THE
HYGIENE OF EARLY LIFE (with Ilg)

BIOGRAPHIES OF CHILD DEVELOPMENT

THE FIRST FIVE YEARS OF LIFE:—A GUIDE TO THE STUDY OF THE
PRE-SCHOOL CHILD

WOLF CHILD AND HUMAN CHILD

TWINS T AND C FROM INFANCY TO ADOLESCENCE (with Thompson)

DEVELOPMENTAL DIAGNOSIS (with Amatruda)

GENIUS, GIFTEDNESS AND GROWTH (THE MARCH OF MEDICINE, 1942)

INFANT AND CHILD IN THE CULTURE OF TODAY

The Guidance of Development in Home and Nursery School

BY

ARNOLD GESELL, M.D.
DIRECTOR OF THE CLINIC OF CHILD DEVELOPMENT
SCHOOL OF MEDICINE, YALE UNIVERSITY

FRANCES L. ILG, M.D.
ASSISTANT PROFESSOR OF CHILD DEVELOPMENT

IN COLLABORATION WITH

JANET LEARNED, M.A.
PRINCIPAL OF THE GUIDANCE NURSERY

LOUISE B. AMES, PH.D.
RESEARCH ASSISTANT

HAMISH HAMILTON LTD.
90 Great Russell Street
LONDON W. C. I.

CONTENTS

※

[v]

CONTENTS

CONTENTS

PREFACE

This book was written and completed in the midst of a war which is bringing untold misery to countless infants and children. And the aftermath has not yet come. This book deals with the amenities of civilization; indeed with the refinements of child care. Were it not that the democratic countries are bent on strengthening the very cultures which are being assailed, one might well wonder why this book should be written at all. Even England, the mother country of the nursery school movement, is at this hour undertaking great programs in the field of child welfare. America has just allocated $6,000,000 for war nursery schools, which with participation of local sponsors may bring a total of 105,000 children into group care nurseries,—nurseries created to make additional thousands of women available for war production. And this is only a beginning. The present cultural crisis is making unusual demands upon our methods and standards of child care. In the post war period these demands will increase.

Now more than ever we need an adequate philosophy of child development to shape our social planning and our practices in home and school. It has become clear that the concept of democracy embraces all aspects of everyday life. This volume considers the deep significance of a democratic culture for the psychological welfare of infants and young children.

The concept of growth has much in common with the ideology of democracy. In the fifteen chapters of Part Two the growth characteristics of the early years are formulated in concrete detail, with special reference to the factors of maturity which must determine our whole outlook upon the nature and needs of the individual child. These growth characteristics are so fundamental that not even the most modern culture can supersede them. A culture is refined through a discriminating recognition of these characteristics. The relationships between a child and his culture are highly reciprocal.

It will be evident from the detailed character of the contents that this book could be written only as a cooperative undertaking. It is the outgrowth of many years of practical experience with normal, near normal and problem children. The experience was correlated with a systematic program of research under the auspices of The Clinic of Child Development of The School of Medicine, Yale University. Infants and young children have been studied with parental cooperation, in the home, at well baby conferences, and in the service division of the Guidance Nursery of the Yale Clinic. The development of personality characteristics of the children has come under consecutive observation by members of the staff. On the basis of this clinical and developmental investigation, detailed methods of individualized guidance have been formulated.

The children studied came from homes of varying socio-economic status in New England. A special group of fourteen Swedish infants was intensively studied by Dr. Ilg, in 1936-37, while she was in residence in Stockholm. The nursery school children have in general been above an average level of intelligence. The parents of all these children have assisted us with a high order of cooperation. We have learned much from them as well as from the children. We are also gratefully indebted to Miss Anne Lockwood, guidance teacher in the Yale Nursery, who assisted in the gathering of observations of children in her charge.

Dr. Catherine S. Amatruda, Assistant Professor of Child Development, read the manuscript in part, and gave us the benefit of valuable criticism. Dr. Amatruda is co-author of a volume on *Developmental Diagnosis: Normal and Abnormal Child Development*, published by Paul B. Hoeber, Inc., Medical Book Department of Harper & Bros. We wish to thank Mr. Hoeber for the special permission to use selected line drawings, based on cinema photographs, which appear as illustrations in Part Two.

J. B. Lippincott & Co. have kindly permitted certain references to an earlier publication by Gesell & Ilg, entitled *Feeding Behavior of Infants: A Pediatric Approach to the Mental Hygiene of Early Life*. The present volume is in many ways a further development of these earlier studies.

We are most fundamentally indebted to the Rockefeller Foundation, which over a period of years has given generous long range support to the systematic investigations which underly the present work. The more recent and extremely timely support of The Carnegie Corporation of New York has made the completion of this work possible.

The general plan and construction of this book are outlined in the Introduction. The practical details of certain chapters and of the Appendix, are clearly and directly addressed to professional and lay workers in the field of early child welfare and education. This would include parents as well as teachers, social workers, nurses and physicians. The material covering the preschool ages has been presented in such a way as to make it serviceable in the guidance of young children whether or not they attend nursery school. We have deliberately drawn no sharp lines between home and nursery school, and infants and preschool children. It is culturally very essential that the whole period from birth to six years should be socially treated as a single area and in consecutive sequence. Even the elementary school teacher might profit by more familiarity with the psychological development of the first five years of life, the most fundamental and formative years in the cycle of the child's growth.

We have used the term culture rather flexibly to denote not only organized institutions and folkways; but also the persons, chiefly parents, in the actual process of expressing those folkways by the rearing of children. We hope that the cultural anthropologist will find in the details of the main body of this volume a concrete documentation of behavior patterns which are delineative of the present day culture and its goals. Cultural anthropology begins at home, and this book deals with domestic behavior in its early relations with the social order.

America, more than any other country in the world, has dedicated its scientific resources and good will to the furtherance of the free development of her children. This is part of the genius of American democracy; and it is a part which should be cherished and protected even in a world crisis.

ARNOLD GESELL

New Haven, Connecticut
July 31, 1942

INFANT AND CHILD
IN THE CULTURE OF TODAY

The Guidance of Development
in Home and Nursery School

INTRODUCTION
PLAN AND PURPOSE

THE general plan of this book is evident from the analytic table of contents. We are dealing with the growing child in a modern culture. He is endowed with innate growth capacities which express themselves psychologically in patterns of behavior. But the culture has heavy demands to make on its children. How are the natural growth characteristics of infant and child brought into harmony with these cultural pressures? What are the relationships between the pressures of natural growth (maturation) and the pressures of the social order (acculturation)? The answers to these questions will determine our attitudes and our practices in the psychological care of infant and child.

The main body of this book, therefore, addresses itself in PART TWO (chapters 7-21) to a factual statement of the mental growth characteristics of the first five years of life. Twelve age periods are separately treated. The most typical traits and growth trends of each age are summarized in

[1]

a *Behavior Profile* (§1) and a *Behavior Day* (§2). By reading the twelve behavior profiles in consecutive series, it is possible to get an impression of the continuous flow of the stream of development. But for reference and comparative study, it is convenient to have all of the facts concerning a given level of maturity assembled in a single chapter. Indeed, this book is so constructed that each chapter is in large measure self-contained and can be read as an independent unit.

We regard the formal concept of chronological age and the functional concept of maturity level as indispensable both for practical common sense and for the science of child development. In the guidance of children it is absolutely necessary to consider the age values of behavior and the behavior values of age. The reader is warned, in advance, however, that *the age norms are not set up as standards and are designed only for orientation and interpretive purposes*. These precautions are discussed in Chapter 6 §4. The prevalence and significance of individual variations are recognized at every turn. Indeed, it is through the norms that we become conscious of such variations. The subject matter of PART TWO is codified in terms of age to clarify the generic, innate sequences of development, and to define some of the more usual deviations which determine the individuality of the child. The ages chosen for discussion are for the most part nodal ages which correspond to periods of relative equilibrium in the progressions toward maturity.

The *Behavior Profile* gives us a picture of the kind of child with which the culture has to deal at a certain stage of his maturity. The *Behavior Day* (§2) in brief informal narrative, outlines the manner in which the culture makes practical provisions for fostering the growth and the activities of the child at advancing ages. Both from a developmental and a cultural point of view, the *day cycle* is extremely fundamental. It determines the distributions and expressions of the child's energies. It reflects the methods and goals of child care in our present day culture.

The behavior day is illustrative and is not set up as a model. It is intended to give suggestive orientation. Behavior days will vary with circumstances and individual differences. Specific variations in behavior and numerous details of child care are summarized in double column under such headings as sleep, feeding, elimination, bath and dressing, self-activity and sociality. The reader may consider these details as elaborated specifications and footnote references which can be consulted for practical purposes. Concrete guidance suggestions are enclosed in brackets.

When a child reaches the age of 18 months, his behavior extends beyond the confines of the home. He goes abroad. He may attend a nursery school. His behavior has an enlarged cultural significance. Accordingly, the chapters which treat the five age levels from 18 months through 4 years (Chapters 15-19) carry special sections entitled *Cultural and Creative Activities* (§3), *Nursery Behavior* (§4), and *Nursery Techniques* (§5). These sections portray the life of the preschool child in the social group. Some of the detail is directed to nursery and guidance teachers; but the subject matter is treated in a functional manner which may be of interest to the general reader, as well as parents, and students of child psychology. The chapter on *The Nursery School as a Guidance Center* was written with the general reader as well as the professional teacher in mind. It is hoped that the chapters in their entirety, both descriptively and by implication, will not be without significance for the student of cultural anthropology. The child's behavior day epitomizes many important aspects of the culture-complex of today.

It will be noted that our presentation makes no sharp distinction between the infant and the nursery school child, also called the preschool child. The nursery school movement in America has been singularly detached and has taken slight note of the two years of infancy which precede nursery school attendance. Every nursery school child was once an infant; moreover, he spends most of his behavior day at home even when he is enrolled as a nursery schooler. The arrangement of Chapters in PART Two is intended to place these considerations in proper perspective. The relationship between home and school is obscured if the perspective is blurred, or if the home-life and the antecedent infancy of the child are overlooked. Certainly the nursery school cannot function intelligently

[3]

as a guidance agency unless the details of home behavior are more intimately appreciated.

Teachers in the elementary school grades also need the perspective which comes from a comprehension of the psychology of child development as opposed to the psychology of learning. The professional training of school teachers should include a liberalizing acquaintance with the developmental psychology of infancy to offset the stilted text-book limitations of an educational psychology too narrowly based on a study of "the learning process."

The underlying concept of the present volume is the concept of growth. This concept is essential not only for estimating the true nature of the child, but the reciprocal relations between the child and his culture. Indeed, one of the crucial tests of any culture-complex is the degree to which it gives scope to the nature and needs of growth, both in its children and adults. This test is of special importance in a democratic culture.

PART ONE, entitled GROWTH AND CULTURE, considers in a broad way the interaction of inner and cultural forces. The family is the pivotal center at which this interaction comes to most significant expression. The household is a cultural workshop for transmitting the social inheritance: a democratic household fosters a way of life which respects the individuality of the growing child. The child as an organism and the environment as a culture are inseparable. Each reacts upon the other. The reactions of the child are primary: he must do his own growing. The culture helps him to achieve his developmental potentialities, helps him to "learn," but the process of acculturation is always limited by the child's natural growth process. Child and culture come into conflict when the two processes are not balanced and accommodated to each other.

Chapters 2 and 3 consider the relations between maturation and acculturation. How does the mind grow? It grows like an organism in *a world of things*. It becomes a person in *a world of persons*. There are general, insuperable laws of growth which govern the patterning of behavior. But infants are individuals. Every child has a unique pattern of growth which is the essence of his individuality.

[4]

The guidance of development requires a discerning recognition of these factors of individuality, discussed in Chapters 4 and 5. Beginning with birth, and indeed before birth, as suggested in Chapters 7 and 8, it is necessary to recognize the import of individual differences. There are differences which cannot be combatted by culture with impunity.

It is rather the task of culture to be alert to the growth needs and growth demands of the child. He must do his own growing. He must achieve a measure of self-regulation. The fullness of that measure depends upon the insight and wisdom of the culture. Chapter 5 considers the problem of self-regulation through cultural guidance,—a peculiarly important problem in the culture of today.

The chapters of PART THREE return to a consideration of this broad problem and its implications. Child guidance is growth guidance. The refinements of the psychological care of normal and deviate child alike depend upon *a developmental philosophy*. A genetic approach is more important than rule of thumb and clever modes of discipline. A developmental outlook permits us to see the total tide of development in perspective. This gives a constructive forward reference to our methods and a more tolerant understanding of the difficulties of immaturity.

"Development" is often an empty abstraction. We have attempted to give form and substance to the concept of growth by formulating in abundance the specific patterns of behavior which express the maturity of infant and child. In chapter 23 we make a sweeping survey of the entire growth complex, including sleep, feeding, bowel and bladder behavior, personal and sex interests, self-activity and sociality. This survey is intended to demonstrate the interrelatedness and the lawful sequences of behavior patterning for the entire period from 4 weeks to 5 years of age. Developmental perspective gives both assurance and direction to the practical procedures of child care and guidance.

The concluding chapter (Chapter 24) reverts to our fundamental thesis: the significance of *a developmental philosophy* for the practice of child guidance, and for the folkways of our culture,—the culture of tomorrow as well as today.

The present tragic status of the world confronts us with three propositions: (1) democracy demands respect for individuals; (2) infants are individuals; (3) the science of human behavior and individuality can really flourish only in a democracy. These three propositions interlock in a significant way and testify to the social importance of a more adequate science of child development in a democratic culture. Such science will also lead to a more equitable distribution of developmental opportunities for infant and child.

A glance at the *end-papers* will give the reader a further indication of the scope of the chapters which follow. Altogether, some sixty-five photographs are assembled in a composite to show the progression of behavior development in the first five years of life. There are ten horizontal rows (five in the front end-paper and five in the back end-paper) covering approximately the following age levels 4, 16, 28, 40, 52 weeks, 18 months, 2, 3, 4, 5 years. The six vertical rows of the front end-paper represent respectively postural behavior, sleep, feeding, and bath behavior, manipulative and play behavior, and social behavior. The six vertical rows of the back end-paper depict postural control, manipulative and play behavior, feeding behavior, and various aspects of individual and social behavior. The pictorial half-title page suggests the various appurtenances and techniques of the culture in which the modern child is reared.

Surrounded by all these gadgets and conveniences, it would seem that his developmental welfare is amply safeguarded. But it is now all too apparent that the matériel of a culture does not in itself insure life, liberty, and happiness even for its children.

No previous culture has ever achieved a product more magnificent than the present body of natural and engineering science. This achievement is our hope, as well as our despair. The despair will not lessen until the techniques of modern science can be more sincerely brought to bear on problems of behavior. Only through profound self knowledge can the human mind bring itself nearer to individual and collective control. This knowledge must begin with an understanding of infants and young children. And that knowledge must extend into the homes of the people; for the household is the "cultural workshop" where human relationships are first formed.

PART ONE

GROWTH AND CULTURE

1

THE FAMILY IN A DEMOCRATIC CULTURE

§1. THE HOUSEHOLD AS A CULTURAL WORKSHOP

THE family remains the most fundamental unit of modern culture. It has been basic throughout the long history of man. The family is both a biological and a cultural group. It is biologic in the sense that it is the best arrangement for begetting children and protecting them while they are dependent. It is a cultural group because it brings into intimate association persons of different age and sex who renew and reshape the folkways of the society into which they are born. The household serves as a "cultural workshop" for the transmission of old traditions and for the creation of new social values.

The spirit and organization of the family therefore reflect the historic culture. A totalitarian "Kultur" subordinates the family completely to the state, fosters autocratic parent-child relationships, favors despotic discipline, and relaxes the tradition of monogamy. It is not concerned with the individual as a person. A democratic culture, on the contrary, affirms the dignity of the individual person. It exalts the status of the family as a social group, favors reciprocity in parent-child relationships, and encourages humane discipline of the child through guidance and understanding.

In a very profound way the democratic ideal is also bound up with the spirit of liberty. Liberty is the life principle of democracy, in the home as well as in the community. The home, like the state, has its problems of government and must give controlled scope to the spirit of liberty which animates the growing child. Every living organism strives to attain a maximum of maturity. The spirit of liberty has its deepmost roots in the biological impulse toward optimal growth. Babies as well as adults are endowed with this inalienable impulsion.

The concept of democracy, therefore, has far-reaching consequences in the rearing of children. Even in early life the child must be given an opportunity to develop purposes and responsibilities which will strengthen his own personality. Considerate regard for his individual characteristics is the first essential.

Considerateness, it has been well said, is in itself a social system. The very word conveys the idea of respect for the dignity of the individual. If parents and teachers begin with the assumption that they can make over and mold a child into a preconceived pattern, they are bound to become autocratic. If, on the contrary, parents begin with the assumption that every baby comes into the world with a unique individuality, their task will be to interpret the child's individuality and to give it the best possible chance to grow and find itself.

Considerateness, as we use the term here, is not merely a social grace. It is something of an art, a combination of perceptiveness and imaginativeness which enables one person to appreciate the psychology of other persons. It is an alert liberalism which is sensitive to distinctive characteristics in other individuals. It is a kind of courtesy to which infants are entitled.

Infants are individuals,—individuals in the making as well as by birthright. To understand their individuality it is necessary to sense the underlying processes of development which are at work.

The child's personality is a product of slow and gradual growth. His nervous system matures by stages and natural sequences. He sits before he stands; he babbles before he talks; he fabricates before he tells the truth; he draws a circle before he draws a square; he is selfish before he is altruistic; he is dependent on others before he achieves dependence on self. All of his abilities, including his morals, are subject to laws of growth. The task of child care is not to force him into a predetermined pattern but to guide his growth.

This developmental point of view does not mean indulgence. It means a constructive deference to the limitations of immaturity. It obliges us to accord more courtesy even to the infant, who is often unwittingly handled in an arbitrary manner simply because we have failed to understand the processes of development.

Only in a democratic climate of opinion is it possible to give full respect to the psychology of child development. Indeed the further evolution of democracy demands a much more refined understanding of infants and preschool children than our civilization has yet attained. Should science ever arrive at the happy juncture where it can focus its full force upon the interpretation of life, it will enable us to do more complete and timely justice to the individual personality in the very young. And this in turn will have far-reaching effects upon the adult population.

§2. THE FUNCTIONS OF INFANCY

IN A biological sense the span of human infancy extends from the zero hour of birth to the middle twenties. It takes time to grow. It takes about twenty-four years for an American youth to reach the stature of maturity. For convenience one may think of this cycle of growth as a succession of four stages of six years each: (1) the preschool years; (2) the elementary school years; (3) the high school years; (4) the preadult years.

We are now beginning to see this cycle of growth in its true perspective. Thus far, for sound social reasons, the middle twelve years have received most of the attention of the public-school system. These are indeed important years for the transmission of cultural inheritance, but the demands of society and the findings of science are compelling us to see the cultural significance of the preschool years—the fundamental years which come first in the cycle of life and which therefore must have a certain priority in all social planning. Coming first, they have a profound formative influence on all the years that follow.

The extreme helplessness of the human infant has provided a perplexing problem for philosophers. Why is man, the king of creation, the most dependent of all creatures during his early life? Over a century ago, Madame Necker de Saussure answered this question in quaint but convincing language:

"If it was the design of the Creator in respect to man that the immortal spirit should receive a strong impulse from the present life, the means of making him pursue the most extended course of development was to place him the lowest degree at its beginning. Hence his state of privation and ignorance in infancy.

"Preoccupied with considering what is wanting in the child, we forget the liberality of nature with respect to him. We do not observe that the order of development made necessary by his ignorance is the most advantageous to morality as well as to the progress of his reason."

These statements show a deep genetic insight into the meaning of infancy. They are all the more creditable, because they antedate the period of modern biological science, which has thrown such a flood of light on the nature and origins of man.

Darwin's epoch-making book, THE ORIGIN OF SPECIES, led to the revolutionary concept that human infancy was evolved to subserve the needs of racial inheritance and of individual growth. Infancy, in this sense, is a positive, adaptive trait,—one of the major end-products of ages of evolution. During these ages the period of human infancy has been gradually prolonged. It is man's distinction that he has the longest infancy.

Some creatures have virtually no infancy at all. Some birds are so precocious that they fly immediately on hatching. The golden eaglet, however, requires eleven weeks before it spreads its giant wings in full flight. Not until the age of 12 weeks is it buffeted by its parents and driven forcibly from home by them. The guinea pig shifts for himself three days after birth. It takes the white rat as many weeks. The chimpanzee becomes an adult at about the age of 9 years. The more complex and advanced the mature organism, the longer the period of infancy. It takes time to grow. Infancy is that time.

Human infancy is also the time for acculturation. The infant emerges out of the racial stream. Birth thrusts him into a man-made world crowded with the furniture, appurtenances and compulsions of a modern culture. One of the durable problems of culture is to bring about an optimal adjustment to this intricate world by supplying optimal conditions of child development.

The infancy of the human species has been prolonged and its plasticity has been greatly augmented; but the new-born baby does not by any means start from scratch. He is at birth already in possession of all the nerve cells he will ever have. These cells have much capacity for learning; but to no small extent their organization has been either fixed or channelized by the countless generations of a past which stretches back into a vista of a billion years. The infant of today is a token of that past as well as a promise of the future.

A baby is not only a specific embodiment of a future adult; he is a generic embodiment of the venerable past of the human race. He represents a vast cloud of ancestral witnesses compacted into a single individuality. He is the inheritor of the ages. His nervous system is the carrier of an immense series of evolutionary adaptations, by means of which the race consolidated its most essential achievements. These achievements are now the common property of mankind; but once they were creations.

The evolution of the human species has been a creative process on a cosmic scale. The human infant as the current custodian of that process revives in telescoped compression its immemorial creativity. He acts like a creator because he is basically a re-creator of what happened long ago, once upon a time. He is an innovator because he is a rehearser. Infancy is both conclusion and preface.

The nineteenth century is sometimes called Darwin's century. Darwin, through the concept of evolution, gave us a better understanding of the nature and the origin of man as a biologic species. The present century is preeminently concerned with man as an individual. If our democratic culture survives, the task of science and society will be to define the nature and the status of the individual. This task comes to its first and fundamental test in the family life of a democratic culture.

2

HOW THE MIND GROWS

THE baby has been born. What will he be like when he is grown? By the end of the first five years we shall have a fairly clear indication of his physical and mental "make-up". Even now, soon after birth, some observers note that "he is the very image of . . ." His nose may already have assumed its typical shape, although his head and other facial features are destined to undergo gradual transformations. Physical growth is a modelling process which produces changes of form, and at the same time preserves a basic constancy of form. That is the paradox of all growth,—the baby remains himself despite the fact that he is constantly changing. It might even be said that he is never so much like himself as when he is changing! This is because he has a distinctive way of developing which denotes the essence of his individuality.

§1. THE PATTERNING OF BEHAVIOR

MENTAL growth, like physical growth, is a modelling process which produces changes in form. Or we might say that mental growth is a *patterning process,* because the mind is essentially the sum total of a growing multitude of *behavior patterns.* A behavior pattern is simply a movement or action which has a more or less definite form. An eye blinks; a hand grasps an object; a tongue protrudes to reject an object,—these are examples of behavior patterns in which a part of the body reacts to some stimulus. Or the whole body reacts as in sitting, standing, creeping, walking. These too are behavior patterns. A baby lying in his crib follows a dangled toy with his eyes: eye following is a behavior pattern. He extends his arms and then closes in on the dangled toy with both hands, seizes it, puts it to his mouth: that is another more complex behavior pattern, one which shows that the baby's mind is indeed growing,—changing and elaborating its forms of behavior with increasing maturity.

Behavior has form or shape in virtually the same sense that physical things have shape. For practical purposes we need not make a sharp distinction between physical patterns and behavior patterns. The baby is a unitary organism and from the very beginning he grows as a single unit. Even in the embryonic period months before birth, the living materials of this organism order themselves into patterned structures. Millions of microscopic muscle cells assemble into bundles attached to ligaments and levers. Millions of microscopic nerve cells, marshalled by forces of growth, penetrate into these muscular tissues. In due time impulses will pass through the nerve fibers into the muscle fibers to bring about movements. These movements will have a certain degree of pattern. We shall call them behavior patterns as soon as they take on a characteristic form. The growing mind consists of countless such patterns of behavior, made possible by the progressive organization of the nervous system.

All growth, whether physical or mental, implies organization. Consider, for example, the early growth of eyes and hands. They are of particular interest because they play an extremely important part in the mental life of infant and child. The eyes are so important that Nature hastens to fashion them as early as the fifth week of the prenatal period. Each eye begins as a tiny cuplike bit of tissue. Within this cup the retina is formed. This retina consists of an extraordinary tapestry of specialized nerve cells which some day will be sensitive to images focused through a transparent lens. A portion of the optic cup becomes narrowed to form the optic nerve which terminates in an extensive jungle of nerve cells in the cortex or gray matter of the brain.

Later when a baby looks at an object he sees with these very brain cells. Looking is an active response. It is not mere sensory impression; it requires motor control. The baby must hold his eyes in position or move them from point to point in order really to see. This control is accomplished through twelve tiny muscles (six for each eye), which are attached to the eye ball and the eye socket. They are so tiny that they weigh only a fraction of an ounce. All twelve of them would easily go into a thimble, but they are among the most indispensable muscles in the baby's whole action-system. With them he fixates his visual attention; with them he scans his surroundings; with them he inspects objects which he holds in his hands.

Vision is so fundamental in the growth of the mind that the baby takes hold of the physical world with his eyes long before he takes hold with his hands. The eyes assume the lead in the patterning of behavior. But he cannot achieve full acquaintance with things through his eyes alone. He must touch them with his hands as well; feel their impact in his palm; and move his fingers over their surfaces and edges. Movement is an essential part of sense perception. He must move his hands to manipulate; just as he must move his eyes to inspect. The nerve cells which determine and direct his hand movements are located in the spinal cord and the brain.

The human nervous system consists of some twelve billions of nerve cells, and of countless nerve fibers which extend to, from, and twixt the bodies of these cells. The fibers are part and parcel of the individual cells

[17]

and by their inter-connections they make the whole nervous system a vast network which pervades every part of the organism,—lungs, gastro-intestinal tract, bladder and bowel, genital organs, secretory glands, heart, and bloodvessels; the sensitive areas of skin, mucous membranes, joints and tendons, a dozen special organs of sense and the muscles of head, neck, trunk and extremities.

The growth of the mind is profoundly and inseparably bound up with the growth of the nervous system. This growth begins remarkably early. Five months before the baby is born all of the nerve cells he will ever possess have already been formed and many of them are prepared to function in an orderly way. At this time the fetus makes movements of arms and legs so vigorous that the movements can be seen and felt through the mother's abdominal wall (quickening); the eyelids can wink; the eyeballs can roll; the hands can clasp; the mouth can open and close; the throat can swallow; the chest makes rhythmic movements in preparation for the event of birth, when the breath of post-natal life will rush into the lungs. All child development is like that; it proceeds with reference to the future. When the time comes the child is normally ready for what we may expect at that time. And he is never ready until the nervous system is ready.

How does the mind grow? It grows *like* the nervous system; it grows *with* the nervous system. Growth is a patterning process. It produces patterned changes in the nerve cells; it produces corresponding changes in patterns of behavior.

Let us examine further the development of eyes and hands. This will give us a concrete indication of the "structure" of the growing mind. The mind has structure in the sense that it is a unified, though intangible fabric constituted of patterns of behavior,—patterns which multiply and elaborate as the baby's nervous system matures.

The eyes of a newborn baby are apt to rove around both in the presence and absence of a stimulus. After several days or even hours, the baby is able to immobilize the eyeballs for brief periods. Later, he stares at surroundings for long periods. When he is 4 weeks old we may dangle

[18]

a ring (a four-inch red embroidery ring attached to a string) in the line of his near vision: he regards it. We move the ring slowly across his field of vision: he "follows" it with his eyes through an arc of about 90°. This means that the nerve cells which control those twelve tiny oculo-motor muscles have ripened and furthermore have made patterned connections with the grosser muscles which rotate the head. The mind must be growing, because behavior is patterning.

The baby has a psychology even during these early weeks when he cannot as yet balance his head on his shoulders. But this ability, too, is just around the corner. At 12 weeks the baby's eyes can follow the ring past the midline, through a full arc of 180°. At 16 weeks he holds his head steady when in the supported sitting position; he can even "pick up" a small quarter inch pellet with his eyes.

The eyes are still in the lead. It may take the baby twenty weeks more before he can pick up that self-same pellet with his hand. The hands and fingers come into their own later (when the requisite nerve cell connections have ripened). However, the infant can hold a rattle and look at it while he is holding it at the age of 16 weeks. That is a significant mental growth gain. It means that eyes and hands are doing team work, coming into more effective coordination. Mental growth cannot be measured in inches and pounds. So it is appraised by patterns.

The 24 week old infant can pick up an object on sight. At 36 weeks he can pick up the aforementioned candy pellet, opposing thumb and index finger. At 40 weeks he can poke it with his extended index finger. At 15 months he can pluck it with precise pincer prehension and promptly put it into the mouth of a bottle,—instead of his own mouth. This is truly a remarkably complex behavior pattern, which denotes a high degree of oculo-motor control; also a high degree of postural control of head, hands and trunk; coordination of guiding eyes and prehensory fingers; suppression of hand to mouth reaction; inhibition of grasp for purposes of release; satisfaction in the accomplished feat. Recall, for comparison, the almost aimless roving of the newborn baby's eyes and hands. The advance in his behavior patterns is a measure of his mental maturity.

Now it may as well be pointed out here that no one taught the baby this progressive series of eye-hand behaviors. He scarcely taught himself. He comes into his increasing powers primarily through intrinsic growth forces which change the inmost architecture of his nervous system. Of course he needs an environment in which to deploy his powers, and a favorable environment insures a favorable realization of his growth potentialities. In the next chapter we shall show how profoundly the organization of the personality of the child is influenced by the culture in which he lives. But the growth of personality is subject to the same growth laws which determine the development of eye-hand behaviors. Environmental factors support, inflect and modify; they do not generate the progressions of development. The sequences, the progressions come from within the organism.

What is the organism? It is living, growing protoplasm. The mind, so far as we can fathom it by direct observation, is an expression of the organization of this protoplasm, manifested in visible patterns of behavior. One of the scriptural parables relates how "the earth bringeth forth fruit of herself: first the blade, then the ear, after that the full corn in the ear." The growth of the child mind is not altogether unlike the growth of a plant. Of itself it brings forth its tokens; it follows inborn sequences. The tokens, however, we shall agree, are infinitely greater in their variety,—and much more exciting!

The plant has no structure which can compare in complexity with the myriad-celled nervous system. The nervous system with its prodigious capacities of growth and learning is the medium through which the mental life of the child is organized in terms of the past, and projected forward in terms of the future. This mental life embraces three levels of reality: (1) *the vegetative functions* of respiration, alimentation, elimination; (2) *the world of things,* in time and space; (3) *the world of persons,* in home and community. The child develops as an integrated unit, and he must simultaneously combine his adjustments at all three levels of reality. His mind does not grow on the installment plan. It grows as a unit.

The vegetative functions are governed by the so-called vegetative nervous system and are already highly organized by the time of birth. But not completely organized; because even physiological processes undergo change with age. Moreover certain rhythms of sleep, feeding and elimination must be adjusted to the culture into which the baby is born. We shall discuss this aspect of mental growth in Chapter 5.

As the mind grows it must become socialized. In some way the individual must preserve not only his vegetative existence; he must become a person among persons in a WORLD OF PERSONS. This constitutes the most bewildering task for the infant and child reared in the complicated culture of today. The organization of his personality depends on the manner in which he adjusts to human relationships. This phase of mental growth is so important that it will be considered in a separate chapter (Chapter 3).

§2. THE WORLD OF THINGS

IT REMAINS to sketch briefly the manner in which the growing mind accomplishes its more impersonal adjustments to the world of things,— the natural and man-made world of time and space. A famous couplet declares that the world is so full of a number of things that we all should be as happy as kings. But the realm of happiness lies rather more in the vegetative functions and in the romantic world of persons. In this chapter we confine ourselves to the physics and geometry of things, the most rudimentary rudiments of the science of Time and Space.

Grown adults take time and space for granted; not so the growing baby. The infant is not a scientist, yet he must master the very first principles on which all physical science is based. His mind is constantly taking first steps into the physical universe from the moment of birth. He has to acquire an appreciation of spatial *here* and *there* and temporal *now* and *then* by the gradual process of development. Perceptions are complicated behavior patterns based on reactions to things. He is not born with full-fledged perceptions; *they grow*. They grow with experience, and with the advancing maturity of his sensory, motor and correlating nerve cells.

It has been picturesquely suggested that to the newborn baby the world is a "big, blooming, buzzing confusion". The accuracy of this characterization may be questioned. Much more probably the young baby senses the visible world at first in fugitive and fluctuating blotches against a neutral background. Sounds likewise may be heard as shreds of wavering distinctness against a neutral background of silence or of continuous undertone. Doubtless he feels the pressure of his seven pound weight as he lies on his back. Perhaps this island of pressure sensation is at the very core of his vague and intermittent sense of self. He also feels from time to time the vigorous movements which he makes with mouth, arms and legs. Doubtless he has delightful moments of subjectivity at the end of a repleting meal and he has episodes of distress from hunger or cold. Such experiences in association with strivings impart vividness to the early mental life of the baby; even though the outer world is still almost without form and void.

It remains formless until he can configure it with experience gained through his eyes and hands. He must first "learn" the art of wakefulness, and then he must "learn" to fasten his eyes on this object and that, and to unfasten them, too. The oculo-sensory and oculo-motor neurones are growing at such an extraordinary speed that he soon gives selective regard to the human face. He probably senses it as a pleasant bobbing blotch, suspended but not localized in space, interesting but undefined. He is still quite unsophisticated as to time and space, quite undiscriminating as to present and past, near and far. His present experiences are so discontinuous that it can scarcely be said that he lives in the present; for there is no present if there is no past or future.

Perceptions of time and space values are so complex that it will literally take the child years to perfect them. Just as his time experiences are at first discontinuous, so his appreciations of space are at first discontinuous; he senses merely the immediate space in which he is immersed; he does not sense its context. He is unaware of distance and depth. For him the visible world is a flat screen or a kaleidoscopic succession of flat screens. Not until he is about nine months old does he begin to probe into the beyond and the beneath. Slowly the relationship of container and contained dawns upon him. At that time he begins to thrust his fist intentfully into the hollow of an empty (or full!) cup. At that time also he extends his index finger to poke and to pry. This is the way in which he "discovers" the third dimension. Immediate space loses its flatness; it takes on the perspectives of depth, hollow, solid. Through ceaseless manipulation of objects he penetrates further into the topography and the solid geometry of space,—the relationship of *in* and *out, on* and *under, in front of, behind, beside.* Through his tireless locomotion, creeping, walking and running, he builds up a sense of *here* and *over there,* of *near* and *far,* of *wall* and *corner,* of *indoors* and *outdoors.* He masters these elements of domestic geography through muscular experience. The sheer processes of development thrust him deeper into the manifold sectors of space.

His conquest of formed space follows natural sequences which are based on the developmental changes of his nervous system. Note what he does with a crayon. At 2 years he makes a vertical stroke (imitatively); the horizontal stroke comes a little later. Later comes the combination of these strokes into a cross and into a square. Still later comes the oblique stroke. An oblique stroke seems quite simple from the standpoint of motor coordination, but it is something so different that it requires many months of additional neuron growth. We do not expect a child to draw a diamond until the age of 6 or 7 years. All of which goes to show how extremely complex are our perceptions and judgments of configured space. The abstract notions of space come still later. They are products of long and almost tedious growth.

The young child comprehends *under-the-bed,* before he comprehends *under-the-chair;* and he is no longer a young child when he comprehends underness in the abstract. At first the relationships are concrete and specific, not general. Only by slow degrees does he master such place and position words as "up", "down", "where", "go-away", "wall", "corner", "across the room", "across the street". As late as 30 months, a bright girl may think (ostrich-like) that she is hidden when she covers her face with her hands; and at the same age a boy's solid geometry may be so defective that he puts both of two legs into one pant leg! The spatial complexities of the game of hide and seek must wait until three or four years. The growth of the child mind is rapid in its general advance; slow in its minuter anatomy.

The sense of time undergoes the same gradualness of development. The psychology and the mathematics of time and space are interdependent. An aviator's sense of time may change when he reaches an altitude of six miles. Infants and young children are subject to the same accordion-like relativity of time and space. When a child is 18 months old he begins to grasp the meaning of "now". Not until he is 2 years old or older does he comprehend "soon". He is learning to "wait". There is little use in telling younger children to wait, in order to delay their reactions. But after the age of two, many children can and do delay when you say "Pretty soon". This shows, incidentally, that the appreciation of time and time words is dependent on motor capacity and motor self-control. The 3 year old begins to use the significant word "when", the temporal equivalent of the word "where". His sense of time has so matured that he uses the word itself, saying "Is it time for orange juice?" He also uses the word "today". He understands when you say "not today". Somewhat later he uses the word "tomorrow". "Yesterday" comes later still. When he says "last night" he usually means anything which happened the previous day or even earlier. Time words, like "morning", "afternoon", "Tuesday", "week", "two o'clock", "year" emerge in the child's speech as he matures. They come in a more or less lawful developmental sequence. They are used in concrete situations long before they are used as abstract notions. At first they are applied on the correct occasions, but without accuracy. There is much dramatic pretense of telling time from a toy wrist watch at four years of age; but a child may be 6 years old before he can make a discriminating verbal distinction between morning and afternoon. Concepts of time (duration) are more difficult developmentally than concepts of space (size). The 4 year old, for example, is conscious that he is "bigger" than the 3 year old. Later he realizes also that he is "older".

The sense of number shows the same slow advance as the sense of time. A 6 months old child is single-minded when he plays with a block. A 9 months old child can hold and bring together two blocks and give attention to a third. At one year he manipulates several cubes one-by-one in a serial manner which is the motor rudiment of counting. At 2 years he distinguishes between one and many. At 3 years he has a fair command of "two" and is beginning to understand the simple word "both". At 4 years he can count three objects, pointing correctly. At 5 years he counts to ten, pointing correctly. He recites numbers in series before he uses them intelligently.

At 4 years he can name one color, usually red. At 5 years he "knows" his colors. He names red, yellow, blue, green. Color is somewhat more advanced than texture. The varied adjectives which describe textures are acquired earlier: hard, soft, sticky, rough, gooshy, crumbly, smooth, etc., etc. While he is a preschool child his vocabulary grows in a rather orderly manner, keeping pace with the maturity of his experience. Sometimes, of course, his words and his experience are out of step. He uses words, with (to us) amusing inappropriateness; but his malapropisms are temporary; the word is soon suited to the reality. A verbal blunder is like a false move of crayon on paper. It is corrected with improvement of coordination. The child has to learn the meaning of words, by the same slow growth processes which pattern his perceptions of things.

Words also are things,—peculiar things. Whether spoken, written, printed, or communicated by mouth, phone or radio, they are both realities and symbols of realities. They are the expressions of desires and the tools of thought. Many young children believe that they think with their mouths, and there is a grain of truth in this confusion of thought with voice. The preschool mind is not mature enough to make clear distinction between inner and outer, between material and immaterial, cause and effect. "What blows?" A 4 year old child may say "Trees blow". He

[25]

thinks that the nodding of the trees stirs the air and makes the wind. At 5 and 6 he is likely to define a word in terms of use. The wind is "to make the clouds come", it is "to push the ships". Ten years later he will give abstract definitions of realities even more intangible than wind:—liberty. evolution, character. Abstract ideas, like concrete judgments, are products of slow, gradual growth.

Time, space, number, form, texture, color and causality,—these are the chief elements in the world of things in which the child must find himself. We have shown that he acquires his command of these elements by slow degrees, first through his muscles of manipulation and locomotion, through eyes, hands, and feet. In this motor experience he lays the foundation for his later judgments and concepts. He does not even count to three until he has learned to pick up and release objects one-by-one with eyes and fingers. Mastery of form, likewise, comes through motor explorations and exploitations. Even the simple relationships of up, down, in, on, under, require a mutual coincidence of maturity and experience. Conceptions of physical causality in the long run are acquired in the same manner. There comes a time when the child asks many questions,—*where, what, why, who,* and *how* questions, and, incidentally he asks them in this genetic order. They must be answered in words; but the words will not be assimilated unless the child's mental maturity and previous experience give them meaning.

In the rearing and guidance of young children there is a tendency to rely too much on the supposed magic of words. Sometimes the adult thinks, naively enough, that if the word is uttered loudly enough and often enough it will finally penetrate. Words do not penetrate. They only register; and what they register in the child's mind is often grotesquely different from what they were intended to convey. Words, however, have genuine power in the guidance of children when they are skillfully used and adapted to the contents and the tempo of the child's mind. In subsequent chapters we shall point out the kind of speech which the nursery school child and the pre-nursery child can comprehend,—words which register and bring about response and release. Attention will also be called to the importance of inflections, intonations and timing. All of these can be more effectively adapted to the guidance of the child when the immaturities of his growing mind are understood. In the present chapter we have indicated the basis and nature of these immaturities. The mind is a growing myriad of reaction patterns which mirror the physical world in which the child is reared. It grows not unlike a plant. But the mind is also a person, and as such it mirrors the reaction patterns of a world of persons. In the following chapter we address ourselves to these personal-social patterns.

3

PERSONALITY AND ACCULTURATION

THE baby grows up in a world of things. He also grows up in a world of persons. These two worlds are not, of course, separated from each other. Often they are almost blended. The baby makes less distinction between them than does the adult. Part of his task of development is to achieve an adaptive and progressive differentiation. For the young baby all things are highly personal, and conversely, persons tend to be regarded as things. It takes time for him to mature a sense of his own self as a person, and also a sense of the selves of others, to say nothing about all sorts of distinctions between physical objects, personal possessions, animals, machines, scurrying clouds, floating boats, moving shadows, reflected images, echoes, rising vapor, animate nature, inanimate nature, heavenly bodies, human deeds, rainfall, wind, snowfall, life and death.

As Thoreau so wisely hinted, the baby is part of Nature and at one with her. The baby grows up in a cosmos as well as a culture,—a universe crowded with impersonal forces and personal agencies. Sometimes these forces and agencies operate with dramatic suddenness, even with violence. More often they operate subtly with concealed but cumulative effect. Somehow the child must find himself in what would be a chaotic welter of stimuli, were he not protected by the ordering forces of his own organic growth. Nature (which is our familiar household name for the cosmos!) intended that he should sustain a certain permanent identity in all the bewildering diversity which surrounds him. Therefore, he has an individual mind: therefore, he becomes a person.

§1. PERSONALITY AS A DYNAMIC STRUCTURE

His mind, as we noted, is an intricate bundle of behavior patterns and behavior potentialities. His personality is the self-same bundle as it functions in a culture. Psychologically speaking, a culture is also an organized body of behavior patterns built up through generations of group experience and mediated by folkways. The infant contributes his mite to this vast cultural complex, because he becomes a focal point for the impacts of culture. As a youth and adult, he both continues and modifies the tradition. The tradition is transmitted by the process of social inheritance, which is only figuratively comparable to the racial inheritance that endows the infant with a nervous system.

This nervous system, as we have shown, in the preceding chapter, is so constructed that it reacts in a patterned and patterning manner to the world of things. It reacts in the same patterning manner to the world of persons,—which is equivalent to saying that personality is subject to the very mechanisms and the laws which govern the growth of perceptions and of intelligence. To be sure the personality reactions are colored by emotions, by feelings of pleasure and pain, by strivings, seekings and avoidances; but all this emotional life is organized and related to patterns of response. Emotions are not free-lance qualities which attach themselves

[29]

to behavior patterns; they are part and parcel of the patterns. Emotions grow and mature in the same sense that perceptions, judgments and concepts grow and mature. In sketching how the mind grows, we have already indicated how the personality develops. The child develops as a whole. What we call his personality is an organized and ever-organizing web of behavior patterns,—particularly of personal-social behavior. These patterns constitute and sum up all his reactions to the culture which reared him. They are neither more nor less mysterious than his sensori-motor patterns of posture, locomotion, and manipulation. They have the same geometry of growth which determines the developmental sequences of vertical, horizontal and oblique. Personality is but an abstraction, unless we agree that it is constituted of genuine patterns of behavior which grow and have being in the sense that cube behavior grows and makes itself manifest in lawful towers and bridges. Personality is not a force behind the scenes which operates a puppet. It is the whole puppet show,—player, stage, audience, acts and scenes. It sums up, as we have just noted, all the impacts of culture upon the growing organism, and since the personality is at once a product and instrument of growth, the infant foreshadows the child; the child the youth; the youth the man.

Any realistic approach to the problems of behavior guidance must recognize the personality as a growing tissue which both yields and resists. In later chapters we shall reduce these generalities to concrete formulations and show how the culture, embodied in parent and teacher, must meet the limitations of immaturity. We can scarcely do justice (and courtesy) to the young child unless we perceive the limitations of personal-social behavior in the same light that we perceive his inability to walk at 20 weeks, and his inability to build a tower of cubes at 40 weeks. The degree and the kind of help he needs as a developing personality are constantly changing with the maturity of his behavior equipment. Let us then attempt to take this subject of personality out of the clouds and envisage it in comprehensible patterns of behavior as they emerge. We shall find that personality development is essentially a progressive finding of the self through reactions to and progressive detachment from other selves.

When and how does the personal life of the infant begin? Not a simple question; for the sense of a personal self is a product of slow growth and the sense of other selves keeps ever changing with advancing maturity. The psychology of the self of a newborn baby must be largely confined to the mass of sensory impressions and feelings which arise from his lungs, his gastro-intestinal tract (many feet in length), his bodily movements, and his enveloping skin which usually fits him quite neatly. The total area of this outer skin and the yet vaster mucous membranes or inner skin is very extensive indeed. His air hungers, his food hungers, his appreciations of warmth, cold, bodily discomfort, and of snugness constitute the core of his psyche. Here is the nucleus, so to speak, of a personal self which grows and elaborates with great rapidity during the first five years of life.

When one thinks how neatly the baby's skin separates him from the impinging universe, one might infer that this dermatological envelope would make a most effective container for a well-defined personality! As a matter of fact this surface so bristles with sensitive receptors that it serves also to merge him with the cosmos in which he is immersed. It takes time, it takes complicated developments of the central nervous system, it takes the distance senses of sight and hearing to disengage him from the contexts to which he is so closely united.

In the beginning he is all universality, or all ego, as you choose. In a few weeks he "sees" a "face" hovering over him. This experience is not a personalized perception of a personal face, but it contains the germ of a sense of *someone else*. In due time through sheer association combined with more matured perceptual power this face will become identified with food, play, and ministering care. It will take many months before that face is apprehended in its true features and in its relationships to head, neck, arms as parts of a personal physique. Even the perception of the physical aspect of other persons takes shape by sketchy stages; analogous to the stages by which the preschool child with a crayon progressively portrays the human form,—first a central mass, from which spring eyes and ambiguous appendages; later head, eyes, nose, mouth, torso, arms, legs, fingers. Development is always a process of progressive differentiation. As the infant matures, his discernment of the anatomy of other persons becomes increasingly particularized. At the same time he learns to interpret the meaning of the nodding face, of the beaming eyes, the smiling mouth, the approaching hands, the glistening bottle, the cup, the spoon, the bib, the bonnet. Somehow or other the experience of these meanings, through the alchemy of growth, becomes organized into a complex of emotional reactions, which at last is sufficiently elaborate to be called a sense of another self. In its early stages this sense is so uncritical and so piecemeal that little distinction is made between a face, a false face, a parent, a nurse, a visitor, a mirror image. The baby smiles more or less indiscriminately at all of these varied stimuli; but by the middle of the first year he begins to distinguish between a familiar person and a stranger; between a frowning and an approving face. His extraordinary ability to read facial expressions is an impressive developmental phenomenon. He distinguishes delicate variations in posture, gesture, and countenance long before he is capable of fine finger coordinations. Sensitivity to the posturings of facial features and to the postural attitudes of other persons lies at the very basis of his acculturation.

§2. THE WORLD OF PERSONS

THIS sensitivity to cultural impress is so great that he acquires a sense of other selves before he acquires a clear sense of his own self. To be sure there is a mutual interaction here; and one may say that his sense of other selves is really an extension or projection of his private self. Even so his perception of other persons is at times in advance of the perception of himself. He is aware of the incoming and outgoing hand of his mother before he becomes acquainted with his own hand as it travels in and out of his field of vision. He spends many moments looking at his hands, fingering his hands, mouthing his hands. These sensory experiences,—visual, tactile, wet, dry, still, moving, stop-go, oral, palmar, touching and being touched, provide him with a medley of data. By gradual degrees he comes to realize that he has a hand which feels when it contacts (active touch), which feels when it is contacted (passive touch), which feels when it moves (sense of motion, or kinesthetic sense mediated by sensory end organs in muscles, joints, and tendons). His ceaseless manipulation, therefore, acquaints him not only with the physical universe and the physical presence of other persons, but with the physical presence of himself.

His mouth as well as his hands serves as an avenue for information. He is under an irrepressible impulse to put "everything" into his mouth, including his own hands, feet, nipple, toys, and food. He learns to distinguish between food and non-food. Every feeding whether by breast, bottle, spoon, by cup, by hand, or otherwise makes a contribution to a growing sense of self and of security. His manipulation of objects also gives him an increasing sense of mastery of his environment. The sense of mastery and the sense of self are more or less ambiguous; because at first he makes little discrimination between himself, on the one hand, and the personal and impersonal features of his environment on the other hand.

Likewise he makes no distinction in the beginning between his own voice and that of others. He probably hears his mother's voice before he identifies his own vocalizations as his own. Sometimes he seems to be startled by sound of his own making; but through his spontaneous vocalizations and through his inveterate banging of objects he comes in time to realize that he is a creator of sound. This again adds to his sense of mastery of his environment. This serves to make him feel himself a person. The culture helps out by repeating the vocalizations he makes and by making other vocalizations for him to repeat. Through nursery games a shuttlecock communication is set up. Pat-a-cake and peek-a-boo are vivid condensations of the mechanism of acculturation which operates similarly though less dramatically throughout the infant's behavior day.

Through the interchange of back and forth play the infant becomes more aware of himself and others. He sees how his actions can be attuned to those of others. A ball is rolled to him. He anticipates the rolling ball. He receives; he reciprocates; he anticipates; he receives again and reciprocates again. It is more than a mere game; for it represents a mode of acculturation. Countless life situations day in and day out call for similar reciprocities. Through these situations the emotions are organized into patterns which correlate with cultural patterns. We can see now why a child who is understimulated in an over-simplified home lacks the patterns of personal-social response which are the substance of personality. The institutionalized baby suffers grievously in personality make-up because he was deprived of the fundamental reciprocities of household living, which build up, that is, make up the structure of personality. A personality cannot take root and cannot flourish except through interpersonal relationships. The psychological impoverishment of the institutional infant convincingly reveals the nature of the acculturation which takes place in the well ordered home. Such a home gives the infant an opportunity to find himself.

Thus bit by bit, pattern by pattern, the personality of the young child takes on structure and design. It is constituted of an infinitude of patterns and attitudes. It is not some mysterious essence which takes hold of the culture and manipulates it to suit some dark subconscious goals. The personality of the young child is more like an organism which is shaped by what it feeds upon. Nature protects this growing organism normally from over-growth. A balance must be struck between self-effacement under cultural pressure and self-assertion under the compulsion of developmental urges.

§3. THE GROWTH OF PERSONALITY

AND so in a tolerant culture the infant one-year-old already has an opportunity to assert his personality. The household obligingly laughs at his performances. He enjoys an audience and delights in repeating performances laughed at. Thus he both acquires and exercises his growing consciousness of self. At this genial age, he also proffers a toy to an outstretched hand and surrenders it with his newly acquired power of prehensory release. This responsive release, of course, has a certain social significance. But Nature cannot carry socialization too far and so at 15 months the child seems to be more demanding, more self-assertive. He may even inhibit release of the toy because he wishes to satisfy his sense of possession.

He also seems to have a high degree of self-dependence at the age of 18 months. He is so engrossed in his run-about activities that he scarcely avoids bumping into other run-about children in his path. He scarcely perceives them as persons like himself, or he would not pinch and pull and stroke them as though they were inanimate objects for manipulation. Nevertheless, such manipulation is increasing his knowledge of the constitution of other persons. He also increases his knowledge by doing a great deal of watching of the social scene. Time after time during the day he interrupts his activity for absorbed inspection of the activities of others. He may lapse into dramatic imitation of activities of his elders. He seizes a broom to sweep the floor just as his mother does.

The 2 year old is an infant-child; but he is more mature than the 18 months run-about. He has a rudimentary sense of ownership; he holds onto possessions,—even hides them. He fights for them (something, of course, which grown-ups never do!). But, no matter, if he has to learn to share, he must first learn *it's mine!* Crawling comes before creeping— backward crawl before forward. The gentler side of his nature is shown in his interest in dolls and babies. Even the boys indulge in doll play.

The 2½ year old has a bad reputation for contrariness and for going to contradictory extremes. In the development of creeping there is a stage when the infant goes neither forward nor backward, so he starts both ways in alternation: he rocks back and forth, supporting himself on hands and knees. The $2\frac{1}{2}$ year old is in a similar two-way rocking stage with respect to his social behavior. He cannot make a single choice, so he makes two,—two contradictory choices; he oscillates between two opposites. There are no one-way streets for him. But, do not despair. He is learning to shift gears. He will forge ahead. Soon he will be a delightful, enjoyable 3 year old.

THREE is a kind of coming-of-age. For one so young, the 3 year old has a high degree of self control. He has himself well in hand. What is more, he likes to please and to conform. "Do it dis way?" is a characteristic question, which shows that he is sensitive to the demands of culture. You can bargain with THREE and he can wait his turn.

FOUR is not quite as docile as THREE. FOUR (and half past) tends to go out of bounds. He is a little dogmatic and self-assertive,—something of a sophomore; a little self-centered; but he likes to dress up and to dramatize and thereby he becomes acculturated.

FIVE is a SUPER-THREE with a socialized pride in clothes and accomplishments, a lover of praise. He is a self-assured, conforming citizen in his kindergarten world. If the development of his personality has been well-balanced and well-timed, he has overcome much of the impulsiveness and naiveté of early infancy. He enters upon higher levels of organization during the elementary school years and keeps advancing during the period of adolescence. If his mental growth is healthy, he integrates and consolidates his achievements as he ascends from one level of maturity to another.

The process of maturing remains essentially the same throughout the whole life cycle. It is a process of developmental morphogenesis. It is a constant building up and interweaving of an infinitude of patterns and sub-patterns, always subject to the mechanisms of developmental physiology. These mechanisms are so lawful and so fundamental that children of similar chronological age are in general most comparable with respect to their emotional characteristics. The intellectual prodigy capable of fifth grade work at the age of six is at heart more like a child of six than a child of eleven. This fact suggests that the make-up of personality depends upon instinctive and innate factors which are so ancient and deep-seated that they cannot with impunity be transcended, even in a highly sophisticated culture.

The foregoing text of this chapter has not attempted to penetrate far into the private world of the child's emotions. These emotions we must infer on the basis of his outward behavior and the historical development of his individuality. We wish to avoid the suggestion that the personality of infant and child is a product of emotions which operate in some mysterious way through the subconscious or otherwise. We should prefer to think of personality in less mysterious and more realistic terms as a structured end product of the child's developmental past. As such, it bears the imprint of the patterns of the culture in which he was born and reared. The early impression of the family life during the first five years leaves the most fundamental and enduring imprint. Acculturation begins in the home and the influence of the larger social groups is limited by the trends initiated through the family. If the child grew up in a natural and not in a social world, he would still be able to achieve some of the fundamental adjustments to life. He would be able to adapt to the world of time and space, the world of things, but he would be almost devoid of personality because personality is constituted of an infinite number of reactions which are released in a socialized world.

Personality is a word to conjure with. In the present chapter, we have, however, deliberately avoided a conjuring discussion of the more speculative and inaccessible aspects of the subject. Our purpose has been to emphasize the central fact that personality is a product of growth, that it is a structured entity which varies enormously with the maturity of the child. It is impossible to describe even in general terms the personality of "the infant" or the personality of "the child". Personality as a living actuality changes so much with age, that a whole series of delineations is necessary to depict the pathways and patterns of its development.

These delineations have been assembled in PART TWO, (Chapters 9-20) where twelve age levels are separately treated. The psychological features of each age level are outlined in a *Behavior Profile*. This profile sketches the personality characteristics of a typical child of a given maturity. How these characteristics function in our culture is further indicated by a summary of the *Behavior Day* of such a child. The behavior day indicates suggestively how a child of a given age distributes his energies and interests in the course of twenty-four hours. When this child reaches the age of 18 months he is also called upon to make adjustments to cultural groups outside of the home. How his "personality" accomplishes these adjustments at advancing ages is concretely described under the headings *Nursery Behavior* and *Cultural and Creative Behavior*. Also under the heading *Behavior Day* and the additional heading *Nursery Techniques,* there are specific statements and suggestive hints of how the personal-social behavior of the child is managed and directed both at home and at school, under the actual conditions of modern life. It is believed that such practical particulars will give a more authentic picture of *personality* than could be derived from an abstract discussion of personality forces.

It is, of course, recognized that there are great individual differences in any age group, but these differences cannot be adequately estimated or understood except in terms of relative maturity. The series of *Behavior Profiles*, therefore, provides a frame of reference for envisaging the growth of personality.

4

INFANTS ARE INDIVIDUALS

INFANTS are individuals. They are individuals from the moment of birth. Indeed, many of their individual characteristics are laid down long before birth. In the shape of his physique the newborn infant already gives tokens of what he is to be. Physical measurements may show which of three body types he will most closely approximate as an adult: (1) round, soft body, short neck, small hands and feet; (2) square, firm body with rugged muscles; (3) spindly body, delicate in construction. Individual differences in physique are due to variations and mixtures of these bodily characteristics.

There is a similar variety in temperaments, corresponding to differences in physique, and in biochemical and physiological peculiarities. Three traits or types of temperament have been distinguished. They combine in varying degrees in different individuals: viscerotonic, somatotonic, and cerebrotonic (Sheldon). The extreme viscerotonic has a good

[39]

digestive tract. He is good-natured, relaxed, sociable, communicative. The pronounced somatotonic is active, energetic, assertive, noisy and aggressive. The fragile cerebrotonic is restrained, inhibited, tense; he may prefer solitude to noise and company. He is sensitive and likely to have allergies.

§1. MATURATION AND ACCULTURATION

SUCH classifications are much too simple to do justice to the infinite diversity of human individualities; but they serve to remind us that there are primary individual differences more basic than the differences acquired through acculturation. In the hey-day of Behaviorism there was a popular impression that all babies are very much alike at birth, and that the differences which become apparent as they mature are due to conditioned reflexes. The child's mind was said to consist of a complex bundle of conditioned reflexes, derived from environmental stimuli. According to this point of view, children resemble each other most while they are infants,—the younger, the more alike.

There is no evidence, however, that infants are not individuals to the same degree that adults are individuals. Long range studies made in our clinic have demonstrated that such traits as social responsiveness, readiness of smiling, self-dependence and motor agility tend to manifest themselves early and to persist under varying environmental conditions. Every child is born with a *naturel* which colors and structures his experiences. The infant, to be sure, has great plasticity, great powers of learning; but there are lawful limits to his conditionability. He has constitutional traits and tendencies, largely inborn, which determine *how, what,* and to some extent even *when* he will learn.

These traits are both racial and familial. The racial traits are those which are common to the whole human species. The familial traits are the distinctive endowment which he inherited from his parents and a long line of grandparents. The child comes into this double inheritance

[40]

through an innate process of growth which we call *maturation*. He comes into the social "heritage" of culture, through a process of *acculturation*. These two processes interact and interfuse, but the process of maturation is most fundamental,—so fundamental that acculturation can never transcend maturation.

Infants are individuals, because the intrinsic forces of maturation operate to keep them from being the mere pawns of culture. The impacts of culture are incessant and often they tend to produce uniformity, but even the tender infant preserves an individuality, through the inherent mechanisms of maturation. We may be duly thankful for this degree of determinism. Did it not exist, the infant would be a victim of the malleability which behaviorists once ascribed to him. He is durable as well as docile. In a boundlessly complex world he says, in effect, "Lo, I too am here!"

§2. THE INDIVIDUALITY OF TWINS

THE meaning of maturation is beautifully illustrated in the development of twins. Fraternal twins are derived from two separately fertilized egg-cells. Each twin, therefore, has a distinctive hereditary origin and a correspondingly distinctive genetic constitution. Such twins are ordinary brothers and sisters. They show family resemblances but they are essentially unlike, even though they are simultaneously reared in the same household and subject to the selfsame culture.

Identical twins are derived from a single egg-cell, and they may indeed be almost identical because they share one and the same genetic constitution. Accordingly they show thoroughgoing correspondences in their physical and mental developments. As Shakespeare, father of twins, put it, "The apple cleft in two is not more twin than these two creatures." One-egg twins may weigh alike to an ounce; their finger and palm prints resemble each other minutely; similarities may extend even to the microscopic structure of the hairs on their heads and to the biochemistry of the body fluids. Simultaneously they may have the same diseases and almost in lock step reach the same stages of maturity in their patterns of behavior. In physique, in temperament, and behavior, they may be virtually indistinguishable.

We have studied such a highly identical pair of twins at the Yale Clinic of Child Development, over a period of 14 years. By repeated physical and mental measurements, by systematic motion picture records of behavior and experimental observations using the method of co-twin control, we have followed the life careers of these twin girls from infancy to adolescence. In the co-twin control studies, we trained one twin (T) and reserved the other twin (C) as a comparative control, to determine the effects of intensive training in such sample functions as stair-climbing, block-building, vocabulary, and manual coordination. These effects proved to be relatively impermanent: the untrained twin attained the equivalent skill as soon as she reached the requisite maturity. Numerous tests at advancing ages revealed an amazing parallelism in their physical and mental growth.

But on close analysis even this remarkably similar pair of twins presented consistent individual differences, many of which could be traced back to infancy. The differences are slight but they are durable. Here are some of them: T is quicker, more direct, more decisive: C is more deliberate, more inclusive, more relaxed. T is a bit brighter: but C is more sociable, more communicative. T shows a predilection for straight and angular lines in her drawings of a house, of smoke, of curtains, and of string balloons. C favors curves. Her curtains are flounced, her smoke curls. In attentional characteristics, T's pick-up is more prompt, she focalizes more sharply, is more alert for details. C's attention is more generally alert, more imaginative, more roving. These differences are slight in degree; but, they are permanent, in the perspective of 14 years. They are permanent because they are constitutional. In terms of temperament, Infant T was somewhat more cerebrotonic. Infant C was somewhat more viscerotonic.

Infants are individuals. When human behavior is organized in a cultural milieu, there is almost an infinitude of available environments; the organism selects from this infinitude in much the same way that a living cell may or may not select potassium from a fluid medium. The structure of the organism, whether conceived in terms of biophysical waves or particles of stereo-chemistry, is attuned to what it selects and averse to what it rejects. For this reason it has proved difficult to find *pure* cultural factors to explain the demonstrated differences in the life careers of Twin T and Twin C. Twins are individuals.

§3. THE INDIVIDUALITY OF GROWTH PATTERNS

THE most fundamental ability is the ability to grow: It is the most fundamental because it includes all other abilities. For the same reason the most important index and symptom of a child's individuality is his *mode of growth*. No two children are exactly alike, but no two (not even Twins T and C!) grow up in just the same way. Every child has a distinctive style or method of growth. The most penetrating question which one can ask about an individual is, "How does he grow?" "How does he learn?" "How does he advance from stage to stage as he matures?" "How did he solve the problems of development as a baby?" These questions are really one. They all bear on the essence of individuality. They concern the growth characteristics which determine the course of personality patterning in relation to patterns of culture.

Growth characteristics in turn must determine the techniques and procedures of child guidance. PARTS TWO and THREE of this volume deal concretely with the growth trends which shape the organization of behavior at ascending age levels. Description, theory, and practice are approached from the standpoint of development. Guidance and hygiene are discussed in terms of maturity. The concept of maturity with all its relativities is the key to an understanding of the individual infant and child.

Temperament and *growth type* are closely related phenomena. Each

[43]

represents the characteristic manner in which an individual reacts to life situations. Growth type is particularly significant because it expresses the long range individual way in which the organism handles the continuous task of achieving maturity. Some children, to use an antique word, are more "growthsome" than others. But they differ yet more profoundly in their styles of growth.

These varied styles are manifested in emotional characteristics, in motor demeanors, in reactions to novelty, success and failure, in dependence upon environment and persons. Consider Children A, B, and C as illustrations of three different modes of development and of self adjustment.

Child A matures slowly: *Child B* rapidly: *Child C* irregularly.

A approaches new situation cautiously and warily: *B* is incautious and cool: *C* is variably overcautious and undercautious.

A is wise with respect to life situations: *B* is bright and clever: *C* is brilliant.

A is equable: *B* is blithe: *C* is moody.

A achieves orientation in total time and space: *B* is oriented to present time and immediate space: *C* is mixed and confused, while achieving orientation.

A takes in the whole and works in from the periphery: *B* operates more in the immediate context: *C* takes in either too much or too little and holds on too long.

A adjusts and shifts focus: *B* is in relatively continuous focus: *C* is well in focus or far out of focus.

A can wait and bide his time: *B* is up and at it, does not need to wait: *C* does not know how to wait and is poor at timing.

A assimilates gradually: *B* combines and adapts expeditiously: *C* overcombines and dissociates poorly.

The foregoing traits are dynamic traits; therefore, they have wide and general applications. They come into expression at all ages from infancy to adolescence and adulthood. They apply to all significant life situations, those of the home as well as community, — to the routines of feeding and everyday living in the nursery. They involve the vegetative **as** well as the sensori-motor and symbolic nervous systems.

The traits, as listed, were not derived from an academic classification, but are based on observations of infants and young children in clinic and nursery school. Even in their present form they may be used as touchstones to appraise the kind of child one is dealing with. It is not possible to diagnose constitutional traits simply by observing occasional behavior patterns. But by watching over a period of weeks, months, and years, the manner in which a child solves the endless succession of growth problems, it *is* possible to become acquainted with very significant aspects of the psychic constitution. The constant task of teacher and parent is to notice how the growing child achieves his adjustments. Only in this way can we understand his individuality.

The A, B, C, traits represent variations in the make-up of the "biological individual" but they also have significance for the "cultural individual." They determine to what extent the child is susceptible or immune to the stimulations of the cultural environment. By implication they even suggest adjustments which the culture must make in behalf of these individual differences in modes of growth and learning. The various traits overlap and do not fall into neat compartments. However, the *A* traits all tend to go together, and in the most typical cases are represented in one and the same individual. This is true of the *B* and the *C* traits also, so that we have, roughly speaking, three major *growth types:* *A, B, C,* the solid, the facile, and the uneven. Which fact leads to a very interesting conclusion as to the responsibilities of the culture. It is clear that the C type will make the most demands, and require constant adjustments; the B type is much less demanding. The A type asks little from the environment and depends on his own resources. The culture should be alert to offer him somewhat more than he asks for. The B type asks more from the environment; he knows what he wants and is so articulate that the culture does not need so much to foresee and plan. The C type is variably overdemanding and underdemanding. The culture must plan,

[45]

foresee, direct, restrict, prod and channelize to bring about mutual accommodations between the individual and his environment.

Between these extremes lie the everyday problems of infant care and child guidance. The beginning of wisdom in the rearing of children is a realistic recognition of the growth factors which shape his conduct, and the acknowledgment that every child has a unique pattern of growth.

5

SELF-REGULATION AND CULTURAL GUIDANCE

IF WE have demonstrated that the infant is indeed an individual, then a very practical question at once arises: How much shall we defer to his individuality? The question cannot be postponed, for every infant from birth has distinctive drives and needs, which must be either ignored, indulged, combatted or controlled. And if they are to be controlled, how can they be reached through the culture; how can they be reached through the child? The very helplessness of the newborn baby, and the obscurity which conceals his individuality make these questions somewhat poignant.

§1. INDIVIDUALS AND SCHEDULES

ONE solution for such perplexities is to "lay down" a fixed feeding schedule and to raise the baby by this schedule. The schedule presumably reflects the wisdom of the race. It is based upon much experience derived from the care of previous generations of babies. It also embodies the cumulative knowledge of the science of nutrition. The physician, as the carrier of this knowledge, lays down or sets up a schedule with a degree of acknowledged authority. The schedule thus becomes at once a symbol and a vehicle of cultural control.

The schedule, therefore, would seem to be the very essence of hygienic science and good will. In actual application, however, the culture often proves to be so inept and the infant proves to be so refractory that conflicts actually ensue between schedule and individual. Difficulties multiply when a hard and fast schedule is rigidly imposed without discrimination on Baby A, Baby B, and Baby C. Veritable contests may occur. The culture, embodied in the parent, insists on feeding at a pre-established hour; the baby insists on sleeping instead; the baby cries when he "should" be asleep; he may even vomit when he "ought" to keep his meal; he may be hungry when he "ought" to be satisfied; he may "refuse" to take solids when he "should," etc. This child-versus-culture conflict is exacerbated when an overwrought parent and an overdetermined physician insist too strongly on schedules and procedures which are not adapted to the infant. It is at this near breaking point of emotional tension that the problem of self-regulation and cultural guidance comes to a genuine issue. And who is to win out,—the schedule or the individual? And who is the wiser,—the household or the baby?

"The Wisdom of the Body",—this is the arresting title of Cannon's well-known volume which discusses the marvellous mechanisms of self-regulation whereby the human body maintains an optimal equilibrium in its chemical constituents and physiological processes. These mechanisms operate with considerable precision even in the newborn baby;

but they do not operate with completed perfection. In many behaviors he is physiologically awkward. He does not know how to sleep, how to wake up, how to keep himself at a steady temperature. In many of these functions he is "learning", he is growing, his body is acquiring more wisdom. But all the time he is preeminently "wise" as to what he *can* not do and what he *should* not do because of the limitations of immaturity.

He is in closer league with Mother Nature than he is with the contemporary culture. There are limits, physiological limits, to his tolerances. He is growing at an extremely rapid rate, and this may add to his difficulties in adjusting to the demands of culture. He is in a somewhat unsettled state of progressive organization and reorganization. He has his ups and downs, his physiological needs seem to vary from day to day; no two days are quite alike, and each month differs from the next. He is under the constant necessity of keeping all his internal organs and body fluids working cooperatively to produce an internal environment favorable for full life and growth. It is not a simple task. He advances as he matures, but not by a straight and narrow path, nor by a simple timetable. *He fluctuates as he advances.* In his wavering he needs help from the culture; he needs discerning guidance rather than rigid regimentation, but fortunately his rapid growth also puts him in possession of new patterns with which to meet the demands of culture.

Self demands and cultural demands must somehow be brought into mutual accordance. This can be done only by appreciating the essential wisdom of the baby's body and behavior manifestations. We must respect his *fluctuations* and interpret their meaning. The fluctuations express his developmental needs. The progress of the fluctuations from one week to another affords a clue to his methods of growth and learning. If we chart his naps and sleep periods over several months, we find that the total sleeping time per day varies in almost a rhythmic manner, as shown in the chart of Child J (Figure 1). The extremes of variation within each week are shown for the period from 4 to 40 weeks. The variations go up and down, but the downs in the long run exceed the ups, so that the average amount of diurnal sleep falls from nineteen hours in the fourth

[49]

week to thirteen hours in the fortieth week. This is what we mean by self-regulating fluctuations.

Development does not proceed in a straight line, it deviates now up now down, now left now right. Sometimes it even seems to deviate now backwards now forwards; but the total trend is forward. If the deviations and the slips are not too many and too extreme, the organism catches its balance at each step and then makes another step onward. The fluctua-

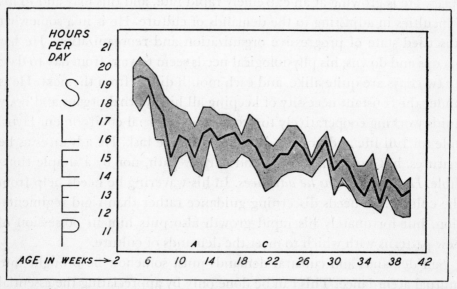

Daily variations in the amount of sleep of Child J from 4 weeks to 40 weeks of age. The extremes of fluctuation are indicated by the solid band. The average number of hours for a week are shown by a solid line (brief respiratory infections occurred at 12 and 21 weeks).

tions are really not lapses: they are groping "efforts" of the organism to reach a further organization.

The enlightened culture attempts to recognize these efforts, and to go along with them. The child is in league with Nature; but he is also growing into his culture. By reading the cues of the child's organism, culture also comes into closer league with Nature. In this way self demands and cultural demands can be brought into accordance. By registering his self-demands and by having them met to a judicious degree the individual is able to accomplish a maximum of self-regulation.

§2. SELF-DEMAND SCHEDULES

How does an infant register his self-demands? By his behavior. The well-being and the ill-being of his organism are summed up in his patterns of behavior and in the alternations of rest and activity which make up his behavior day. The infant's diary is represented in his behavior day, and as we shall presently see, it is an interesting and significant diary if it is duly recorded and read in perspective.

The infant does not have words at his command, but he has two sets of signs and signals: the negative and the positive; those which express *avoidance and rejection;* and those which express *seeking and acceptance.* The negative signals include crying, fretting, uneasiness, refusal, anxiety. The positive signals include quiescence, relaxation, satiety, cooing, smiling, and pleasurable self-activity. By such behavior language the infant reports his status and his self-demands. He tells us whether and when he is hungry, sleepy, tired, contented, uncomfortable. By taking cognizance of these cues the culture (through the parents) can devise a flexible schedule of care adapted to the infant's needs as they arise. This would be a *self-demand schedule,* as distinguished from an imposed schedule. An inflexible schedule based on a more or less arbitrary norm would ignore the infant's signs and signals. It would insist on regularity of intervals despite the infant's irregular fluctuations. It would regularly insist on waking even when the infant insists on sleeping.

There are two kinds of time,—organic time and clock time. The former is based on the wisdom of the body, the latter on astronomical science and cultural conventions. A self-demand schedule takes its departure from organic time. The infant is fed when he is hungry; he is allowed to sleep when he is sleepy; he is not roused to be fed; he is "changed" if he fusses on being wet; he is granted some social play when he craves it. He

is not made to live by the clock on the wall, but rather by the internal clock of his fluctuating organic needs.

It is a relatively simple matter to initiate such a self-demand schedule, to keep it in operation, and to chart its course from day to day and week to week. The accompanying bar chart (Figure 2) illustrates the method of recording a behavior day. The total length of a single bar represents a 24 hour period from midnight to midnight. The behavior events of the day can be plotted along the course of this time bar. Sleep is indicated by

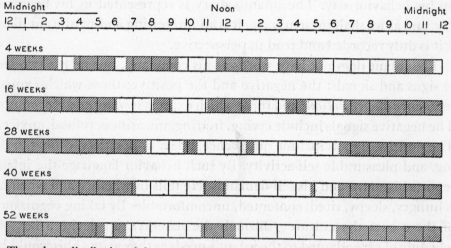

The 24 hour distribution of sleep and waking time of Infant S at 4, 16, 28, 40, and 52 weeks of age. The records are abstracted from a *behavior day chart* as described in Appendix A.

cross-hatching; waking periods are left blank. Specific events like feeding and elimination may also be included in the record by conventional devices which are illustrated in sections from actual charts as pictured in Appendix A. These charts show how the behavior days of the infant change as he matures. Through self-adjustment and cultural guidance he progressively works out his individual schedule. Even a glance at Figure 2, which consists of excerpts from five different ages, will show a definite trend in the organization of sleep and waking periods in the Behavior Day.

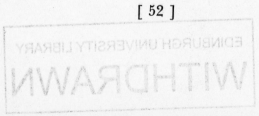

§3. SELF-REGULATION THROUGH CULTURAL CONTROL

THE principle of self-regulatory fluctuations is so fundamental in child development that it has vast cultural implications. The principle applies not only to such "simple" functions as sleeping, eating, and infant play; it applies to the higher forms of learning and of mental organization. The organism during the entire period of active growth is in a state of formative instability combined with a progressive movement toward stability. The so-called growth gains represent consolidations of stability. The opposition between two apparently opposing tendencies results in seesaw fluctuations. Stability and variability co-exist not as contradictory opposites, but as mutual complements. Therefore we must look upon many fluctuations as positive thrusts or efforts toward higher maturity. They may be construed as self-demands, which if adequately satisfied by the culture result in optimal growth of personality organization.

Such is the underlying theory stated in broad terms. This volume conceives cultural guidance in terms of the optimal needs of the individual organism. The cultural pattern must be adapted to the growth pattern, because in final analysis all individual development depends upon intrinsic self-regulation. There is no adjustment to culture other than self-adjustment.

But self-demand is only the beginning of the story of fostering the infant's healthy development. We have seen only too often within recent decades how self-demands may lead to excess. The bewildered parent is shocked when a 4 year old child tells her to "shut up". She has tried hard to have him live by his inner laws; but she comes to realize that he does not live by inner laws alone, for these are of no use to him unless they have come into equilibrium with the laws of the world in which he moves. She may have seen that her child made a good start, but she did not know how to help him finish, how to help him round out his patterns of behavior.

This is why it is so important for the parent to learn the mechanisms of innate and cultural regulation within the first year of the child's life when the patterns are relatively simple. She hears the urgency of the hunger cries of the 4 week old child which can only be controlled with food. She realizes that at 16 to 28 weeks this cry is less frequent and that the child can wait for his feeding. His hunger pains are now less intense, his gastro-intestinal tract is subordinating itself at times to other demands. For now the infant's overflow energy is diverted into active discovery of his own body, his hands, his feet, and also the persons who people his environment. His own inner growth is a controlling and organizing factor.

But this inner ability to wait is specific rather than general. It fails to show itself at the age of 18 months when it is time for juice and crackers. There is a developmental reason for this behavior. The child is acquiring a new control, namely that of demanding food when he sees the table at which the juice and crackers last were served. *Now* is all he knows at this stage of maturity. His mother, realizing the significance of this passing stage of maturity, manages accordingly. She has his mid-morning juice and crackers ready before he sees the table at the expected time. She also knows that she can help him to wait when he is 2½ years old by saying, "Pretty soon". By three years he understands, "When it's time", and by four, he wishes to help in the preparation of a meal. Thus culture in its greater wisdom has led the child steadily onward in relation to his innate readiness to make new adjustments and to curb himself. This is the wisdom of growth guidance as opposed to absolute discipline.

The old and pithy word "curb" harks back to a control that was used in earlier days. The word lives with us in our curbstones. These ancient stones help us in the control of behavior quite as much as do modern traffic lights. But the young child grows only slowly into the realization of what a curbstone means as a limit of safety. His culture having put him in a world of swiftly moving cars, must protect him from dashing out into the street at 18 months. He needs to be harnessed. At two, he not only sees curbstones but has the motor capacity and balance to walk on them endlessly as long as he has a helping and protecting hand available. It is not until two and a half years that he visually sees and is aware of the danger of a car backing up toward him. At three, he continues to accept his mother's hand as he is crossing a street. At four he is more watchful, more conscious of objects coming from both directions, and longs for the independence of crossing a street absolutely alone. The culture knows that he often overstates his abilities at this age, but responds to his eagerness by allowing him to cross narrow, safe, streets (though not thoroughfares) without holding of hands. By five he is less eager and more self-regulated and accepts the new and helpful control of traffic lights, with his ever watchful eyes. It is now that he is capable of greater independence. Culture recognizes the cue.

If he cannot adjust in this orderly fashion, there may be two possible causes. He may be holding on to earlier modes of adjustment (C-type growth pattern). The culture must then wait and watch knowing that the time will come when his behavior equipment will be ready. Often, however, the child cannot make the final step alone, but needs a lift from the environment at the moment when he is ready to accept the help. The custodians of the culture need to realize that sometimes life becomes too complex and must be greatly simplified in behalf of the child.

Through such mutual accommodations between culture and child, human relationships are improved at all age levels. The "culture" teaches the child, but the child also teaches the "culture",—makes it more intelligently aware of the laws, the frailties, and the potentialities of human nature.

§4. THE CULTURAL SIGNIFICANCE OF SELF-REGULATION

DOES this philosophy of self-regulation imply overindulgence or excessive individualism? By no means; for we always conceive of our individual as growing in a democratic culture which makes demands on individual responsibility. The danger of overindulgence is fictitious, for the goal of self-regulatory guidance is to increase the tensions and the fullness of growth. In the infant the self-demand type of management builds up body stamina and a corresponding organic sense of secureness. The most vital cravings of the infant have to do with food and sleep. These cravings have an individual, organic pattern. They cannot be transformed nor transgressed. Only by individualizing the schedules can we meet these cravings promptly and generously. By meeting them with certainty, we multiply those experiences of satisfied expectation which create a sense of security, a confidence in the lawfulness of the universe.

It is too easy to forget that the infant has a psychology, and that our methods of care affect his mental as well as physical welfare. The individualization of food- sleep- activity schedules is a basic approach to the mental hygiene of infancy. The education of the baby begins with his behavior day.

The mother's specialized education with respect to this particular baby also begins with the selfsame behavior day. The first year of life offers her a golden opportunity to become acquainted with the individual psychology of her child. And what she learns during that first year will be of permanent value, for throughout childhood and adolescence this child is likely to display the same dynamic characteristics which come into transparent view in early life.

The adoption of a self-demand schedule policy creates a favorable atmosphere for the kind of observation which will enable the mother to really learn the basic characteristics of her infant. She escapes the vexation which comes from forcing unwanted food and from waiting for long spells of hunger crying to come to an end. Instead of looking at the clock on the wall, she shifts her interest to the total behavior day of the baby as it records itself on the daily chart. She also notes in what manner and in what direction these days transform as the infant himself transforms. This is a challenge to intelligent perception. Thus she satisfies her instinctive interest in the child's growth and gains increasing insight into the growth process and the growth pattern. It simply comes to this: She

[56]

has made the baby (with all his inborn wisdom) a working partner. He helps her to work out an optimal and a flexible schedule suited to his changing needs.

Although this seems very simple, it has profound consequences in the mother's attitudes. Instead of striving for executive efficiency, she aims first of all to be perceptive of and sensitive to the child's behavior. Thus she becomes a true complement to him; alertly responsive to his needs. The child is more than a detached individual who must be taken care of at stated clock intervals. And he is more than a treasured possession. He is a living, growing organism, an individual in his own right to whom the culture must attune itself if his potentialities are to be fully realized.

The first year of life is by no means all-determining, but it is the most favorable of all periods for acquiring the right orientation toward the child's individuality. During this first year one does not use sharp emotional methods of discipline. One comes to understand in what way the child's immaturity must be met and helped. We expect the child to creep before he walks. We do not punish him for creeping. We do not prod him unduly into walking. Growth has its seasons and sequences.

The child must do his own growing. For this reason we should create the most favorable conditions for self-regulation and self-adjustment. But this means neither self-indulgence nor laissez faire. The culture intervenes, assists, directs, postpones, encourages and discourages at many turns; but always in relation to the child's behavior equipment and maturity status. When the baby is young we meet his hunger needs promptly. As he grows older he is gradually accustomed to waiting a little longer before his hunger is gratified. He thus acquires increasing hardihood by slow degrees as he is able to bear it. But this method of gradual induction is not possible unless we take fundamental notice of his self-demand cues and shape our guidance on a self-regulatory developmental basis.

This philosophy of child development and of child guidance assumes a democratic type of culture. A totalitarian type of culture would place the first and last premium upon the extrinsic cultural pattern; it would mould the child to this pattern; it would have little patience with self-demands. Cultural guidance, as outlined in the present volume, is essentially individualized. It begins in earliest infancy. It remains individualized not only in the home, but in the nursery school group and in the larger social world.

6

THE CYCLE OF CHILD DEVELOPMENT

SOME three billion years ago a fiery mass was hurled from the sun. Ever since, this mass which is now our earthly home, has been revolving around its parent sun, and has also been spinning on its own soft axle. Year in, year out; day in, day out.

About a billion years ago the first simple forms of animal life appeared in the waters which bathed the earth. A million years ago, a dawn man walked upon the breast of the earth. A few thousand years ago the descendants of this ancient man began to name the seasons of the yearly cycle and the hours of the daily cycle. Only yesterday did man achieve an insight into his racial ancestry and the origins of his own life cycle.

This life cycle is vastly more complex than the orbits of earth and sun; but like the heavenly bodies the human life cycle is governed by natural laws. In surety and precision the laws of development are comparable to those of gravitation.

§1. STAGES AND AGES

THE life cycle of a child begins with the fertilization of an egg cell. This almost microscopic particle undergoes prodigious developmental transformations. It becomes in swiftly moving sequence a living, palpitating embryo, a fetus, a neonate, an infant, a toddler, a preschool child, a school child, an adolescent, an adult. In a biological sense the life cycle is already nearing completion when the individual is mature enough to produce germinal cells competent to perpetuate the species.

Psychological maturity, however, in a modern culture is a more advanced condition. It might be defined as a stage of personal maturity which is competent to undertake the responsibility of parenthood. This kind of maturity is long in the making. In a more primitive epoch, infants became adults early. Civilization prolongs the period of "infancy" and is itself dependent upon such prolongation.

Development takes time. It is a continuous process. Beginning with conception (the fertilization of the egg-cell) it proceeds stage by stage in orderly sequence. Each stage represents a degree or level of maturity in the cycle of development. To ask how many stages there are in this cycle would be like asking how many moments there are in a day. A stage is simply a passing moment, while development, like time, keeps marching on. This does not, however, prevent us from selecting significant moments in the developmental cycle to mark the progressions toward maturity.

This is one reason why it has become a cultural custom to celebrate birthdays. Each anniversary marks one more revolution around the sun; but it also marks a higher level of maturity. It takes time to mature. We express the amount of time consumed by age. Age differences figure to an extraordinary degree in social practices and legislation. This is the scientific as well as cultural sanction for defining maturity stages in terms of calendar ages.

We recognize, of course, that the factor of individuality is so strong that no two children are exactly alike at a given age. But individual variations cling closely to a central trend, because the sequences and ground plan of human growth are relatively stable characteristics. Study of hundreds of normal infants and young children has enabled us to ascertain the average age trends of behavior development. We think of behavior in terms of age, and we think of age in terms of behavior. For any selected age it is possible to sketch a portrait which delineates the behavior characteristics typical of the age. A series of such maturity portraits is presented in the *Behavior Profiles* of Chapters 9 to 20.

For the convenience of the reader, twelve age levels are represented in these profiles, namely: 4, 16, 28, 40 weeks; 12, 15, 18 months; 2, 2½, 3, 4, 5 years. The developmental changes which take place in the first five years are so swift and variegated that they cannot be taken in at a single glance. It is necessary to still the moving tide with a cross-sectional view at spaced intervals. And to obtain a consistent conspectus we must choose our intervals with some care.

The rate of child development in the first year is so fast that five age intervals are necessary to do justice to the psychological patterns and needs of the infant. In the second year the transformations are so great, and from a cultural standpoint so important, that special consideration is given to the ages of 15 months and 18 months. In the third year the intermediate age of 30 months proves to be so significant that it needs separate discussion. All told there are twelve advancing stages.

This does not mean that development proceeds in a staircase manner or by installments. It is always fluent and continuous. The stage by stage treatment helps us to make comparisons of adjacent levels and to get a sense of the developmental flow. Without norms of maturity we cannot see the relativities in the patterns of growth. The cycle of child development eludes us unless we manage to envisage the bewildering pageantry of behavior in terms of stages and ages.

The accompanying chart affords a bird's eye view of the scope of early development. The fetal period is included to indicate the continuity of the growth cycle. The organization of behavior begins long before birth, and the general direction of this organization is from head to foot, from

[61]

proximal to distal segments. Lips and tongue lead, ears and eye muscles follow, then neck, shoulders, arms, hands, fingers, trunk, legs, feet. The chart reflects this law of developmental direction; it also suggests that various fields of behavior develop conjointly and in close coordination. Four fields are distinguished: (1) *Motor Behavior* (posture, locomotion, prehension, and postural sets). (2) *Adaptive Behavior* (capacity to perceive significant elements in a situation, and to use present and past experience to adapt to new situations). (3) *Language Behavior* (all forms of communications and comprehension by gestures, sounds, words). (4) *Personal-Social Behavior* (personal reactions to other persons and to the social culture). Characteristic behavior in these four fields will be outlined in the behavior profiles, and also in the outlines of nursery behavior, and of the illustrative behavior days.

The first five years in the cycle of child development are the most fundamental and the most formative for the simple but sufficient reason that they come first. Their influence upon the years that follow is incalculable. The trends and sequences of this fundamental development may be summed up tersely:

In the *first quarter* of the *first year,* the infant, having weathered the hazards of the neonatal period, gains control of his twelve oculomotor muscles.

In the *second quarter* (16-28 weeks) he gains command of the muscles which support his head and move his arms. He reaches out for things.

In the *third quarter* (28-40 weeks) he gains command of his trunk and hands. He sits. He grasps, transfers and manipulates objects.

In the *fourth quarter* (40-52 weeks) he extends command to his legs and feet; to his forefingers and thumbs. He pokes and plucks.

By the end of the *second year* he walks and runs; articulates words and phrases; acquires bowel and bladder control; attains a rudimentary sense of personal identity and of personal possession.

At *three years* he speaks in sentences, using words as tools of thought; he shows a positive propensity to understand his environment and to comply with cultural demands. He is no longer a mere infant.

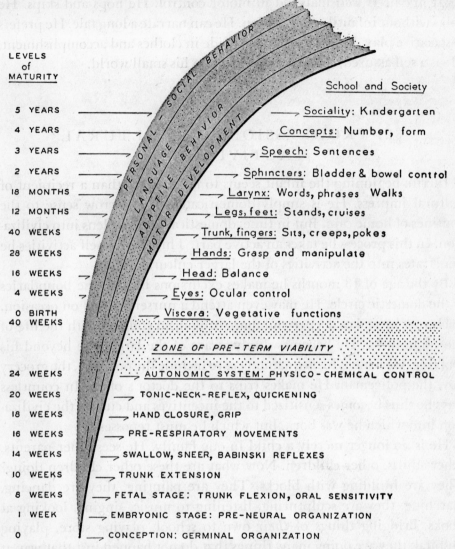

LEVELS
of
MATURITY

School and Society

5 YEARS ——————→ ———→ Sociality: Kindergarten

4 YEARS ——————→ ———→ Concepts: Number, form

3 YEARS ——————→ ———→ Speech: Sentences

2 YEARS ——————→ ———→ Sphincters: Bladder & bowel control

18 MONTHS ——————→ ———→ Larynx: Words, phrases Walks

12 MONTHS ——————→ ———→ Legs, feet: Stands, cruises

40 WEEKS ——————→ ———→ Trunk, fingers: Sits, creeps, pokes

28 WEEKS ——————→ ———→ Hands: Grasp and manipulate

16 WEEKS ——————→ ———→ Head: Balance

4 WEEKS ——————→ ———→ Eyes: Ocular control

0 BIRTH
40 WEEKS ———→ Viscera: Vegetative functions

ZONE OF PRE-TERM VIABILITY

24 WEEKS ——→ AUTONOMIC SYSTEM: PHYSICO-CHEMICAL CONTROL

20 WEEKS ——→ TONIC-NECK-REFLEX, QUICKENING

18 WEEKS ——→ HAND CLOSURE, GRIP

16 WEEKS ——→ PRE-RESPIRATORY MOVEMENTS

14 WEEKS ——→ SWALLOW, SNEER, BABINSKI REFLEXES

10 WEEKS ——→ TRUNK EXTENSION

8 WEEKS ——→ FETAL STAGE: TRUNK FLEXION, ORAL SENSITIVITY

1 WEEK ——→ EMBRYONIC STAGE: PRE-NEURAL ORGANIZATION

0 ——→ CONCEPTION: GERMINAL ORGANIZATION

A diagrammatic representation of the trends and fields of behavior growth from the embryonic period through five years of age.

At *four years* he asks innumerable questions, perceives analogies, displays an active tendency to conceptualize and generalize. He is nearly self-dependent in routines of home life.

[63]

At *five* he is well matured in motor control. He hops and skips. He talks without infantile articulation. He can narrate a long tale. He prefers associative play. He feels socialized pride in clothes and accomplishment. He is a self-assured, comforming citizen in his small world.

§2. PROGRESSIONS IN CULTURAL ACTIVITIES

IN THE beginning the infant seems to be no more than a recipient of cultural impress. He is simply domesticated in a narrow sense to the routines of home care. But in time, domestication broadens into civilization. In this process he takes an active part. Through his self-activities he penetrates into the activities of the larger cultural group.

By the age of 18 months he makes excursions beyond the boundaries of the domestic circle. He may even attend a nursery school on occasion. Each year he makes deeper and more prolonged contacts with the life of the community. He becomes dimly aware of the larger life beyond his roof tree. He widens his acquaintances to include the postman, the grocery boy, the policeman. He makes trips to the doctor's office. In countless ways he thus becomes sensitized to the incentives and cues of the civilization into which he was born, but which he must repossess.

He is no longer merely a child in one family. He sees other parents, other adults, other children. Now what are these other children doing? They are building with blocks. They are painting, they are dancing, marching, they are sculpturing, listening to music, singing, looking at books, bringing things of *their* own to school, playing store, playing hospital, they are doing many things that do not happen just that way at home. Indeed these *other children* are carrying patterns of culture to each other at the very time that they themselves are acquiring the patterns. Here is the soul of the mechanism of acculturation. The most important function of adults in this process is to create the optimal setting in the arrangement of groups and the planning of environmental apparatus. Through sensitization and desensitization to cues in the group life, the child becomes socialized. This is civilization.

There was once a rather attractive theory called the Culture Epoch Theory, which held that the child in his individual development passes through the same cultural stages as the race. He progresses from savagery to barbarism to civilization! Parallelisms were even found between the child's play activities and successive periods of cultural evolution: the root-and-grub stage, hunting and capture, pastoral, agricultural and commercial stages.

Now, of course, such pretty parallelisms can nowhere be found except in the pages of a book. Modern culture presses so closely upon the child that he is scarcely out of his diapers when he begins to press electric buttons and operate radio dials. However, in his back yard sand-box, he will root and dig and build in patterns which are at least reminiscent of primitive levels of workmanship. There is, after all, a grain of truth in the principle of the culture epoch theory, for the modern child does not accumulate culture in a piecemeal manner or by artificial installments. He grows into his culture by the exercise of natural patterns of exploitation and by dramatic enactments through play and imitation. His assimilation of the arts, the folkways, and the technologies of his complicated culture is a developmental process, subject to the same laws of growth which determine his sensori-motor maturity.

In following chapters we shall outline the cultural and creative activities by means of which the modern child makes developmental thrusts into the culture which surrounds him. These thrusts spring from his own spontaneity because by nature he is a creative artist of sorts. Remembering that the infant is, culturally speaking, a novice, we may well be amazed at his resourcefulness, his extraordinary capacity for original activity, inventions, and discovery. Thanks to this workmanship combined with a certain degree of docility, he domesticates himself in and is domesticated by the culture in which he is domiciled!

Civilization cannot be imposed. It must be newly achieved by each generation. Even babies and young children must acquire it in order to possess it. They acquire it by gradual stages which correspond to the basic sequences of developmental maturity. These stages will be suggestively outlined under the heading Cultural and Creative Activities in Chapters 15 to 19. To emphasize the developmental progression, the various activities will be listed by chronological ages. The outline is merely suggestive. There is a wide range of individual differences in culturability and in native talent.

Society is now learning that such differences in talent have social importance. It is very significant that they show themselves in the preschool period. Some day we shall identify various forms of giftedness in cultural and creative abilities before the child reaches school age. These abilities may show themselves spontaneously in the home, but more often they need the catalytic fillip and the motivational directive of the cultural group,—the neighborhood play group or the nursery school.

In miniature the nursery school represents and anticipates the universal cultural pattern. This pattern, which Wissler has demonstrated is common to all cultures from the most primitive to our own, consists of the following traits: (1) *Speech* (language, writing systems, etc.). (2) *Material Traits* (a. food habits, b. shelter, c. transportation and travel, d. dress, e. utensils, tools, etc., f. weapons, g. occupations and industries). (3) *Art* (carving, painting, drawing, music, etc.). (4) *Mythology and Scientific Knowledge.* (5) *Religious practices* (a. ritualistic forms, b. treatment of the sick, c. treatment of the dead). (6) *Family and Social Systems* (a. the forms of marriage, b. methods of reckoning relationship, c. inheritance, d. social control, e. sports and games). (7) *Property* (real and personal, standards of value and exchange, trade). (8) *Government* (a. political forms, b. judicial and legal procedures). (9) *War.*

Now it is very interesting to analyze the foregoing components of the culture-complex of today and to note the significant degree to which these components enter into the group life of the preschool child. He does not in his own person create or transmit a finished culture, but he is more than a mere dependent within a mature culture. He participates as a genuine member in cultural activities which are within his abilities.

Activities which are beyond him he approaches through dramatic imitations, pictures, and stories. Festivals and rituals take him somewhat into the realm of religion. Government and war are furthest from his ken; but he gets glimpses even of these "essential" activities.

After the child reaches the age of 18 months his cultural and creative activities begin to take on recognizable form in building, painting, modeling, music, pictures and books, dramatic expression, tools, possessiveness and sharing, festivals and celebrations. These various patterns of cultural activity will be listed in PART TWO for the age levels from 18 months through four years. By the age of five, the child has attained a considerable degree of social maturity. Acculturation has proceeded at a fast pace.

The progressions in this acculturation are neatly suggested by the patterns of doll play exhibited by the preschool child at advancing ages. Picture a doll, a doll crib, and a chair in the corner of a nursery school:

18-Month-Old toddles over to the crib, seizes the doll by the leg, drags it out, hugs and lugs it a short distance, drops it on the floor.

2-Year-Old picks up the doll more discriminately and holds its head up; he may even restore it to the crib and pull over the cover to keep the doll warm.

3-Year-Old may dress and undress the doll, seat himself in the chair and say something to the doll.

4-Year-Old dramatizes a complex situation, summons the doctor to the bedside and takes the patient's temperature.

5-Year-Old may make the crib and doll the center of a yet more complex project,—the children's ward of a hospital and may carry the project over imaginatively from one day to the morrow. He no longer lives from moment to moment as he did at 18 months.

§3. THE CYCLE OF THE BEHAVIOR DAY

THE world has been spinning a long time. All organisms from the morning glory to the roosting hen are in some way affected by the diurnal rotation, with its successions of night and day. The daily cycle has had a far-reaching influence in the partitioning and patterning of cultural practices. It has also become ingrained in some measure in the protoplasmic constitution of the human organism. One of the developmental tasks of the baby is to make a working adjustment to this immemorial cycle of 24 hours, reckoning from midnight to midnight.

Every organism, as we have noted in Chapter 5, is a storer and distributor of energy. The problem of infant and parents is to work out by self-regulation and guidance a satisfactory *behavior day* in terms of sleep, naps, feeding, cleansings, and toiletings, dressing and play. The behavior day will be subject to innumerable variations, including temperature, humidity, illness, distractions, and fatigues, to say nothing of the natural fluctuations of growth. Seasons also exert their influence and leave an imprint on the patterning of a whole series of behavior days. But the basic factor which shapes the general pattern of the day is the factor of maturity. For this reason we have sketched for each age level a *sample* behavior day, derived from actual clinical records. *This sample is in no sense a standard or model.* It is, however, from age to age, illustrative of the way in which the baby's daily life changes under the joint influence of maturation and acculturation.

§4. THE USE AND MISUSE OF AGE NORMS

NATURE abhors identities. Variation is the rule. No two children are exactly alike; and it has been said, perhaps with too much intellectual gravity, that there is no such thing as an average child. This has led some skeptics to suggest that age norms are very misleading. Why should we set up such norms, when not even brothers and sisters grow up in precisely the same way? We shall attempt to answer this question, for the reader has already observed that this volume is built around the concepts of age and maturity.

In the present stage of our scientific culture it would be very awkward to abandon the notion and the fact of age in any treatise on child development. The human life cycle is inextricably bound up with the factors of agedness and of aging. Duration and development are inseparable, metaphysically and also from the incontrovertible standpoint of common sense.

What is almost the first question we ask of ourselves when we are introduced to a baby or to a child? We ask, *How old is he?* If the mother is very proud of his accomplishments she has already told us in advance. In a general way we know what to expect of a given age; and we feel better acquainted with a child when we learn how old he is. There is something strangely mysterious about a foundling whose age is unknown. If a foundling is to be adopted in early infancy, it is extremely important to adjudge his chronological age by whatever age norms are available!

Then there is the story about the very modern boy, not much higher than a table, who wore a pair of horn-rimmed spectacles. A kindly lady leaned over and asked him tactfully, "How old are you, my little boy?" He removed his horn-rimmed spectacles and reflectively wiped them. "My psychological age, madam, is 12 years; my social age is 8 years; my moral age is 10 years; my anatomical and physiological ages are respectively 6 and 7; but I have not been apprised of my chronological age. It is a matter of relative unimportance." Thereupon he restored his horn-rimmed spectacles.

Although this boy has told us a great deal, we shall not feel acquainted with him until he tells us how old he is. We cannot see him in focussed perspective, not knowing his chronological age. Vice versa, we should know very little about him, if we knew only his chronological age. We celebrate the birthdays of a growing child not because the earth has made another revolution, but because the child is progressing toward maturity.

[69]

Feet and inches tell us how tall a child is; pounds and ounces how heavy. In somewhat the same way norms of behavior development tell us how mature he is. Norms are standards of reference to which a child can be compared. They must be used with the same judiciousness as norms of height and weight. Although these physical norms represent an average trend, we expect most children to exceed or to fall somewhat short of the specifications. The norms must be applied intelligently, and often only the expert judgment of a physician can determine whether the child is undernourished or malnourished. Intelligent parents have learned that such "standards" must be applied with discretion and caution.

Norms of behavior development, as measures of maturity, must be applied with even greater caution. The lay person should not attempt to make a diagnosis on the basis of such norms. This would constitute a misuse of norms. Refined and responsible application of maturity norms requires clinical skill based on long clinical experience.

Nevertheless the lay person wishes to know how the child mind matures, how the patterns of behavior normally change with age. We cannot appreciate the changing psychology of personality without an understanding of the pathways and patterns of development. The map of child development is so complicated that we can neither orient our observations nor locate our findings without the aid of longitude and latitude. The meridians locate durational time (age); the parallels of latitude locate developmental distance (maturity) . For the psychological orientation of the reader we have drawn up a series of behavior profiles for advancing age levels. These are mere thumbnail sketches of maturity; but they are concrete enough to give bearings. And that is their purpose. They do not permit mathematically precise readings; but they do indicate approximate locations. When the profiles are read as a consecutive series, they give a time-flow-map of the way in which a child matures. It is not intended that a single profile should be used to determine whether a given child is bright or dull, good or bad. Individual deviations are almost as normal as they are numerous. The norms enable us to detect the deviations.

The behavior profiles as a series outline the sequences of development. By following this continuity the reader is in a better position to interpret the sequences and patterns of maturity in a growing child. The *mode of growth* is the most important thing to study and to understand.

Babies pass through similar stages of growth, but not on the same time table. Variations are particularly common in postural behavior. For example, we observed five healthy babies, all of whom are now intelligent school children in their teens. At 40 weeks of age, one of these babies was backward in locomotion; one was advanced. The other three were near average. Baby ONE *"swam"* on his stomach without making headway. Baby TWO *crawled*. Baby THREE *creep-crawled*. Baby FOUR *crept on hands and knees*. Baby FIVE *went on all fours*. There were special reasons why Baby ONE was behind schedule in this particular item. Her general development in language, adaptive and personal-social behavior was quite satisfactory. It would have been regrettable if the mother of Baby ONE had worried unduly over this bit of retardation. Likewise the mother of Baby FIVE had no reason to be unduly elated, since the total behavior picture was near average expectation.

From this example it is clear that age norms and normative character sketches always need critical interpretation. They are useful not only in determining whether a child's behavior is near ordinary expectations, but also whether the behavior is well-balanced in the four major fields (motor, adaptive, language, and personal-social). It is especially desirable that there should be no serious deviations in the field of personal-social behavior. If there are extreme defects or deviations in any field of behavior, the advice of the family physician may be sought and a specialist consulted.

The behavior guidance and general management of a child should be based on the maturity level of his personal-social behavior. If the parents, for example, find that their 3 or 4 year old child is consistently functioning like a 2½ year old child, it will work advantageously for the child if his parents are aware of his level of maturity. Naturally, he should be treated as a 2½ year old child and not be held up to 3 year old "standards". At this age such a degree of retardation will have less serious consequences if his psychological care is determined by his psychological maturity.

The guidance of development must reckon judiciously with norms in one form or another. In final analysis, the child himself is the norm of last resort. We are interested in his growth. From time to time, that is, from age to age, we compare him with his former self; and this gives us an insight into *his* method of growth. This is supremely significant, because that method is the most comprehensive expression of his individuality. Under considerate and wise auspices he is not likely ever to fall below the indications of a former self, because the long-range tendency of growth is toward a maximum realization rather than a decline. This trend toward an optimum is inherent in the self-regulatory mechanisms of growth, particularly when aided by an enlightened culture.

There is also a principle of relativity which should afford us some comfort. It is whimsically stated in two stanzas by John Kendrick Bangs:

> I met a little Elfman, once
> Down where the lilies blow.
> I asked him why he was so small
> And why he did not grow.
>
> He slightly frowned, and with his eyes
> He looked me through and through.
> 'I'm quite as big for me', he said,
> 'As you are big for you.'

PART TWO

THE GROWING CHILD

7

BEFORE THE BABY IS BORN

§1. THE FIRST BABY

HUSBAND and wife choose each other, but they cannot choose their children. The parents cannot determine in advance the kind of children who will be born of marriage. That is the great adventure of life. Nature in her wisdom has so contrived it that not even the sex of the child can be pre-determined, much less the temperament, the physique, and the personality characteristics. The newborn infant is an individual in his own right and must be accepted as such.

Indeed, the individuality of the infant is to a significant degree determined before birth; well before the fourth month of gestation the prenatal child has taken on certain fundamental features of the individuality which will become apparent in infancy. Through no process of maternal impression or of wishful thinking is it possible to determine in advance whether this child will be boy or girl, blond or brunet, athletic or retiring; whether he will love the sea better than the mountains.

[73]

After the child is born, a parent with an overweening faith in the influences of environment may continue to harbor a preconceived image with excessive determination. In extreme and not too normal instances there is a positive fixation upon a specific type of child. This fixation later impels the mother or father or both to attempt too strongly to make over the child in terms of this image. Matters grow still worse if the father has one ideal and the mother another. Such fixations are detrimental to the developmental welfare of the infant. From the very outset, parents must temper their wishes and school their affections. They must accept the infant for what he is. They should become consistently inquisitive about one permanent question, namely: *What kind of child is he,—what is his true nature?*

This question is shrouded in darkness before birth, but will be ultimately answered in visible patterns of behavior. Even during the prenatal period the behavior characteristics of the future infant are undergoing a preliminary development. So-called quickening is more than a mere index of life. It is the product of a patterned behavior response made possible by the maturing nervous system. The 20 weeks old fetus is already so far advanced in his bodily organization and in the sculpturing of his physiognomy that he is distinctly human in his lineaments, and assumes in the fluid medium of the uterus, postures and attitudes not unlike those which he will display when he lies safely ensconced in his bassinet.

Although the mother's imagery cannot be too precise, the realization that the individuality of the child is in the making puts her in a better position to identify herself during the period of pregnancy with the developmental welfare of the child.

The impending crisis of the first birth is sometimes so magnified that the anxieties and fears of the mother prevent her from building up a natural, constructive outlook. The supervision of the obstetrician may relate itself too much to the birth episode alone. The expectant parents would greatly benefit from a pre-pediatric type of guidance, directed toward the postnatal career of the child. For example, it is probable that breast feeding would be more widely adopted in the interests of the child if both obstetricians and pediatricians encouraged the mother to nurse the child during his early months.

Such anticipations are especially important in the case of the first born child when the mother has so many new orientations to accomplish. These orientations are physical or biological on the one hand, and cultural on the other. The attitude and expectancies of the mother during the period of gestation, therefore, have far-reaching implications for the early career of the forthcoming child.

The care and management of the child will depend not only upon the practical details of technique, but also upon the philosophy of the parents. The welfare of the child is best safeguarded by a developmental philosophy which respects at every turn the individuality of the child and the relativities of immaturity. The foundations of this philosophy are best laid before the baby is born.

§2. A SECOND BABY

THE first baby makes the greatest demands upon the mother, both physically and psychologically. The second benefits thereby. The parents are now in a better position to see the meaning of birth and of child development in truer perspective. But the very fact that there is another baby already in the picture adds new problems which justify a little frank discussion.

Needless to say the second baby is just as important as the first and just as much an individual. To a certain extent he too must be reared as an only child, entitled to his own distinctive rights. Parents sometimes envisage the second child as a reforming influence, who will be used to mitigate the selfishness and the aggressiveness, perhaps mistakenly ascribed to the first child. If such motives determine the second pregnancy, the home may really not be ready for the newcomer. If the parents are too completely wrapped up in the first child, the second is likely to suffer in some measure. The stern virtues of impartiality begin even before the second child is born.

Current theories have exaggerated the dangers of a jealousy reaction toward the arrival of a new baby. The result is that parents in their anxiety to forestall such a reaction, go to extreme lengths to build up fortitude and hospitality in the already entrenched first-born. Some of this build-up is nothing short of amusing (in the dispassionate light of what we know about child development). Perhaps a sense of humor can prevent us from going to unnecessary or unwise extremes in getting Junior ready for the New Baby who several months hence will make him a Senior!

To begin with, Junior has a very limited presentiment of events which have not taken place. If he is two years old he has no sense of the future. If he is somewhat older, he may be disappointed and bored by unending references to an event so distant that day after day it is heralded and yet never comes! His age, his temperament, and his maturity should determine how much is told and how it is told. It must be remembered that young children are not adept in thinking in words. They can scarcely be told anything for which they have not had equivalent experience. Or rather, they may be told, but they will not understand. Or they will interpret so literally that their imagery becomes a travesty of the truth you attempt to impart.

A little lesson on seeds and flowers will hardly elucidate the complexities of child-bearing. Even with a bright child such a botanical approach has its hazards as was illustrated by an incident in an Episcopalian Cathedral, when a certain bright preschool child broke the solemn silence of a marriage ceremony by bursting out aloud with the question: "But, Mother, when is he going to put on the pollen!?"

Concrete minded children do not think in analogies. They think in terms of seeds in the stomach. An experimental child may swallow a tomato seed or even a prune pit in order to induce pregnancy. Then there was the girl (or was it a boy?) who swallowed two seeds because the objective was twins!

Such amusing misconceptions should remind us of the limitations of the child's intellect and imagination. His comprehension is dependent upon experience and upon growth which proceeds by slow degrees. It is idle to give him information in advance of his capacity to assimilate. Too much information will actually confuse him, if at the age of four or five he is offered sophisticated ideas and images in the form of words and pictures. His questions are not as profound as they sound. They should be met with casualness rather than ecstasy. Reserve combined with a disarming smile is better than misplaced candor. One need not resort to concealment and old-wives tales; but in general it is wise to respect the child's primitive notions and to give him a minimum response which will satisfy him for the present, and provide him with a nucleus for another advance in his thinking. He cannot be told anything complex at one fell swoop. "To inform the understanding is the work of time." His adjustment to the new baby does not so much depend upon advance information as on a kindly planned protection of his sense of status and prestige.

The planning includes the spacing of children. Many factors bear on this question. One of these is the age of the first born. Usually the 3 year old child is becoming psychologically ready to make a good adjustment to a new baby. He has just come through a stage of reliving his own babyhood emotionally and is well on his way to adjusting to the larger world beyond the home. The 3 year old is ready to go to grandmother's when his mother goes to the hospital. He thinks about the trip almost more than he thinks of the new baby. He may even stay on for an extra two weeks after his mother and the new baby have returned to their home. Frequent postcards hold his contact with his parents. If he stays at home, the mother's voice over the telephone continues a bond, although for some children this makes her absence more difficult.

For the younger child, 12 to 18 months old, special preparations may not register at all. He may not react unfavorably to the mother's hospitalization or the homecoming of the baby, but unwittingly he may be deprived of many accustomed privileges and even some necessities if the household has not been careful to plan for him in his own right.

The 2 year old child can take part in a simple way in the physical preparations perhaps a month or two before the baby comes. The bassinet, the blankets, the baby powder and doll play help to initiate him into the impending event. At this age, he will probably cleave to his mother as the time for her departure draws near. He may miss her severely during the two weeks when she is in the maternity hospital if he has not become accustomed to a caretaker beforehand. In general, it may be best to have him remain in his own home during this period, for to place him in unfamiliar surroundings might add to the strain of the separation from his mother. The daily homecoming of the father gives support to his sense of security. The 2 year old responds well to some physical token of his mother, such as a scarf or a pocketbook, and wants his repeated query, "Where's Mommy?" answered with the self-same words, such as "Mommy's on Ivy Street in the big house." He may even come to answer his own questions by himself if they are tossed back to him.

It is rather surprising to see how slow is the 3 year old, and even the 4 year old, to notice the enlarging of the mother's abdomen. At 3½ to 4 years he is often very conscious of marked deviations in the symmetry of the body such as an amputated arm or a limping leg. But a slowly changing form before his own eyes does not register. If it is perceived he often gives his own immediate interpretations that his mother has eaten too much breakfast so that her stomach has grown large. He may even try to duplicate her prowess! The wise mother does not impose more knowledge of the coming event than the child has shown himself perceptive of and capable of handling. As with the 2 year old, the orientation of the 3 year old is accomplished through participation in the physical preparations a month or two before the baby arrives.

The 4 year old, and sometimes the 3 year old, is ready for further information and elementary interpretations. In Chapter 23, we shall attempt to outline the steps and developmental stages by which the young child grows into a deepening knowledge of the meaning of birth and babies.

A great fuss is naturally made when the new baby arrives home. This is the critical period which calls for finesse. It is easier for all concerned if the older child, especially the 3 or 4 year old is away from home. Then the mother has a simpler home adjustment to make and can give all of her attention to the newborn infant. After the four week period has been passed, when the mother can again move freely about the house, the return and adjustment of the older child is much easier. At whatever age the older child may be, the first sight of the new baby is the most difficult for him. If initial jealousy does occur, it usually passes rapidly within the first few days. The recurrence of this feeling is most apt to come if the older child (not usually beyond 4 years) sees the new baby nursing at the breast. He should not feel dispossessed. He should participate in the fuss of welcoming and be given simple tasks, such as fetching diapers and administering the bath powder, to afford him a sense of participation. Perhaps much of the fuss should be strategically and ostensibly shifted from the new baby to himself. His prestige should be preserved at all hazards. Indeed, in the happiest households, the prestige of all members is equally safeguarded. When there are two or more children in a family, the most skillful mother plans separately for each individuality.

Whenever a second baby comes into a household, there is danger that we shall try to do too much and consequently overlook the simplest things which are the most important. Explanations have their limitations. The shortest path to the young child is not through the intellect. He is not ready for a preschool course in embryology and obstetrics. There is even some danger in magnifying the role of the physician before the new baby is born. We know of a boy who betrayed unmistakable disappointment as he looked upon the florid face of his newborn brother. In his wisdom, the elder brother exclaimed, "I knew this would happen if you had a *country* doctor!"

We also know of a girl who had been beautifully "prepared" for the new baby, but, alas, was visibly dejected when she saw the new arrival. Why? Because nightly she had prayed for an *older* sister!

8

A GOOD START

WHEN does the baby's mental welfare begin? Before birth. And not, of course, because of the effect of maternal impressions upon the unborn child; but, rather because the mother, even during her pregnancy, is developing attitudes, expectancies, and decisions which will inevitably influence the course of the baby's mental growth, particularly in the four fundamental months which follow birth. It is well to make a good start.

The mental hygiene of the child, therefore, begins with maternity hygiene, and for this reason the obstetrician has a more important role to play than he frequently suspects. Naturally his concern is focused upon the critical event of birth and the preservation of the mother's health in the face of this crisis. But granting this, the expectant mother still turns to him with many questions which have potential importance for her own personal psychology and for the psychological welfare of the expected

[80]

child. There are still other questions which she does not formulate at all, but which the obstetrician should formulate for her through his guidance.

§1. BREAST FEEDING AND
SELF-REGULATION

FIRST and foremost comes the question of breast feeding. Too often the decision on this crucial question is allowed to drift until a short time before the baby's birth. This dilatoriness has an adverse effect upon the mother's emotional orientation. It also tends to have an adverse effect upon her capacity for lactation. For one thing, the breast and nipples may require regular and systematic attention three months prior to the birth, the anointing and massage of the nipples preventing the cracking which so often interferes with successful breast feeding. This regular attention to the nipples also prepares the mother mentally for the duty of breast feeding, when the time arrives. Perhaps the word "duty" has been misplaced. Our culture in America has shown an increasing tendency to give the mother a choice between nursing and artificial feeding, and often has weighted the choice in favor of the bottle as opposed to the breast.

On the other hand there is the pediatrician who, in cooperation with the obstetrician, judiciously encourages breast feeding in the absence of decisive contra-indications. Certainly the pediatrician's difficulties will be greatly reduced if breast feeding is successfully undertaken during the first four months (to say nothing about mother and baby) .

In the circumnatal period it is natural that there should be cooperation and a certain overlapping in the professional services of obstetrician and pediatrician. In the family physician both services are combined in one person. The obstetrician is concerned with mother,—and child: the pediatrician with child,—and mother. The pediatric responsibility begins, at least technically, with the severance of the umbilical cord. We shall assume that the pediatrician favors breast feeding and that he wishes to avoid excessive adherence to an iron clad clock schedule. This would set the stage for a self-regulated regime, based on a sensible interpretation of the self-demands of the infant. Breast feeding is the most favorable condition for the initiation of a self-demand schedule.

For two weeks the newborn infant remains in residence in the hospital. Prevailing hospital conventions in our present culture require that the baby should spend nearly all of this fortnight in the nursery dormitory. The nurse is permitted to bring the baby to the mother from time to time and is also permitted to hold him up behind the plate glass for the inspection of admiring visitors, essential or non-essential. Under such hospital auspices the baby is fed according to a fixed schedule laid down by the supervising physician. The sporadic and congregate crying of the babies in the nursery is taken as a matter of course. The individual crying of individual babies is not in general subjected to individual attention. Each baby is fed when the clock indicates that he should be fed.

§2. A ROOMING-IN ARRANGEMENT FOR THE BABY

Now let us assume that we take our point of departure from the internal physiological clock of the infant himself and give regard to his individual cries. We might then suggest a rooming-in arrangement which would bring both bassinet and baby into the mother's room. It is a movable bassinet which may be put in a secluded corner or more intimately at the foot or side of the bed, in accordance with the mother's wishes. For is it not also desirable to place the mother on a reasonable self-demand basis? When her strength permits and when her wishes so dictate it may prove very wise to keep the baby within her vicinity during the course of the day. Naturally after the evening or night feeding the baby will be restored to his dormitory.

This arrangement will actually reduce the amount of manipulation to which the baby is subjected. It simply means that when he cries to be fed, he will be fed. It also means that the baby will benefit from the added oversight of the mother, during the intervals between feedings. There is no evidence that under proper safeguards such a rooming-in procedure increases the hazard of infection. If anything, the hazard will be reduced because of other attendant advantages.

The presence of the baby gives the mother a profound sense of security. Vague worries and misgivings as to the identity of her baby lose their insistence. She is in a favorable position to build up a sense of relationship with the infant, a sense of familiarity which will fortify her confidence when in the very near future she herself takes over the ministrations and infant care. She is spared the uncertainty which comes from being unable to visualize exactly where her baby is and how he is faring at any given moment, and throughout the many moments of the day. This proximity of mother and child is so natural and can be made so simple that it will dissipate tensions and much of the hospital haste and hurry. The presence of the baby will serve in a salutary way to protect her against an excess of visitors. He sleeps most of the day. The mother keeps a weather eye on the baby. The incidental oversight makes her perceptive of his self-demands. All this increases the advantages of the self-regulatory program of care on which she and the physician have embarked. There is no excessive strain upon the mother. She is within easy reach of a push-button and controls the situation by summoning the nurse whenever she needs help. The rooming-in self-regulatory arrangement is not rigid; it is flexible and can be altered to meet the needs of both mother and child from day to day. It applies to bottle-fed as well as breast-fed babies.

From the standpoint of the infant there are obvious advantages; that is, if we grant that the infant is subject to psychological influences in this early neonatal period. He enjoys more natural and diverse stimulations under rooming-in conditions. His rhythms will not escape notice and he will be spared unnecessary crying. He is in a position to be his natural self. He will communicate his individuality to his mother even in this first fortnight. The more intimate reciprocal relationship between them serves to give the mother more insight into the baby's needs as expressed in his patterns of behavior. The rooming-in arrangement, however, should be kept flexible. It may be adopted in varying degrees subject to the physician's judgment. In some instances for special reasons it may be unsuitable either for the mother or for the baby.

In any event, the mother's perceptiveness of behavior signs is fostered by a very simple device, namely, the behavior chart previously mentioned (p. 52). Each one of the days which the baby spends in the hospital is recorded by a simple line-a-day method, with a total daily expenditure of less than five minutes. The records will be kept by the nurse, but they are so useful that the mother will wish to continue them after the homecoming. This chart records by figures and conventional signs four major items in the baby's behavior day: namely, *feeding; elimination; sleep; crying*. The entries are made on the basis of a 24-hour cycle from midnight to midnight, as described in Appendix A.

Each entry is made immediately on the spot. The adjacent lines automatically summarize the changes from day to day. The chart itself does not bake us any bread, but it constitutes a helpful diary for the mother and an informative indicator for the physician. If the baby is breast fed, he is weighed prior to each feeding and immediately after each feeding. The difference is the amount of the intake, for the baby is weighed with clothes on.* From the record the pediatrician will always know how much the baby takes at any given feeding. The chart makes such a revealing cumulative record that the mother will wish to continue the daily recordings after she leaves the hospital. The chart in this way serves to bridge the gap between home and hospital.

---

* At first sight this may seem like a formidable procedure but since the baby's clothes do not need to be removed, the weighing takes very little time and the figures are accurate. Convenience is served if the scales are available in the mother's room.

§3. FROM HOSPITAL TO HOME

AT HOME the mother takes over the recording which she learned from the nurse. Under the rooming-in conditions of the first fortnight at the hospital, she has seen so much of her baby that he is no stranger to her. He looks much less precarious because she has seen his adaptations from day to day. She has seen him dressed and undressed. She has witnessed several baths. This introductory familiarity with the details of infant care stands her in good stead when she is thrown on her own after the homecoming. She may not even need the demonstrating services of a visiting nurse. She will escape the nervousness which so often occurs in the transition to home surroundings. The most comprehensive commendation, therefore, of the rooming-in arrangement is this: it strengthens the bonds between mother and child; it heightens poise and confidence because it achieves a more complete mutual adaptation.

The homelikeness of the rooming-in arrangement at the hospital has made the whole transition to the home less of a crisis. The transition becomes still less of a burden to the mother if the conditions at home at least for another fortnight can be made to approximate the indulgences of the hospital. The mother should not take over increased activities too suddenly. It is a great advantage if she can live on a separate floor or in a somewhat detached part of the house. If possible, the baby should sleep at night in a separate room, as he did in the hospital. Indeed, the rooming-in arrangement of the hospital can be more or less duplicated. Perhaps the father will be in a position to bring the baby to the mother for the night feedings. The domestic policy should be to divide the labors! The home waits on the mother; the mother waits on the child.

The mother's sleep schedule should be adjusted to that of the infant, ample rest being provided to enable her to continue with the breast feeding. Increase of liquid intake is indicated from time to time if there are signs of reduction in lactation. Her interest in continuing the breast feeding is strengthened by a realization that the breast feeding has a favorable effect upon the post-partum involution of the uterus.

It is remarkable to what extent breast feeding is sensitive to cultural impress. Among many peoples from the most primitive to the highly civilized Swedish, breast feeding is taken for granted as established custom. It is the exceptional mother in these cultural groups who does not nurse her infant.

In America the adoption and duration of breast feeding depends to a surprising degree on more or less fortuitous cultural influences. We know of a pediatrician with a wide metropolitan practice who through sheer exercise of his own professional abilities has induced three-fourths of his maternal clients to adopt breast feeding in preference to bottle feeding. In many other instances this ratio is reversed. The authority and opinions of the physician constitute an important part of the cultural impact. Sometimes it is a lack of accommodation between obstetrician and pediatrician which brings about a premature termination of breast feeding. The obstetrician may stop the nursing early to prevent a breast abscess,— a potential though rare occurrence. This danger may well be lessened if the pediatrician in the interest of the child (as well as mother) recommends nursing at both breasts at each feeding with alternation of the first breast. Positive cooperation between obstetrician and pediatrician favor prolongations of breast feeding. The initiation of breast feeding may even hinge upon the professional solicitude and skill of the physician in charge. He should supervise the very first nursings which are so critical in establishing a successful adjustment to the breast.

Even after breast feeding has been initiated in a lying-in hospital, the mother often resorts to artificial feeding on discharge, influenced, perhaps, by gossip which she has heard on the ward, or by suggestions she has gratuitously received from a nurse, an intern, or a neighbor. The neighbor says, "I nursed my first child, but why bother. I put my second child on a bottle and he got along just as well." The "custom" of breast feeding often hangs upon such slender contingencies in America, which fact is itself proof that a strong consolidation of both lay and professional opinion might soon make breast feeding much more nearly universal, at least during the first four months.

§4. THE EVOLUTION OF THE BEHAVIOR DAY

THE behavior day chart serves to smooth the transition from hospital to home. The chart helps the mother to a fuller understanding of the child because it both symbolizes and directs her growing insight into the **baby's** individuality. The lengthening chart will also impart a significant impression of the baby's growth. She will detect in the chart not only the manner in which the baby distributes his daily quota of energy, but also the manner in which he blocks out and consolidates his various behaviors. His staple and significant behaviors consist of the following: Sleeping; Crying; Fussing; "Talking"; Playing; Sense-perceiving; Sleeping; etc. The chart (Appendix A) will show how these behaviors undergo developmental changes from week to week. The changes achieved by the baby give some foretaste of changes yet to accrue in the future. This will have orientational value for the mother during the first four months, giving a sense of perspective just at the time when it is most needed.

These first months are inclined to be somewhat stormy, but the weather will seem much less erratic and take on much more meaning if the child's behavior is not regarded as erratic but is interpreted as an expression of his organic needs and interests. The chart facilitates such interpretation. The baby's most articulate mouthpiece is his crying. Crying is essentially language even though at times it appears to be indulged in for purposes of sheer self-activity. From the standpoint of a self-demand regime the major task of the mother is to be alert to all forms of crying and fussing, to read their meaning and to give as prompt attention as possible. Punctual response to crying in the early weeks reduces the total amount of crying, for if there is a delay in the response there is likely to be a resumption and prolongation of the crying after attention has been given. It is a comfort to realize in advance that ordinarily there is a steady reduction in the frequency and amount of crying. During the first 8 weeks hunger crying is virtually universal. After about 8 weeks the hunger cry tends to diminish in intensity and frequency. The child begins to substitute fussing for crying and he has longer intervals of quiescence because he is becoming interested in various forms of non-feeding behavior. His crying is consequently more intermittent, less sustained.

By the age of 16 weeks his hunger cry may be almost entirely limited to the morning feeding. During the first six weeks he also cries when his diapers are wet or soiled. He may even cry out for this reason during a sleep period. After about the age of 6 weeks he accepts this condition with a nonchalance which may continue to the age of 12 or 15 months, or even later.

At about the age of 4 weeks a new type of cry emerges: the baby shows a tendency to cry prior to sleep. This is not a hunger cry. The cry is a mixture of cause and effect, a symptom of his growing capacity to stay awake. It is a developmental symptom of a thrust toward a higher level of activity. This wakefulness crying tends to occur in the afternoon and evening. It loses its prominence after about the age of 10 or 12 weeks, forsooth because the baby has scaled the higher level. At about this time there is an increasing metamorphosis of crying into fussing and into "talking" vocalization. With advancing age the crying which occurs toward the end of the day is frequently related to a higher order of psychological hungers. The child wishes to exercise his growing sense-perception abilities, to experience color, light, sound, musical notes, singing. He wishes to watch movements; he likes to feel movements too through his kinesthetic sense perception. He may like to be talked to, or even to receive play objects toward the end of the first four months. These new appetites or interests come in small snatches, often punctuated by brief intervals of crying and fussing. The mother is well advised not to over-stimulate the child in response to this type of crying, but inasmuch as it is symptomatic of psychological growth needs, it deserves discriminating consideration.

For similar reasons a little gentle rocking prior to sleep may assuage a fretful cry. While the mother carried her unborn child he was frequently subjected to translations in space. He does not suffer from mild transportations and an occasional jostle after he is born.

With increasing age the child cries less readily on provocation. Whereas in the early weeks a startle was typically followed by a cry, he may by the age of 12 weeks and later, startle without crying. He is building up margins of reserve and margins of exploitive activity. Viewed in perspective his behavior is manifestly becoming more configured, more defined. He terminates meals more decisively by symptoms of positive refusal. His appetite is more clear cut. His demand to be moved from the crib for a brief sojourn on the couch may become so clearly defined to a perceptive mother that he could not express it better if he had a vocabulary of spoken words.

His behavior becomes relatively so effectively defined that there may be a temptation to feed him solids even as early as 12 or 16 weeks. Such a premature attempt to introduce solids during the first four months sometimes invites regrettable results. The baby's neuro-muscular system is not mature enough to handle solids competently. His tongue projection and lip constriction patterns are so dominant that they interfere with normal swallowing mechanisms. Moreover, if supplementary food is added too early the mother's milk balance is upset. A premature administration of solids may result either in marked reduction or over-production of the mother's milk supply, for the baby consumes less at the breast. Not until about the age of 20 weeks is he likely to be mature and interested enough to handle solids acceptably. Fortunately at this period the mother is capable of maintaining an adequate milk supply over a full 12-hour interval without the stimulus of the infant's nursing. This circumstance permits the introduction of solids without prejudicing continued breast feeding and also gives more freedom to the mother. Breast feeding continues to be advantageous both to mother and child for a few months more. It is especially advantageous if the child persists in demanding an early morning feeding.

[89]

The expanding behavior chart builds up a perspective which reaches into the future as well as the past. This sense of perspective is further increased when the mother is informed in advance that her child at 16 weeks is very likely to show well defined behavior patterns. But she should understand that the trend toward focused and defined behavior is not altogether smooth and even,—the baby has "bad" days as well as "good" days. And paradoxically enough, from the standpoint of development the "bad" days may be his best days because they are days of high tension in which he is making a thrust (as previously suggested) into a more advanced sphere of behavior. These are the high tension days when his crying is not so much expressive of a frustration as of "thrustration"! The pendulum is swinging to a new extreme. He is wriggling upward. He may briefly display a behavior pattern which will not become part of his established equipment until several weeks later. After a high tension episode or a high tension day he may revert to a lower level of apparently vegetative functioning which on the surface seems like a "good" day.

Actually both types of days have their justification in the economy of development. Development proceeds consistently toward a distant goal but it fluctuates from day to day while advancing toward that goal. It is therefore not surprising to find that after the baby has consolidated many of his abilities at the end of four months, he will begin in another month or two again to show perturbances and irregularities reminiscent of the first four months. Nevertheless the trend of normal development is always toward increasing organization and consolidation. Realization of this trend has practical value because it gives the mother a sense of proportion. Things are not as bad as they seem. Patience does not cease to be a virtue; for the higher order of abilities cannot be hastened. Everything in season. "Time bringeth all things."

In the following chapters we shall try to outline in an orderly manner the behavior traits and the behavior trends which Time brings to the growing infant. We have already emphasized that Time travels in divers paces with divers persons. No two infants develop in precisely the same manner at precisely the same pace in every detail. But the ladder of maturity is made of rungs. The following series of behavior profiles is simply intended to show *in a general and approximate way* how a somewhat typical child, as a representative of his species and his culture, mounts the tall ladder with rungs placed at advancing ages. First we delineate the baby four-weeks-old.

9

FOUR WEEKS OLD

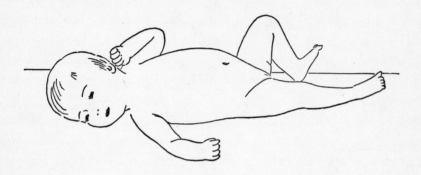

§1. BEHAVIOR PROFILE

WHAT is the mind of the 4 week old baby like? He cannot tell us; and you and I cannot recall what it was like. The inmost psychic processes of infant and child are always veiled from view. Nevertheless, we can gain a just and useful picture of the "psychology" of a baby, even at the tender age of 4 weeks, if we examine the different kinds of behavior of which he is capable. His behavior patterns, his behavior traits, tell us what he really is.

In 4 weeks the baby has made considerable progress. He is not quite as limp and "molluscous" as he was at birth. His body muscles have more tone; they tighten in tension when he is picked up. Therefore he seems less fragile, more organized.

Indeed, he *is* more organized. Growth is a process of progressive organization. It is not simply a matter of getting bigger and stronger. The

4 week old baby is much more mature than a new born baby because his whole action-system is more elaborately built up, more closely knit together. Multimillions of nerve fibers from millions of nerve cells have made new connections with each other and have improved their old connections with his internal organs and with his muscular system.

His breathing is deeper and more regular; his swallowing is firmer, he does not choke or regurgitate as freely as he used to. He is less susceptible to startling, jaw trembling, and sneezing. His temperature regulation is steadier. All his vegetative functions are under better control, because the chemistry of his body fluids as well as the "vegetative" part of his nervous system has made adjustments to his postnatal environment.

But he is by no means a vegetable. He evidences an unmistakable psychological interest in his bodily functions and bodily experiences. He gives manifest attention to the well-being that suffuses him after a meal; he enjoys the massive warmth and tingle of the bath; he responds to the snugness of being wrapped up or of being securely held. He reacts positively to comforts and satisfactions; he reacts negatively to discomforts and denials. By crying and other sign language he expresses demands and desires. He is far from empty-minded. He is far from being a mere automaton. There may even be a trace of volition in some of his behavior. At any rate we cannot think of him as being a mere bundle of reflexes. From the standpoint of 4-week-oldness his behavior is patterned, meaningful, significant.

He still sleeps most of the day and night, as much as twenty hours out of the twenty-four; but his waking up is more decisive and more businesslike than it was even a fortnight ago. His eyes roll less aimlessly; the twelve diminutive but all-important muscles that operate the movements of the eye balls are assuming directive control. He is now able to hold both eyes in a fixed position, staring vaguely at a window or wall. This does not mean that he actually perceives the outlines of the window; the nerve cells of the brain cortex are not sufficiently grown for that. Yet he is especially regardful of the human face when it comes noddingly into his field of vision. His general body activity diminishes when this "interesting" optical and social stimulus meets the eye. In yet another month he will converge both eyes upon a near object. Then we may say he has truly begun to use his binoculars.

At 4 weeks his range of eye movements is limited by incomplete head control. He tends to keep his head to one side. You can entice him to look at a dangling toy held directly before his eyes, and he will follow it a short distance when it is moved toward the midline; but it will take another month or two before he will follow way across from one horizon to the opposite horizon.

At 16 weeks his head will prefer the midline, facing the zenith. If during the first few months the head prefers the horizon or side position, it is for good developmental reasons. This position enables the baby to catch glimpses of his hand, for he often holds his arm extended toward the same side to which his head is directed, the other arm being flexed at the shoulder.

This sideward attitude of head and arm (sometimes called the tonic-neck-reflex) is a normal stage of growth which should not be tampered with simply because it appears asymmetrical. It is a natural form of asymmetry which serves to bring eyes and hands into coordination, and such natural postures are entitled to respect. At 4 weeks the baby's hands are usually fisted. (Another natural posture,—how silly it would be to keep prying open the hands; they will remain open in due course when the baby is ready to reach.)

Just now, at the age of 4 weeks, the baby is beginning to reach, but he does so with his eyes rather than his hands. The eyes take the lead in the organization of his growing brain. He cannot hold a rattle prolongedly until about the age of 8 weeks; at first he merely holds without looking. In another month he both holds and looks,—still later he seizes on sight. The coordination of hands and eyes is a long and complicated process. It takes time. It needs understanding.

The 4 week old baby is not ready for social stimulation. His vegetative needs, his sensori-motor experiences are most important. He is often busiest when he is apparently quiescent. His behavior patterns are undergoing organization and re-organization, through immobilization as well as through activity. He cannot tell us what is happening because his laryngeal vocabulary is limited to a few throaty sounds. But he makes his developmental needs articulate in many other ways. This will become clear when we describe the daily cycle of his home behavior.

§2. BEHAVIOR DAY

THE behavior profile which you have just read summarizes the behavior capacities and characteristics of the 4 week old baby. How will he display these characteristics; how will he use his capacities in the course of a day? He answers this question for us in the form of his behavior day. If he could keep a log book, he could record for us all of his activities and interests, and from such a record we could gain a picture of the manner in which he stores and distributes his energies.

On the basis of our own observations of the day-by-day living of the 4 week old infant, we can draw up a suggestive profile sketch of a more or less typical behavior day. We cannot set down any hard and fast hours because we must allow for many individual variations and because we shall assume for purposes of illustration a breast-fed baby on a self-demand schedule. The Egyptians reckoned their day from midnight, the Babylonians from sunrise, the Athenians from sunset; we shall reckon the baby's day from midnight and shall consider the full series of twenty-four hours which span the interval between two successive midnights.

Assume that the baby is sound asleep, at least on the first midnight. He may awake at almost any hour between 2 A.M. and 6 A.M. He awakes with a decisive, piercing crying. He awakes because his economy requires that once again he should have a ration of food. He wakes to eat. His cry is a more or less articulate statement of this extremely fundamental fact. Incidentally, it serves to announce his presence. Vaguely it may even express a sense of isolation, for he quiets momentarily when he is taken up, whether by his father or his mother. But crying renews if he is not soon put to the breast. He needs a little help to secure the nipple. Crying ceases when he establishes contact.

He nurses for a period of from twenty to forty minutes. He may be seemingly satisfied with one breast but often when offered the second breast he takes it with revived vigor. His eyes are closed during the nursing. As he approaches satiety the sucking becomes more intermittent and he gradually tapers off into sleep.

A similar satiety response occurs if his tiny stomach is distended by air. The wise mother, therefore, "bubbles" the infant when shifting him from one breast to the other and at the termination of the meal. The baby is now under the benevolent anesthesia of natural sleep. The mother exploits this opportunity to change the wet diapers. By postponing the change in this way, the baby's impatience is circumvented. If, however, the diapers were soiled before the feeding, the change is made earlier.

The baby is put back into the bassinet. He sleeps for a period of from two to five hours and wakes up as before for the prime purpose of feeding again. We call this a sleep period rather than a nap. A nap is a restricted and well-demarcated interval of sleep immediately preceded or followed by an equally well-defined period of wakefulness. But at 4 weeks the feeding-sleeping-waking-feeding sequence is so closely merged that the baby's day resolves itself into five or six zones of sleep; each terminating typically with a hunger cry. The baby has not yet learned to wake up for more advanced reasons. He does not nap. His capacity for wakefulness is very immature.

In the late afternoon (typically between four and six o'clock), however, he has a wider margin for perceptual and pre-social behavior. This, therefore, is an optimal time, although not the conventional one, for his daily bath. Where he might show resistance in the morning, he now enjoys the experience of immersion in the tepid water. His eyes open wider; his general body activity may abate. He often gives tokens of pleasurable response to the sound of the voice and to the handling which gives him a feeling of tactility, and to being tucked in when he is dressed and restored to the bassinet for another sleep period.

Whether the infant cries because he is awake, or whether he is awake because he cries poses a philosophical problem. The 4 week old infant is maturing his capacity to wake up and to extend his areas of sense perception. Hunger is the chief cause of his crying but his cries are beginning to differentiate and there are distinctive features in the cries associated with various kinds of discomfort.

He frets or cries when his alimentary tract and his eliminative organs are not functioning smoothly. He basks with contentment when his physiological wellbeing is at least temporarily achieved. In these brief periods he has a margin for more advanced perceptual adjustments. He may give absorbed attention to his sense of wellbeing. He likes to gaze in the direction of his accustomed tonic-neck-reflex attitude and sometimes his fretfulness subsides if he is given an opportunity to fixate his restless eyes on some large and not too bright pattern.

Needless to say, these evidences of perceptual and pre-social interest are slight and fugitive. Some children do not show them at all until the age of 6 or 8 weeks. At times this early crying seems to be quite without reason; almost as though it were crying for its own sake. But the very fact that the baby quiets recurrently to slight environmental changes suggests that he is entitled to some of these changes. The handling should be restricted to his actual needs. He is not ready for social stimulation. At this age no two behavior days are likely to be identical. Some are stormier than others. Excess storminess may mean that the appropriate adjustments between the organism and the environment have not been attained. All of which suggests that it is well to be alert to such signals as the baby is able to give during the course of his behavior day.

The foregoing behavior day is not set up as a model, but as a suggestive example. This also holds true for the behavior days at later age levels

[97]

presented in Chapters 10-19. They are merely illustrative behavior days. Individual differences are to be expected.

Further child care details for each age are given in the double column text. [*Specific guidance suggestions are enclosed in brackets.*]

SLEEP

Onset—The baby gradually drops off to sleep toward the end of the nursing process when sucking becomes intermittent. He will not accept the nipple when sleep is associated with satiety. If wakefulness follows one of the feedings, he may cry prior to the next sleep period.

Waking—The baby cries as he awakens. He may stop momentarily as his diaper is changed, especially when it is only wet. Crying usually continues until he is fed.

Periods—Four to five periods in twenty-four hours. The reduction from seven to eight at birth is accomplished by the merging of two sleep periods. Further reduction may be accomplished by the dropping-out of a sleep period between two successive feedings.

[The infant should be cared for as soon as he awakens crying. If crying precedes going to sleep, release from crying into sleep may be assisted by mild and brief rocking of bassinet or carriage, perhaps accompanied by singing.]

FEEDING

Number—The infant spontaneously cuts down his feedings from seven to eight at birth to five or six at 4 weeks. This is accomplished by merging two adjacent feedings. This reduction may not hold for long but returns later.

Amount—The total amount may fluctuate between 18 ounces and 25 ounces from 2 to

4 weeks of age, after which there is a more rapid rise to 32 or 36 ounces by 6 to 8 weeks of age. There may be no more than a one ounce fluctuation in the amount of each feeding at 4 weeks of age, but this rapidly increases to a three to four ounce fluctuation by 6 to 8 weeks.

Duration—Sucking time varies greatly from child to child but is usually 30 to 40 minutes and may even be longer during the evening feedings.

Breast and Bottle Feeding—Crying demands may be quieted by placing the baby on the mother's lap, but more frequently they are quieted after he secures the breast. He needs help to secure the nipple. The tongue has become more efficient in grasping the nipple and in exerting back-and-forth suction. With satiety the infant falls asleep, will not accept the re-introduction of the nipple, and may show transient facial brightening.

[The majority of infants know when they are hungry and are able to express their hunger by crying. They become more proficient in this innate ability if they are allowed to exercise it. Their proficiency is also promoted if their demands are answered with promptness and if satiety both for food and sucking is insured. This is most easily accomplished with breast feeding. Both breasts should be presented at each feeding. The first breast is alternated from feeding to feeding even though the child may refuse the second breast at times. The amount taken should be recorded. This can most easily be accomplished by weighing the breast-fed baby before and after each feeding with the same clothes on, the difference being the intake of milk.]

ELIMINATION

Bowel—One to three or even four movements, on awakening from sleep.
Bladder—The baby may cry when his diaper is wet and quiets when changed. This pattern is only occasional and does not last beyond 6 weeks of age.

[If crying is associated with wet or soiled diapers, changing will quiet the infant. This cause of crying is to be differentiated from hunger crying.]

BATH AND DRESSING

The baby now enjoys the bath. He does not like to be dressed and undressed.

[Clothing should be as simple as possible. Preferably it should not be put on over the baby's head.]

SELF-ACTIVITY

The infant stares at lights and windows. He favors turning his head to one side or the other, according to his tonic-neck-reflex. He may become angry if turned on the side away from the light. He quiets as he is shifted toward the light. This desire for light and brightness, apart from sunlight to which he makes a violent negative response, is later shown at 8 to 10 weeks in an interest in red and orange colors. Intense crying may be controlled by having a bright-colored cretonne pillow to gaze upon.

Visual experience with light and bright colors is important to the child as well as is the food in his stomach.

SOCIALITY

The baby stares at faces that are close by. If he cries in the evening—which is his way of asking for social stimulation—he quiets if he is picked up and held or if he is allowed to lie naked on a table where he can hear voices and look at lights for an hour or two. This demand is most frequent from 6 to 8 weeks, and its total duration is so related to a growth process that the end-results appear to be similar whether he is allowed to cry it out or his demands are satisfied. By 8 weeks he likes to follow movement and enjoys seeing people move about the room.

10

SIXTEEN WEEKS OLD

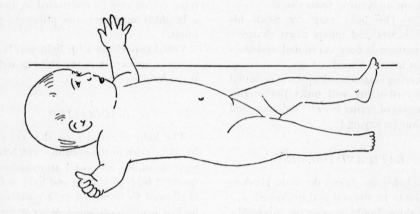

§1. BEHAVIOR PROFILE

THE FOUR WEEK OLD infant was quite content to lie on his back. He could not support his head on his own shoulders. But the 16 week old infant glories in the exercise of his growing capacity to hold his head upright. He likes to be translated from the supine to a propped sitting position. His eyes widen, his pulse strengthens, his breathing quickens as he is shifted from horizontal to perpendicular. He holds his head quite steady while bolstering pillows or his mother's hands supply the necessary support for his wobbly trunk. For some ten minutes at a time he relishes his new commanding outlook upon the surrounding world.

He no longer stares blankly. He rotates his head freely from side to side as he lies in his crib,—indeed so freely that the rubbing produces an erosive bald spot. (The spot is oblate and favors his preferred side.) He moves his eyes in active inspection. He fixes them on this and that. He looks at his own hand; he looks at the kitchen sink; he looks at a toy which his mother dangles before him; he may even look from the toy to his mother's hand, and then back again at the toy, a sign of his increasing discrimination. He is becoming perceptive. He is also becoming more expressive. He smiles on the mere sight of a face. He coos, bubbles, chuckles, gurgles, and even laughs aloud.

The provocations for these vocalizations are both internal and external, but he is much less "subjective" than he was at the age of 4 weeks, much less wrapped up in himself. He is more bound up with his environment: he is sensitive to cultural cues, he "notices" sounds, especially those of the human voice; he "recognizes" his mother; he is so accustomed to certain routines that he expects certain things to happen at meal time and bath time. He betrays these expectancies in his countenance and in his postures. So the household is also becoming sensitive to his cues. The two-way reciprocity of cues is the basis of acculturation.

Having gained elementary management of the muscles which direct his eyes, and the muscles which erect and rotate his head, the next developmental task calls for a better management of his hands. (It is interesting to note that he can "pick up" a small object with his eyes long before he can pick it up with his fingers!)

At 16 weeks the hand is no longer predominantly fisted. It has loosened up. The fingers are more nimble, more busy. The baby still looks at his hands on occasion, but he has a new trick; he brings them together over his chest, and engages them in mutual fingering play. His fingers finger his fingers! Thus he himself touches and is touched simultaneously. This double touch is a lesson in self-discovery. He comes to appreciate what his fingers are; and that objects are something different. Putting fingers into the mouth and putting objects into the mouth also help to clear up these fundamental distinctions. The baby has to learn his physics and his anatomy as well as his sociology.

And so in the next three months he lays hold of the physical world with his hands as well as his eyes. As once he showed visual hunger, now he shows touch hunger. He is ravenous in his desire to approach, to contact, to grasp, to feel, and to manipulate. Whether lying in a crib or seated in a lap, he shows a psycho-motor eagerness when an object comes within reach. At 16 weeks his shoulders strain, and his arms activate as a toy is brought near. In another month his hands close in on the object, corral it, grasp it on contact. In yet another month or two he makes direct one-handed approach on sight. These advancing coordinations are organized through the steady process of growth. At 16 weeks he clutches rather than prehends. He clasps his coverlet, pulling it over his face quite uncritically. This behavior pattern is immature but it foretokens more advanced forms of grasp and manipulation.

A baby is never complete. He is always in the making. But even his incomplete abilities are charged with potentialities. Accordingly there is much promise in the cooing, the expectant inspection, the excited breathing, the mutual fingering, and the coverlet clutching of the socially smiling, just sixteen baby.

§2. BEHAVIOR DAY

WHEN DOES THE SIXTEEN WEEK OLD baby awake? Anytime between 5 and 8 o'clock in the morning. One can scarcely list the clock hours of a typical behavior day at this age, because the organism is in a highly transitional stage of readjustment. Besides, the baby's waking hour may depend upon whether he was roused for a feeding at 10 o'clock of the previous night. If he wakes at 5 or 6 o'clock he is likely to show in the next few weeks a steady trend toward a later hour. This trend is rather consistent. He does not exhibit the wide fluctuations in waking time characteristic of 4 weeks of age.

He may wake with a prompt cry to announce that he is hungry. But to say that he wakes simply to eat would do him an injustice, for often instead of crying he "talks" to himself for fifteen minutes or more. All his behavior, including his self-waking, is more demarcated. His hunger cry is business-like. He quiets promptly when his mother comes; but he also breaks into a renewed spell of crying if his patience span is imposed upon.

His morning appetite is acute. He approaches the breast with mouth open and lips poised. He no longer needs help in establishing contact, and sucks strenuously.

His mother "talks" to him a little after feeding because he has a surplus margin of interest in sights and sounds. He is not perturbed by wet or soiled diapers, which, however, are changed before the next sleep period. The length of this period varies. If he is on a five meal schedule he takes a short morning nap. After perhaps an hour he spontaneously wakes and once more begins to play. His wakefulness is more defined, more purposive in character than it was at 4 weeks. His sleep is less closely merged with feeding; it may be both preceded and followed by an active playful wakefulness. Such a sleep interlude is truly a nap, quite different from the vaguer vegetative somnolence of the newborn.

He awakes to play and he plays to be awake. In this play he exercises his growing sensori-motor powers: he deploys his eyes and rotates his head to inspect his surroundings, brings his fingering hands together, clutches his dress, coos, laughs.

Another nap now follows. He likes to take this long morning nap in his carriage on an outdoor porch, or in an airy room, away from the din and activity of the household. He may resist briefly when a bonnet is placed around his actively shifting head, but if not further molested he falls into a deepened slumber, to wake again both for play and for food. Play has become an occupation as essential for his psychological growth as sleep. He is working toward a three phase cycle of Play activity—Feeding—Sleeping—Play activity—Feeding—Sleeping. But the phases do not always occur distinctly in this sequence. After the early afternoon sleep, he may wake up with a rather prompt hunger cry. Then he will be ready to play only after he has been fed.

The most elaborate and well-defined period of wakefulness is likely to occur in the late afternoon or evening. Having been replenished he plays by himself contentedly for perhaps a half hour. Then he may fuss, not for food but for attention and judicious stimulation. His wakefulness is deeper and wider. He likes to be shifted from the confines of crib to the vaster expanse of couch or bed, perhaps with partial removal of constricting clothes. He enjoys the novelty of such change of scene; he may relish for a short period a well-propped partial sitting position, from which he sees and hears the world at new angles. Dangling toys intrigue him; he may hold a rattle for a few minutes. He is content with mild and brief variations of experience.

The curve of sociality mounts so high that late afternoon is a favorable time for the traditional "morning" bath. The bath has no greater sanitary importance at this transposed hour; but its behavior value may be enhanced thereby both for mother and child.

After his evening meal, which may include mashed banana, the baby "talks to himself." He may suck his fingers for several minutes, for the hand to mouth reaction is so strong at this age that it usually occurs after each feeding.

At night he is capable of a twelve-hour span of sleep. He is stretching the length of nocturnal sleep and the length of day-light wakefulness. In obedience to his private alarm clock he sleeps till the following day. He wakes partly from necessity (to eat); partly from predilection (to be up and doing).

SLEEP

Night

Onset—The baby falls asleep fairly soon after his 6 P.M. feeding.

Waking—Time of waking varies, with different infants, from 5 to 8 A.M. Those who wake early do not usually cry, but talk and play with their hands or with the bedcovers until they are hungry. Desire to be fed is indicated by fussing.

Nap

Onset and Waking—The infant does not usually fall asleep at the end of a feeding, but talks to himself or plays with his hands for a while. Crying may precede sleep, though not at every nap period. If crying does occur, the child may need the quieting effect of back and forth movement of either carriage or crib, especially after the 10 A.M. and 2 P.M. feedings. He appears happy when waking from naps and does not cry.

Periods—Three naps in 24 hours are characteristic of this age, though there may be two or four instead of three.

Naps occur in the early morning, late morning, afternoon and evening. The early morning nap may merge with night sleep, particularly if waking is late (around 8 A.M.) The late morning nap may alternate with the afternoon nap. An evening nap is unusual and comes in only with a recurrence of the evening wakefulness characteristic of a younger age.

Place—The napping place has shifted from bassinet to crib. The baby carriage is usually the best place for the morning out-of-door nap.

FEEDING

Self-Regulation—A clear-cut crying demand on waking becomes less frequent from 12 weeks on, usually being associated only with the first morning waking. At other feedings the infant is more able to wait and can to some extent adapt to the demands of his environment. He may indicate a desire to be fed by fussing. At this age there may be occasional refusals (even to the extent of screaming) of the noon or 6 P.M. feeding. The poorer feeder may have a tendency to split one of these feedings into two parts, taking the second part after a one hour interval.

[If pre- and post-feeding weighing causes crying, it may be discontinued since it is no longer necessary to keep a very strict check on intake.

There is often a decreased appetite for milk at this age and vomiting may occur with the poorer feeders.]

Number—There are from three to five feedings at this age, the two earliest morning feedings often merging. The infant no longer spontaneously wakens for a 10 to 11 P.M. feeding.

Amount—The total daily intake may vary between 25 and 32 ounces. The poorer feeders do not fluctuate as much as the good feeders and are apt to hold close to 25 ounces. Individual feedings for the good feeders may vary in amount by five or six ounces; for the poorer feeders there is little fluctuation. Both breasts are preferred, except at the 10 A.M. feeding when usually only one is taken. If the baby is still waked for a 10 P.M. feeding, then only one breast may be taken at the early morning feeding.

Duration—Both breasts—fifteen to twenty minutes. One breast—ten to fifteen minutes. The 5 to 6 P.M. feeding may take as long as twenty-five to thirty minutes.

Breast and Bottle Feeding—The infant may fuss before feeding but often waits until approximately feeding time. Some cry vigorously on the scales or as the mother exposes her breast, in anticipation. When the nipple is presented, finger or tongue sucking gives way to poised lips and grasping with hands. Hands may come to the breast or may grasp at clothes as the infant secures the nipple with very little assistance from the adult. During nursing he may shift his regard from the breast, to his mother's face, to the surroundings,—and especially to other people who may be present. Lips are pursed at the corners and sucking is strong. It may be so much stronger than the swallowing ability that choking results. Also, in bottle feeding the infant is frequently called upon to adjust to the deflation of the rubber nipple. The harder he sucks the flatter the nipple becomes until finally he is able to release the nipple and wait until air distends it.

After initial satiety the infant may release and re-secure the breast repeatedly in a playful manner, with smiling. With final satiety he arches his back and may growl if forced back to the breast. He usually burps spontaneously after finishing the first breast. Though he may seem satiated as he is shifted to the second breast, his impatient eagerness usually leads him to make a good response to it. With final satiety he is apt to suck his tongue or thumb, and is often very talkative.

[Sucking demand is so strong at this age that it is best to satisfy it before solid foods are given.]

Spoon Feeding—Tongue projection is still so marked that little food is swallowed unless it is placed on the back of the tongue. Though the patterns for handling solid foods are very inadequate, mashed banana is a uniformly preferred food at this age.

Cup Feeding—Approximation of the lips to the rim of the cup is still very inadequate and much spilling results. In spite of this, the infant often enjoys the process of drinking water or fruit juices.

ELIMINATION

Bowel—There are one or two movements a day though a day is frequently skipped. The time of occurrence varies from child to child though it is usually consistent for any one child. The most common time is after a feeding, and it may be delayed long enough for a response to a pot to be obtained, though if such a response is secured it does not usually continue for longer than seven to ten days. If the movement does not follow a feeding it is apt to occur during the wakeful period from 6 to 10 A.M. If it occurs during a feeding, the baby may regurgitate.

BATH AND DRESSING

At this age the baby expresses his love of his bath by kicking and laughing. He does not like to have the bath too deep and may like to lie on his stomach as he is bathed. Around 20 weeks he may hold onto the side of the tub, and may express disappointment when taken out.

SELF-ACTIVITY

Waking periods are now longer and are often spent in physical activity, such as kicking, rotating head from side to side, or rolling to one side. The infant is now able to grasp objects, and particularly enjoys a dangling toy. He also likes to clasp his hands together, and may suck his thumb or fingers before and after feedings. He is now very talkative, often vocalizing with delight, especially in the early morning and afternoon. Talking and crying may follow each other closely. He blows bubbles less than formerly. He enjoys a shift to a couch or large bed in the afternoon and may be good alone for as much as an hour, from 3 to 4 P.M., though he is also interested in people. He likes to have a light after 6 P.M. but no longer demands it. If it is left on it may keep him awake.

SOCIALITY

There is at this age an increased demand for sociality. This may come in relation to feedings, often before each feeding, though with some infants it occurs during or after the feeding. Demand for social attention is especially strong toward the end of the day, around 5 P.M. The infant likes to be shifted from his bed for this social period. He particularly likes to be in his carriage. There is, at 12 to 16 weeks, a marked interest in the father and also in young children. Social play with the father may go more smoothly than with the mother since the baby does not associate food with the father. He likes to have people pay attention to him, talk to him, sing to him. He is apt to cry in supine and seems to prefer sitting. By 20 weeks he so much enjoys being talked to that he may cry when people leave.

[He is apt to be more demanding of social attention if he sleeps in the same room with his mother, especially if she stirs in the early morning.]

11
TWENTY-EIGHT WEEKS OLD

§1. BEHAVIOR PROFILE

THE TWENTY-EIGHT WEEK OLD infant likes to sit in a high chair (or it may be for safety reasons a lower chair). When he wakes from a nap he is quite likely to lift his head, as though straining to reach a perpendicular position. He wishes to sit up and take notice; and above all he wishes to get hold of some object (a clothespin will do), which he can handle, mouth, and bang.

This is a heyday for manipulation. The baby has "learned" to balance his head; he can almost balance his trunk; he knows how to grasp on sight; he is eager to try out his rapidly growing abilities.

His eagerness and intentness show that his play is serious business. He is discovering the size, shape, weight, and texture of things. He is no longer content merely to finger his hands, as he did at 16 weeks. He wants to finger the clothespin, to get the feel of it. He puts it to his mouth, pulls it out, looks at it, rotates it with a twist of the wrist, puts it back into his mouth, pulls it out, gives it another twist, brings up his free hand, transfers the clothespin from hand to hand, bangs it on the high chair tray, drops it, recovers it, retransfers it from hand to hand, drops it out of reach, leans over to retrieve it, fails, fusses a moment, and then bangs the tray with his empty hand, etc., etc., throughout his busy day. He is never idle because he is under such a compelling urge to use his hands for manipulation and exploitation.

His hands are not quite as paw-like as they were. He is beginning to use his thumb more adeptly, and to tilt his hand just prior to grasp. But his fine finger coordination is crude compared with what it will be at 40 weeks. He still is more expert with his eyes than with his hands, he keenly looks at a small object which he cannot yet pick up deftly.

His urge to manipulate is so strong that he can play by himself happily for short periods. At these times he should be left to his own devices. It is characteristic of him to be self-contained as well as sociable. He will show a similar self-containedness at a higher level when he is in the 18-months-old run-about stage.

Now he is sedentary. So he sits in his chair; he watches with interest the activities of the household. He vocalizes his eagerness not to say impatience when he spies a bottle or a dish and sees his mother preparing a meal for him. He may reach for a dish quite out of reach, because he still has something to learn about distance—and time too. But his mouth and throat muscles are much more highly organized than they were at 16 weeks. He can now "handle" solids, which before tended to make him cough or choke. Nor does he extrude his tongue with the infantile ineptitude of earlier days. His lips sweep competently over the spoon in his mouth; his tongue smacks and on satiety he keeps his mouth tightly closed. All this denotes a great advance in his neuro-muscular organization.

But, of course, he cannot grasp a spoon adaptively by the handle nor use it as a utensil. At one year he will be able to insert a spoon into a cup. Not until about 2 years can he put the burden of a laden spoon into his

[109]

mouth, unaided, without excessive spilling. The spoon is a complicated cultural tool. The 28 week old infant in his manipulation is laying the foundations for the motor mastery of this tool.

All told the 28 week old baby presents a mixture of versatility and of transitional incompleteness. He is vastly superior to the 16 week old baby in the combined command of eyes and hands; but he is only at the brink of abilities which will come to maturity during the rest of the first year. He is at the brink of sitting alone; at the close of the year he will stand alone. He can hold two objects, one in each hand; in time he will combine them. He is vocalizing vowels and consonants in great variety. Soon they will take on the status of words. Through his ceaseless manipulations, transfers and mouthings he is building up a wealth of perceptions which will make him feel more at home in his physical surroundings. Similarly he is amassing a wealth of social perceptions; he is reading the facial expressions, the gestures, the postural attitudes and the goings and comings of the domestic routine. These social perceptions are not yet very sophisticated, but they are sensitive; they are patterned; and they are essential to the continuing growth of his personality.

At this age the child's abilities are in relative balance. The behavior patterns of the 28 week old baby are in good focus. His interests are balanced; he is both self-contained and sociable; he alternates with ease from spontaneous self activity to social reference activity. He likes to sit up (with support) but he is also quite content to lie supine. He likes to manipulate toys, but almost any object will do; or no object at all will do, for then he moves his hand across the field of vision for the pleasure (and educational value) of seeing it move. All in all his behavior traits are well counterpoised. But the tensions of growth will soon again throw them out of their comparative equilibrium as he forges ahead to a still higher level of maturity.

§2. BEHAVIOR DAY

OUR TWENTY-EIGHT WEEK OLD baby wakes up at almost any time between 6 and 8 A.M. He is reputed to wake up "soaking wet." His urinary output apparently has increased since the age of 16 weeks. But he is quite indifferent and typically amuses himself with play of his own devices. Now and then an infant of lusty appetite may demand a prompt feeding on waking, but 28 weeks is a relatively amiable and equable age, and mothers report that children of this age usually wake up "good," playing contentedly for twenty to thirty minutes. A corner of the blanket, a loose end of tape, or even his own free moving hand will serve his playful purposes. He may vocalize but not as much as at 16 weeks, for 28 weeks is the heyday of manipulation and visual-manual play.

Breast feeding may still be in his regime. If so, he takes the breast most satisfactorily for the morning feeding, but he is beginning to show a preference for bottle and solids at later feedings. Incidentally, the mother has found this early breast feeding very convenient because there is considerable variation in the morning waking hour during the interval between 16 and 28 weeks, and often an immediate demand for food. Whether at breast or bottle he displays increased efficiency in sucking.

Typically the period from 6 to 8 A.M. is one of pleasant wakefulness. During this period the baby is most comfortable in a room by himself. He will play by himself contentedly for twenty minutes, then likes to be given a toy, and at the end of another twenty minutes or so is propped up in his crib to survey his surroundings.

At 9 o'clock he is ready for a trip to the kitchen where he is placed in a safe chair, which gives him a commanding view of the preliminaries of his next meal. He is not without anticipation and he becomes excited when the food approaches. He is fed in his chair, or if his postural and temperamental characteristics so require, he is fed on a lap. He poises his lips cooperatively for the spoon and a smile of satisfaction and satiation terminates the meal.

[111]

His daily bowel movement may occur at this time or before the morning feeding. In the period from 16 to 20 weeks he displayed some adaptive response to placement on the toilet, but thereafter he began to show a strenuous refusal. The mother has by this time accepted his refusal and is delaying systematic "training." He gives no evidence of being perturbed by soiled diapers.

At 10 o'clock he is put into his carriage which is wheeled out of doors or onto a porch, and after a draught at the bottle he goes to sleep with relative promptness. He wakes at about noon or 1 o'clock. He wakes happily and again plays contentedly by himself in the carriage. If he fusses slightly he is readily appeased by a toy and later by being propped up in a supported sitting position.

By 2 o'clock he is ready for his vegetable meal followed by a bottle which he takes in his chair or crib. Weather permitting, it is time for a trip in his carriage. He does not altogether acquiesce in the application of a bonnet but he definitely enjoys the sight-seeing opportunities offered by the perambulator. This is the first age when the baby is very "good" on these trips.

The afternoon nap comes at about 3:30 and lasts about an hour. He wakes somewhat more slowly from this nap and shows somewhat less self-dependence. As at earlier ages, he likes a little afternoon sociability as well as orange juice. Five o'clock, therefore, proves to be a favorable hour for the bath, unless an early waking from the morning nap made a noon bath more acceptable for the household. In any event he enjoys the bath hugely. Divestment of clothes is both a pleasure in itself and an anticipation of things to come.

The last feeding comes at about 5:30. It may be at breast but more usually at bottle. And so to bed at 6 o'clock when he falls promptly to sleep for a twelve hour stretch.

SLEEP

Night

Onset—The baby tends to fall asleep directly after his 6 P.M.* feeding.

Waking—Very few babies of this age are awakened for a 10 P.M. feeding, and even fewer wake themselves at this hour. If they are awakened, they take very little milk or refuse the feeding entirely; but if they wake voluntarily they can be quieted only by a feeding. The majority sleep right through the night, for eleven to thirteen hours, waking around 6 A.M. or later. Babies of this age are usually "good" for half an hour or longer after waking before they demand a feeding.

Nap

Onset and Waking—There is now no difficulty in going to sleep or in waking. Sleep is usually closely associated with the 10 A.M. and the 6 P.M. feedings.

Periods—There is at this age a fairly wide variety of nap patterns. There are usually two to three naps a day. The mid-morning and afternoon naps are the most stable. Some children have a consistent pattern of a long morning and a short afternoon nap (or vice versa) whereas others alternate the length, depending on the length of the morning nap. An evening nap does not usually occur unless it is defined by a 10 P.M. waking.

Place—Babies nap best in their carriages out of doors, for the morning nap. Some have their afternoon nap while being wheeled in their carriages. If not, they usually have this nap in their cribs in the house, during the latter part of the afternoon.

FEEDING

Self-Regulation—Self-demand occurs mainly for the first morning feeding. The time of this demand fluctuates according to the hour of waking. Some infants demand this feeding immediately on waking, but most will wait for half an hour or so. Other feedings are accepted at the times determined by the mother in accordance with the baby's growing needs and the ease or difficulty of his adjustment to the demands of the household schedule.

The baby is beginning to show a preference for the bottle and for solid foods rather than the breast, and takes the breast best at the first morning feeding. Solids are taken best at 8 to 10 A.M. and at 2 P.M.

[With the decrease in sucking demands, solid foods may now be given at the beginning of each meal.

From 32 to 36 weeks the infant is very impatient as he watches his meal being prepared. This can be remedied by having the meal ready before he sees it.]

Number—Three to four a day. Four persists if the child demands a 6 A.M. feeding or if the 10 P.M. feeding is continued.

Amount—The total amount is now difficult to judge because of the addition of solid foods. However, the poor feeders still keep to a consistent level of intake without fluctuating more than an ounce or two at a feeding, whereas the good feeders may show as much as a ten ounce fluctuation at a feeding. The early morning and the 6 P.M. are the best meals (ten to eleven ounces), and the 2 P.M. is the poorest (four to five ounces). If the breast is given at the 2 P.M. feeding it is usually taken poorly or refused.

Duration—Eight to ten minutes for breast or bottle feeding.

---

* We refer to a 10 A.M., 2 P.M., 6 P.M. feeding simply for convenience.

Breast and Bottle Feeding—The infant vocalizes his eagerness when he sees the breast or bottle. He places his hands on breast or bottle, securing the nipple with ease. He exerts good continuous sucking, with the lower lip rolled out and forward and with good pursing at the corners. During the feeding, hands repeatedly grasp and release the breast or bottle. This grasp and release is similar to the 16 week old tongue pattern of grasp and release. The infant regards the nipple as he withdraws from the breast or pulls the bottle away from his mouth.

With satiety he tries to sit up, and when helped to sit smiles at his mother or at others present, and may shake his head from side to side as though saying, "No, no."

[Since the infant is apt to bite the nipple, especially after the 2 P.M. feeding, after taking only a few ounces, it may be best to omit this bottle and to give whatever milk the infant will take from a cup.]

Spoon Feeding—The baby at this age anticipates spoon feeding with eagerness, poising his mouth as he reaches toward the spoon with his head. Hands may be fisted at shoulder level or may rest on the tray of the high chair—if he is capable of being fed in a high chair. He sucks the food from the spoon. With succeeding spoonsful he shows increasing eagerness and may grasp the spoon or the adult's finger. With satiety he bites on the spoon, and smiles after the feeding.

Cup Feeding—The infant shows a new awareness of the cup and spontaneously makes demands to be cup fed. He apparently associates the running of water with the filling of the cup, and on sight of the cup he reaches forward with head rather than with hands, and with poised mouth. There is better approximation of his lips to the rim of the cup, but he has difficulty when the cup is removed in retaining the fluid in his mouth. He is incapable of taking more than one or two swallows at a time. He definitely prefers water or juices to milk, and may refuse milk from a cup.

ELIMINATION

Bowel—One movement a day (in the diaper) usually from 9 to 10 A.M., though it may occasionally occur in the late afternoon. The earlier response to the pot is no longer present. In fact strong resistance to the pot may be shown. There is no demand to be changed except on the part of a few fastidious girls who cry vigorously until they are changed. Babies of this type are more apt to be trained easily and early to the pot, and this behavior, once established, is usually sustained.

Bladder—Urination is still frequent and so excessive in amount that the child is often very wet when changed. Sex differences are noted at this age in that some girls are establishing a longer interval—as long as one to two hours—after which they may respond to the pot.

BATH AND DRESSING

Bath—The baby enjoys being undressed for his bath at this age, and he also enjoys his bath. His hands are so active that objects are no longer safe on the bath table. In the tub, the baby splashes vigorously, usually with his hands though sometimes with his feet. He may close his eyes at the sight of the washcloth. It may suit the demands of both child and household to shift the bath hour ahead to the noon hour.

[When the infant is unhappily conscious of the approach of the washcloth, it is wise to approach him from the rear, washing his ears and cheeks from the back toward the front.]

Dressing—The baby likes to remove his bootees and also likes to play with the strings of his bootees or of his sweater.

SELF-ACTIVITY

The infant again enjoys supine. He hummocks, kicks, extends his legs upward, grasps his feet, brings them to his mouth, pulls off his bootees and stockings. He likes to watch his moving hand. He brings his hands less often to his mouth, and this occurs mostly after feeding or before sleep. He enjoys play with string, paper, soft rubber squeaky toys, and rattles. These he brings to his mouth and bites on. He vocalizes happily to himself, gurgling, growling, and making high squealing sounds. He is happier alone in both morning and late afternoon during his wakeful periods, until he indicates, by fussing, a desire for companionship.

[Around 32 weeks, the infant may frequently cry and need help in getting out of some awkward position.]

SOCIALITY

Babies of this age enjoy people not only for themselves but for what the people can do for them. Once the adult has given a toy or propped the baby sitting, the baby can let the adult go and can enjoy himself alone until he makes his next demand. He enjoys being wheeled along the street in his carriage, and although he enjoys sitting up for short periods, he is also content to lie down. He is beginning to respond to more than one person at a time, and likes to be handed back and forth from one person to another. He also likes rhythm, and enjoys being bounced on someone's knee. He differentiates between people, and demands more of the one who feeds him. He is lively with those whom he knows and is beginning to be shy with strangers, especially in new places.

[Around 32 weeks, though the baby enjoys the company of others, he may easily become over-excited. Instability of emotional make-up at this time is expressed in the close interplay of crying and laughter.]

12

FORTY WEEKS OLD

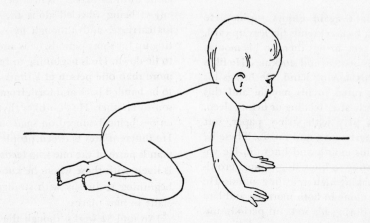

§1. BEHAVIOR PROFILE

THE FORTY WEEK OLD infant no longer takes kindly to the supine position. For the sleeping infant it may do; but when FORTY WEEKS awakes, he rolls over and sits up. He may even rear himself to a standing position, pulling himself by the palings of his crib. Man was meant to be a biped. There is an unmistakable hind-legs urge toward the perpendicular, which puts the baby on his feet. But the horizontal alignment is still under better control. For a few months the baby remains a quadruped, using his hands for locomotion as well as for manipulation.

In the evolution of the race, the upright posture was assumed for the purpose of emancipating the hands, freeing them for nobler and more refined uses. The 40 week old baby is developmentally in this transition phase of emancipation, and the higher uses of the hand are already well in evidence. He brings index finger and thumb into delicate pincer-like

[116]

opposition; he extends the index finger to poke and probe, to palpate and pluck. He can pluck a string and give it a tug. He is beginning to grasp things more adaptively by their handle. His inquisitive index finger will take him further and further into the third dimension. He will probe into holes and grooves and into the depths of a cup. Through these more refined manipulations he acquires a sense of hollow and solid; container and contained; up and down; side by side; in and out; apart and united.

The 40 week baby, therefore, is not nearly as naively single-minded as he was at twenty-eight weeks. He is beginning to see and to handle things in the depth of perspective. The universe is less flat, less simplex. He is conscious of *two* as well as *one*. Indeed, he puts two things together. He needs two clothespins instead of one to satisfy his impulse to combine and to bring together what is apart. This dim awareness of twoness is reflected in his experimental exploitation of play objects. He is more discriminating and sometimes actually dainty in his manipulations.

Socially, likewise, he is more discriminating, more perceptive of small variations in sight and sound. This greater perceptiveness makes him seem more sensitive, as indeed he is. He is sensitive to more events in his social environment; he is becoming responsive to demonstrations and to teaching. He has a new capacity for imitation. Accordingly he "learns" new nursery tricks like pat-a-cake and bye-bye. He could not "learn" them when he was twenty-eight weeks old, because he did not have the same perceptiveness for the actions of others, nor was the appropriate movement pattern as yet in his repertoire. His repertoire of movements depends upon the maturity of his nervous system. He cannot imitate any action until he is already capable of that action as the result of natural growth. If at the age of forty weeks you try to engage him in a game of back and forth ball play, he may disappoint you by holding onto the ball and merely waving it. But, of course, one *should* not be disappointed. In due time he will mature the motor capacity of release, and then he will roll the ball to you. Everything in season.

§2. BEHAVIOR DAY

THE FORTY WEEK OLD baby wakes anytime between 5 and 7 o'clock. He is likely to be wet but his fussing is often primarily for social attention. He is also likely to be keenly hungry and he imbibes his bottle with dispatch. He holds and pats his partially propped bottle. Should the nipple become deflated during the sucking, he is now an expert in waiting until it reflates. After his bottle, he is wheeled into another room for partial isolation, unless he is already in a room of his own. If he does not have this isolation he is likely to be too demanding. He plays contentedly for an hour or more, if he has two or three shifts of toys.

At 8 o'clock he is ready for breakfast. He may take this in his high chair. He vocalizes "ma-ma" and "nam-nam" in his eager anticipation; but he has learned to inhibit some of his excitement and waits for the presentation of the dish of cereal. The demanding eagerness, however, returns if the mother is too slow in following one spoonful with the next. He associates an empty dish with the termination of the meal and he makes a ready transition to a period of play.

Between 8 and 10 o'clock he likes to be part of the household group. He is content to play in his high chair, pen or crib and may enjoy a shift from one station to another by way of variety.

He may have a bowel movement during this morning play period, or in some instances there is a toilet placement immediately following breakfast.

Ten o'clock often proves to be a convenient time for the bath. He greatly enjoys a bath and expresses eager anticipation when he hears the water running and sees the preparation. The bath is completed almost too soon for his preferences. He is likely to enjoy by way of playful contest the washing of his face with the washcloth. He plays with a water toy during the sanitary ministrations.

By about a quarter past ten he is ready for sleep. He sleeps well indoors.

[118]

This is his long nap. He wakes at about 1 o'clock and again usually wet. (Girls are more apt to be dry.) He may play contentedly for a brief period and then fusses for social attention.

He lunches at about 1:30 on spoon-fed vegetables. He opens his mouth decisively as the spoon is presented and swallows rapidly. He eats with new efficiency, moving steadily toward the completion of the meal. He becomes playful toward the end of the meal, manipulating empty dish or spoon. He finger feeds on spilled particles, thus exercising his new powers of precise pincer prehension.

At 2 o'clock, weather permitting, comes a carriage ride. He does not even yet accept his bonnet with full grace, but he enjoys sight-seeing. Nevertheless, he is not totally preoccupied with the scenery. He is in the early stages of independent sitting and of digital manipulation. He therefore likes to occupy himself with a toy even on his outdoor trips. His propensity to stand may be so strong that he needs a safety strap.

If he returns home dry at about 3 o'clock, he may respond to placement on the toilet. By this time he may be showing signs of sleepiness. He falls asleep promptly and naps from half an hour to an hour. He may wake up dry at about 4 o'clock. His nap is usually followed by orange juice which he relishes. This is typically the most social period of the day. He enjoys being a member of the household group. He enjoys social types of play including the usual nursery games. His sociality may lead to over-stimulation. He is beginning to show a temper by way of resistance or as a mode of communication, not to say environmental utilization. He is not yet using words but his vocalizations are more articulate, more insistent.

A supper of cereal and fruit follows at about 6 o'clock. He is usually ready for the night's sleep in a quarter of an hour. He may "talk" to himself for from fifteen minutes to an hour, or he may promptly fall asleep. He may cry out momentarily during the course of the night, without waking and without requiring attention.

SLEEP

Night

Onset—The baby still tends to fall asleep directly after his 6 P.M. feeding. A few infants who have had more difficulty in going to sleep and who have previously cried before some sleep periods may now talk for fifteen minutes to one hour before falling asleep.

[If there is resistance to being put to bed at the usual 6 P.M. hour, delay bedtime a half hour or more.]

Waking—Most infants sleep right through till 5 to 7 A.M., the trend being toward the later hour. Night waking seems to depend both on household conditions and on the child himself. The infant who sleeps in the same room with his parents may awaken when his parents go to bed, but usually falls right back to sleep after his diaper is changed. Some cry out in their sleep momentarily without waking, and require no attention. A few are beginning to have occasional wakeful periods of an hour or more between 2 and 4 A.M. During this period the baby may talk happily to himself or may crawl out from under the covers and play. Toward the end of this period he may fuss and may be unable to go back to sleep unless his diaper is changed or he is given a bottle.

Early wakers (5 to 6 A.M.) may want to be "changed" at once and then enjoy either vocal play lying down, or play with a toy sitting up. They are most contented in a room by themselves at this time and will remain so for 1 to 1½ hours provided they have two or three shifts of toys, before they fuss for their food. Late wakers (7 A.M. or later) tend to demand food shortly after waking.

Nap

Onset and Waking—The baby indicates his need for sleep by fussing, turning his head to one side, sucking his thumb or a piece of material, wriggling his pelvis, or pushing with his feet, and if he is put into his crib at such times he falls asleep fairly quickly. If no such need has been indicated he may accept being put down at the usual time but may remain awake.

The morning nap most often follows the 10 A.M. bath period (if the bath is given then) and the afternoon nap may follow a ride in the carriage—around 3 P.M.

Periods—There is not quite such a wide variety of nap patterns as at 28 weeks. There may be four short nap periods—one at each of the four periods of the day—or there may be only one long mid-morning nap. The most usual pattern is a long mid-morning and an unstable afternoon nap which comes and goes.

Place—This is a transitional period of sleeping indoors in preference to out of doors. Some infants give a clue to their demand for less light by placing their hands over their eyes, and usually sleep better indoors with the shades pulled.

FEEDING

Self-Regulation—The baby may indicate an early morning demand, but this demand is as much for company as for food. Breakfast is not usually served before 7 or 8 A.M. This meal is often preceded by a solitary play period of 1 to 1½ hours.

The infant takes his bottle alone for the first morning feeding if it is given then. It usually needs to be propped, though the baby will hold it alone toward the end of the feeding. At other feedings he demands that his bottle be held, and often enjoys the bottle after he has had his solid food, sitting in his high chair. Most solid foods are taken well, and some preference is indicated by a razzing refusal of disliked foods. One ounce of milk may be accepted in a cup, but the tendency is to blow bubbles in the cup with a very rapid satiety of drinking. Orange juice and water are, however, taken well from a cup.

Although he is still eager for his feedings, he is not usually as impatient when he sees his meal being prepared as he was from 32 to 36 weeks. He tends to vocalize in anticipation rather than fussing and crying.

[The infant still needs to have some sucking at the bottle. If he does not, feedings are more difficult and prolonged because he will suck his fingers between spoonsful.]

Number—Three meals a day, with fruit juice in the mid-afternoon. A bottle may be given as an extra first morning feeding as soon as he awakes. Night bottles are very rare. Some infants receive only two bottles, at 7 A.M. and 6 P.M., and others still continue on three bottles a day.

Amount—The total intake depends to a certain extent upon how much is offered. The infant now has a sense of finishing his bottle and therefore asks for no more than his bottle of eight ounces. He also "cleans up" his dish and takes it for granted that that is the end. Some infants have eaten a larger quantity before this age, others are just increasing their quantity at this time. The point of satiety indicates whether too much is being given, and the absence of any satiety patterns may indicate that more could be given.

Duration—Three to four minutes for a bottle. Five to ten minutes for solid food.

Bottle Feeding—Bottle feeding patterns are similar to 28 weeks patterns except that sucking is now more forceful and more rapid and the hands are taking more part

in holding the bottle. For the first morning feeding, which the baby usually takes alone, the bottle may be propped to one side or on his chest. This is necessary because the full bottle is too heavy for him to hold, though he manages it well, tilting it easily, as it empties. He may be able to resecure it if he loses it. Otherwise he fusses for assistance. At other feedings he likes to have someone hold his bottle for him.

Spoon Feeding—Most infants are fed in a high chair at this age. They express their eager anticipation with such vocalizing as "dada" or "nam-nam." They open their mouths as the spoon is presented, swallow rapidly as they draw in their lower lips. Lateral movements of chewing are just beginning. The infant may reach toward the dish or show eagerness if the mother is slow in presenting the food. Satiety is clearly expressed coincidentally with the emptying of the dish. If satiety precedes this, it is indicated by biting of the spoon or the infant's own tongue, by shaking the head "No," and by razzing good-naturedly but determinedly. The baby enjoys a short period of play with the empty dish and spoon.

[A few infants may still need to be fed on the mother's lap or half-propped in their cribs.

It is best to provide an unbreakable dish that can be used for play at the end of the meal.]

Cup Feeding—The baby drinks one ounce, one to two swallows at a time, with good lip approximation. There is still a tendency to spill out of the mouth as the cup is removed. The baby enjoys blowing bubbles and also enjoys playing at drinking from an empty cup.

Self Help—The baby finger feeds with spilled bits from his tray.

ELIMINATION

Bowel—One to two movements a day, at 8 to 10 A.M. and/or 6 to 7 P.M. The baby may respond to the pot, especially if the bowel movement occurs after a meal. Some, especially girls, fuss to be changed. *Bladder*—The baby may be dry after an hour's nap or a carriage ride and may respond to the pot if put on at once. However he may not urinate till just after he is taken off the pot. He may fuss to be changed in the middle of the night.

BATH AND DRESSING

The bath hour may continue to be at noon or in the late afternoon, but a morning bath is often most convenient for the household. The baby vigorously expresses anticipation when he hears the bath water running. He often prefers to lie prone in the bath tub, creeps better in water than on the floor, or rocks back and forth. He may cry as his face is being washed, but many enjoy the combat of face washing, which can be accomplished easily if the baby is occupied with water toys or is standing in the tub.

SELF-ACTIVITY

Vocalization is varied at this age. The baby has given up growling sounds. He now says "mama," "papa," "nana," "gaga," "dada." He enjoys making lip noises, vocalizing at a high pitch, and trying out a variety of pitches with some such syllable as "dada." He often stops short and laughs at his own sounds, especially the high ones.

He concentrates on inspection and exploitation of toys. He enjoys playing with a cup and pretends to drink. He brings objects to his mouth and chews them. He clasps his hands or waves them.

He recognizes the absence of objects to which he has become accustomed, such as his mother's wrist watch or a water toy. He enjoys gross motor activity: sitting and playing after he has been set up, leaning far forward and re-erecting himself. He re-secures a toy; kicks; goes from sitting to creeping; pulls himself up and may lower himself. He is beginning to cruise. He likes to roll to the side or to prone and may get caught between the bars of his play pen.

[Because of increased motor abilities it is now dangerous to leave the baby unguarded even for a moment on a bed or bath table lest he fall off.]

SOCIALITY

Though the infant will play by himself for relatively long periods, he is quick to articulate his desire for a shift of toys or company. He particularly likes to be with the family group from 8 to 10 A.M. and in the late afternoon (4 to 6 P.M.) and happily stays in his crib, play pen, or chair at these times. He also likes a carriage ride in the late morning or early afternoon—depending on his naptime.

Social activities which he enjoys are peek-a-boo and lip play (which consists of patting his lips to induce singing), walking with both hands held, and being put prone on the floor or being placed in a rocking toy.

Girls show their first signs of coyness by putting their heads to one side as they smile. This occurs most frequently in the bath.

The baby is still shy with strangers and seems particularly afraid of a strange voice. [The baby continues to demand more of his mother than of other members of the family. He is often better when alone with one person.]

13

ONE YEAR OLD

---

§1. BEHAVIOR PROFILE

THE FIRST BIRTHDAY, of course, is a great occasion. The folkways call
for a cake and one lighted candle to punctuate the event; and properly
so, from a chronological standpoint. But biologically speaking, this birthday does not mark an epoch; for the year old baby is in the midstream of
developmental changes which do not come to their fulfillment until
about the age of fifteen months. It will help us to better understand his
behavior characteristics if we think of him as a 15 month old child in the
making.

At fifteen months the modern child has usually achieved the upright
posture; he can attain the standing position unaided; he can walk alone;
he prefers to walk; he has discarded creeping and begun to jargon in a
manner which promises the most human achievement of all, namely
speech. The year-old child is still on the way toward these abilities. He

can attain the sitting position unaided, but often prefers to creep; he can pivot in the sitting position; he can cruise and climb if he gets ample purchase with his hands. But these are quadrupedal rather than bipedal patterns. Many children near the close of the first year walk on hands and soles rather than hands and knees. This is the last of a score of stages which finally lead to the assumption of the upright posture. When feet become the fulcrum, the hands will soon be emancipated.

Nevertheless, the year-old baby is already capable of finer coordination in his eating and in his play activities. He picks small morsels of food from his tray with deft forceps prehension, and masticates and swallows with much less spilling from the mouth. Finger feeding comes before self-spoon feeding. But the year-old infant may seize a spoon by the handle and brush it over his tray. He can also dip it into a cup and release it; all of which shows that he is advancing in his mastery of tools and of the solid and hollow geometry of space. Watch his play closely, and you can tell by his self-activity what patterns of behavior are growing. One can almost see them sprout, he exercises his newly forming powers with so much spirit.

He likes to play with several small objects rather than a solitary one. He picks them up one-by-one, drops them, picks them up again, one-by-one. This behavior appears a little disorderly on the surface; but it is really very orderly from the standpoint of natural growth, for this one-by-one action pattern is a rudimentary kind of counting. It is not as complex as a counting-out game, but it is a developmental prerequisite.

The baby has another reason for this picking up and dropping manipulation. He is exercising his immature but maturing powers of release. Having learned how to grasp he must now learn how to let go. If he seems to overdo it, it is because the extensor muscles are not yet under smooth control. Hence his expulsiveness; hence also his momentary inability to let go at the right time.

But start a simple game of back-and-forth rolling ball play with him and you will see what a significant advance he has made since the age of forty weeks. At forty weeks he perhaps regarded your overtures soberly, looking at your movements without actually reciprocating them. Instead he held the ball, mouthed it or surrendered it in an ill-defined manner. By one year his release is responsive; it has an element of voluntary imitation and initiation. In another month he releases with a slight but defined cast—all of which reminds us how complicated these simple patterns are and how much they depend upon maturation.

Socialized opportunities undoubtedly facilitate the shaping of the patterns and favor a healthy organization of accompanying emotions. The year-old child likes an audience. This is one reason why he is so often the very center of the household group. As such he shows a Thespian tendency to repeat performances laughed at. He enjoys applause. This must help him to sense his own self-identity, just as he learned better to sense a clothespin when he brought it bangingly down against his tray. He is defining a difficult psychological distinction,—the difference between himself and others.

He is capable of primitive kinds of affection, jealousy, sympathy, anxiety. He may be responsive to rhythm. He may even evidence a sense of humor, for he laughs at abrupt surprise sounds, and at startling incongruities. He may be a prodigious imitator. Demonstrate the ringing of a bell and he will wave it furiously by way of social reciprocity. But suddenly in the very midst of the waving he stops to poke the clapper with his inquisitive index! This poking was not part of the demonstration, but it is part of the child. We may be grateful that Nature has protected him with this degree of independence. After all, we do not wish to swamp him with acculturation!

§2. BEHAVIOR DAY

THE YEAR-OLD baby wakes between 6 and 8 o'clock in the morning. He usually wakes with a communicative call rather than an infantile cry. The call is a guttural "eh" or some equivalent vocalization. He may play by himself for as much as twenty minutes before he calls out. He jargons with some excitement when his mother or caretaker arrives. He wakes up wet and is changed and toileted, and put back into his crib where he amuses himself with manipulative toys and satisfies his moderate appetite with a cracker or zwieback.

Breakfast follows in half an hour or an hour, say at 8:30. The breakfast usually consists of cereal, a strong preference being expressed for whichever kind he likes best. He eats with moderate appetite, but has a margin of self-activity through the meal. He likes to play with a toy in either hand; one toy a container and the other toy an object which he can thrust into the container. His manipulatory drive is so strong and uncritical that the dish is not safe unless it is held out of reach. At the conclusion of the meal he pulls himself to a standing position. It may be that he takes his cup of milk in this position or while he is still sitting.

He may be toileted after the meal. A morning bowel movement at this time is common. He is content to be restored to his crib where he romps and plays by himself with manipulative toys. Perhaps at 10 o'clock he is put in his play pen in the yard, if the weather permits, or on the porch, where he is self-sufficient and happy for say another half hour, when he begins to fuss, partly by way of anticipation of his morning bath which he greatly enjoys. If he kept a diary he probably would record this as the high peak of the day's routine. He prefers to sit in his bath and he is no longer engrossed with mere aquatic play.

He is ready for a nap by 11 A.M. He may prefer to take this nap indoors in a semi-darkened room. This midday nap is often two hours long. He usually wakes wet. In any event he may be toileted and changed. He is given a cracker and he looks on as his mother prepares the midday lunch. He usually takes this lunch, as he did his breakfast, in a high chair.

At 2 o'clock he is ready for a carriage ride which he enjoys, but in a manner which reflects more than 40 weeks maturity. At 40 weeks his playthings still absorbed much of his attention. Now he enjoys following the movements of pedestrians and automobiles and inspecting the landscape. He may be dry when he returns from his journey. Routinely he is again toileted.

Late afternoon again proves to be a social period. Although he has been relatively self-contained during the day, he now likes give-and-take play with adults and with children. If he is learning to walk he likes to take a walk up and down the room, hands held. Similarly he enjoys cruising from chair to chair. He is ready on the slightest cue to reciprocate in nursery games such as, "Where is the baby?", or repeatedly giving and then taking back some object. By way of conclusion of this social play he likes to climb into an adult's lap, rubbing his face against the adult's hand or giving other tokens of affection.

A supper of cereal and fruit follows at about 5:30. And so to bed at 6. As a nightcap he has a bottle which he may discard by the age of 15 months. He falls asleep between 6 and 8 P.M. which neatly completes a 12-hour cycle.

SLEEP

Night

Onset—The year old baby usually falls asleep sometime between 6 and 8 P.M. A few infants still have an eating-sleeping association. A number, however, refuse to go to bed before they are ready, then go happily and fall asleep quickly. Others go to bed at the normal time directly after supper, and play on top of their covers or walk about in their cribs before they fall asleep on top of the covers.

Waking—Most babies sleep through till 6 to 8 A.M. They may be "good" for twenty minutes after waking but more usually they call for their mother by crying or by vocalizing "eh." After calling, they seem definitely to wait for a response, and when the mother comes they greet her with excited jargon and may even look behind her as though expecting the other members of the family.

After being placed on the pot, or changed, the baby is given a piece of zwieback or cracker (which he now prefers to a bottle). He plays happily in his crib, eating his zwieback and enjoying his manipulative toys for half an hour to an hour. Breakfast follows this play period without the baby's having made any demand for it.

Nap

Onset and Waking—If the nap follows a morning bath or an early lunch, the infant accepts it readily and goes off to sleep shortly, but if it occurs in the middle of a morning play period he shows his desire for sleep by fussing or pulling at his ears, and goes to sleep fairly rapidly after he is put to bed. As with the early morning waking he demands attention at once, is glad to see his mother, is put on the pot or changed, and may tolerate a half hour alone in the play pen with zwieback and toys before his lunch.

[If the infant interrupts his nap by crying before he urinates, it may be best not to pick him up and toilet him, for he may not go back to sleep. If he is allowed merely to urinate in his diaper he usually falls right back to sleep.]

Periods—Usually there is only one nap a day, from 11 or 11:30 to 12:30 or 2:00. Occasionally an early morning or a late afternoon nap persists irregularly.

Place—The carriage is no longer a safe place for the nap and babies sleep better and longer in their cribs in a darkened room.

FEEDING

Self-Regulation—Gross motor drives may still be so strong that it may be easier to conduct the feeding with the baby strapped in his carriage in a sitting or standing position. If the baby is in his high chair he needs some toy, preferably two toys that can readily be combined, to occupy the margin of his attention. He does not usually demand to have the dish on the tray, where it is not safe from his grasp and would probably be turned over, so long as he has something else to occupy his hands.

Many refuse milk from a bottle at this age (or even younger), especially if some change like a shift in style of nipple has been made. This does not necessarily mean that the baby takes the milk better in a cup, for some refuse milk from a cup off and on up to 18 months or even later. The preferred bottle is the 6 P.M. bottle which may still be clung to.

Preferences for certain foods are becoming fairly well defined. Cereal may be refused in the morning but may be taken well for supper. A wheat cereal may be refused but oatmeal taken with eagerness. Or, hot cereal may be refused and a cold cereal chosen. Certain vegetables may be preferred.

Number—Three meals a day with mid-afternoon fruit juice. A zwieback or cracker may be given both on morning waking and after the nap. If a bottle is still given it is usually only one a day, directly after supper or after the baby is in bed.

Appetite—Appetite is usually good for all meals though it may be somewhat less for breakfast.

Spoon Feeding—Similar to 40 weeks. The baby shows less eagerness for food, and a margin of his attention is given to other things than food. He enjoys some finger feeding of food and may remove food from his mouth, look at it, and then reinsert it. He may rub spilled food on the tray. Toward the end of the meal he often pivots in sitting, flexes his legs on the chair seat, and may pull himself to standing.

Cup Feeding—Patterns are similar to those observed at 40 weeks, but now the baby enjoys holding his cup alone. His hands are pressed flat against the sides or bottom of the cup. His head tilts backward to enable him to drain the last drop.

[If only an ounce or two is given in a cup the baby can have the satisfaction of finishing it.]

Self Help—The baby usually finger feeds for part of one meal, either lunch or supper. A few boys, of a dominant but emotionally dependent type, demand to feed themselves at this age. They absolutely refuse any help even though they need it and results may be very messy. These same boys often ask for help at 2 to 3 years of age.

ELIMINATION

Bowel—One to two movements a day, at 8 to 9 A.M. and during the afternoon. The infant may respond to a pot if the bowel movement occurs directly after breakfast. "Successes" on the pot are less frequent than they have been and more resistance is expressed. An earlier indication that the bowel movement is about to take place (grunting) is no longer present, but the baby may fuss to be changed after the movement occurs.

Bladder—Dryness after nap, and occasionally when the baby awakes during the night and in the early morning, if he is put on the pot immediately after waking, is more frequent now, though some have relapses. Girls often laugh as they urinate, from 40 to 52 weeks, are interested in the process of urinating and look in the pot afterward to see what they have done. They may want to put their fingers in the urine or to put toilet paper in the pot, and may desire to flush the toilet. Fussing to be changed is beginning to be the rule though some show delay in this response.

BATH AND DRESSING

Bath—Bath is still a favorite part of the day's routine. It may be given at any time of the day that fits best into the household schedule, often in the late afternoon. Most babies prefer to sit in their baths at this age, and are no longer absorbed by play with the water or by their own gross motor activity. They are now interested in the washcloth, the soap, and water toys. They grasp and release these objects in the tub or extend them outside the tub, for instance dabbling water onto the floor from the washcloth.

[Bath toys can be controlled more easily than the washcloth. If the baby refuses to give up the washcloth he can often be induced to place it in a container which can then be put out of sight.]

Dressing—Hat, shoes and pants are the chief interests in dressing, and there is more interest in taking off than in putting on. When asked if he wants to go bye-bye (out for a walk), the baby may pat his head to indicate his desire for a hat. Shoes are played with for themselves and their laces, as well as for the pleasure of taking them off. The infant of this age is beginning to pull his pants off by himself, especially if his diapers are soiled or wet, and he is alone in his crib. This does not occur often. He now cooperates in dressing, putting his arm into an arm-hole or extending his leg to have his pants put on.

[A baby with an excessive drive to walk with his hands held may be inhibited, after he has had sufficient opportunity to express this drive, by taking off his shoes. His attention immediately turns to playing with the shoe, and walking is forgotten.]

SELF-ACTIVITY

The baby enjoys gross motor activity in his play pen and crib, pulling himself to standing, cruising, standing alone, creeping. He enjoys creeping on the floor, rather than in the play pen. He will usually be good in his play pen in the backyard or in the house for an hour in the morning, occupied with gross motor activity and with playthings. He enjoys placing things on his head, such as a hat, basket, or cup. He often throws things out of the play pen and then has difficulty in re-securing them.

Activities most enjoyed are gross motor activities; putting objects in and out of other objects (for instance putting clothespins in and out of a basket); and play with buttons, which consists of looking at the buttons and fingering them.

[The Taylor-tot device may prove useful for those babies whose sitting and creeping are poor but who like to stand.]

SOCIALITY

Fifty-two weeks is the heyday of sociality. The baby enjoys social give and take, and social occasions are apt to come about spontaneously, without planning. He is usually out alone in his play pen during the morning, though there may be some play with the family group. Most of his sociality, other than in relation to regular routine, occurs in the afternoon. He enjoys his carriage ride—enjoys standing up in his harness, and is especially interested in moving objects such as automobiles or bicycles. His playthings no longer absorb his attention.

He enjoys walking with his hands held, and loves the game of being chased while creeping. He enjoys hiding behind chairs to play the game of "Where's the baby?"

or waving "bye-bye." He is interested in opening doors. He says "eh" or "ta-ta" as he gives something to an adult, but he expects to have the object given right back. He throws things to the floor with the expectation that they will be restored to him. He whimpers or cries when things are taken from him.

He enjoys rhythms. He may be inhibited by "no-no" or may enjoy a game of smiling and laughing and continuing his activity in spite of such admonitions. He may be just coming into a period of being shy with strangers, or if he has gone through this period he may be friendly again.

14

FIFTEEN MONTHS OLD

---

§1. BEHAVIOR PROFILE

AT ABOUT FIFTEEN MONTHS of age the American baby becomes something more than a "mere" infant. He is discarding creeping for toddling. He is discarding his nursing bottle in conformance with cultural custom. By virtue of other cultural pressures, he says "ta-ta" on more or less suitable occasions; by gesture language he calls attention to wetted pants; he makes an imitative stroke with a crayon; he helps to turn the pages of a picture book, albeit several leaves at one swift swoop. Numerous patterns which were in the making at one year now come to relative fulfillment. He is ready for a new chapter of acculturation.

But having graduated from "mere" infancy, he does not by any means settle down. On the contrary he seems to feel and to exercise his newly formed powers almost to excess. He becomes demanding; he strains at the leash. While being dressed he may have to be bodily held. In his chair he stretches forward importuningly for things out of reach. He wants to hold and carry something in each hand. He is beginning to insist on doing things for himself. He likes to take off his shoes. He likes to empty and at least to overturn waste-baskets, not once but many times. If he is not equally ready to refill the waste-basket, it is because his nervous system is not quite ripe for this higher pattern of behavior.

For the time being, his gross motor drive is very strong; he is ceaselessly active, with brief bursts of locomotion, starting, stopping, starting again, climbing, and clambering. He likes to go out for a ride by automobile or by baby carriage, but even then he is prone to stand up and to be on his own self-activated move. If confined to a pen, he is very likely to throw out his toys.

Casting is a very characteristic trait. And what is casting, but emphatic release? The voluntary power to release hold of an object is a complicated action pattern which requires an elaborate development of the controlling nerve cells of the brain. It takes time to bring about these developments; the child must learn to modulate his release, to time it accurately, to make it obedient to his intentions. Like any other growing function, it needs exercise,—practice as we say, although the practice is primarily a symptom rather than a cause of the growth.

The year old child could poise one block over another; the 15 month old child can let go of the block, neatly enough to build a tower of two. Likewise he can release a tiny pellet into a bottle. The maturing power of release also enables him to play a better to-and-from game with a ball. Indeed, he can throw it after a crude, casting fashion. At 18 months he can hurl it. Even primitive man was once awkward in hurling stones. It takes years of neuro-motor organization before a child can throw in a mature manner. Casting is a rudimentary first step in the development of this complicated ability. It must be a very important action pattern, or it would not figure so strongly in the behavior traits at 15 months of age.

We have said that the 15 month old child is "demanding." Perhaps it would be more accurate to say "assertive"; because he is not so much demanding things of us, his caretakers, as he is demanding things of himself: he is asserting his embryonic self-dependence. He wants to help feed himself. He grasps the cup executively with both hands (and of course tilts it to excess). He boldly thrusts his spoon into his cereal and, upside down, into his mouth (of course with spilling). It will take almost another year before he inhibits the turning of the spoon in this manoeuver. (It took primitive man a long time to master the principles of the lever.) The significant demands are those he makes upon himself.

Now, as always, it is necessary to achieve a working balance between the individual and society. The danger is that the culture itself will place too heavy repressions upon this growing organism which is graduating from mere infancy. He does not enjoy the same kind of protectiveness which he had at the age of one year. The 15 month old baby is at the threshold of behavior capacities which already foretell nursery school and kindergarten. He is dimly aware of pictures in a book; he can fit a round block into a round hole; he jargons and gestures; he is actually beginning to build a little with blocks; he can imitate a stroke of crayon upon paper; he is no longer a "mere" scribbler. These are foretokens of his educability, but he is still very immature.

The temptation may be for the adult carriers of culture to press him too fast and too heavily in the direction of civilization. It is well to remember that Nature requires time to organize his burgeoning neuro-muscular system,—postural, manual, laryngeal, and sphincter. Everything in season!

§2. BEHAVIOR DAY

THE PATTERN OF THE BEHAVIOR DAY is changing. It shows the accumulative effect of cultural impress. Even at 15 months, although the child still needs constant care, he is not as much a baby as he was at 12 months. Our illustrative 15 month old child wakes between 6 and 8 o'clock in the morning. He does not demand to be changed even though he wakes wet. Nor does he need toys. He is content with simple self-improvised manipu lative and postural play in his crib. But when he hears someone stirring, the pattern suddenly changes to alert anticipation, which becomes overflowing joy as soon as his mother or caretaker greets him. He is now very sensitive to visual and auditory cues which have a social meaning.

The task of dressing him may fall to the father. The baby enjoys the tug and pull of dressing.

He is now capable of bipedal locomotion and so he walks to his breakfast. (This is a new behavior day event.) He nibbles his zwieback while he observes the family breakfast, and at about 8 A.M. is ready for his own, usually stationed in his high chair. His morning appetite is strong. He accepts being fed with a spoon, and demands that the dish be left on the tray. His motor drive is under better control so that the dish is now safe on the tray though it may need to be guarded. He likes to hold the spoon and likes to dip it occasionally into his cereal. He is more competent with the cup.

At about 9 o'clock he is changed and toileted. He is not likely to resist toileting at this age. He is then returned to his crib where he amuses himself with manipulative toys,—a ball, a doll, a tin pan, clothespins, or containers of various sorts. Vigorous hurling, banging or casting of toys may be a signal for a change of scene. He is transferred to a play pen. At 12 months he was quite content when the pen was in the rear yard. Now he prefers a play pen in the front yard or on the front porch. He likes to watch the traffic. He is about to graduate from the play pen and the scope of his interest is widening. He likes to look into the neighbor's yard or onto the neighbor's porch, particularly if on this porch there is another play pen with another preschool child. This tendency to penetrate beyond the pen can be anticipated by placing some of his toys outside of the pen. He manages to pull these toys into the pen and having secured them in this manner he is probably a little less likely to cast them out. Casting, however, is a developmental, and not a regrettable, behavior pattern.

He plays contentedly until about noon, when he is ready for his midday lunch. He definitely wants this lunch. He is not too much interested in preliminaries, but he is a little more eager to contribute his own self-help during this meal, even though the spoon is likely to enter his mouth bottom side up. He is quite ready to accept help in feeding toward the end of the meal, although he may insist on holding the cup to drink his milk or water.

At about 12:30 he is toileted and may have his first or second bowel movement, after which he is returned to his crib. The effects of acculturation now become evident. Typically he makes no protest against the impending nap. He snuggles down under his covers. He likes to watch the shades go down. He is happy to be in bed and with an inflection of satisfied conclusiveness he says, "there," or "bye-bye," and falls off to a sleep of an hour or two.

He is quite likely to wake wet. He is changed and toileted. He usually wakes in high mettle, eager to get out of his crib to continue with his behavior day. Already he is making definite associations between times and events. He is building up a sense of his own behavior day which was scarcely present in earlier infancy. He realizes that he will soon be enjoying a trip in the carriage and he waits with a certain degree of patience before the journey,—the patience being supported by a cracker which he munches while he waits.

Having arrived in the park or in a neighbor's play yard, he likes to be set free on the wide expanse of a lawn or a sidewalk. He indulges in a diversity of play, postural and manipulatory. Somewhat acrobatically he bends over and looks between his legs; he picks up sticks and strokes the dirt; hands them to an adult with an inflected "ta-ta" and does not expect a return as he did at 12 months. He jargons; he has a more sophisticated interest in his own sounds. Where formerly he was somewhat startled by them, he now listens to them suggestively. In his jargon he thus communicates with himself as well as with others.

He returns home at about 4:30 and continues his characteristic play activities, utilizing the apparatus of the living room, with a special interest in all containers, particularly waste-baskets. But he also likes to listen

[135]

to music, to dance in rhythm to it, or even with the help of an adult to look in brief snatches at a picture book.

The daily bath may come at 5 o'clock. It is preeminently a play period. He likes to continue in his bath for a quarter of an hour. A favorite activity is the pouring of water from a receptacle.

Supper follows. He helps a little in the feeding but amiably accepts administered feeding. Supper over he likes to come back to home base in his mother's lap or his father's lap, giving tokens of affection. He holds out his hand to have it kissed or caressed. And at about 6 o'clock he is again happy to be back in his crib for a sleep of some twelve hours. He is making increasingly definite person to person contacts, and after he has been tucked in bed he extends his hand through the palings for a good-night greeting.

The fact that we have so many greeting and intercommunication patterns emerging during the course of a single day at 15 months is a convincing reminder that acculturation is well under way and that much still lies ahead.

SLEEP
Night

Onset—Bedtime now comes between 6 and 8 P.M. and follows the happenings of the day in a regular, orderly fashion. The order, for instance, may be supper, bath, bed. The baby seems to have acquired a sense of "time to go to bed," an expectation that going to bed will follow certain events on the day's program. (At a later age this order and timing may change.) There may be initial crying by some, but most seem to have a feeling of being glad to be back in bed again. There may be talking for half an hour to two hours. The more active children may crawl out from under the covers and may be very active in their cribs until they finally fall asleep, perhaps at the foot of the crib.

[If falling asleep has been delayed, it is better not to go in to the child until he has fallen asleep or is nearly asleep. Otherwise the presence of the mother may stimulate him and further delay his falling asleep.]

Waking—Night waking is largely an individual matter and more common with the active child. Many children awake crying (more frequently before midnight) and are usually not quieted merely by being held. They can often be quieted by looking out of the window at lights, or by having someone play "This little pig went to market" with their fingers and toes. It is unwise to put them back to bed before they are ready, and the transition may often best be accomplished with a cracker, or by letting them hold something like a toothbrush which they may have fastened upon in the bathroom.

Morning waking occurs between 6 and 8 A.M. The child is usually good at this time, lying under his covers and talking to himself. He may later crawl out from under the covers and play around in his crib, without the need of toys.

Nap

The nap usually follows a noon lunch. A common indication of the child's readiness for sleep is his trying to get off his shoes. He usually settles down at once and goes right to sleep. A few children delay sleep, and play for a few minutes with toys before settling down on top of the covers. They awake after a two to three hour period and are ready to get up at once.

FEEDING

Self-Regulation—The gross motor drive is now under much better control than formerly. The child is able to sit through his meals, and commonly demands to help feed himself. Boys still lead in these demands. They do an especially creditable job with finger feeding, and this is definitely their preferred method of feeding. They still are apt to turn the spoon en route to their mouths, and are thus apt to spill the contents of the spoon unless the contents stick to the spoon. With fatigue they are more apt to allow the mother to feed them.

An even more usual demand is to hold a spoon and dip it into the food in the dish, which is now safe on the tray. The child accepts being fed as long as he is happily occupied. Spilled bits on the tray are usually finger fed. Many children differentiate as to the preferred method of being fed at different meals. Breakfast may be accepted

without any demands for self-feeding. Lunch may be accepted partially, with some demands for self-feeding. Supper may be completely taken alone, with the one possible exception when the child may allow his father to feed him. Many also enjoy feeding the father or mother and may do better at this than at feeding themselves.

Those who have clung to their evening bottle—either on their own demand or because their parents have felt it is the surest and easiest way to insure an adequate milk intake—most frequently have this bottle on going to sleep and often call it "ba-ba." They may even ask for it in anticipation of going to bed.

Preferences and refusals have their ups and downs but are on the whole quite similar to the patterns described at 1 year of age.

Number and Appetite—Same as at 1 year of age.

Spoon Feeding—This is an age when a large majority of children make some demand to participate in meals and want to have a try at the spoon. They grasp it pronately near the bowl, and have difficulty in filling it since they dip it rather than scoop it into the food. What sticks to the spoon is then carried to the mouth, but the journey to the mouth is a hazardous one and the spoon may be turned upside down and the little contents there are may be spilled. If it does reach the mouth right side up it is usually turned after it is inserted. The free hand is quite inactive and only comes in to help in an emergency. The child usually allows his mother to feed him so long as he is allowed to do some of the feeding himself.

[The child will often best accept help from the mother if she fills his spoon from her spoon, and then supports the handle of his spoon as he lifts it to his mouth.]

Cup Feeding—The child now enjoys manipulating the cup by himself, grasping it more with thumb and forefinger or with the tips of his fingers. He drinks more continuously (five to six swallows) and now tilts his cup by the action of his fingers rather than by the tilting of his head. However he is apt to tilt the cup too quickly so that some spilling results.

[Though the child demands to hold his cup alone, he may allow his mother to help by holding her finger under his chin to restrict the wide excursions of the chin.]
Self Help—Demands are similar to those expressed at 1 year with the addition that a demand to spoon feed is coming in and the child may insist on feeding himself one whole meal, preferably lunch or supper.

ELIMINATION

Bowel—One or two movements a day, though occasionally a day may be skipped. With some children it still occurs in the morning, either on waking or around breakfast time. With a few it has shifted to a more consistent afternoon pattern, either after lunch or in relation to the nap. A resistance to the pot common from 12 to 15 months is now giving way to an acceptance. If the child is put on at a favorable moment such as after a meal—usually breakfast—he may have a bowel movement easily on the pot. However at other times he will not "go" until he is removed from the pot even though he remains contentedly on it for as long as he is left there.

Another favorable time is when the mother observes that the child has suddenly become very quiet, or when he looks at his mother, or stoops as he grunts. He is beginning to be conscious of a bowel movement in his pants and may fuss, say "uh," or grasp at his pants to indicate his desire to be changed, especially when he is with an adult. He is less demanding of attention when he is in his crib or play pen and may even try to take off his pants by himself.

[Occasionally episodes of stool smearing may occur at this age, when the child is alone either in his play pen or crib. It is important that his clothes should fit securely and also that he be watched, preferably without his seeing the adult. Then he may be cared for immediately after he has had his movement.]
Bladder—The child may be dry after his nap if he is taken up immediately. At this age he appears to be more conscious of being wet than earlier. If he is in training pants and makes puddles on the floor, he may point to the puddles, use a special word such as "tee-tee" or "pee-pee," or may just say, "see." He may splash his hands in the puddle and may be interested in mopping it up with any nearby cloth. He responds fairly well to being put on the toilet, especially at favorable times such as after meals and before and after sleeping periods. He may not urinate until taken off the toilet, which also occurs with the bowel movement. Resistance to the toilet is shown if he is put on when he does not need to be, or during the mid-morning and the mid-afternoon. Some children may now be (temporarily) increasing their span to two or three hours.

[A "potty chair" may be the most successful toilet equipment at this age, particularly for those children who like to do things for themselves.

Since many children will not urinate or have a bowel movement until after they are removed from the toilet, it is best not to leave them on too long. Leaving them on for longer periods will not produce the desired results.

Punishment for wetting has little or no effect. If the child is punished, he is apt to stop telling after he is wet. Dressing him in diapers and rubber pants is preferable.

If the child resists being placed on the toilet, his resistance should be respected.]

BATH AND DRESSING

Bath—Now that the nap is usually in the afternoon, and supper is at 5 o'clock, there is little time for the bath in the afternoon. It may be best to postpone it till just before bedtime. Then it is heartily enjoyed, especially if it is taken with an older sibling.

Washcloth and soap are still grasped. Water is often sucked from the washcloth, or the washcloth may be placed on the head like a hat. Favorite water toys are containers such as cups or watering cans. The child may try to drink the bath water. He may fuss when taken from the tub but usually quiets when given some distracting toy.

Dressing—Dressing can be very difficult at this age. The child's attention is usually on other things. This is the age when the parent needs to hold the child tightly and pour him into his clothes. In the morning he may be dressed best on his mother's lap with the mother seated beside the crib so that he may reach for and occupy himself with his toys. Or he may be dressed standing on a high restricted place with a shelf at chest height for his toys.

His chief clothing interests are still his hat, shoes, and pants, and these are usually in relation to specific times: the hat when going out, the pants when soiled or wet, and the shoes when he is sleepy and ready for his nap.

[After waking from his nap his chief interest is often to go outdoors, clothes or no clothes. Therefore dressing him near a window or open door, if weather permits, may make the ordeal less difficult. Giving him a cracker often helps.]

SELF-ACTIVITY

The child occupies himself happily and contentedly at the following times: until he is picked up in the early morning; for an hour in his room or crib; and then for another hour out in his play pen in the morning. He cannot stay too long in one place at one time and enjoys a shift. His demands increase as the day goes on. He does not demand toys on waking, but plays happily, with gross motor activity. He wants his toys when he is returned to his room and he likes a little action, such as watching traffic or seeing people walk by, when he is out in his play pen. His favorite playthings are balls, spoons, cups, clothespins, boxes, and some fitting toys. His best play with toys often occurs in his room from 9 to 10 A.M. after his early gross motor workout. Then he puts things into things and takes them out again, throws balls and goes after them, and with fatigue throws his playthings out of the crib or play pen or puts them behind him.

SOCIALITY

The shy period which occurs at 1 year has usually passed, and the 15 month old child is eager to go out into the world in or with his carriage. Some still sit or stand in their carriages and especially enjoy the noises of the world. They hear a dog bark, a horse trotting, the whirr of an airplane. A sudden sharp noise may even cause them to whimper. They watch, too, but more than that they listen. Some, whose gross motor drive is strong, fuss to get out of their carriages after fifteen to thirty minutes, and wish to push the carriage themselves.

An hour's carriage ride is quite enough at this age. The 15 monther wants to be about his own intimate business of walking, stooping to pick up sticks, bending over to look between his legs, bringing odds and ends to the adult, and exercising what small vocabulary he has. He delights in dogs and often says, "bow-wow." He enjoys imitating smoking, coughing, nose blowing or sneezing, and blowing out matches.

In fact he is becoming so aware that he has to be restricted in his activities. He is apt to demand anything in sight if he is at the table. He is "into everything" in the living room and no longer plays the game of "no-no," but boldly demands his own

way. If he plays in the living room, things must be put out of reach. His primary interest in the living room, however, is the waste paper basket. His eyes search around a living room and seem invariably to pick out waste paper baskets. He enjoys pulling things out, and less often, putting them back in.

Toward the end of the afternoon he may enjoy looking at colored pictures and turning pages, and may also respond to rhythmic music with the swaying of his hips.

[When the child makes demands which cannot be met—such as a demand to walk in some forbidden place—he may respond favorably to being picked up. The shift in posture seems to cut off the demand at once.

Some children will not accept things directly from the adult hand but will accept things from a container.]

15

EIGHTEEN MONTHS OLD

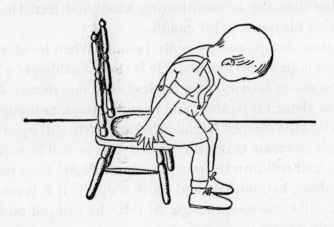

§1. BEHAVIOR PROFILE

THE EIGHTEEN MONTH OLD is so charged with run-about compulsions that he prefers to push his baby carriage rather than ride in it. His loco-motor drive is so strong that he is constantly running into nooks and corners and byways, or going up and down stairs by one device or another. For the same reason he likes to chase and be chased. He is con-stantly introducing variations into his movements, as though he were trying out the versatilities of his motor equipment. He walks backward, he pulls his carriage backward. He does this partly because he is "learn-ing" to shift the gears of his physiological automobile,—namely, his nervous system. This neuro-automobile is far from complete. He can start and stop pretty well (when he is so minded!); but he cannot turn corners; and he will have to double his age before he can pedal his tricycle or stand on one leg.

He has not even fully attained the upright posture. He walks on a broad base, feet wide apart; he runs with a stiff, propulsive flat gait. He squats a good deal; his abdomen is rather prominent; his arms extend out bi-laterally from the body, almost like flippers; he uses whole arm movements in ball play and "painting"; his hands are not agile at the wrists; he has difficulty in coordinating hands and feet. He even has trouble getting his spoon to his mouth.

He lugs, tugs, dumps, pushes, pulls, pounds. When he seizes a teddy bear he clasps it grossly to his chest. He is also something of a furniture mover. Gross motor activity takes the lead over fine motor. There is a primitiveness about his postures and manipulations, as though a reminiscent touch of the stooped Neanderthal man were still upon him.

But there is no reason to despair. At two years he will be more nimble at the wrists, and will turn the pages of a book singly! Even now he can take off his shoes, hat, mittens, and unzip a zipper, if it is not too fine. Much more will come soon enough. At three he will put on his shoes; at four he will lace them.

His attention, like his body activity, is mercurial. He attends to the *here* and the *now*. He has little perception for far off objects. He runs into them headlong, with meager sense of direction. You may talk to him about the future, but he will not listen, because for the time he is color-blind to the future. He is immersed in the immediate; but even now the push of growth is lifting him out of the immediate by giving him a sense of "conclusions."

This spontaneous interest in conclusions is one of his most interesting psychological characteristics. He likes to complete a situation. He puts a ball in a box and then utters a delighted exclamatory "oh" or "oh my!" in a burst of conclusive satisfaction. He likes to close a door; to hand you a dish when he has finished, to mop up a puddle, to flush the toilet, to "tell" after he has soiled himself. When he sits down in a chair it is with a decisive manner, as though to say, "now, that's done."

These are elementary judgments, even if they are not yet put in words and sentences. He is thinking with his body rather than with his larynx, and his mind is already operating on a distinctly higher level than it did at one year. His attention is sketchy, mobile, works in swift, brief strokes. In his play he likes to carry objects from one place to another. In this way he learns what a place is. He even likes to put things back in place,—an embryonic orderliness soon outgrown. But this bit of behavior is a good reminder that a great deal of organization is going on in spite of the apparent aimlessness of his activity. How can you discover without exploring? And how can you explore without traveling? And how can you find out where you started from without going back? So there is a logic, after all, in this back and forth behavior,—the logic of development.

This logic cannot be hastened by words. The child must begin with a practical logic. Things must be acted out first. He has only about a dozen words at his command. He relies on a more abundant vocabulary of expressive gestures and odd little clucking sounds (again reminiscent of a very primitive human). Favorite words are "all gone," "thank you," "bye-bye," "oh, my,"—all of which register completions. He responds to a few simple verbal directions, but he must be managed chiefly through things rather than words. If he is to remain still, he usually must have an interesting object in his hands. The manipulation of this object serves to drain his locomotor drive. Music may do the same thing. He will stay on the spot, and sway accompaniment with whole body rhythm. He may hum spontaneously. If he attempts singing, it is by repetition of a single word. He is not very sedentary, nor ready for the finer arts, though he likes to stroke in the dirt with a stick.

With such an action system, and with such very elementary insight into time and space, we do not expect elaborate or refined interpersonal relations. It is doubtful whether he even perceives other run-about children as persons like himself. He pulls, pinches, pushes and strokes them as though they were objects for manipulation. He is quite content with solitary play, back to back with one of his contemporaries.

And yet he is laying the basis for a more intellectual grasp of what another person is. He does a great deal of watching. He learns by looking a hundred times a day. It is by brief strokes and spans of attention but they count up. Sometimes he even imitates the wonderful adults upon whom he gazes: he crosses his legs; he reads a newspaper! He likes to play more elaborate peek-a-boo games; to hide and be found. This reciprocal kind of play helps to build up an identification of himself as distinct from, but like others. If he seizes a broom to sweep, he holds it by the end and shoves it shovelwise, a reminder of how much he still has to learn about spatial as well as human relations.

§2 . BEHAVIOR DAY

THE EIGHTEEN MONTH OLD child is relatively self-contained even though he is often described as a run-about. He wakes between 6 and 8 o'clock in the morning and plays contentedly until his mother arrives. He greets her, but not with the bubbling and excessive overflow of even three months ago. He is changed and restored to his crib with a cracker and toys. He is content to play for half an hour or more until breakfast, which comes at about 8:30, and may not begin until the father has left home. Breakfast is often served on a low chair and table unit. He likes the confinement of such a unit. He accepts feeding by his mother although he insists on holding his cup while he drinks.

After breakfast he is toileted. He may have a bowel movement, but irregularity is quite typical of this age. If it is summer time he spends a play period from about 9 to 11:30 out of doors on the porch or in a protected corner of the yard. If his enclosure gives him a free run so that he can exercise his locomotor abilities and if it is provided with a sand box and other toys, he is quite content to remain in it. He needs only marginal supervision. It may be necessary to go to him if he falls or cries, and he reacts favorably to shifts of toys when needed. He is so busy and preoccupied with his play activity that he does not need to be changed during the course of the morning. His rubber pants serve their purpose, and if he is interrupted he may resist toileting.

The noon luncheon may be served in his room. He is more insistent on helping himself at this meal. After luncheon he is toileted and is soon ready for his afternoon nap of, say, two hours. He wakes happy and cheerful from this nap. He is anxious to be up and doing. He is even interested in dressing to the extent that he helps with socks and shoes. However he is more skillful at undressing than at dressing.

After a snack of juice and crackers, he is taken out for a ride in his carriage. He does not like to stay too long in the carriage and is happier to get out and push. He may have to be restrained in a harness. He returns home willingly by carriage and plays perhaps for a quarter hour in the living room, dancing to the radio, looking at magazines, playing with the wastebasket. Being relatively self-contained, he is quite agreeable to being left in his room with the gate closed while his mother prepares supper.

Supper comes at about 5 o'clock. Having had his fling of self-feeding at the noon meal, he accepts a measure of help at the evening meal. He is toileted again and may have a second bowel movement.

His daily bath comes a little before 6 o'clock. He enjoys it as he did at 15 months but he is somewhat less reckless in his play, more sedate and more wary. After his bath, he joins his father for a brief period of good-night play.

Shortly after 6 o'clock he is put to bed with his teddy bear, to whom he jargons more or less sociably. In spite of his locomotor capacities, he stays under his covers and falls asleep sometime between half past six and eight, to awake in the morning for another active day.

SLEEP

Night

18 months—Bedtime still comes between 6 and 8 P.M. The child of this age likes to take some of his toys, as his teddy bear or his own shoe, to bed with him. He may play for a while with this object before dropping off to sleep, usually under the covers. Evening or night waking occurs intermittently and is usually associated with an active or too exciting day. He is easily quieted by being talked to, given a drink, or toileted if that is necessary.

He wakes between 6 and 8 A.M. He usually stays under the covers, talks to his teddy bear or plays with his shoe, and when he feels that it is time to get up, he may fuss or call. He is happy to see his parent and is eager to be taken up.

21 months *—Sleeping up till now has gone quite smoothly, but this is often the beginning of a period of sleeping difficulties which may continue through 30 months. Difficulties occur not only on going to sleep and during sleep, but also on waking. Difficulty is especially evident on going to sleep, when the child though he seemingly has settled down with a book, doll or teddy bear, then calls his mother back for the first of numerous demands for toileting, a drink, a handkerchief, a kiss, or anything that comes into his mind. Sleep is more disturbed at this age and there is more night waking, but the child usually quiets readily after being toileted, or given a drink or a cracker. A few children remain awake talking to themselves for an hour or more, early in the morning. Total sleeping time is further cut down by the fact that they wake earlier in the morning than they did when they were younger. They are apt to fuss, but if the mother goes to them and cares for them they may go back to sleep for an hour or more.

Nap

18 months—As at 15 months, the nap follows the noon meal. The child may or may not take toys to bed with him, but is often so ready for bed that he goes right to sleep. A few children, as at 15 months, may delay sleep. The nap lasts for 1½ to 2 hours. The child usually awakes happy and wants to get right up. Occasionally he awakes crying and then responds best to a motor workout of running about before being toileted.

21 months—As with night sleeping, there is difficulty in release of consciousness, but most children play well by themselves and do not call their mothers. Sleep may be delayed an hour or more and is finally induced only by the mother's putting the child under the covers at an opportune time. He sleeps longer (2 to 2½ hours) and although he usually awakes happily he may awake fussing. If he fusses it is best to let him take his time and awaken slowly.

FEEDING

Appetite—Appetite may be decreasing and is usually less than the robust infant appetite. The noon meal is frequently the best meal. Appetite for milk from a cup is less than appetite for milk from a bottle.

[If giving milk from a cup instead of a bottle has markedly reduced the amount which the child will take, it may be better to continue at least one bottle a day.]

Refusals and Preferences—18 months—Refusals and preferences are fluctuating and not clearly defined.

21 months—Preferences are becoming more positive. If canned baby foods have previously been given, the child may demand the continuance of a specific brand.

Spoon Feeding—Grasp of the spoon is pronate. The baby holds the spoon horizontally, raises his elbow as he lifts the spoon to his mouth. The spoon is aligned to the mouth half-point, half-side, and may turn after it enters the mouth. The free hand is ready to help as needed, pushing food on the lips into the mouth or placing spilled food in the spoon. The child may even carry food from the dish with his fingers and place it in the spoon bowl before putting the spoon into his mouth. Discrete particles such as peas and pieces

---

* The age level of 21 months is a transitional age. It has not been given separate chapter status, but is separately discussed in this section under the six behavior day categories (Sleep, Feeding, Elimination, etc.)

of meat are preferably finger fed. Food that cannot be swallowed is removed from the mouth.

The child cleans off the spoon well by tilting the spoon handle upwards as he removes the spoon from his mouth. He adjusts his head as with cup feeding. There is a lateral chewing movement of jaw and tongue. The tongue selectively licks in bits of food from the chin or the side of the mouth.

Cup Feeding—The child holds the cup with both hands, holding and tilting it securely. He now has good control of his fingers as he tilts the cup, and spills very little. As he comes up for air he exhales audibly. He soon returns to drinking and usually finishes his glassful. The hazard in cup drinking lies in the fact that when through drinking the child automatically extends the cup to his mother, and if she is not there or does not come at once when he calls, he is apt to drop the cup or to throw it across the room.

Self Help—18 months—Most children enjoy feeding themselves and may be able to handle all three meals. The mother may need to help fill the spoon. Some children, who have previously expressed occasional desire to feed themselves, may now prefer to be fed. Each dish is handed to the mother as it is emptied. Cup drinking is handled entirely by the child, except for the mother's accepting the cup.

21 months—If the child feeds himself, he eats better alone, with his mother moving about the room but not paying attention to him until he calls. If more than one dish is on the tray, he loves to pour things from one dish to another. He is not really able to handle more than one dish at a time. He likes to have patterns repeated—the same bib, the same spoon.

[Since the child at this age is sensitive to peripheral stimuli, it is important not to have his meal interrupted by small or large distractions. The dessert within sight, too much interference on the part of the mother, or the father coming home—any of these may serve to interrupt and perhaps terminate his meal. It is therefore often easiest to control such stimuli by feeding the child alone in his own room.]

ELIMINATION

Bowel—18 months—There is a variety of times and contexts for the bowel movement at this age, but each child is fairly consistent to his own pattern. However, at this age fluctuation and incompleteness are the rule. Therefore, any one child may set up a meal relationship for a time, then shift to midmorning, then to midafternoon. This makes successful "training" difficult. The child is beginning to request the toilet either by a word or by fetching his pot, and often the mother may judge by his unusual quietness that he is about to function.

There appear to be two distinct types of children, one with a close meal association with the bowel movement; the other more irregular and functioning at some time between meals. Those who have a meal association are usually trained more easily. The two daily movements usually occur after breakfast and after supper. These children often have a high language ability and refer to the bowel movement by name, i.e. "pot," "pee-pee," "toidy,"— a word which is not different from that used by them for urination. These words are more commonly used after functioning than before.

Those who have an irregular time of functioning commonly have their movement when alone, most commonly in the midmorning, and preferably standing at their playpen or crib rail. They usually want to be changed, and therefore may tell afterwards by making a meaningful sound ("uh-uh" or "k-k"). Or, they may merely gesture by pulling at their pants. These children usually resist the toilet and often have occasional episodes of stool smearing, initiated as they try to take care of themselves when alone in their playpens or cribs. If they do respond to the toilet in the morning they frequently do not finish, and then they may have one or two more movements in their diapers throughout the day, particularly when they are alone.

21 months—Similar to 18 months. More smearing episodes occur, especially after naps. Some children still refuse the toilet while others are completely trained, especially those who have a regular time. Some who have been well trained earlier, often have a relapse at this age, associated with a diarrheal episode. This may be related to teething, but may also be related to a new but too powerful release mechanism. Many are reported to have an explosive bowel movement which indicates a forceful casting release mechanism.

They are also quite conscious of the process and the product. Often if they soil their diapers, they seem unable to move, and stand screaming in distress, and continue screaming while they are being changed. This response is not necessarily related to any previous punishment. Sometimes they are able to inhibit release when it has started too soon, which may also bring on a screaming response. When they are successful in responding to the toilet they are often overjoyed at their success. Some children, **chiefly boys**, are unable

to have their bowel movement unless they are completely undressed. This may be associated with the 21 months' tendency to undress and to run about naked.

Bladder—18 months—Most children do not object to the toilet at this age if they are not put on too often. They may even enjoy sitting on it. However there are some who still resist strenuously. Some children now take the initiative themselves by occasionally asking in advance, in which case they use the same word that they use for bowel functioning. Or they may fetch the pot. They respond best to being asked whether they want to go, before they are taken. Their answer is usually quite accurate. The response to the toilet is fairly prompt.

If the child is in training pants and makes puddles on the floor, he continues to point to them saying "See," or "pee-pee," and enjoys mopping them up. This is the age when punishment and shame are often introduced by the adult, since something in the child's awareness makes the adult feel that the child could have done better. If punishment and shame are used, the child will point to the puddle and say "ooh-ooh" as though it were quite awful; and when asked, "Who did it?" he may blame it on the cat or on his grandfather, and when further asked if he did it himself may reply, "No, nebber." Another shame response is to show undue and sudden affection toward the mother just after wetting.

The child is increasingly dry after his nap, but still more frequently wet than dry. Keeping dry may depend on how quickly he was put on the toilet after waking.

This is an age when picking the child up at 10 P.M. for toileting is often started.

He is usually wet at this time, and may not awaken when changed or put on the toilet. He may, however, resist the toilet, in which case this practice should be discontinued. The child is usually wet in the morning even though picked up in the evening, but a few are consistently dry on waking with the help of this 10 P.M. toileting.

[Because bladder control is in a transition stage, it is still best to keep the child in diapers or in padded training pants and rubber pants, especially during the morning play period when he does not like to be disturbed, and during the night when they may prevent him from feeling wet and waking up. Training pants plus rubber pants are more comfortable, and if the child is away from home he may need them since he is apt to refuse to respond to a strange toilet.]

21 months—Though the child may resist the toilet at specific times when he does not need it, there is very little general resistance to the toilet at this age. The child may use words or gestures, and many are beginning to go to the bathroom by themselves even though unable to care for themselves. Accidents are more common in the afternoon, when the span is shorter than the morning span of 1½ to 2 hours. Children are more apt to ask for the toilet at night after being put to bed than at naptime.

The majority are wet after their naps, even though they may have been previously dry. Dryness depends largely on how quickly the mother gets to the child after he has awakened.

Resistance to being picked up at 10 P.M. is strong with many, so that many are not picked up at this time. They are usually wet in the morning.

BATH AND DRESSING

Bath—18 months—As at 15 months, the bath is usually given after supper. There may be occasional short periods of resisting the bath, the cause of which is hard to determine. Perhaps the child has fallen in the tub or has felt unsure on the slippery tub bottom, or has been disturbed by the noise of water gurgling down the drain.

[A rubber mat placed on the bottom of the tub may help to give a feeling of security.

Children who are stimulated rather than relaxed by a bath just before going to bed should have their bath at an earlier hour.]

21 months—There is an interest in helping to wash out the tub, an expression of the child's urge to imitate domestic activities.

Dressing—18 months—The child at this age is becoming interested in the process of being dressed and is on the whole quite cooperative. He even tries to put on his shoes but he is better at undressing than at dressing. He takes off his mittens, hat, socks, can unzip zippers, and is beginning to have an interest in undressing for itself.

21 months—The child undresses completely down to and sometimes even including his shirt, if that is easily removed. He does this when alone, usually in his room or out in the back yard. It is a common sight to see a 21 month old child frisking about the back yard without any clothes on— only the chill and cold of winter may inhibit this removal of clothes.

SELF-ACTIVITY

18 months—The 18-monther is indeed a busybody. He is both secure on his feet and secure in his own interests. He is not yet enough aware of people to be overdemanding, and demands occur mainly when he gets into trouble with his own activities. He has usually graduated from the playpen, though if his motor drive and activity are low he may prefer his 15 month old station of being in his play pen in the front yard. If he refuses the pen, his refusal is strenuous and should be respected. He will settle down to a happy play time either alone in his room, on a closed in porch or in a closed in yard space which is not too big but which gives him space to run around. He may prefer to be in any of these places for most of the morning, although he may enjoy being shifted from indoors to outdoors.

The success of his play depends upon the presence of interesting playthings and the absence of hazardous equipment. Because he is such a furniture-mover and is beginning to be such a climber, it is wise to remove chests of drawers and small tables and chairs which he can move, while he is playing in his room. If a chest of drawers remains, the drawers should be locked to keep him from getting into them, or the dresser turned to face the wall. Windows and screens should be securely fastened.

Indoors he endlessly shifts from pull toys to doll to teddy to pots and pans to balls to fitting toy to blocks or a hammer toy to magazines (especially those with colored advertisements). He hugs the doll one moment, drops it and runs over to finger the light plug the next, runs over to sit down and look at the magazine, tears out a page when he is finished, gets up and goes to his hammer toy. He may become angry when things do not work the way he thinks they should, but he does not usually call the adult for help. Out of doors on the porch or in the yard he also enjoys his indoor toys, but most of all he enjoys play

with sand and can sit for long periods filling and dumping sand, especially outside of the sandbox.

Besides the morning play periods alone, the 18-monther will accept being put alone in his room with the gate closed for fifteen to thirty minutes while his supper is being prepared, provided that he has had a happy social afternoon. If he is not to be put to bed at the usual 6 o'clock hour, it is wise to build up an evening play period in his room if his parents have an early dinner hour. This is initiated best with a new toy and should not continue past the time when he starts to fuss.

[Toys which are too difficult to handle and which for this reason bring on crying should be removed from the child's room and reserved for social play periods. Books which the child can tear should be removed from his room, though he may be allowed discarded magazines for his tearing play.

Light plugs in the child's room should be either disconnected or covered over, because of the danger of an electric shock resulting from the child's inserting sharp metal objects such as hairpins.]

21 months—The prolonged busyness of the 18-monther is now lessening because of the child's new awareness of people. His play periods alone are now more frequent but shorter. He likes to linger in the kitchen in the morning until 9:30 or 10:00 before he will go to his room or to his outdoor play space, and then he may stay only if he himself closes the door.

Indoors, a toy telephone, circles on a peg, or a small cardboard chest of drawers delight him. He enjoys acting out many of the household tasks he has seen performed, as dusting, opening drawers, or putting things on shelves. He still tears magazines, but his eyes may hit upon the wall paper and he may have the kind of hands that become busy picking at it. There are apt to be more interruptions of the play period at this age. He is more likely to fall or to get stuck. He quiets with affection after a fall.

He may scream for assistance as well as from fright if he suddenly has a bowel movement in his pants. After his mother has come to him, the child may refuse to return to solitary play. However he will later remain happily in his room as his lunch or supper is being prepared if he is told that his mother is "fetching the num-num." He also may build up a longer evening play period, as long as one hour, during his parents' early dinner hour.

SOCIALITY

18 months—This is the age when the child is "into everything" as soon as he is given the run of the house, and he never stays in one place for long. He is, however, becoming interested in the activities of the household such as sweeping and dusting, and enjoys mimicking these. He is beginning to know where things are kept, likes to fetch things (father's slippers when he comes home), and especially enjoys putting things back. He can also go to places where things are kept and ask for them, if they are out of reach, by looking or pointing, making the sound of demand ("eh-eh"), or sometimes by naming.

His main time for social demand is not until after his nap. Then he wants to go out for a walk. He may even prefer to leave his carriage at home, though he may ride in it for a while and then want to push it. He likes to be on his feet and to go exploring. He darts into every by-way that he sees or up any steps. He also rushes into the street. He refuses to be touched or to have his arm held, but generally tolerates a harness if it is used only when needed. The harness should be used with a loose rein except to break a fall, and the reins should be looped up whenever they are not needed. The 18-monther does not need to travel far from home since he so enjoys his weaving back and forth and his penetration into all by-ways.

When he plays indoors with an adult he can tolerate only a short time in the living room before he gets into things. He now enjoys dumping the wastepaper basket. He also enjoys turning the knob of the radio to get music to dance by. For a short period he may enjoy looking at picture books, turning pages, pointing to objects, and occasionally naming them.

But as soon as he fatigues, he is apt to grab objects and strenuously resists inhibitions. Then a sit-down temper tantrum may ensue, which can be terminated only by letting him have the desired object or by picking him up. Sometimes when he realizes he is taking something he shouldn't, he runs away and drops the object as he runs. After a very short time in the living room he plays happily with the adult in his own room, which is his favorite place.

After his evening play period of fifteen to twenty minutes he enjoys coming to the dining room, and sits happily if confined, looking at a book or chewing on some food. He especially enjoys sociability with his father before bed, with a little rough-housing.

21 months—At 21 months the child is not only more aware of people than formerly, but also knows what belongs to different people. He now understands, "This is mommy's," "This is daddy's," and "This is Bobby's" (his own). A sense of property rights is dawning in his mind. He likes his own place on the bookshelf, his own drawer in his parents' desk, his own corner in his mother's room with some of his toys there. In fact, each room acquires new meaning to him if he has something of his own in it. Then he always knows what to do in each room as he enters, and when he has exhausted the possibilities of his own things it is time to leave that room, for it is then that he begins to get into other people's things. He cannot be trusted alone in any room except his own.

He is now more aware of household activities and wants to participate in them. A favorite room is the kitchen. He likes to fetch things out of drawers, use them, and put them back. He delights in putting the groceries away and really knows where they go. After play in the kitchen he will happily go to his room for his morning play period, or else out-of-doors. He usually demands company by 11 A.M. and wants to go on a late morning walk before lunch. But before he goes for his walk he will gladly help pick up his toys and put them away.

The walk is similar to that at 18 months except that it involves more awareness on the part of the child. Whereas at 18 months he went hither and yon impulsively, he now goes to the same places knowingly and with remembrance. His eyes are already picking out walls and it will not be long before he will want to walk on them. He responds less quickly to requests and is apt to do the opposite of what is asked of him, such as going in the opposite direction. This is especially true when it is time to go home. However some incentive such as a constant repetition of "Go see Susie" (who may be the dog, cat, maid or a doll) causes the homeward path to be taken in one direction.

The child is now both more responsive to and more demanding of the adult. He now grasps the adult's hand and pulls him to show him things. He is now more conscious of his acts as they are related to the adult and to the adult's approval or disapproval. He is conscious of disapproval of his tearing off the wall paper, and very adroitly directs the adult's attention away from the marred place on the wall.

He also can control the adult by calling his name. Many, especially boys, do not call their mothers "ma-ma" before 21 months. They now also have words for their desires, and combine the giver and the gift as when they call, "Mommie wa-wa," or "Mommie toidy."

This is the age when this new acquisition (language) may be used repetitively, and when going to bed is beginning to be fraught with frequent calling back of the mother. This is especially evident if the child has been put to bed at the usual 6 P.M. hour when he actually does not go to sleep before 7 or 8 P.M. The adult must then realize that the child has outgrown his infantile ways and needs a more mature type of handling.

§3. CULTURAL AND CREATIVE ACTIVITIES

BOOKS

1. Attends to pictures of familiar objects in books.
2. Listens to short rhymes with interesting sounds, especially when they are accompanied by action or pictures. Likes to have them sung.

3. Enjoys tactile books such as "Pat the Bunny" or "The Tactile Book."
4. May look at books upside down.
5. Needs supervision while looking at books as frequently tears them at this age. Cloth and heavy cardboard books are recommended.

MUSIC

1. Spontaneous humming or singing of syllables.
2. Wide range in tone, pitch and intensity of voice.
3. Very much aware of sounds such as bells, whistles, clocks.
4. Rhythmic response to music with whole body activity.

PAINTING

1. Whole arm movements.
2. Very few strokes on a page, often in the form of an arc.
3. Shifting of brush from one hand to the other.
4. Satisfied with only one color.

BLOCKS

1. Carries blocks around the room, pounds them together, or dumps in a mass.
2. Only building may be a tower of three or four.

POSSESSIONS

1. May have a special toy, blanket or other object to which he is attached. Unable to sleep without it.
2. Definite relationship of possessions to their owners—takes hat or pocketbook to its correct owner.

EXCURSIONS

1. Enjoys short walks; runs ahead of adults; interested in all by-ways.

§4. NURSERY BEHAVIOR

IF EIGHTEEN MONTHS attends a nursery, it is on a very special basis and for a short session. He needs constant watching. The vigilance of one adult cannot be spread over more than two or three children of this runabout age. The conditions on which he is permitted to attend a nursery will be stated elsewhere. The following sketch of his hour in the nursery does not attempt to describe individual differences; nor does it describe a model child; it simply outlines the kind of behavior which is illustrative and typical of this interesting stage of immaturity.

EIGHTEEN MONTH OLD arrives at the nursery at about 9:30 in company with his mother. After the first few visits he shows an interest in his new surroundings. He is likely to break into a smile on arrival. The mother in her zeal may try to have him say "how-do-you-do," but he in his wisdom remains mute or simply jargons to his guidance teacher. He tends to loiter as he approaches, perhaps touching the walls of the vestibule.

He takes off his cap; his mother takes off his wraps. He does not hang them up, but strains to get away even before the wraps have been completely removed. Without leave-taking ceremonies, he darts into the room, and makes for the toy shelf, giving almost no regard for his teacher. He touches one toy after another, the blocks, the rings, the telephone and then climbs up the stairs. He finds a doll in the crib, picks it up with dispatch, hands it to the teacher, exclaiming "oh!"; then hands her a toy dog, slides down to the main floor; runs across the room; spies the nested blocks, runs over to them laughing. He sits down a moment, takes a few of the blocks apart and then toddles over to another focus of interest, the peg and hammer toy. He carries a block with him, but drops it heedlessly on the way to give heed instead to the hammer and pegs. After a brief period of pounding he makes for a favorite toy, a collection of rings on a pole. He picks up several and deposits them in the teacher's lap, less interested in the social than the fetch and carry aspects of the situation. He makes very few overtures to her; he does not wait for her direction but he likes to have her around, misses her if she is absent.

He is not as heedless of persons as appears on the surface. Often he stands and watches the other children and responds with bits of mimicry. The teacher removes the turtle from the aquarium and places it on the floor. The group of children gather around to watch; they assume the squatting position characteristic of this age. There is a moment of concentrated group attention; then the group disperses, each child renewing his independent succession of activities.

There are no idle moments. When EIGHTEEN MONTH OLD is not exploiting a toy he is usually transporting it. His postural sets and postural control are put to ceaseless, varying tests,—he goes up and down the three-flight staircase, front-wise, back-wise and with other permutations; he slides, he crawls through a tunnel, he moves chairs and table about; he pulls a wagon, pushes a doll carriage, but without clear destination or purpose, quickly abandoning one type of activity for another.

After perhaps twenty minutes, the sight of the table may remind EIGHTEEN MONTH OLD of the fruit juice which he enjoyed the week before. He brings a chair to the table, seats himself by backing into the chair and by demeanor and gesture rather than words, declares his readiness for refreshment. He cannot pour his juice, but he manipulates his cup, drinks noisily and restores the cup to the table, with at last a verbalized "more." In a semi-automatic manner he stretches out his hand for crackers.

Luncheon over he inspects a picture book with the help of his teacher, both cooperating in the turning of the pages. He listens to music for a few minutes, responding with a bouncing rhythm.

He is dressed for outdoors. This may take five minutes for he cannot offer much assistance in the process. He makes ready adjustments to the change of scene which takes him to the slide, the jungle gym, the sandbox, the dump truck, and the water-paint. He takes a brief journey on the kiddy-car. His favorite sedentary occupation is a repetitious filling and dumping of sand. He takes an inarticulate pleasure sitting back to back with a companion, while both dump and fill and fill and dump; each apparently self-engrossed.

If instead of continuing to play with the sand, he should revert to thumb-sucking or inactivity, we should regard it as a symptom that he has overstayed his hour. In the interests of his psychological hygiene, the mother's return is punctual and her return is welcomed by the child.

§5. NURSERY TECHNIQUES

PHYSICAL ENVIRONMENT

SIMPLIFY the physical environment to prevent over-stimulation. Provide gross motor equipment, such as stairs with railing, and slides, to suit the child's gross motor drives. Manipulative materials are also necessary.

The simplicity and freedom of the outdoors are suited to the psychology of the 18 month old child. Outdoor activity reduces tensions and resistance. He enjoys the outdoors and this puts him at his best.

A sandbox is a necessity at this age, providing as it does a focal center capable of holding interest without the restrictions of bounds, as well as an opportunity for filling and dumping play.

ADJUSTMENT

Adjustment should be effected at this age through *things*. It often consists of gradual luring of the child away from the mother by rolling rings which he follows, by moving manipulative toys farther and farther away from the mother, or by centering his interest on some part of the room or on toys at a distance from and if possible out of sight of the mother. This gives her a chance to slip out. This is not an age for formal goodbyes. "Out of sight out of mind" applies here.

ROUTINES

Do not attempt to set up elaborate routines (as toilet, washing hands, resting) too soon after entrance. These activities are not only associated with home and mother but are often not yet well established and the child may resist them in school for several weeks or longer. His adjustment to school may be jeopardized if these routines are pushed. Diapers and rubber pants to keep the child dry, a short stay at school to avoid the necessity for rest, are desirable.

The one routine which is accepted and heartily enjoyed is midmorning lunch of juice and crackers.

He also enjoys some participation in undressing, such as taking off his hat and mittens, and putting his clothes in his cubby; but the rest of undressing and dressing has to be done by the teacher.

The child at this age has a strong desire to "put things back" and enjoys clearing up the room before midmorning lunch.

[156]

TRANSITIONS

Avoid resistance to sudden changes by utilizing methods of gradual transition. (Verbal transitions are usually futile at this age.) Allow the child to take a favorite toy with him. Use the toy as a lure to get him from one room to another. Utilize his responsiveness to gross motor humor by picking him up as a bag of rags. He may accept this, while resisting simpler touching approaches such as having his hand held. He likes chasing someone and being chased. Do not expect to control him through hypnotism or solemn discipline.

TEACHER

For his safety each child needs the close and constant physical supervision of an adult teacher. Children of this age are quick and adventurous and frequently tumble. Therefore groups should be kept small.

Direct the child through objects and physical orientations and gestures. Use language sparingly.

When contacting the child it is important for the teacher to be on his physical level by squatting or sitting on a low chair or on the floor.

The teacher's role is more passive at this age than at the immediately following ages. Her chief role is protecting and supplementing.

Once the initial adjustment is made, this is one of the easiest ages to handle because the child goes on his own steam and is not likely to get into conflicts with his contemporaries.

VERBAL

Use language sparingly. Simple well chosen words such as "all gone," "thank you," "bye-bye" are most effective. The child responds better to one word or a short phrase than to complicated explanations. For instance, "Hat?", or "Outdoors?".

Use the child's name in addressing him rather than the pronoun, as "Bobby wash hands."

Situations can be terminated by "thank you," or "bye-bye."

It is important for the teacher to employ a rising, expectant inflection when she speaks to the 18 month old child.

Gestures are often needed to reinforce language.

The 18 month old has an immediate time concept and only understands "now" or association with routines, such as "after juice."

HUMOR

Children may respond to gross motor humor as hiding and peekaboo, and being lifted in bag of rags fashion. Such humor can be used in effecting transitions.

OTHER CHILDREN

The 18 month old child tends to treat another child as an object rather than as a person. He resorts to experimental poking, pulling, pinching, pushing, and sometimes hitting. The teacher needs to be on guard to direct this experimentation into harmless channels. She should not attempt to force socialized cooperativeness at this age.

GROUP ACTIVITY

These children are not ready for group play. Most of their time is spent in solitary activities. Group activities are largely confined to gathering for midmorning lunch, or for short glimpses of nature specimens or new toys.

16

TWO YEARS OLD

§1. BEHAVIOR PROFILE

AT TWO YEARS the child cuts his last milk teeth. He is no longer an infant though compared with a 3 year old child he is still very immature. There is danger of overestimating his capacities, simply because he is sturdy on his feet and is beginning to put words together. He is still an infant-child. He has so much behavior to coordinate, to organize in this third year that we must stress his limitations as well as his prodigious capacity for growth.

He does not yet walk erect. There remains a little of the angularity of the ancient man in his posture. Knees and elbows are slightly bent, shoulders are hunched. He holds his arms out and backward. His abdomen, however, does not protrude as much as at eighteen months. When he picks up something from the floor, he half bends at the waist as well as at the knees; whereas at 18 months he squatted. Stooping is a more ad-

[159]

vanced behavior pattern than squatting. But the 2 year old still leans forward as he runs. Should he fall he would bruise his forehead; at $2\frac{1}{2}$ years he will hit his nose; at 3 years, his teeth. These are consequences of his physical make-up, just as his behavior traits are consequences of the make-up of his action system.

To get up from a sitting position on the floor, he leans forward, pushes up buttocks first, and head second, instead of raising an erect trunk as he will later. He goes up and down stairs mark-time fashion, without alternating his feet. He can kick a ball, whereas EIGHTEEN MONTHS merely walked into a ball; but he cannot stand on one foot as he will in another year. There is not much spring in his knees. The knee joints become flaccid or rubbery when one tries to slip on his leggings. He is rather hard to dress even though he is cooperative.

He is still geared to gross motor activity, and likes to run and romp, lug, push and pull, but with better coordination than at 18 months. His fine motor control also has advanced. He manipulates more freely with one hand, and alternates from one hand to the other. He rotates his fore-arm, which enables him to turn a doorknob. He can crudely imitate a circular stroke. This increased manipulatory skill expresses itself in his marked interest in fitting one thing into another. "It fits" is a favorite and sometimes triumphant sentence. He also likes to take things apart and fit them together again.

The muscles of eyes and face are more adept. He moves his eyes more freely and is sensitive to marginal fields, whereas at 18 months he ran headlong as though he had blinders on. He stops and engages in long periods of looking. The muscles of the jaw are coming under full voluntary control. Chewing is no longer as effortful as it was at 18 months, and mastication is becoming more rotary.

The whole linguistic apparatus, mouth, lips, tongue, larynx and thorax, is undergoing rapid organization. Jargon is dropping out, sentences are coming in. Soliloquy is taking the place of the babbling of the 6 month old child, as though on an advanced level the 2 year old is under a similar compulsion to exercise his vocal abilities, to repeat words, to name things, to suit words to action and action to words. Vocabularies vary enormously in size from a half dozen to a thousand words, but the third year is ordinarily the year when words burgeon.

The third year is also the year when the sphincter muscles of bladder and bowel are coming under voluntary control. Culture seems to conspire to increase the burden of development. For this reason home and nursery must be on their guard not to expect too much all at once in the correlation of postural control, fine coordination, speech, sphincter control, obedience, courtesy and neatness.

The action system of the 2 year old is not yet sufficiently advanced to effect delicate and long sustained interpersonal relations. He still prefers solitary play to parallel play and seldom plays cooperatively. He is in the pre-cooperative stage; watching what others are doing rather than participating. He cannot share; he cannot as a rule let someone else play with what is his own. He must learn "It's mine" first. He does so by holding on and by hoarding. This is not a vice. How can he possibly acquire pride of ownership any other way? It is the method of development. Keeping and sharing are not separate virtues, they spring from the same developmental root. The hitting, patting, poking, biting, hairpulling and tug of war over materials so characteristic of Two need to be handled with understanding and sensible techniques on the part of parent and guidance teacher. The infant-child is still too young to be reached by words alone; he must organize his experience through touching, handling, holding, clasping and even a little hoarding and running away.

So to sum him up, what are his dominating interests? He loves to romp, flee and pursue. He likes to fill and empty, to put in and to pull out, to tear apart and to fit together, to taste (even clay and wood), to touch and rub. He prefers action toys such as trains, cars, telephones. He is intrigued by water and washing. Although he is not yet an humanitarian, he likes to watch the human scene. He imitates the domesticities of feminine laundry work and doll play. He has a genuine interest in the mother-baby relationship.

[161]

§2. BEHAVIOR DAY

THE TWO YEAR OLD child wakes somewhat slowly at, say 7 o'clock in the morning. He is happy to wake but not interested in getting out of his crib at once. He wakes wet but tolerates this condition and plays contentedly for about half an hour. He has a ready greeting for his mother, who toilets him and puts him in a bathrobe for an interim. He likes to go to the bathroom during this interim to watch his father shave. He is also content when he is returned to his room where he munches a cracker and plays behind the closed gate. At breakfast he accepts considerable help from his mother but contributes in small dabs of self-help. (He will take over more completely at the noon meal.)

After breakfast he is toileted and is likely to have a bowel movement at this time. He is dressed and again he offers some self-help. He plays in the kitchen for a while and then, at about 9:30, if it is not a nursery-school day, he returns to his room and remains behind the closed gate without protest. If he should catch sight of his mother he may clamor for release. Otherwise he plays by himself for perhaps an hour. At 10:30 he is toileted and, weather permitting, is taken out of doors. He makes no resistance to toileting because he takes it to mean a transition to new play experiences in his sand box.

In his small enclosed play-yard he engages in gross postural play activity, pulling toys, trundling his baby carriage, and climbing on boxes, and near noon he has acquired a vigorous appetite for luncheon. This is the big meal of the day. He helps in its preparation. He also insists on feeding himself at this meal. He may even ask his mother to leave the room as he does so, calling her back for a next course.

After luncheon he is toileted and put to bed for a relaxation period which usually terminates in a nap, though sleep may be delayed until about 2:30. The nap may last an hour. He wakes slowly. He usually wakes dry and responds to toileting. He takes some interest in dressing. He is beginning to show a well-defined liking for certain garments. He likes to listen to his mother's conversation and to make a few contributions of his own.

After juice and crackers, he is ready for outdoors. He prefers a stroller to a carriage. He likes to walk, does not object to being held by the hand. He likes to walk on walls. He is not averse to an auto ride, and particularly enjoys the traffic, assisting the stop-and-go lights with his own commentary announcements.

He likes to watch the preparations for supper. He may even help a bit He feeds himself in part during the evening meal.

He is toileted again and may have a second bowel movement.

By 6 o'clock he is ready for a period of solitary play in his room. He likes to climb in and out of his crib when the arrangements so permit. He also takes off his shoes as though by way of anticipation of going to bed. Frequently he has a brief session of play with his father. He is somewhat demanding about this bit of "life with father" for he insists that father should come directly to his playroom, without delaying to read the newspaper!

The daily bath comes after this play period. Here too the baby likes to offer some assistance and helps to wash himself with the washcloth.

He is off for bed at half past seven. He likes to have a book and some soft animal toy. After about a quarter-hour of play he may call his mother, requesting the toilet or a drink. He resumes play, and, after another interval, he is quite likely to call back again. By about 8 o'clock he is ready to say "goodnight," and this usually announces a release into sleep.

SLEEP
Night

The time of falling asleep depends to some extent on when the child is put to bed, but his falling asleep is usually delayed till 8 or 9 P.M. The nap tends to displace night sleep, and if he has no nap he falls asleep earlier. His going to sleep patterns are similar to those at 21 months, there being many demands and requests. Children in whom these demands began at 21 months are often decreasing their demands by 24 months. Those who do not begin them till 24 or 30 months continue these patterns often until 36 or 42 months. By 24 months, demands before going to sleep include a request for two or three stuffed animals, a book or two, and a pillow. The child still calls his parent back with various requests, though these may be decreasing. Going to sleep is not an easy thing for the 2 year old and tensional overflows may occur in various avenues—play, gross motor activity like bouncing, calling for the mother or demanding the toilet. The child may actually need the toilet three or four times and even if he does not urinate he very likely has sensations that make him ask. Having the door slightly ajar or a light on in the hall seems for some children to make the mother more accessible and relieves their anxiety.

If the child can handle going to sleep by himself he sings, plays with his toys, takes the case off the pillow, bounces, and may even finally crawl back under the covers by himself. When he is once asleep he often resists being picked up for toileting, and this waking may actually disturb his sleep pattern. Some, however, awake by themselves, especially girls, and demand the toilet as often as three to five times a night. They not only demand the toilet, but may also demand a drink of water or a cracker.

When the child awakes, between 6:30 and 7:30 A.M., he usually plays happily in his crib with his toys. If he calls, he is quickly satisfied with being changed and given a cracker and a few toys. He is then happily occupied until it is time to get up, when he especially likes to join his mother or father in the bathroom.

[This is the age when the child begins to hold on to the mother as he is being put to bed. This does not occur as much with the father and may occur even less with a maid. Thus bedtime may be smoother if someone other than the mother puts the child to bed.

Some children wake at the slightest disturbance during the night. In these cases it is best to make every possible prepara-

tion for the child's safety and comfort before he is left, and then not go into his room again.]

Nap

Going to sleep patterns are similar at nap time to those at night time, with the exception that demands for the adult, at nap time, are put off till it is time to get up. Some give up sleeping at nap time for a few weeks or a few months, and others once or twice a week, but they will play happily in their cribs or rooms for an hour or more. If they do finally get to sleep, it is often induced by the adult's putting them under the covers, and they usually sleep well for two or three hours. Some do better if allowed to waken by themselves but too long a nap does displace night sleep and some children need to be wakened. When they awake by themselves they often awaken slowly and do not wish to be rushed through routines.

EATING

Appetite—Fair to moderately good. Breakfast is now relatively small. The noon meal is usually the best, but with some the one good meal is supper.

Refusals and Preferences—This is the age when the child is spoken of as "finicky" or "fussy." Now he is able to name many foods and has more definite ideas about what he likes. "I want," or "Billy wants" is a common expression at this age. His affection is not only shown toward his mother but also toward the foods that he eats. His sense of form makes him prefer whole things—whole beans, whole pieces of potato—unless he demands the extreme opposite, i.e., the continuation of puréed foods. He does not like foods mixed up, such as gravy on his potato or milk on his cereal, unless, of course, he does the mixing himself. His preferences may be related to taste, form, consistency or even color, red and yellow foods often catching his fancy. He is apt to repeat his demand for one food, but finally he drops that food completely and goes off on a different food jag.

[It is best to allow the 2 year old to have his food jags. Introduce new foods under new or pleasant situations. A great variety of foods is not needed by the 2 year old. If he holds food in his mouth, this may be considered a sign of satiety.]

Spoon Feeding—The child now shows less experimental interest in the spoon and dish as play objects. The spoon is grasped more between thumb and index (more common with girls), and pronately. Filling of the spoon may be accomplished by pushing the point into the food without utilizing the free hand to push on the food. The point of the filled spoon is inserted into the middle of the mouth. There is still considerable spilling, and those who are disturbed by spilling may refuse to feed themselves, but accept food readily when they are fed.

Cup Feeding—The child may now hold his cup or glass in one hand, with the free hand poised, ready to help if needed. He is able to lift, drink from, and set down the glass skillfully.

Self Help—Some 2 year olds are able to feed themselves entirely and will accept no help. They seem to know that they do better alone, and dismiss the parent with, "Mommy way!" If the mother remains in the room she may have to be careful not even to look at the child.

There are some, however, who eat better when partially fed. They may eat their main dish better if they are given a spoonful of dessert now and then. With still others who are the really poor eaters, the further distraction of stories, told or read, may be needed, especially when they are eating foods that they do not like.

The two extreme groups, the messy and the spotless eaters, are rather clearly defined at 2 years. The spotless are more apt to demand to be fed, to hold onto rituals, even to demand a special mat under their dessert dish if this has once been provided, and also to hold onto a repetition of certain foods.

ELIMINATION

Bowel—Accidents are rarer, though they come in periods. The two daily bowel movements usually occur after meals. Those who have a nap relationship are slower in being trained. The child now differentiates bowel and bladder functions verbally. He may ask with such phrases as the following: "Make movement," "I have to go grunts," "Make a mess." Although he needs to be helped to go to the toilet, he wants to be left alone and often speaks imperiously to his parent with, "Get out," "Go downstairs," or "Go away." But when he is finished he calls the parent back again to help him. Some children will not have a bowel movement if they are put on the toilet, but will only go if they put themselves on.

[The 2 year old who will not have his bowel movement when placed on the toilet may do better if allowed to go by himself. This is often best accomplished by allowing him to run around in or near the bathroom without his pants on at the time when the bowel movement ordinarily occurs. Toilet facilities should, of course, be of a size and kind that he can use by himself.]

Bladder—There are fewer daytime accidents, though they may still occur in periods. The child's span is fairly long now (1½ to 2 hours) and he often asks for the toilet. "I have to go potty (toidy)," or "Do wee-wee" are common expressions. He does not usually resist routine times before and after sleep, and mid-morning and afternoon except when he does not need to urinate. With most children there is an increased frequency period as short as twenty minutes between 5 and 8 P.M. Some are trying to go by themselves and may successfully remove their pants but cannot reach the bathroom in time.

They are now beginning to be proud of their toilet achievements and are apt to say, "Good boy" or "Good girl" when they have finished. They are also more concerned about their failures. They may suddenly cry as they urinate and find it difficult to move with wet pants on. Or they do something about it, taking off their wet pants and putting them in the hamper.

They are now more frequently dry than wet after their naps. Some may have a week's period when they wet daily and others may revert to wetting once or twice a week.

There is a good bit of variation in night wetting, with girls achieving dryness considerably ahead of boys. A fair majority of all children at this age are dry at 10 P.M. They usually wake when picked up and may or may not mind being picked up. Even when they do not object they may have difficulty in getting back to sleep. If they are not picked up they may in any case awake during the night to be taken to the bathroom. A few are dry in the morning but the majority are wet even though they have been picked up at night.

[If children are picked up at 10 P.M. they need not be awakened, though they usually do awake of their own accord at this age. If the child still wets at night it is still desirable to continue diapers and rubber pants.]

BATH AND DRESSING

Bath—The child is now becoming more interested in helping to wash himself, and may prefer the washcloth to the bath toys. He is especially interested in washing and drying his hands, though he does neither very well.

[If the child refuses his bath, accept his refusal. He may, however, enjoy the change of having a sponge bath or of being washed on the hamper with his feet in a basin.]
Dressing—The 2 year old can take off his shoes as well as his stockings and pants. He may try to put on some of his clothes by himself but is not very successful. He almost invariably puts both feet into one pant leg and puts his hat on backwards. When being dressed he is not only cooperative but definitely helpful. He finds large armholes and thrusts his arms into them, and lifts his feet to put on his pants. Some children still like to undress over and over again as a game and enjoy running about without their clothes on. However, at 2 years, the recurrence of this undressing pattern comes only for short periods, as is true with so much of their other behavior.

SELF-ACTIVITY

If the snags of 21 months were not properly handled or ironed out, the child may be unable to adjust to a morning play period alone. Fortunately it is most frequently the child who is too stimulated by being with people who often does best alone, and the child who plays nicely beside the adult without getting in the adult's way who refuses to play alone.

The 2 year old may, on the days when

he does not attend nursery school, go happily to his room after a spell in the kitchen, if the doorway is guarded by a gate. But he may allow his door to be closed in anticipation of having something such as a letter or card slipped in under it.

He is now quieter at his play and has more continuity in doing things. He especially likes things that move and turn, such as little cars and wheels. In the kitchen the meat grinder and egg beater delight him. Screw toys and even a screw driver, which he cannot handle alone, are also enjoyed. He now lines up his blocks and enjoys the blocks that stick together and fit into each other. The 2 year old often chooses little things like pebbles, pieces of string, marbles, beads, little bottles, and little books. Christmas cards are also cherished. Within the domestic line he now both feeds and toilets his doll and teddy and may even put them to bed, or take them for a ride in a doll carriage.

It takes the 30 month old child to conduct a proper tea party, but the 2 year old enjoys the fitting together and matching of cup and saucer and the pouring of water. Out of doors, sand still holds his interest, with digging becoming more efficient. The addition of water is more than desired by the child, but is not the easiest thing for him to handle when he is alone, and always seems to lead to a demand for more water. Pushing a wagon or a baby carriage, along with other gross motor activities of running and climbing, are favorite out of door occupations.

SOCIALITY

The 2 year old child is now becoming quite an acceptable member of the household. With his further understanding of property rights he gets into fewer things. However he has now reached the stage of possessing as many things as he can, often with only the slightest reason for claim, and he insists upon his rights with "It's mine." The strength of his home demands is often in rather marked contrast to the meek compliance of his behavior away from home.

He enjoys helping in the house, running errands, helping make beds or clean the bathroom, and placing the table silver. He enjoys bringing ash trays or passing things to people. He seems so mature in so much that he does that he is sometimes not watched closely enough. When left to his own devices he can completely wreck a room, especially his mother's bedroom, in a very short time, by emptying bureau drawers, pulling scarfs off bureaus, and getting into powders or creams.

His walks are now more sedate. He likes to hold the adult's hand. He may stop to pick up sticks or pebbles, but he does not linger long. He delights in walking on walls or curbstones with his hand held. This is one way in which he can be given the sense of the boundary of the street. If he lingers behind his mother he usually comes running when she starts off and says goodbye to him. He will now accept a ride in his stroller, and if he still uses a carriage he enjoys hiding back under the hood especially as he passes strangers.

His afternoon play period in the house is happiest with books and music. The nursery rhymes strike a responsive note in the 2 year old and any kind of tactile book demands repeated feelings. Dancing to music now includes running, turning in circles, and the beginnings of bouncing up and down.

The father is still a great favorite at this age, though the child may want his mother if he is in any trouble or at night when he is tired, and especially during the night.

He may show considerable dependence on his mother and is apt to demand all of her attention if there are others present. This is the age when affection is shown for parents or for those caring for the child, especially in the evening before bed.

The 2 year old with his increasing awareness of people goes through a shy period with strangers, especially adults. Indoors he may put his fingers to his mouth, hide in the folds of the curtains or against his mother's skirts. Out of doors he may act the same, or may walk a large circle around a passerby, or hold the adult's hand and keep very close to her. But when he once becomes acquainted with a stranger, and especially if the stranger is of a preferred sex, he generously brings all of his toys and places them in the stranger's lap.

He is now enlarging his vocabulary from "baby" to "man," "lady," and even "boy" and "girl." He is delighted to be with other children and plays especially well with older children. He has passed through his earlier aggressive stage and is able to play parallel with another child. He almost always needs close supervision when playing with another child, especially after the first twenty minutes of play.

It is best for either the mother or the father to handle the child alone. This prevents conflicts. Many children find it difficult to be with both parents together until they are much older.

§3. CULTURAL AND CREATIVE ACTIVITIES

BOOKS

1. Enjoyment of simple pictures with few details and clear color.
2. Likes to talk about pictures, having adult turn back the child's "Whassat?" with "What *is* it?" or an explanation. Likes to have the adult ask, "Where is the kitty?" etc.
3. Enjoys having stories simplified by interpreting them to him using his vocabulary, people and experiences he knows and especially his own name.
4. Interested in sound and repetition, as in "Ask Mr. Bear."
5. Likes listening to nursery rhymes and repeating them with the adult.

MUSIC

1. Sings phrases of songs, generally not on pitch.
2. Enjoyment of rhythmical equipment such as rocking boat, swing and rocking chair. These often stimulate spontaneous singing.
3. Rhythmical responses as bending knees in bouncing motion, swaying, swinging arms, nodding head, and tapping feet are favorites.
4. Likes holding something as block, bells or another's hand while walking to music.
5. Interested in watching victrola operate while listening to records.

PAINTING

1. More wrist action than at 18 months.
2. Less shift in handedness, though often paints with a brush in each hand.
3. "Scrubbing" paper with little regard for color. Paints several colors over each other vigorously, with muddy effect.
4. More variety of strokes when only one color is presented.
5. Process, not end result, important to the child.
6. Easily distracted and does not always watch hand movements.
7. Social enjoyment of painting on same paper with another child.

FINGER PAINTING AND CLAY

1. Initial objection to feeling of paint and getting hands dirty, but enjoys it after a few trials.
2. Manipulates clay—pounding, squeezing and pulling off small pieces; often handing to adult.
3. Often experiments with the taste of clay.

SAND, STONES, WATER

1. Fills pails and dishes with sand and stones, dumping and throwing.
2. High interest in water play—extensive hand washing, washing clothes, filling and emptying dishes.

BLOCKS

1. Used manipulatively filling wagons, dumping and rolling.
2. Some building of towers and lines, often combining various sizes of blocks in random order.
3. Preference for colored blocks.

POSSESSIONS

1. Pride in clothes—especially shoes, socks and handkerchief.
2. Strong feeling of ownership in toys. "It's mine" is a constant refrain.
3. Difficulty in sharing toys; hoards them.
4. May bring small token such as marble, orange section, etc., to school and hold onto it all morning, objecting to anyone's taking it.
5. Enjoys naming possessions of others, and telling to whom they belong.
6. Much interest in money but almost no understanding of its use. Likes to use it manipulatively, carrying it around and handling it.

HOLIDAYS AND FESTIVALS

1. Birthday—Enjoys a party with just family or perhaps one other child. The best time for this is the child's regular mealtime. The food is the party for the 2 year old.

2. Christmas—The tree is important. He enjoys Christmas cards and plays with them long after Christmas.

3. Valentine's Day—Enjoys receiving Valentine cards and may carry them around for days.

4. Easter—Interest in the Easter Bunny.

5. Hallowe'en—Not much interest in this holiday.

6. Thanksgiving—Has little meaning except for naming the turkey. May not enjoy the day because shy with guests.

7. Religion—Some are ready for Sunday School if it is run on nursery school principles. Enjoy repeating the last phrases of prayers.

EXCURSIONS

1. Out-for-a-walk he is interested in touching things he sees along the way. Picks up sticks and stones, touches animals. Likes to walk on curbs or walls. Dawdles and concentrates interest within a small area.

2. No thought of destination.

§4. NURSERY BEHAVIOR

EIGHTEEN MONTHS darts and dashes. TWO YEARS is not such a quick shifter. Indeed he is something of a dawdler. He is more wary and a little more conservative. When he comes to the Guidance Nursery in the morning he likes to linger over the preliminaries. They are not mere preliminaries for him; they are genuine experiences. He is not stalling, nor is he indolent; he is taking time to absorb and assimilate each experience. Perhaps now it would be *superficiality* to flit too rapidly from one thing to another.

While his outdoor garments are being removed he likes to talk to his

[170]

teacher about his shoes, socks or handkerchief. He recognizes his teacher and accepts her in this familiar setting (if she has not made too radical a change in her attire); but even so his mother may have to help him make the re-transition, by withdrawing gradually and slipping away opportunely. He is fond of the familiar and an altogether strange new teacher might baffle or disturb him. (He may even be perplexed by a familiar assistant teacher. He prefers a relationship with one adult at a time both at home and at school.)

On leaving the cloak room for the nursery, he makes at once for some favorite toy such as the spindled blocks, and begins to play by himself. This self-chosen play engrosses him almost completely for a while and then he gradually shows awareness of the other children and their activities. He begins to watch at first with curiosity and then with deepening insight. Solitary play gives way to parallel play.

He watches a girl, whom he may call by name, ironing a coverlet. She is surprisingly deft at this particular bit of domesticity. She smooths out the wrinkles by hand, shakes the cloth, applies the iron, smooths and shakes again. He watches actively (he can scarcely watch any other way); the sight of the ironing induces corresponding movements in his own action system; he is impelled to seize another iron (fortunately there are two), and he duplicates with somewhat less deftness, but without embarrassment the whole series of manoeuvers. Before the morning is done there will be many brief episodes of mimicry, imitation, and dramatic rendering, particularly of the best known household events.

Doll play is therefore far advanced beyond the 18 month level. The TWO YEAR OLD wraps a blanket around the doll, clasps it to his bosom, places it adaptively in bed, and tucks it in at least crudely. This is all done in a quick touch and go manner. Attention span is still short; but he makes up for the shortness by doing the same thing over again at intervals and with variations.

So he, or she, goes blithely from one activity to another without much rhyme or reason in the transitions. For example, when she is through

[171]

with her ironing, what will the aforementioned 2 year old girl do in the next three minutes at her disposal:

9:22 She walks over to the aquarium table; pats the table; points at the salamander.

9:23 Moves to a chair, straddles the chair, pokes more bravely at the salamander, saying, "Go away."

9:24 Mounts the rocking boat, rocks heartily, smiles at her teacher. Gets up, strikes an akimbo pose, watches a playmate; picks up a wooden hammer; offers it to him, saying, "See!"

9:25 Goes back to her ironing, which her playmate again imitates.

But it is a brief session of imitation. He wanders off on his own initiative. It is really a wandering of attention. We follow his journeys and find that in the next fifteen minutes he makes at least seven trips to the tower gym and return; sometimes he goes empty handed; more often he transports and deposits a toy.

At first blush this activity looks like 18 months run-about behavior, but on close examination it proves to be much more complex in its adaptive moments, and less mercurial. At 18 months he pulled a cart a short distance and then dropped the handle and went on to other things. At two years he pulls the cart and "parks" it in the corner before he shifts to the next activity. He still acts in snatches, but the snatches are more organized and on each repetition with variations, the process of organization continues. This is the present logic of his development. And the nursery program is designed to favor this mode of development.

After toilet routine, it is time for mid-morning juice. He climbs or backs into a chair, and is none too skillful in placing either himself or the chair. He pats the table, saying "caca (cracker) too," as the juice is poured. He grasps the cup with both hands, drinks with spilling, puts down the cup, watches the other children intently. He wipes his face with a napkin, with a crude back and forth swab, runs over to the phonograph, listens to the music for a brief space, and returns to his ironing.

Next, he goes to a small table for clay play. He allows his teacher to sli-

[172]

an apron over his head. He pulls off pieces of clay, saying, "roll, roll." He pats little daubs of clay onto the board and then returns them to the mass of clay. Occasionally he varies his play by poking and slapping at the mass. He picks off a large lump and pushing it along the table top pretends that it is a train. (At this age children often pretend that a block is a cooky or something else which they desire and lack.)

Clay play over, he follows the teacher into the washroom for hand-washing. Then, on suggestion, he runs to bring his outdoor clothes from his cubby. He puts on his hat himself and thrusts his hands into mittens. Leggings and coat are put on by the teacher.

He runs to the doorway, pausing on the threshold, and then walks slowly out into the yard. He goes to the sand-box and sits in it, playing quietly in the sand while he watches some of his more active playmates racing about the yard. For the first ten minutes outdoor play is usually solitary, but gradually the play builds up till parallel play predominates, whether children are chasing each other about the yard, racing in and out of the playhouse, or playing more quietly side by side in the sand-box. The group often play better out of doors than they do inside. Although there is little actual conversation, they laugh together, and there are numerous physical contacts as well as parallel play. There are eddies and bursts of contagious humor.

Outdoor play holds up nicely whether the child is racing around or playing in the sand, for about half an hour. If fatigue sets in, bumps and tears are inevitable for one or two in the group. Nearly all are glad to see their mothers, who take them home directly from the playground. Going indoors again makes the transitions more complicated and difficult even for the 2 year old.

§5. NURSERY TECHNIQUES

PHYSICAL ENVIRONMENT

18 months' equipment can all be used at this age. In addition there should be a doll corner and climbing apparatus.

[173]

ADJUSTMENT

This is perhaps the most difficult age for adjustment. The child is increasingly aware of and affectionate toward his mother and therefore finds it hard to leave her. He is also shy of new people and new places. If there is difficulty, it is often best to have some relative or neighbor bring him to school instead of his mother. Adjustment is effected through *people* at this age. Therefore one special teacher greets him, stays near him, and helps him to initiate activity.

The initial adjustment may be better outdoors, and it may be necessary for the teacher to carry him out and attempt to interest him in sand, filling and dumping, rolling toys, etc.

There may be initial crying at this age, which usually stops quickly as soon as interest is caught and held.

ROUTINES

The child accepts elaborate routines at this age, though he may still resist toileting. He has a tendency to prolong hand washing, and may need the teacher's help in stopping. He may respond to, "Goodbye water," combined with having the plug removed, and being led to his towel.

Mid-morning lunch is still the high point of the morning. He can wait for the group to collect and enjoys having everyone there. He should not be expected to conform to one cup of juice and one cracker, though often he will respond to "One (cracker) for each hand." He should be allowed a second helping, and is usually satisfied when he sees that the supply is "all gone." Some may demand and need more than others, and some may even refuse crackers.

The child is not yet ready to relax for a mid-morning rest, but music and books provide a period of relaxation.

Two is interested in dressing and undressing though he does not help himself beyond removing his hat and mittens, and zipping and unzipping zippers, which are a new interest.

TRANSITIONS

Two is prone to dawdle, but can be shifted by such devices as the following:

a. By leading him away, if he is not resistant.
b. By talk of next thing: "Go find the soap;" "Time to get crackers now."
c. By telling him to "Say goodbye."
d. By leading him away by means of an enticing toy.

[174]

e. By picking him up bodily and carrying him to the next situation. Two often dislikes to be touched—led by the hand—but can be picked up bodily, as at 18 months.

f. By warning him in advance of a proposed transition. "Pretty soon we'll go to the bathroom and then have juice."

TEACHER

Two still needs almost constant physical supervision. Added to this is his need for emotional security. Therefore it is necessary to keep the group small and to have a minimum of two teachers.

Since children of this age do not as a rule ask for help or come to get help, teachers must be alert to note when help is needed. This in regard to handling disputes, terminating play that is deteriorating, protecting the rights of individual children, protecting the child from fatigue and from physical harm. On occasion, stimulating play and widening its scope builds up the play of the group.

The teacher is now more of a person to the child and he usually knows his teacher's name. He usually responds to one teacher in preference to any other.

Sometimes the teacher can work through other, perhaps older, children when a child refuses to comply. "Betsy, will you bring Jane to wash?"

VERBAL

Verbal handling is now beginning to supersede physical handling whereas at 18 months the opposite is true. The teacher's language should be modelled on the level of the children. Typically useful phrases are: "Have clay after juice." "When it's time." "Now John can have it." "Find your hat." "This is where it fits." Emphasize important words with a positive, calm, reassuring tone.

Be ready to shift level of verbal techniques to a level above or below the child's age as the situation requires. Often 18 months' verbal techniques, as "Goodbye water" to terminate washing; or "Goodbye turtle" to terminate play with turtle, are useful. Some children, however, will be found ready for 2½ verbal techniques.

Try to get the child himself to substitute verbal for gross physical approaches to other children such as screaming or hitting in disputes. Say, "Jane can *talk* to Jimmie. Say, 'No, Jimmie.'"

Imitation of the other children's activities may be induced by use of a repetitive phrase such as, "Ann is drinking her juice, Judy is drinking her juice."

Interest in specific rather than general concepts is characteristic. The child will not respond to a general statement, as "Let's put the toys away," but may respond to, "Teddy goes in the bed," "Cars go on the shelf." Also the teacher can use the specific when two children are fighting over a toy, to direct one of them to a similar toy. "Ann could find the *blue* carriage."

Use such popular words as "again" and "another."

There may be need for continued use of supplementary gestures to make clear the meaning of new words.

HUMOR

Humor is largely gross motor as peek-a-boo and chasing, but may at this age be initiated by the children and may be carried on by them without adult support.

OTHER CHILDREN

Two shows an awakening interest in his contemporaries. Children at this age are both an absorbing interest and a thorn in the flesh to each other. Play is still predominantly solitary but affectionate approaches such as hugging, patting, and kissing often occur. Parallel play is beginning. They also spend much time just watching each other.

One of Two's chief difficulties is his dislike to give things up and to share. He likes, however, to find substitutes for other children to use. He will respond to, "If you have the car what can John use? He could use the train. I'll hold the car while you get the train for John." Two-and-a-half can respond to just the first sentence, but Two needs more definite suggestions. Do not expect disputes to be settled "fairly" from an adult point of view. "It's mine" may have to be respected in a demanding child at the expense of more docile children. This may violate the adult's sense of fair play but does not unduly disturb other 2 year olds. They generally accept the adult's comment, "Johnny *needs* it"; whereas at 2½ they reply, "I need it."

GROUP ACTIVITY

There should not be too much planning for group activity. Since solitary or parallel play naturally predominates, group activities should be spaced and brief. All children should not be expected or required to cooperate. Flexibility is needed in music, reading and similar activities. They need to see the music (victrola) going around; they need to touch the book that is being read. Groups that can be kept within touch are best. Some children will stray immediately. Juice time is best for collecting the whole group.

17

TWO-AND-A-HALF YEARS OLD

§1. BEHAVIOR PROFILE

IF A GROUP of nursery school parents should cast a secret ballot to determine the most exasperating age in the preschool period, it is quite likely that the honors would fall to the TWO-AND-A-HALF YEAR OLD because he has a reputation for going to contrary extremes. The spanking curve therefore comes to a peak at about this time. Needless to say, we do not subscribe to this low estimation,—nor to the spanking.

TWO-AND-A-HALF YEAR OLD is in a transitional period. He is fundamentally the same interesting child that he was at two; and he is growing into the thoroughly enjoyable child of three. Indeed even now there is something delightful about his energy, his (apparently) misplaced exuberance, and his unmistakable tokens of embryonic sociability, helpfulness and imaginativeness. If these tokens are sketchy and offset by their very opposites, it is because TWO-AND-A-HALF YEAR OLD is at an intermediate crossroads stage in the growth of his action system. He has to do a great deal of intermediating between his own contrary impulses. Once more we must remind ourselves that he acts that way because he is built that way. And if he is managed rather than disciplined in terms of his peculiar limitations, he becomes tolerable and amiable.

Why does he go to such trying extremes? It is because his command of *Yes* and *No;* of *Come* and *Go; Run* and *Stop; Give* and *Take; Grasp* and *Release; Push* and *Pull; Assault* and *Retreat* is so evenly balanced. Life is charged with double alternatives. Every pathway in the culture is a two-way street to him, because he is most inexperienced. (But remember, at eighteen months every path was a mere one-way street). His action system likewise is a two-way system, with almost equally inviting alternatives, because he is so immature. His equilibrium is unstably balanced, because his inhibitory mechanisms are very incomplete. Moreover, life and environment are so complex at this transitional stage, that he is almost obliged to go *both* ways, to experience both alternatives so that he may find out which is really the right one. Do not despair if he tries out both, and tries you. When he is 3 years old he will be comparatively so much more mature that he will actually take pleasure in being asked to choose between two familiar alternatives.

At present his capacity for voluntary choice is weak; so he chooses both alternatives, not because of downright stubbornness, but because he lacks facility in balancing alternatives and of thinking of one alternative to the exclusion of another. Instead of following one line he follows two (and one of them seems obstinate to the observer). The nerve cell organization which presides over inhibition is poorly developed. This shows itself even in such "neurological" actions as grasping and releasing. He does not have his flexor and extensor muscles in check and counter check. He tends to grasp too strongly and he releases with over-extension. He has not learned to let go. He has difficulty in relaxing readily to go to sleep. And when he sleeps he may even show a tendency to sleep too much. Similarly he may not easily release the sphincters of bladder control and so he withholds elimination too long,—another instance of going to extremes which can scarcely be set down to innate wilfulness.

The peculiar limitations of his action system, therefore, account for his characteristic inability to *modulate* his behavior. He has such difficulty in making transitions that he tends to dawdle as though it were hard for him to go from the familiar to something different. He is so conservative that he combats innovations. He wants to have things done the accustomed way. Sometimes he is actually a ritualist, particularly at home, and insists on having things *just so*. On these occasions he may be so insistent that he seems positively imperious. His "imperiousness" is really not tyrannical; it is simply an unmodulated intensity,—the same kind of uninhibited propulsive release that he shows when handling objects. Even so, it is best to take this fictitious domineering with a grain of humor and let him be King within manageable bounds. By using a few of the techniques outlined below, you can *activate* him in the "right" direction. He cannot be forced; the activation must finally come from within himself. Our guidance teacher has revealingly told us that to handle him you must be something of a "juggler." This means that he himself is something of an equilibrist entertaining opposite alternatives,—trying to keep two balls in the air when he "should" be tossing only one. But he does this on account of his inexperience. Also he does it because it is the developmental method by which he learns opposites. Such behavior is the psychological equivalent of growing pains. It is helpful to think of him as a preschool edition of a slightly confused adolescent who has not yet found his way.

Nevertheless in this very process the Two-and-a-Half Year Old is finding his way. His adhesiveness, his vacillation, his oscillations between extremes are temporary. By the age of three he will amaze us with his conformance, his desire to please, his interest in making not two choices, but one. At present he is learning to make *one* by exercising *two*. And we can afford to be philosophical because he is giving us a glimpse of Nature's favorite method of growth,—the method of reciprocal inter-

[179]

weaving by means of which she brings flexors and extensors, yes and no, come and go, grasp and release, push and pull into balanced equilibrium.

These characteristic traits are not, of course, equally marked in all children. They are particularly pronounced in those of a perseverative type. High tension and sudden fatigability sometimes evidence themselves in a kind of stuttering, which is "outgrown." Equable temperaments are least likely to show conspicuous symptoms; but it is relatively normal, from a developmental standpoint, for children at this age to show to some degree the extremes which have been suggested,—the sudden shift from intense activity to passive quiescence accompanied by transient thumb sucking; shifts from exuberance to shyness; from keen desire to possess an object to indifference when it is possessed; from clamor for food to rejection of it; from shriek and scream to whispering and monotone; from herd-like imitativeness to shrinking isolation; from laughing to whining; from precipitateness to dawdling.

These swings from one extreme to another are not mood swings. They are fluctuations caused by narrowness of base. The base will broaden as the child matures, as he makes an increasing number of distinctions between paired opposites and paired alternatives. Experience will organize the choices he will make with ease at three, four and five years of age. He needs developmental time; he deserves discerning patience.

Moreover is he not at least interesting, as he so transparently betrays his intellectual limitations? And is he not attractive with all his promising mixtures of exuberance and shyness, his overtures to adults, his friendly questions, his imaginativeness, his conquests of difficult words, his socialized imitativeness, his tribal chants, and his generosity? For he *is* generous when he eagerly brings his toys to school to show to his companions, and then cannot let go of them! How can you possibly prize a toy without showing it to others? And how can you share it without keeping it? Life and culture are full of paradoxes for all of us. Two and a half years is the paradoxical age.

§2. BEHAVIOR DAY

THE TWO-AND-A-HALF YEAR OLD child may wake up at almost any time between 5 and 9 o'clock in the morning. He tends to waken toward the later hour, say between 8 and 8:30. He calls for his mother fairly promptly after waking and is immediately toileted.

If he does not attend nursery school on this particular morning, he enjoys the leisure of bathrobe and slippers while he takes a light breakfast. After breakfast he is dressed. Dressing is facilitated by the confinement of the bathroom. He ordinarily has to be helped during the whole process.

He is now ready for an hour's play in his room which is set up and prearranged to meet the needs of his abundant self-activity. He talks to himself a great deal during a happy, active hour. The sound of heightened gross motor activity during which he may turn over the chair in his playroom calls attention to the termination of this hour of play. His mother comes and toilets him. He likes to linger in the bathroom, but he is also ready for a session of outdoor play.

The luncheon at noon is usually his largest meal. He likes to feed himself for at least half of the meal, during which he selects the foods which he most prefers. He may assert his self-dependence by asking his mother to leave the room, but he calls her back and accepts her help for the last half of the meal, reverting again to self-feeding for dessert. He is toileted, and often has a bowel movement at this time.

The scheduled nap may begin at about 12:30, but usually he consumes an hour or more in self-activity before going to sleep. He likes to have the side of the bed down and he may get in and out of bed two or three times. He talks a great deal to himself during this pre-nap period. He may finally fall off to sleep after he has been tucked in by his mother. He sleeps for an hour or more, wakens slowly, and usually dry. He does not call for his mother until he has gone through a transitional period of progressive wakefulness.

[181]

By 3 o'clock he is ready for a walk or a visit abroad, though if he attended nursery school in the morning he may play from 3 to 5 o'clock in his own backyard. On his return from his walk he may have a snatch of play in the living room.

Supper comes at about 5 o'clock. He accepts more help during this meal than he did at luncheon. He is content to return to his room after supper and to play by himself for perhaps a full hour with the door closed. He also enjoys a round of play with his father. It may be active play: it may be more receptive,—listening to music, or looking at a book.

The bath, which comes at about 7 o'clock, is still a favorite experience. The 2½ year old likes to handle situations in a somewhat commanding manner. He insists on certain routines; likes to have things done in an accustomed way and likes to find things in accustomed places. By these demands he asserts his increasing insight into what he thinks is being demanded of him. He insists on comparable routines when he is put to bed. These are somewhat "ritualistic" and may, therefore, be time-consuming. He continues his soliloquies and also talks to his teddy bear. He may call to his mother to adjust a pillow or render some other specific help. He falls to sleep about 8:30. He may be picked up between 10 and 12 o'clock and is toileted without being awakened. He sleeps the clock around.

SLEEP

Night

Bedtime depends very definitely on the length of the nap, which can vary from no sleep to a three, four or even five hour nap. It is not uncommon for the hour of going to sleep to vary from 6 P.M. to 10 P.M. Bedtime, therefore, has to be shifted according to the child's needs, but should preferably not be delayed beyond 8 P.M.

Going to bed is also complicated by a new intrusion, for the 2 year old bedtime demands have often grown into an elaborated and rigid structure that may now take as long as one half to one hour to enact. There is the going upstairs ritual, the taking a bath ritual, brushing the teeth ritual, getting into bed, pulling down the shades, kissing, and even a specially worded good-night ritual. If the plug is pulled out of the bathtub the wrong way the entire going-to-bed routine may be disturbed and a temper tantrum may occur. Even the shades have to be pulled down just to the proper height.

The 30-monther makes most of his demands before getting into bed. When he is once in bed and has said goodnight, he calls his parent back less often than at 2 years, and usually his demands express real needs. When he finally settles down he often sings and talks to himself. Those who have had snuggle duckies up to now may be giving them up, though some cling to them until 3 years of age and cannot sleep without them. Those who fall asleep early are more apt to awaken during the night. They may or may not cry, and often ask for the toilet or a drink. The 10 to 12 P.M. picking up for toileting is more often successful at this age than formerly, but when it is unsuccessful, the disturbance it causes is very real.

Morning waking is as variable and has as wide a range as going to sleep. With some children, the later they go to sleep the earlier they will awaken. Therefore going to sleep at 10 P.M. may cause a 5 A.M. waking. However the majority are "sleep the clock around children" and often do not awaken before 8:30 or 9:00 A.M. If they awaken early they will often play with their toys and look at magazines before they call the adult. Sometimes shifts of toys will help the early waker to stay in his crib, but after an hour or so he demands to get up. There is no problem with the late waker for he is taken right up for his breakfast.

[The child will leave pre-sleep activities more easily if he can have an active share in putting away play materials. The mother should not leave in the middle of pre-sleep preparations to attend to some other household demand. Such preparations once started must be carried through to completion, or they will have to be started all over again. If the mother tries to complete them, after an interruption, without starting again, the child may have a temper tantrum.]

Nap

The nap is often a real problem at this age. Children of this age do not usually mind going to bed for their naps and enjoy taking a number of toys to bed, but they do not stay in their cribs for long. They can now climb out with ease and keep coming out of their rooms, unless the door is tied. The 30-monther does not usually mind his door being tied as long as he can freely get in and out of his crib and has his toys in the room to play with. *The windows must be very safe,* for he is apt to climb on the window-ledge.

Many children refuse to nap in their cribs at this age. They may nap better in another room on another bed, but the novelty of this may wear off soon and then they are much worse than they were in their own rooms. If some variation (under their own control) can be made in their own room they will respond more quickly, more continuously and with less interference with the rest of the household. They especially like to sleep on the floor, under their crib, or in a bureau drawer. If they cannot handle this themselves after preliminary arrangements and suggestions have been made by the parent when they are put into their rooms, they may respond to a little help from the adult around 2 or 2:30 when they are more ready for sleep. Then the barricading of a blanket bed on the floor may be just the needed touch. Some will accept the bed if it is imaginatively turned into something else, such as a bus or a railroad train.

The parent must not only decide whether she should help put the child to sleep, but also if she should awaken him from his nap before he is ready to wake himself. A few children can have a long nap and still go to bed at the usual bedtime. With others, the displacement of the night sleep caused by a long nap makes evenings at home a bit troublesome for the parents. However, if the child cannot stand being waked at 3 to 3:30 and merely cries for the rest of the time when he would have been asleep, it is wise not to awaken him. Some will respond well to the ring of a telephone or to an alarm clock in an adjoining room when they will not accept being awakened by a person's voice. Trial and error is probably the only way these decisions can be made. And eventually the child will handle the whole problem for himself by not sleeping at all or by taking a shorter nap.

[If a child awakes crying from his nap, wait until the cry changes to a more agreeable note before going into his room. Engage in tasks such as pulling up the shade without approaching the child until he has made an initial approach, such as saying sweetly, "Hello, mommie."]

EATING

Appetite—The appetite often fluctuates between very good and very poor. Usually one meal, either the noon or evening meal, is a good one.

Refusals and Preferences—These are quite similar to those of the 2 year old child, with the patterns of demand being held to more rigidly. In general, the child prefers meat, fruit and butter, and dislikes green vegetables. He is now taking milk fairly well.

One may think of his preferences and refusals in a gradation of those foods he likes so well that he will eat them by himself, those that he likes well enough to be fed, and those that he absolutely refuses. As at 2 years of age, he still goes on food jags and a food which was once in the first place of preference may become an outrightly refused food.

[It is best to allow swings in appetite. The parent may keep a chart if necessary to convince herself that good days balance poor days. Allowing the child to pour his milk from a pitcher may increase his appetite for milk.]

Self Help—Patterns of self help are also quite similar to those of 2 years. The parent can now readily set up a sequence of courses and can tell the child to "Call me when you are ready for your . . . dessert" (for example). The child may feed himself half of his dinner and this will usually include foods that he likes. He will then be ready to be fed the remainder of his dinner if this does not include currently refused foods.

The ritualisms of the ritualist are at this age more clearly defined in eating as well as in going to sleep patterns. He demands the repetition of foods, of dishes, and of arrangement of dishes, and even of time when a certain food is given. If, for example, egg is given at supper time it may be taken with relish but refused at lunch time.

This is the age when between-meal snacks are in greater demand; and often they interfere with appetite for regular meals. A few children eat very poorly at mealtimes but will eat well between meals.

[It is best to try to establish a set time for the in-between-meal snacks, such as 10:30 A.M. and 4:00 P.M., and to see if the child can be held off verbally until these times. Crackers and dried fruits along with fruit juices are probably preferable both from the point of view of ease of handling and of what is best for the child. Candy had best be out of sight and out of reach, even out of the house, or the demand may be very excessive at this age. Special infrequent occasions when candy is allowed establish it within the treat realm and not within the incessant demand realm.]

ELIMINATION

Bowel—The number of movements varies from one to two a day, with an increased tendency to skip one or even two days between bowel functioning. Accidents are rare. The general tendency is for the child to ask to go even though he needs no help. Some still tell after they have gone by themselves. They prefer to go by themselves and to climb up onto the toilet seat themselves even though they need help with taking off their pants. Those who have been slow to name the bowel movement, often now name it with some such action word as "plop" or "bang poo-pee."

Very few now resist the toilet seat though some seem to persist in the postural need of functioning either standing up or lying down. If the child who still refuses the toilet seat or any type of receptacle shows a localizing tendency of going to a corner of a room or behind doors, he is often ready to be shifted to the bathroom, where he may function on a paper in the corner. When once he has begun to function in the bathroom, he more rapidly adjusts to a potty chair or the toilet seat, but should not be expected to adjust to the flushing of the toilet.

Even if the mother helps to put him on the toilet, he does not usually wish her to stay in the room and requests as at 2 years of age, but now a little more personally, "You go away," or "Mommie go downstairs?" He now can leave on his shoes and socks and shirt, but wants his pants or overalls all the way off.

As was also true at 2 years of age, he will call out, "Mommie, all through," and wait to be wiped and put back into his clothes.

The time of occurrence has a wide variation, with some still having a meal relationship and others being more irregular, with a definite trend to having the movement in the afternoon, especially in relation to the nap. The child usually asks to go at these times. Stool smearing is relatively rare at this age.

[Though it is common for children to skip one or two days at this age between bowel functionings, the parents should check on this, and if the interval is longer than this, fruit laxatives may be given. It may help the child to function to have the adult remain in the room, or to allow the child to look at a book.]

Bladder—There are very few daytime accidents. Most children go by themselves, according to the ease of removing their clothing and facilities available for climbing up on the toilet. Some, however, always tell beforehand, even though they need no help. They do need verbal help, however, such as being given permission to go. This is an age for long spans, especially with girls, who often have a morning span of as much as five hours (from rising till after lunch).

When they hold off too long they may start to dampen their pants before reaching the bathroom. They are very conscious of wet pants even though the wetness is only a drop, and want to be changed at once. (This type of long span and holding off is more common with boys from 3 to 3½ years of age). Many find it difficult to urinate on a strange toilet.

[If the child has difficulty in urinating after a long span, he may respond to such helpful stimuli as the sound of running water, or taking a drink. It may help to tell him to close his eyes and listen for the sound that the stream of urine will make.]

Those who do not tell can be readily routinized. This function is now coming so much under the child's own control that he is beginning to be conscious of the control of others. He is interested in watching other people go to the bathroom and also is very much interested in watching animals out of doors. However, he usually reserves his comments until 3 years of age. Boys often urinate out of doors if they are allowed to.

It is difficult to generalize about nap dryness because individual differences are so marked. Some who have previously been dry, especially boys, are now wet again. Girls are more consistently dry. The length of the nap may have something to do with the relapse since the nap is now sometimes two or even four or five hours long. Therefore they may be dry if awakened from the nap, wet if allowed to sleep it out. The consciousness of being wet is probably most dependent on cultural handling, and with adult stimulation of shame, an opposite response on the part of the child of pride in a "methy bed" may be elicited.

Dryness at night is dependent upon a number of factors. There are a few children who go through the night without wetting. These may go through the night without waking or may call two or three times during the night to be taken to the bathroom. The majority, however, need to be picked up and even then may still be wet in the morning. If they are wet by 8 or 9 P.M. the chances are that they will wet two or three times more during the night. If they are dry at 10, the chances are fifty-fifty that they will be wet in the morning. If they are still dry at 12, they will usually be dry in the morning. Picking up is, however, not a simple matter, for many children resist it. With any sign of resistance the practice should be discontinued until later acceptance. Picking up is more palliative at this age than instructive. Rubber pants and diapers are still in order to make the child more comfortable physically and emotionally, to restrict the laundry and to eliminate the uriniferous smell which can be so distasteful in a child's room.

BATH AND DRESSING

Bath—The bath, which is now given around 7 P.M., is quite a favorite at this age. As with most of his activities at 30 months, the child "takes over" even though he is not capable. He wants to handle the faucets and the plug and to build up a ritual around them. He also likes to shine the fixtures and has often lost all sense of the bath as being a time when he is washed. He loves to slide back and forth in the water and would go on endlessly if not stopped.

Getting the child out of the tub is quite dependent upon the ingenuity of the parent. The removal of the plug with the subsequent running down of the water makes some children fearful that they will be sucked down, too. Therefore they hop out at once. But there are many who are not in the least fearful and who continue to slide back and forth even when the water is all out. Then tricks of getting out, as counting or any other helpful transitional devices, need to be used.

Dressing—The 30-monther is still better at undressing than at dressing. He can usually take off all of his clothes but his dressing abilities are limited to putting on his socks and sometimes his shirt, pants or coat. His dressing is not, however, very effective and usually needs correction. The heels of his socks are almost invariably on his instep, both feet are in one pant leg, his shirt is on backward and his coat is often twisted. If he insists upon dressing by himself, he will usually accept helpful preliminary orientation of the garment, i.e., the shirt on the floor with the back uppermost. He will also accept some verbal help but will not allow his mother to touch him.

This demand for independence alternates with a demand for complete dependence when he will not do the things he can do for himself, and even withdraws from the most rudimentary beginnings of helping with dressing, such as thrusting his arm into an armhole. At this time he may go limp and say he is a doll or a baby. If the parent is not fully aware of the swings of the 30 month pendulum, or will not accept them, she will undoubtedly get into trouble.

This is the age when temper tantrums over dressing are common. Besides his demands to dress himself or be dressed, the child often runs away as soon as his mother starts to dress him. He particularly enjoys being chased and as soon as he is caught he runs off into another room or corner. He becomes violent if he is really caught and picked up, but usually comes running if he is left by himself with the suggestion, "Come to the bathroom when you are ready." If the mother closes doors behind her, this will almost immediately martial the child's forces to right about face and he runs in the direction which the mother desires. He comes calling, "I'm ready, I'm ready." When he is once in the bathroom it is wise to close the door and even to lock it. A high hamper is a good place on which to dress a child of this age. He fools less because he does not want to fall off, and he wants to have dressing over with so as to get down as soon as possible.

[The game of discovering parts of the body, such as the head, hand or foot, as they emerge from clothing, is a delightful game at this age.]

SELF-ACTIVITY

If the 30-monther is attending nursery school three times a week, his morning play period at home takes on a new character of relaxation and of re-discovery. He is happy to go to his room after breakfast, but with his proficient ability to right about face, he will just as rapidly reverse his direction if his room is not sufficiently attractive and enticing. Therefore it is very essential to set up his room as though it were a stage, with the planned beginnings of spheres of interest—a doll corner here, fitting toys over there, a magazine on the bed and a tray of plasticene on the table.

The child is usually happy to linger in the bathroom washing his hands and making soap bubbles while the mother is accomplishing this bit of stage craft. As a last touch she might hide something under a box for him to discover. His interest is quickly secured, he leaves his washing, and is whisked into his room. While the door is being shut, and tied (if necessary) he is discovering his "surprise," and then happily sets about his morning activities.

His play is accompanied by constant talking. All of his past experiences are flooding in in bits of this and that. There is something enchanting about a verbatim record of the speech of a 30 month old child talking to himself in his room as he plays. Speech is now coming in with a rush and it is so uppermost in his mind that he uses it constantly. Words and activities that he has been hearing and observing at home and away from home are now put into practice in the simple security of his own room. Seeing his doll reminds him to put it on his lap the way grandmother does, or to tuck it in bed the way he saw it done at nursery school.

His play and equipment are similar to

those of the 2 year old child. There may be the addition of a bed, an iron and ironing board in the doll corner, a few extra cars on the shelves, a simple puzzle and sometimes plasticene. Scissors and crayons are not yet sufficiently under his control for him to handle alone in his room, though they are definitely in his realm of interest. Even plasticene may at times be too difficult for him to control, and he is then likely to spread it all over the room.

Some children want all their toys within sight or reach and have a strong sense of ownership and place for them. They are very orderly with their toys and stand guard as the room is being cleaned so that nothing will be disturbed. The majority of children, however, have only a momentary relationship with their toys. They actually do better with a shifting scene. Therefore the mother in her preliminary arrangement decides what is best for the child at the moment. He may even help her decide by asking for certain things. It is impractical to have either too many things in a child's room or too few. Some desire play with only one or two fitting toys whereas others demand variety.

When the 30-monther has finished with a toy he drops it, often in back of him. He may, however, return to it later. With fatigue, usually at the end of an hour, he shifts to more gross motor activity, jumps off a box, runs into a closet and closes the door, and finally may end by turning over all of the chairs. He may occasionally return to wall paper or plaster destruction. If he does he has improved his technique and is now using some object as a tool to increase his efficiency.

With the sounds of gross motor activity, the mother knows it is nearing time for shifting to out of doors. Nothing delights the 30-monther more than to have his mother knock on his door at this moment and to invite her to "Come in." If she knows the ways of development she will not say, "My, what a mess your room is in"; but will rather say, "My, what a wonderful time you've had."

She will also know that this is no time for him to help in re-ordering the room. Toileting and out-of-doors where space and bodily movements are freer should follow immediately. His 2 year old outdoor play equipment is still of interest to him. He can also handle hollow boxes which he loves to lift, carry and jump from, and he enjoys paper cartons that he can climb into. A pail of water that he can dip into and pour on his sand delights the 30-monther. He plays happily until it is time for lunch and then often does not want to leave his play. It is then up to the mother to lure him into the house without his realizing that he is being lured.

[Successful lures include the mother's mentioning some preferred food, giving the child something "important" such as a loaf of bread to carry into the house, or playing the game of "find mommy" when he knows from previous experience what door she is hiding behind.]

SOCIALITY

The ritualism so characteristic of 30 months may weigh heavily on the entire household. The child of this age is likely to know where everything belongs and to insist that everything remain in its place. This is no time to rearrange the living-room furniture. Chairs must be placed at specific angles and certain pictures must remain on certain tables.

This is the age when father learns to hang up his coat, for his 30 month old child may not tolerate his throwing it down on a hall chair. The child is, however, much more efficient about handling other people's affairs than his own which are often in a very chaotic state. He also may remember exactly how all household routines have been conducted and may insist always on an exact repetition. Father must put on his bedroom slippers whether he wants to or not. Milk bottles must be brought in only by the child. If he gets up late and finds the milk bottles in the ice box, the only thing to do may be to put them back out on the porch, close the door, and then go through the whole routine as though nothing had occurred.

His imperial domineering ways are sometimes hard for others to accept. He may command one to sit here, another to do something else, and still another to go away. If the parent realizes that the child is only passing through a temporary regal, dictatorial stage, he may respond to the child's orders more graciously, more whimsically. The child actually needs to be treated with a little subservience to take him off his guard. A little humor added to the subservience may produce the desired effect.

During his imperiousness the child may actually be a very useful member of society. He may be of considerable help in putting things away and in carrying out simple household tasks such as emptying the ash trays.

He is usually more independent on his walks and he is apt either to run ahead or to linger behind. He makes definite requests as to what he wants to do, and carries out going to a destination with real dispatch. However on the homeward journey he is apt to lapse into dawdling or going up other people's steps. Therefore it is wise to have some means of conveyance such as a wagon, a doll carriage in which

the child can ride, or a stroller, to help him home again. One either stays close to home, or encompasses distances in a car. The afternoon social play period in the house still includes music, dancing and books. But the child also likes to color with crayons, to snip with scissors and to do puzzles with help.

Most children at this age exhibit a definite preference for either father or mother, though the preference varies from child to child. Sometimes the child prefers one parent for one time of the day and for certain activities and the other parent at some other time of day. He is usually less dependent than he was at 24 months. His affection has not the overflowing warmth of the 2 year old's, but is often expressed in a rigid pattern of something to be gone through, such as a kissing ritual. As with the 2 year old he is more apt to demand his mother when he is in trouble and during the middle of the night. However, he may quiet more quickly for his father, if he will accept the father.

The shyness and withdrawal of Two have now gone into reverse. However the 30-monther includes both poles of shyness and withdrawal on the one hand and approach and aggression on the other hand. He responds according to the demands of the situation. He may demand his mother's hand when he meets a stranger on the street or he may suddenly "sock" a stranger with few or no premonitory signs.

He wants very much to be with people, both adults and children, but he cannot handle them. This is the snatch and grab age, especially when he is with younger children. However the same child may swing from a period when he is habitually too compliant to one when he is too domineering. On the whole he plays best with one other child out of doors, and he does much better with a 5 or 6 year old child whom he respects and also accepts. Play with children of his own age is often best handled under supervision, away from home, for instance at nursery school.

Some children play best at their own homes with other children, others play better away from home. Those who play best at home are usually the ones who adjust poorly to new places. But they are also the ones who have difficulty in letting other children play with their toys. Therefore it is best to plan with them to put away their most prized possessions before another child comes to call. Then it is easier for them to share their less prized toys.

Those who play better away from home are more often the quick adjusters, the quick shifters. They want novelty and find it easy to adjust to the child who clings to the old. To lead these two types into a fuller realization of themselves, the environment helps the stay-at-home child finally to release his home and his things by going abroad, whereas it helps the going-abroad child to hold on a little tighter to the things at home by adjusting him to play with other children at home. This process of adjustment to others becomes more urgent at this 30 months period.

§3. CULTURAL AND CREATIVE ACTIVITIES

BOOKS

1. Pretends to pick up objects from pictures, pats kitty, etc.
2. Spontaneous language (of the child) is often rhythmical and repetitive.
3. Enjoys rhythm and repetition in rhymes and stories.
4. Wants repetition of same story day after day.
5. Slow acceptance of new story.
6. Attends to short, simple stories of familiar subjects, as "The Little Family" and "The Little Auto."
7. No demand for plot in stories but enjoys a simple one, as in "Cinder."
8. Likes books giving simple information about animals and transportation, as "Ask Mr. Bear" and "Saturday Walk."
9. Enjoys having adult improvise story about what the child does throughout the day or what his contemporaries are doing.
10. From 33 to 36 months wants to hear elaborate details of the babyhood of himself and later of each member of his family and friends. The story of "Little Baby Ann" is a favorite during this stage.
11. Reading in which he takes some part holds him longer, as naming kinds of animals or filling in words or phrases of a sentence he knows.
12. Enjoys looking at books alone.

[190]

MUSIC

1. May know all or parts of several songs which he reproduces at home or spontaneously at school, but is often inhibited in singing with others in school.
2. Spontaneous singing on minor third of such phrases as "coal man, coal truck."
3. Absorbs music and particularly enjoys repetition of old, familiar tunes.
4. High interest in listening to instruments, especially victrola.
5. Enjoyment of marked rhythm as Ravel's "Bolero" or band music.
6. Musically talented children with sensitive ears may show fear of victrola at this age.
7. Less individuality in rhythms because of imitation and awareness of others.
8. Majority of group will run, gallop, swing, etc., to music, watching others.
9. Enjoys simple group activity as ring-around-a-rosy.

PAINTING

1. Experimenting with vertical and horizontal lines, dots and circular movements.
2. Good form at beginning but generally quick to deteriorate.
3. May go out of bounds, painting on table, easel, floor, own hands, other children.
4. May paint many pages with little variety.

FINGER PAINTING

1. A better medium for this age than painting on easels because hands are in direct contact with the medium and do not have to adjust to a tool and container, such as brush and paint jar. Since this is a tangled age, the simpler medium is preferable, because it does not add complications.
2. To see the enjoyment of a child having his hands legitimately in paint, makes one know the wise choice of this medium.
3. Needs more supervision than at any other age. Stimulus of group in school controls it somewhat, but apt to go far out-of-bounds at home.
4. Pure enjoyment of manipulation and color with little feeling for form.

CLAY

1. Excellent medium for this age because each child can have identical materials for parallel play, thus reducing to a minimum the characteristic desire for the equipment of others.

2. Good medium for working off tangles and surplus energy by pounding, squeezing and poking.
3. Affords relaxation as it inspires a long span of attention, which is seldom true of other materials.
4. Out-of-bounds behavior can be legitimatized and interest span lengthened by using other materials in combination with clay, such as tongue depressors, cars and animals.
5. Like to pass products around to each other, naming them pies, cakes, etc.

SAND, STONES, WATER

1. Makes pies and cakes with sand and mud, patting and smoothing them.
2. Continued high interest in water, which is also an excellent medium for this age. Likes blowing soap-bubbles, "painting" with water, washing clothes and hanging on line, sailing boats and scrubbing.

BLOCKS

1. Continued vertical and horizontal building with beginning of symmetry.
2. Some simple structures are named, as bridge, bed, tracks.
3. Sometimes blocks are used imaginatively as coal, ashes, lumber.
4. Uses larger blocks more than when younger.
5. Some color matching with blocks.

POSSESSIONS

1. Brings favorite toy to school to show to others, but generally not able to share it with others. May bring same toy each day. Is happier if toy is stored out of reach of others until time to go home.
2. Clings to favorite possession when insecure.
3. May cling to old clothes and dislike new ones.
4. Especially fond of hats and mittens.
5. May go through elaborate rituals with possessions at home.
6. Interest in acquiring possessions of others, but seldom plays with them.
7. Like to have a few pennies in their pocketbooks and are very possessive about them.

EXCURSIONS

1. Enjoys going to the park to see other children or to use play equipment.
2. Likes short excursions to nearby farms to see animals or flowers.

3. Enjoys watching trains go by at a distance.
4. Beginning to have thought of a destination in mind, and may even insist on going along a special route.

§4. NURSERY BEHAVIOR

THE TWO-AND-A-HALF YEAR OLD does not make transitions readily. He likes to do certain things in just the same way that he has done them before. He shows a kind of tenaciousness (rather than obstinacy!) which makes him resistant to change. And he has other private reasons that we know nothing about for the deliberateness which makes him seem a dawdler. He moves slowly in the short journey from the street to the entrance of the Nursery. He insists on coming by a standard route and himself lifting the latch as he and custom demand. His mother reports that at home, "He is the same way!",—almost ritualistic in his insistence on certain routines. However, he dismisses her with a more or less perfunctory "good-bye" and perhaps a kiss.

He attempts to undress himself, and makes a show of taking over the whole procedure, but usually the guidance teacher must come to the rescue with her assistance. He asserts his independence by saying, "Me do it myself!"

Preliminaries and rituals done, he makes for the nursery. He walks into the playroom and first spies a cart, takes the handle of it, but quickly changes his mind, drops the handle and grabs a car. But four of his contemporaries are already in the room, and problems of interpersonal relations arise very promptly. Let us designate these children by initials as follows: A and B are boys; C, D, and E, girls. These five children scarcely constitute a community, even under the mandate of the guidance teacher; but they do create a sociological mixture of independent, parallel, non-cooperative and incipiently collaborative activities. These activities are so intermeshed that nothing less than a play-by-play account for a period of fifteen minutes can tell the story.

[193]

9:12   A walks into the playroom, spies a cart, seizes the handle, pulls the cart a short distance. Drops the cart and grabs a tractor. B comes up and tries to take it away from him. Both say "Mine" in loud, angry voices and pull at the toy. When the teacher asks, "What can B have?" A replies, "Fire engine. I want zese sings." After getting the tractor, he runs to the animal box and squats before it. Takes toy animals out onto the floor asking C, "What zis sing? You broke that one off."

9:14   Throws one of the animals. Tries to pull several at a time out of the box. Closes cover of box, kneeling before it. Plays on the floor with an animal. Then runs over and hugs D, at the same time trying to take her toys from her, saying, "I want zese sings." Tells D she broke one of the toys. "I can't fiss 'em no more." Doesn't notice when D walks away. Pushes a tractor across the floor and watches as it rolls away.

9:15   Goes over to where teacher is helping children build a "car" of the big construction blocks. Says "I wanna bridge." All sit in car but A, who leaves and goes to a shelf in the corner for small blocks. Others sit in the car, pretending to go for a ride. A returns with small "driver" blocks. He grabs E's driver, trying to give E a different one. E holds both, saying loudly, "No, no, no." A says, "I'm goin' down in the cella" (under the block car), and slaps E.

9:17   Allows the teacher to lead him to the "cellar under the jungle gym." Says, "I need a screwdriver." All in the car watch him intently. B climbs out of the car and says he needs a hammer.

9:18   A comes out from under jungle gym and pounds at side of gym with block "screwdriver" which teacher has given him. B does same thing on other side of gym.

9:19   A gets another block from the shelf and then climbs up steps into the jungle gym, pounding from inside. Throws his blocks and then climbs way up the side of the gym. Complains that B, who is shaking the gym, "Makes me fall."

9:21   A climbs down stairs toward teacher and takes "screwdriver" which she gives him from a basket of blocks. Then grabs the basket and selects another block. Several other children run over, saying, "I want a screwdriver too." A returns to the gym and pounds again, then goes to the shelf for still more blocks. B says, "Here, A." A pays no attention.

9:22   A goes over to the table and picks up toy telephone. Lifts the receiver, paying no attention to B who has followed him. A says, "I'll call, myself." Sits, throwing leg over chair, and takes up receiver, getting cord tangled as he does so. Holds receiver in right hand and dials with left, saying, "Speak to Daddy pease? Daddy?" Listens, dialing. Replaces receiver; lifts it again; dials. Replaces. Picks nose. Receiver off again, in one hand, puts to ear, looks around room, staring at teacher and at E, holding receiver to ear.

9:24   B wants to phone. A says, "That one over there." Dials again, again saying, "Daddy? Daddy, I'm at school." Repeats whole performance. Says, "I want zose turtles, pease"; and takes toy monkey from C. Then D comes over and tries to take monkey from him.

9:25   A goes over to B and tries to push B out of the chair. Says, "It's mine." B says, "It's mine." C puts her arms around B, from behind, and says, "It's B's."

9:26   A goes over to where children are building with large blocks. Says, "I say, I want to build this way, I say. I go along tunnel. *Get that big board away!*" Has very definite ideas about where things go and removes blocks placed by the others.

Similar activities continue for almost an hour. When an entanglement threatens to become too intricate the guidance teacher intervenes by introducing a new material like modelling clay, which can be parcelled out to all the members of the group. This permits congregational parallel play and reduces the tensions for the time being. The plastic clay has a mollifying effect. Each child picks off small lumps, pats them flat on the board, and then returns them to the mass for another lump. A pie, a cake, a snowman, and a worm take shape. The sculptures may be named spontaneously. The guidance teacher demonstrates rolling of the clay between two hands. The children imitate readily but crudely. Some tire of the clay sooner than others.

The sticky hands are now ready for washing. The teacher announces conversationally that, "It is time to wash hands." The children as they finish modelling go a few at a time to the washroom. The 30-monther washes his hands in a purposeful manner with back-and-forth but not rotary rubbing. He is now comparatively efficient and does not indulge in repeated and supernumerary washings after the manner of the 2 year old child. He is toileted unless, as often happens at this age, he shows temporary resistance, or has an unusually long span.

On re-entering the nursery room characteristic self-dependence asserts itself and each child tends for a while to engage in independent activity: one looks at books; one builds with large or small blocks; others play with manipulative toys; or chase each other about the room. One child builds a tower. The tower persists in falling. He empties a whole basket of blocks onto the floor, puts the basket over his head, and hurls the basket into space; and then stands sucking his thumb, defeated.

With such symptoms premonitory of possible fatigue it is time for serving the mid-morning juice. The guidance teacher hands each child a napkin to take to the table. Our typical TWO-AND-A-HALF YEAR OLD goes to the cupboard for a cup and then returns to the table, waiting for the group to collect. He helps pour the juice, empties his cup in a few gulps. He indulges in very few words during the refreshments. It takes about five minutes to finish the mid-morning luncheon. He leaves the table in a decisive manner and on the suggestion of the teacher dabs his mouth with his napkin, puts the napkin in the cup and places it on the tray.

At this time it is customary for the nursery group to break into small sub-groups of three or four who gather about the teacher to look at books, and to listen to stories read from the books. In another ten minutes the children are ready for an hour of free play out of doors.

The 2½ year old child acquiesces quite passively in having his outdoor things put on. He helps a little by thrusting his arms into sleeves and hands into mittens, but for the most part leaves the task up to the teacher. Dressed, he hurries to the outdoor play yard.

Out of door play follows the general pattern of indoor play. Each child appears to play by himself, following his own devices; but little groups form themselves in the sand-box, on the jumping board, or at some other center of interest. Once congregated, each child again appears to follow his own devices; but they join in mass imitation on slight provocation: let some one begin to throw sand outside the sand-box with a large spoon, the others follow suit. When one child starts jumping up and down, with both feet, on the jumping board, so do the others, often causing considerable confusion. The sight of a man going by causes one of the children to call, "What you doing man? What you doing man? What you doing man?" This chant is taken up by the whole clan. The children rather hoped that the man himself would join in by repeating their chant.

Although much of their activity is communal, imitativeness and acquisitiveness are poorly differentiated. There are enough spoons and pails for all, but if one child takes a pail of sand from the sand-box to a different part of the yard, he is usually followed by a would-be snatcher and a tussle often ensues. Two-and-a-Half Year Old has a fairly robust sense of possession for himself, but not for others.

There is a great deal of activity and moving about the yard, but most of the activity is self-centered. There is little variety and play does not build up as a result of group stimulation. On the contrary it is apt to disintegrate into running and shrieking. Occasionally one child holds out a helping hand to another. More often it is a pushing or a clutching hand. These engagements however may not be aggressive; often they seem to be without emotion, even when one child is hurling sand at another. (This may be in direct contrast to the strong emotion often shown in a similar situation at home.)

After about an hour of outdoor play it is time for the children to go home. They do not have a spontaneous sense of time. It is not easy for them to detach themselves from the activities in which they are engaged. The Two-and-a-Half Year Old on leaving the nursery shows the same kind of adhesiveness which he displayed on entering. His attachment to familiar objects may be so great that he renews his contact with them once more before he goes; he touches them one by one as he makes his exit.

§5. NURSERY TECHNIQUES

PHYSICAL ENVIRONMENT

Environmental handling is most important at this age. Doors should be shut; distracting materials removed.

Two small rooms are preferable to one large one. This makes possible shifting the group from one room to another, or the isolation of one child or of small groups.

Climbing apparatus indoors as well as out is most desirable at this age.

ADJUSTMENT

Most children adjust easily at this age. There are few adjustment problems. The mother may still need to slip out; or the child may require a formal goodbye. Usually children of this age, with their interest in school, are oblivious to their mother's departure.

The shy child may adjust best if the teacher pays little or no obvious attention to him and makes her approaches indirectly.

ROUTINES

Children of this age enjoy a few routines such as washing, toileting, and mid-morning lunch. They cooperate in dressing and undressing on some days but on others the adult may have to do most of it.

Their ability to rest on cots varies, but in any event rest should be short and may be more relaxing if accompanied by music. Rest should not be forced or continued if it meets with too much resistance. This age group often relaxes best merely by sitting in a comfortable position looking at books. Shifting to a room other than the playroom is more conducive to relaxation.

TRANSITIONS

This is a perseverative age. Transitions are difficult. Expect a slow adjustment to new materials, a strong holding on, and slow release even after interest has waned.

Do not try to hurry children too much, since two and a half is a strong dawdling age. If rituals have been set up by the child, make use of them instead of trying to break them down.

Verbal handling alone can be used to effect transitions much more successfully than at two, when verbal handling had to be supplemented by physical handling or by a lure.

TEACHER

Do not trust the child too much. He appears self-reliant and unneedful of restraints, but cannot really be relied upon. His repetition of a rule or prohibition does not mean that he can carry it out. This is no age for promises from the child. "Me do it myself" cannot always be carried out. "You do it" may express a real need for help.

Children may need adult direction in their play at this age. They are often not sufficiently mature to carry out their own ideas unaided, and deteriorate without adult assistance.

Give yourself and the child leeway so you both will not lose face in situations. By saying, "You *have* to wash your hands before juice," you may get resistance from the child, and the adult may have to back down. Save face by suggesting, "You need to wash your hands," and if the child resists, say, "Maybe tomorrow you will be ready to wash your hands."

Never make too much of an issue of discipline with two-and-a-half. Comprehension is low at this age and disciplining emphasizes contrariness and fosters repetition.

Do not expect children to respond to direct questions or to direct commands. Do expect them to respond to a statement which has *meaning* to them, if it is made with assurance. For example, "Now it's time for juice. First we wash hands," or "*First* we wash our hands *and then* we have juice."

Use other children in the group, as in noisy situations. Say, "Dicky doesn't like so much noise. It hurts his ears." "Dotty uses a whispering voice." These suggestions often do not work immediately but are for future reference. The immediate action is to take the noisy child out of the group—preferably outdoors.

The child at 2½ deteriorates easily and the group follows in a mercurial flow in a negative direction. A complete shift is essential when this happens.

VERBAL

Verbal handling has now superseded physical handling. The child's rapidly increasing comprehension and use of language make it possible for both the teacher and himself to express themselves through language.

(The reader will note that most of the techniques discussed at this and following ages are verbal in character.)

Certain key words help to organize the child's vacillating tendencies and thus give him a thrust in the forward direction. Some of the most potent words are "Needs," "Have to have," "When he's finished," "It's time to," "You forgot."

Questions may be used advantageously to activate the child if he demands answers that he already knows such as, "Where does your coat go?" "What did you forget?" "What do you do with your cup?" Avoid questions that can be answered by "No" such as, "Can you hang your coat up?" which is usually answered by "No."

HUMOR

If you treat the more annoying characteristics of the 2½ year old such as perseveration, vacillation, and negativism by using them in humor, you not only give them a legitimate outlet but also loosen their grip. Use these characteristics as foils for activating techniques; for example:

> *Perseveration and Vacillation:* "No, no, no." Adult: "Yes, yes, yes," etc., with laughter.

> *Negativism:* Ask silly questions that are answered by "No."
> "Does Nancy go home with Panda?" "No."
> "Does Nancy go home with Daddy?" "No."
> "Does Nancy go home with Mary?" "Yes."
> (When Nancy has had trouble, formerly, going home with Mary.)

OTHER CHILDREN

The teacher needs to have a wealth of techniques to draw upon, because more disputes occur at this age than at any other. Disputes are best handled with the teacher on hand to give the children sufficient suggestions, but also sufficient leeway to settle things according to each individual's needs. Often at this age the more mature child gives in to the less mature. The solution will often not conform to adult standards of justice.

Substitutions are still one of the best methods of handling disputes. "What else can you use?" or "What can we get for Bill, then?" etc. Some children are not able to give things back to other children, but like to find a substitute for the other child to play with. The runaway teaser will return toys in response to, "You *could* give it back to Dicky."

Take advantage of the fact that the child is beginning to use substitution techniques himself, not directed by the teacher. For example, Dotty wants to get her monkey away from Bill. She says, "Bill, I need that monkey. Bill wants to get dressed now to go out of doors?"

GROUP ACTIVITY

The quality of 2½ year group activity is fluctuating because of the unpredictability of the individuals composing it. Some of the stormiest days which appear tangled and give the guidance teacher a sense of failure may in reality be the precursors of more coordinated group activity.

Rising tension at this age may be relieved by the adult's setting up parallel group play, with each child using identical material such as clay, beads, etc.

Though parallel play still predominates, there are glimpses of cooperative group play including two or three children. Children may sit momentarily in a block train, may bring medicine to a "sick" child, or may pull others in a cart.

18

THREE YEARS OLD

§1. BEHAVIOR PROFILE

THREE IS A coming of age. The strands of previous development converge and come to a focus. The conflicting extremes of a half year ago give way to a high degree of self-control. For one so young the THREE-YEAR-OLD has himself well in hand. Far from being contrary, he tries to please and to conform. He even asks, "Do it dis way?", as though he were sensitive to the demands of culture. He is susceptible to praise and he likes friendly humor. He is remarkably attentive to spoken words, and often displays a quaint seriousness. If a group of nursery school parents should again cast a secret ballot to decide on the most delightful age of the preschool period, the honors would perhaps go to the THREE-YEAR-OLD, even if once upon a time he was TWO-AND-A-HALF.

The greater self-control of three has a motor basis. He is more sure and nimble on his feet; he walks erect, and he can turn sharp corners without going through the studied manoeuvers of earlier months. His whole motor set is more evenly balanced, more fluid; he no longer walks with arms outstretched, but swings them somewhat like an adult. He likes to hurry up and down stairs, but he also enjoys sedentary pastime which engages fine motor coordination. It is significant that he can delimit and orient his crayon strokes sufficiently to imitate the drawing of a cross. He has an eye for form, which suggests that the small muscles which operate his eyes are more facile than they were. He also has gained considerable inhibitory control of his sphincters; and he can almost toilet himself during the day. Not to overlook another domestic detail, he can unbutton buttons without popping them!

There is something "threeish" about the scope of his attention and insight. He can repeat three digits, he is beginning to count to three; he enumerates three objects in a picture; he is familiar with the three basic forms, circle, square, and triangle; he can combine three blocks to build a bridge. Many of his sentences and questions consist of three units. He likes to compare two objects and this requires a three-step logic.

He listens to words with increased assurance and insight. He even likes to make acquaintance with new words, apparently intrigued by their phonetic novelty. He has learned to listen to adults and he listens to learn from them. He uses words with more confidence and with intelligent inflection; although he may not overcome infantile articulations until the age of four or five. For practice he soliloquizes and dramatizes, combining actions and words. He creates dramatic situations to test out and to apply his words. In this way he extends the range and depth of his command of language. These action-thought patterns like his postural patterns will come into evidence in his nursery behavior.

The group life of the nursery will also reveal the advances which he is making in his management of personal-social relationships. These relationships are the most difficult and complicated which the growing child has to encounter. Nature has endowed the THREE-YEAR-OLD with an interest in persons. He watches their facial expressions for the purpose of finding out what these expressions indicate. He is not reading

[203]

from a book; but he is reading the expectations of his elders. He is making an important distinction between a physical obstacle and a personal one. Sometimes, however, he still strikes out at either, in spite of the fact that he generally desires to please. He is capable of sympathy. The infantile indifference has gone with other ineptitudes. Emotion as well as intelligence grows.

His sense of time is meager but well defined within his limitations. He distinguishes between night and day. He can say and understand "When it's time." Accordingly he can be put off a bit by the culture, and he can hold himself in anticipation. In other words, you can bargain with him, and he can wait his turn.

This constitutes a remarkable psychological advance and betokens well for the future,—if the culture is able to organize his growing capacities for mutual aid behavior. These capacities and his limitations are revealed in the ordered freedom of a well conducted nursery group. But it should be remembered that his cooperativeness is only in a nascent stage. He is still a preschool child. His collaborations in the nursery will be desultory, sketchy. He must also develop independence through solitary play. Too much must not be expected of him.

§2. BEHAVIOR DAY

THE WAKING HOUR is still variable although the margin of variation is not quite as large as formerly. The 3 year old child may wake at, say, 7 o'clock. He may wake dry. Often he whines a little during this first waking and calls to his mother, who promptly toilets him. If he still seems tired, as often happens, he goes back to bed, perhaps to doze off for a supplementary nap. Such an awakening is a thawing out process. By 7:30 he may be ready to come into the parents' room, and now, being thawed out, he likes to romp rather actively on the floor or bed.

He dresses while his parents are dressing, needing only a little help along the way.

[204]

He breakfasts alone in his room at about 8 o'clock and manages the meal almost entirely alone. He may even toilet himself. He is growing more self-reliant and he likes to help others when he can. Accordingly, he lends a hand in clearing the breakfast table; he carries the silverware. He assists in getting his own room in order.

He is ready for a session of independent play at about 9 o'clock. This play is somewhat less harum-scarum than it was half a year ago. When his mother comes for him he gladly helps her put his toys away. He goes to the toilet on slight suggestion.

By 11 o'clock the day's program may permit him to accompany his mother to market. It is a welcome experience supplementary to nursery school on the previous day. He also likes to go out doors for a tricycle trip or for a round of play on the domestic back-yard gym.

At the end of the play period, he goes to the toilet on a casual hint and washes his hands after a fashion by himself. He has his noon luncheon in his own room. This, as at $2\frac{1}{2}$ years, is his best meal. He manages most of it alone. He likes to have his mother near. She intercedes with occasional help but she does not have to complete the meal for him to the same degree as formerly. The luncheon is still best served in courses.

At the next toileting he may have a bowel movement.

The routines of the day do not have to be rushed. He makes comfortable transitions and adaptations. He feels his own increasing independence and demands that his afternoon nap at 1 o'clock should be a "play nap." This is a relaxation and rest period. He utilizes it for that purpose. He gets in and out of bed a few times and he may finally fall asleep without further aid from his mother. He is content to play at "napping" from one to two hours. If he should not fall asleep, he presents himself to his mother as if to say, "Time is up." If the allotted time is not up, he returns to his "play napping" usually without protest.

He goes to the toilet again on suggestion at 3 o'clock. He needs very little help in this toileting.

He likes to go on an excursion to a friend's house in the afternoon. He plays best out of doors.

On returning home, he is not likely to make any excessive demands. He likes to help in the preparation of the evening meal and even initiates suggestions as to the things he would like to have for his supper, which occurs at about 5:30, and is again best managed in his own room. He needs, perhaps, a little more completion help from his mother at this evening meal.

He plays contentedly until about 6:30, often preferring dramatic or puzzle playing. He enjoys a half-hour of play with his father. He is fond of quiet social play, listening to records and to stories.

The bath may still come at about 7 o'clock. Again he is interested in helping with the arrangements but his "ritualisms" are much less rigid. They are developing into more adaptive cooperation. Time-consuming demands are abating and he is in bed by about 7:30, and may fall asleep within a half hour. He does not need much external assistance in achieving release into sleep, but his mother may tell him a simple bed-time story about what he did when he was a little baby.

He may not need to be picked up during the night for toileting. He sleeps the round of the clock.

SLEEP

Night

There are many tag ends of 30 months' behavior that linger on into 36 months. The maturity of the 3 year old during the daylight hours seems slowly to leave him as night approaches and he again becomes, at least in part, what he was before. He is, however, giving up much of his ritualism and if he does continue it, it can be handled by such devices as the mother closing her eyes and saying she won't look until the child is under the covers. At 2½, the mother had to remove her whole person and shut the door. Now she has only to remove her seeing self by closing her eyes. As at 2½, the child will often go to sleep faster for another person than for his mother.

The 3 year old does not usually mind being picked up for toileting at 10 to 12 P.M., though the majority of 3 year olds do not need to be picked up. Wakefulness is, however, common at three years and this is often the time when a night life begins. One type of child gets out of his crib easily by himself, goes to the bathroom, goes downstairs, gets some food from the ice-box, "reads" a magazine after turning on the light in the living room, and may be found asleep on the couch next morning. Another type of child talks to himself for an hour or two in bed; and still a third type insists upon getting into his mother's bed.

This is the age when dreams begin to be reported. Though they may wake the child he is rarely able to tell them.

Morning waking is more difficult than going to sleep. As with 2½, the time of waking varies between 6 and 8 A.M. The child is often tired on awakening, sucks his thumb, whines, and in general has a difficult time in starting the day. He is more apt to call to be taken up than to get up by himself. If he is allowed to come into his parents' bed (when it is time) to romp and play, he starts his day more gaily and more easily.

[Some children wake early in the evening while their parents are out, and cry until they vomit or until the parents return. Some children may be able to accept being told ahead of time that their parents are going out. It may be sufficient for the child to be told just as his parents are leaving the house, or he may need to be warned even a day or two in advance. If such warnings are not adequate and the child continues to cry, the parent may have to stay at home evenings until the child can adjust at a later age.

If the child gets up and wanders around the house during the night without calling anyone, tying his door loosely may necessitate his calling. Many need to be toileted and need to be given food.

If the child insists upon getting into bed with his mother it may be wise to accede to his demand, but to warn him ahead of time that after he has fallen asleep he will be put back in his crib. If he wakes and cries when returned to his crib, the mother may have to allow him to sleep with her. This type of demand is often self-limited to a week's duration. If, however, it continues, the child may respond better to having his father take the mother's role in the situation.]

Nap

This is the onset of the "play nap." Even the naming of this time when the child is resting in his room a "play nap" often seems to make it more acceptable. There may be a period of two to three months from 30 to 36 months of age when the child does not sleep. He often returns to a real nap at 36 months but this is not constant. If the child of this age does go to sleep he usually falls asleep more quickly than at 30 months. The length of the nap is cut down to one or two hours and waking, though slow, does not involve the conflict that it often does at 30 months.

EATING

Appetite—The fluctuations of 30 months are now settling down to a fair appetite. Breakfast and supper are now more frequently the best meals, though there are many variations. The milk intake is definitely on the rise.

Refusals and Preferences—These are less marked than they were at 24 to 30 months. Meat, fruit, and milk are now on the preferred list. Desserts and sweets are more desired, but cannot yet be used as a goal toward which to work (48 months). Vegetables are now slowly being accepted. The child often wants foods that require more chewing, such as raw vegetables, potato skins, or meat on a bone.

Spoon Feeding—The spoon is now grasped more between thumb and index. Some girls hold it adult fashion with the palm turned inward. Boys, however, are more likely to direct the palm downward. The filling of the spoon is easily accomplished both by pushing the point of the spoon into the food and by rotating it inwardly. The bowl of the spoon may be inserted sidewise or by its point.

There is good rotation at the wrist and little if any spilling results. A fork is often demanded, especially to pierce pieces of meat.

Cup Drinking—The cup is now held by the handle in adult fashion. The free hand is no longer needed to help. The head again tilts back to secure the last drop. This function will later be taken over by the hands alone.

Self Help—Although the 3 year old child is eating well alone, he may not eat well at the family table. The situation is usually too complex. He is apt to demand everyone's attention and wants to have everything in sight. Because of his dawdling he is either coaxed, fed, or left at the table to finish alone after the rest of the family has left.

He is now beginning to ask for special foods he likes during the preparation of his meals.

ELIMINATION

Bowel—The number of movements varies from one to two a day with only an occasional skipping of a day. If there is only one movement, it most frequently occurs after lunch and if there are two the other more frequently occurs after breakfast. Very few have a bowel movement associated with their nap at this age. Many go to the toilet by themselves with or without telling, but still want help when they have finished.

Bladder—Most children go at routine times, with a fairly long span and no accidents during the day. If an occasional accident does occur, they insist upon having their pants changed at once. The most common asking is expressed in general terms such as, "I'm going to the bathroom."

The majority of children are consistently dry after their naps and also in the morning without being taken up during the night. A number of children are still dependent upon being picked up at 10 o'clock and a few wet once or twice a week, or are alternately dry or wet for a few weeks at a time.

BATH AND DRESSING

Bath—Many of the 30 month bath patterns linger on, though bath rituals are less complicated and more subject to change. Children are now more insistent upon helping to wash themselves at least in part. Getting out of the tub is still resisted, but surprising the mother by getting out while she closes her eyes, usually works.

Dressing—Dressing at this age is likely to go more smoothly than at 30 months as the child is more interested in doing what he can to help and is therefore less likely to run away. Undressing is still carried out with greater interest and ability than dressing. Most children of this age undress well and rather rapidly. Undressing is further facilitated by a new ability to unbutton front and side buttons.

Dressing includes putting on pants, socks and shoes and sometimes sweaters or dresses. However they cannot consistently distinguish the back from the front or button buttons, and though they may try to lace their shoes it is usually done incorrectly. Self-help in dressing is also dependent upon their mood, for they do well one day and poorly the next.

SELF-ACTIVITY

The planning for the child's activity is now much more relaxed. Techniques can now be used with less rigidity and often the handling of a 3 year old is so simple and natural that no conscious techniques are needed. As with the younger ages, the mornings when the child is not at nursery school are best handled by play alone either in the child's room or in a closed-in yard. He happily accepts these places arranged for his own use as long as he does not have to stay in them too long. But he usually plays so happily and well that it is now the mother who may interrupt the play to suggest that he move on to the next activity. The child makes his own self-demand here and need only be helped more specifically with warnings in advance when it is time for the routines of toileting and eating.

A whole new imaginative world is opening up for the 3 year old. He now may have the addition of a fire-engine, larger building blocks, a new puzzle, and if he is capable of handling crayons alone without scribbling on the wall, he may have a coloring book and crayons. This is the age when sex differences in choice of play materials are becoming more marked than earlier.

It is interesting to see a 3 year old's room after he has had an hour's play alone. It has none of the chaos of the 2½ year old child's room. There are remnants of his play activity, and he may have stories to tell about what he has done. He likes to linger on and even helps to put his toys away though he has no initiative for this and only does it from a sense of comradery with the adult, and only on suggestion.

After toileting and maybe a mid-morning snack he is happy to be out of doors. His tricycle, which may be his latest acquisition, is often his chief interest. He usually knows how to ride it, but if he does not he likes just to push it around. Another addition to his play yard may be a gym with ladders, a swing, and trapeze rings. He can play endlessly on these and may find it hard to leave when it is time for lunch.

SOCIALITY

The 3 year old has fewer definite ideas about how the household should be run than does the 30 month old child. He is now more ready to accept suggestions, and may be of considerable help to his mother in wiping dishes, putting things away, and in running simple errands. He is an easier child about the house now that he no longer meddles excessively with things he should not touch.

He enjoys his afternoon excursions out of doors and often prefers to go on his tricycle. If a destination has been planned, he holds a definite idea of it in his mind, but he makes few spontaneous demands to visit his friends.

He is happy when the planned excursion is to another child's home. He actually prefers the afternoon companionship of other children, but cannot quite make his wants known unless it is usual for him to see a certain child quite often. Two 3 year olds play best out of doors with gross motor equipment and may play alone well for twenty to thirty minutes. After this, they usually need supervision and guidance. (For a discussion of this supervision and guidance see §5 of this chapter.) If the 3 year old is not supervised, he is apt to withdraw from his companion or to attack him with biting, scratching, pushing or kicking.

If he has difficulty in adjusting to children of his own age even with supervision, it is best to handle him alone and to plan short excursions to see things and places, or to arrange his play with a 5 or 6 year old who will demand a reasonable amount of fair play from the 3 year old but will give in to his immature wishes when he cannot be handled otherwise.

As discussed under 30 months behavior, there is one type of child who plays best at home and shares poorly, and another type who plays best away from home and shares generously. The former is the child who does best with an older child.

The mother is more commonly the favored parent. The child enjoys speaking of himself and his mother together as "we." He has just come through a new emotional awareness of himself. From 30 to 36 months he has progressed past the feeling of "I" and its needs, and "you" with its demands from the other person. "I" and "you" are their own counterparts, for he sometimes demands to do what he cannot do and asks help from the parent with things he can do.

With growth and reorganization he partially loses this sense of "I" and "you" and somehow sinks back into babyhood. Emotionally he relives his whole life, with help from his mother. With fatigue he asks to be carried and wants to be a baby. He actually may say, "I'm a little baby. I can't talk, I have no teeth, and I have no hair." If he takes himself literally he may actually pull out hair. But if he holds more closely to his present reality, as is more usual, he may say, "I'm a little baby. I have to have a bottle. I sleep out in the carriage, *but* I can talk."

The wise mother helps the child to relive his babyhood. She answers all of his questions and tells him about himself. He wants to know about what he wore and how he cried, how he talked and laughed, where he slept, how he was fed. He even likes to hear about the fears he has conquered. He especially likes these stories after he is put to bed and may enjoy hearing them over and over.

But finally toward three, he is a little older and has relived step by step much of his past life until he has reached his present age. Then he is ready to go forth from the parent, to look forward rather than backward, to think of himself in his relation to the future, whether the future is tomorrow, the next school day or the next holiday. Some cling to this reliving of their past lives and especially their babyhood even into the fifth year.

[The child may be ready at this age to choose between two alternatives and may enjoy making simple choices, i.e. when he is slow to come in for lunch he may be asked, "Do you want to come in the front door or the back door?" Or, if he is slow in dressing, he may be asked, "Do you want to wear your blue overalls or your green ones?"

Those who cannot take choices need to have planning ahead of time. "We're going to buy the chocolate cookies at the store." If this type of child is allowed his own choice, he will be sure to shift his choice halfway home and have a temper tantrum because he does not have his way.

Do not divide authority about any specific situation between the mother and the father. The child should know that his mother decides about clothes, candy, etc.; his father, about the repair of toys, excursions to the railroad station, etc. Particularly do not allow the child to play one parent against the other.]

The imaginative life of the child rises slowly until it reaches a high peak at $3\frac{1}{2}$ years, in the form of an imaginary companion. At 4 years this transforms into more dramatic social play involving two or more children. Even during the second year of life the child may pretend to pick something off the wall and give it to the adult. By two he may pretend to pick food out of a magazine. By two and a half, he is conducting a very creditable tea party even without the real aid of water. The realist, however, insists upon having water in his tea pot and cannot imagine having a tea party without "tea."

The interest in imaginative playmates has its beginning at about 2½ years of age. At the same time, he makes shifts in his identity; he becomes an animal. All this is coincident with the self-discovery of his own identity. These imaginative constructions are tentative at first, but become more defined and strong by 3 and especially by 3½ years of age. There are wide individual differences. Some children do not indulge in this imaginary life. The stimulus comes quite spontaneously from within the child. One 3 year old girl who longed for playmates saw little girls looking through her window. Some children cling to a friend who has gone away by holding on to him as an imaginary companion.

Probably all imaginative life in the child satisfies some inner need, whether it is for companionship, someone to "beat," someone to look up to, someone to do things with, someone to do things for or someone to boss. Probably the intricacies of individual emotional development are being worked out by the child through these imaginative devices.

By 3½ years the child's imaginary life often has more definite pattern, is bound up more intimately with his own activities. The imaginary companion may need a place at the table, he may sleep in or under the child's bed, he may go for a ride in the car. The child is often very demanding about the rights of his imaginary companion and very solicitous in teaching him many things.

He most often relates this companion to his own home life. It is only rarely that the companion is brought to nursery school, though he may be brought as far as the schoolroom door. If he is brought into the room, this may well be an indication of a difficult adjustment which the child is handling through these imaginative means. The same is true of the child who takes on the role of an animal. This role is much stronger at home, and exercises such complete domination that the hand becomes a paw, the speech turns into animal noises, and the tongue becomes a lapping instrument when it is time to drink milk. This imaginative shift of personality is more likely to be carried into the nursery school than is the imaginary companion.

Any of these imaginative outlets should be respected by the parent, and even utilized, but not exploited. With a fuller experience and a growing ability to adjust to the social structure, the child shifts his imaginary impersonations into his group play by becoming the doctor, the fireman, or the mother. But as with other behaviors, there are recurrences of this imaginative life even up to 8 or 9 years of age.

§3. CULTURAL AND CREATIVE ACTIVITIES

BOOKS

1. Increasing span of interest in listening to stories.
2. Can be held longer when stories are read to small groups.

3. Continued enjoyment of familiar experiences with repetition and more detail as, "Bobbie and Donnie were Twins."

4. Likes information about nature, transportation, etc., woven into story form as "Beachcomber Bobbie" and "Four Airplanes."

5. Likes imaginative stories based on real people and real animals, as "Caps for Sale," and "Little Black Sambo."

6. Enjoyment of riddles and guessing, such as "The Noisy Book."

7. Enjoys widening of horizon through information books as, "Sails, Wheels and Wings."

8. Makes relevant comments during stories, especially about materials or experiences at home.

9. Some insist on stories being re-told and re-read word for word without changes.

10. Likes to look at books and may "read" to others or explain pictures.

MUSIC

1. Many can reproduce whole songs, though generally not on pitch.
2. Beginning to match simple tones.
3. Less inhibition in joining group singing.
4. Can recognize several melodies.
5. Experimenting with musical instruments.
6. Simple explanations concerning songs and instruments delight them and encourage interest.
7. Marked individual differences in interest and ability to listen to music.
8. Enjoy a diversity of musical experiences.
9. Most members of the group participate in a variety of rhythms.
10. Watchers will often participate when approached through another child, or through dramatizing.
11. Children gallop, jump, walk and run in fairly good time to music.
12. Enjoy dressing up in costumes for rhythms.

PAINTING

1. Strokes are more varied and rhythmical.
2. Beginnings of design are emerging.
3. Often child covers whole page with one color, or with blocks of various colors.
4. Sometimes names finished product, but seldom any recognizable resemblance.

[212]

5. May be stimulated by watching an older, talented child paint, or by observing more advanced paintings of other children.
6. Joy and pride in product; exclaims, "Look what I made!"
7. Works with more concentration and precision.
8. Dislikes to share paper with others.

FINGER PAINTING

1. Experimenting with finger movements as well as whole hand movements.
2. Some feeling for design.

CRAYONS

1. Demands a variety of colors.
2. Enters representative stage earlier with crayons than with paint.

CLAY

1. Enjoyment of manipulating with hands, patting, making holes with fingers and squeezing.
2. Beginning of form: making flat, round "cakes," and balls. Rolls long, narrow strips, etc.
3. Some naming of product with general approximation in shape.
4. Makes products for others outside of school, especially mother, but often forgets to take them home.

SAND

1. Makes cakes, pies, roads, tunnels, etc.
2. Combines with other materials, such as pegs, stones, shells, cars.

BLOCKS

1. Likes a diversity of shapes and sizes.
2. Order and balance in building.
3. Combining with cars, trains, etc.
4. Often names what he is making.
5. Enjoys the process of construction more than playing with finished product.

POSSESSIONS

1. Enjoys new clothes and likes to exhibit them to others, especially to teacher.
2. Beginning to share toys; less hoarding.

3. Brings possessions to school to share with others, books for instance.

4. May enjoy exhibiting possessions then forgets about them for the morning. Generally brings different things every day.

5. Dislikes having others wear his clothes.

6. Likes to have pennies to put in the bank. Knows that money is used in making purchases but has no idea of how much. Play money may be very satisfactory as a substitute.

HOLIDAYS AND FESTIVALS

1. Birthday—The moment the cake arrives, the child is three. He enjoys a small party of two or three friends. Best time for this is still mealtime.

2. Christmas—Interest in Santa Claus. Much interested in his own presents. Cannot keep secret the presents he is giving others.

3. Valentine's Day—Likes sending valentines to others and making a personal mark (as a scribble or the first letter of his name) on the back. Often brings valentines to school to show to other children.

4. Easter—Interest in Easter bunny and eggs.

5. Hallowe'en—Delighted with Jack O'Lantern, which is the whole meaning of Hallowe'en to him. Likes watching adult make Jack O'Lantern and gives some help.

6. Thanksgiving—The whole meaning of Thanksgiving is the turkey, which he knows about beforehand. However he also enjoys the party aspect of this holiday including guests or a trip to visit relatives.

7. Religion—Greater interest in going to Sunday School. Also enjoys the quietness of church. May enjoy saying short prayers.

EXCURSIONS

1. Enjoys excursions to airport, railroad station, fire station, harbor, zoo or farm.

2. Fascinated watching men at work, as carpenter, painter, mechanic. Likes to watch steam-shovel, cement-mixer, in operation.

3. Interested in planning visits, as an afternoon with another child or lunch with grandmother.

4. Enjoys everyday excursions as going to market.

5. Definitely has thought of destination in mind and enjoys talking about it beforehand.

§4. NURSERY BEHAVIOR

THE THREE YEAR OLD is becoming a man of the world. He displays a certain abandon and also some savoir faire when he makes his entrance to the nursery. If he is exuberant he may shout and sing as he comes along. He is likely to be sociable and communicative if he meets a familiar adult on the way. He may begin to tell some interesting story before he even enters the cloak room and he is very likely to continue his story because of the fullness of his utterance.

He readily sheds his dependence on his mother. While he is reciting his tale she may have to remind him that it is time to say "goodbye," and she must be content with a somewhat perfunctory leave-taking. He is not mature enough to do two complicated things at one time. Although he can remove his outdoor garments without much assistance, he stops midway in the process when he begins to talk. His talk is usually directed to the guidance teacher. His companions are equally eager to impart some story to her. As a result there will be several children talking at the same time, not too concerned whether every word is listened to.

The desire to talk is so eager and the guidance teacher herself is so interested that the preliminary period in the cloak room becomes a kind of social prologue to the morning in the nursery. All this is quite different from the inertias and dawdling so characteristic of younger age groups. The atmosphere reflects the advancing maturity of the THREE YEAR OLD and his strong tendency to establish social contacts, particularly with adults. With adult cooperation the conversation can be continued indefinitely. Three's conversational approaches to children of his own age are briefer and are more touch and go. It is as though he recognized the cultural significance of the adult in a new way. The mere presence of the guidance teacher influences the flow of his behavior. At 'juice time' and 'story time' he will again project his narrations upon her. More frequently they are stories of the interesting things which happened at home.

[215]

He is weighted with home experiences even when he has crossed the threshold of the nursery.

He enters the nursery room with some deliberativeness. When he was a year younger he tended to run forthwith toward some particular toy. Now he may survey the scene for a moment and when there are other children in the room he will choose a child or an activity which engages his interest. There is an element of choice in what he does. There is an element of sociality in his approach. After a brief greeting or interchange with one of his playmates he may engage for a while in independent play. The following stenographic account with its time record illustrates the range, diversity and sequences of his behavior. The several children are alphabetically designated.

9:35   R and S are building with large blocks. They build slowly and watch the other children riding in portable house. S says, "Building a house. Look at this house: one-two-three (blocks)." Long pauses occur as they watch others. R leaves and S keeps on building alone. "I think I will do this. This is mine, mine, mine. Who, who, who? This is mine." Watches R climbing ladder.

9:41   S has walked to the middle of the room and after standing for some time watching the other children she climbs on the "train" beside J. Says, "Bee" to J and he says "Bee" to her. She says "You"; and he replies, "You." She sits on the train. The teacher puts up a gangplank and J says, "You take that thing down." Three of the children take turns walking up the gangplank. S says, "I wanna try that."

9:44   S climbs up the gangplank. Four children are now standing on the train. The teacher says, "Here comes the engineer." R replies "Here's a passenger. Here's a passenger." Smiles at her own remark. R and S stand quietly and the others walk up and down the gangplank.

9:45   J, the engineer, "starts" the train which now contains three children and the teacher.

9:47   On suggestion, P collects tickets and then goes around selling sandwiches.

9:48   S wants to drive. J pushes her away and slaps her. She squeals. The others watch neutrally. S leaves and J again drives. The passengers watch.

Passengers pretend to share a "chocolate bar" block with the teacher. Sandwich seller brings around more refreshments.

9:50 Teacher suggests that children be baggage men and put the baggage (building blocks which are scattered around) in the baggage house. All cooperate. Children are asked how many trunks they can carry. S says, "I can carry just one." J says, "I can carry four." R says, "I can carry two." S and R stay with this putting away longer than do the other three who go over to the portable house. R says, "Dese go here." S says, "Yes, yes. An' here's some more. Here's some. I think I can carry all of these. See how I can carry these!" R, "We're all tidy." S, "There's no room for these now."

The foregoing is a random sample of group behavior at the THREE YEAR OLD level. It will be noted that although the THREE YEAR OLD is capable of initiatives, he is almost more susceptible to social suggestion. His behavior tends to elaborate as soon as the teacher supplies a prompting. Promptings would have been without effect at a younger age; but the THREE YEAR OLD almost demands them. And so the teacher becomes a kind of catalytic agent or energizer. She simply gives cues. It is not her task to get the child to do something which she thinks should be educationally imposed upon him.

For similar reasons the THREE YEAR OLD is now responsive to verbal suggestions. Toward mid-morning the teacher says, "It is time to wash"; "You could go with M——." The ablutions are executed with moderate efficiency. The THREE YEAR OLD may have to be reminded to turn off the faucet, but he does not go out of bounds as he will at three-and-a-half, when he will wash the mirror as well as himself.

He returns to the nursery room and helps the teacher with the setting of the table for the mid-morning lunch. R may remark, "I want some juice." S declares, "I want some crackers." The conversation is at a simple level, but it elaborates at once as soon as the teacher drops a catalytic remark. She says, "It will soon be spring." Immediately R, S, and J chime in as follows:

R: "I know, mummy told me." J: "We wear spring coats." R: "Did you know it rained last night? I didn't get wet because I had a rain and snow-suit on." S: "I had a umbrella." R, pouring juice: "Up to the bump." S chimes in "Up to the pump." R: "Bump, not pump."

Each child puts his glass on the tray as he finishes and then in obedience to routine makes directly for the relaxation cots. He offers no resistance: he likes to relax with the aid of music or of a quiet story read by the teacher. He keeps his eyes open but remains moderately quiescent for a period of about ten minutes. Then on verbal suggestion he returns to the cloak room to be dressed for outdoors.

By this time the level of his integration has somewhat subsided. More-over, it is more difficult to dress than to undress, and so he needs the help of the teacher at critical points. His speech and inflections have less pat-tern and control than they had earlier in the morning. He welcomes the transition to the out of doors. Outdoor play has a beneficial effect on his mood and movements. He favors the use of his grosser motor muscles. He rides the tricycle; he climbs; he digs; he slides. At the same time he dramatizes himself as a fireman, an engineer, or a roadman, without carry-ing out any elaborate dramatic sequence. Two or three children, however, are likely to congregate and engage in some type of activity.

After about an hour of outdoor play the THREE YEAR OLD is ready to welcome his mother. But he wants one more turn before he goes. He also likes to demonstrate some athletic feat in which he has both a per-sonal and social pride. If the pride were not social as well as personal he would not make this reference to his mother. He is very much in charac-ter when he does so, for he likes to please. He himself is pleased when he pleases others.

§5. NURSERY TECHNIQUES

PHYSICAL ENVIRONMENT

Fewer environmental restrictions are necessary. Since the gross motor drive is reduced, children can hold more to spheres of interest in various sections of the room. They can also be helped to hold to these spheres of interest longer through verbal suggestions from the adult, i.e. "Is your supper ready?" when playing in the doll corner; or "Does anybody need any groceries?" when playing in the store.

More materials for dramatic play, such as a costume box, and more constructive materials, such as large blocks, are important at this age.

ADJUSTMENT

Adjustment difficulties are rare at this age, and when they occur can be handled through familiar "surprises" or through favorite toys.

ROUTINES

Children at this age move easily through such routines as washing, toileting, mid-morning lunch and rest. They can handle undressing almost entirely by themselves but need some help in dressing, mostly in starting their ski-pants and jackets. (More help is usually needed at home than at school.) Dressing and undressing can both be speeded up through humor.

Very few refuse to rest on cots at this age, but they will not rest for more than ten to fifteen minutes. Relaxation can best be accomplished when music or stories are used.

Children do not put toys away spontaneously, but enjoy doing so in a group if putting away is dramatized and they can pretend that they are lumbermen, movers, or some other specific persons. The whole group often work together in the spirit of a game.

TRANSITIONS

Transitions are seldom difficult at this age. New ways of doing things, of going from one place to another, can be used. Since the gross motor drive is now more under the child's control the suggestion to run, jump, or hop into the bathroom or elsewhere becomes a new game.

TEACHER

This is a social, imitative, "Me, too" age. Therefore it is better to point out positive rather than negative factors (referred to more safely before three), as children are apt to do the thing mentioned. "We stand on the floor" gives them the positive suggestion rather than, "We don't stand on the table."

One has to decide at three years when the child's behavior is deteriorating whether to handle a situation at a younger level or at a higher level. For instance when a child runs away from putting on his outdoor clothes at the end of the morning the adult may need to dress him in the bathroom with the door closed (30 months behavior), or to interest him in some new information about animals or the next holiday (48 months behavior).

If a 3 year old is in constant conflict and is lowering the behavior of the group, he may become smoother after visiting a younger group where solitary play predominates. A dynamic, aggressive 3 year old who takes over the direction of his group completely may by visiting a 4 year old group acquire more subtle techniques and at the same time give his group a rest.

One of the most effective measures to use as a last resort is isolation. Because of the increased sociability of the child, he is strongly affected by removal from the group plus the explanation that, "You bother the other children," or "You are too tired to play with them." Isolation should not last very long and should be accompanied by an adult or by toys. If a group situation occurs which the child particularly enjoys, the adult can point out, "It's too bad you missed the fire engine story today because you bit Sally." Also project into the future, "Next time you will remember that we don't bite *any more*." The next day during the story situation the adult may remark, "It's nice to have Bill hear the story today, *too*." If a child repeats some unacceptable behavior, the phrase, "You forgot," or "You made a mistake" may terminate the behavior.

VERBAL

The 2½ year old child's demand for repetition of the same words and phrases is now giving way to an interest in many new words and new uses of words.

a) Key adjectives—"new," "different," "big," "strong." "Could you make a *different* kind?" stimulates the child within a situation without giving him a specific idea. "Can you carry two *big* ones?" may be the needed challenge to put the blocks away.
b) Key nouns—"surprise," "secret." "When you finish going to the bathroom I have a *surprise* for you" may organize a scraggly group.
c) Key verbs—"help," "might," "could," "guess what." "You *could* help John fill the cart" may not only produce the desired action but also the satisfaction as expressed in "I'm helping."
d) Key adverbs—"Maybe," "How about," "too." "You could help, *too*" helps the child to join in group activity which he craves. By 3½ the group rings with the spontaneous remark, "Me, too."

The 3 year old listens well when he is reasoned with. He will sometimes do things he does not like to do if he is given a good reason, e.g. "Let's pick up the blocks so we'll have more room to dance." A good reason for doing something should include a specific step by step suggestion. Children withdraw from general demands such as "Pick up your room." or "Tell me what you did at school today." They respond readily, however, to "First let's pick up the big blocks and then . . ." or "Did you paint at school today?"

The use of "maybe," "you might," "perhaps," "you could" gives the child a graceful way of refusing in situations where complying is not important, e.g., "Maybe you could help Bobby pull the wagon."

One of the best ways to simplify a group pressure situation is by whispering to the child. The same question such as, "Where does your cup go?" may not be responded to when spoken out loud, but may be immediately responded to when spoken in a whisper. The whispering not only gives the enjoyment of a secret, but also restricts the child's influence to only one other person.

HUMOR

The gross motor humor of the 2 year old is steadily giving way to verbal humor by three. Simple repetitions as "golly, golly, golly" tossed back and forth between the child and the adult like a verbal ball give a joyous air to activity.

Humorous wrong guesses from the adult delight the child. E.g., as the child is taking off his outer things the adult may ask, "Are your socks purple today?" "No," says the child with a smile.

Adult: "Then they are red?" "No" laughs the child.

Adult: "Then they must be blue." "No, wrong again" laughs the child as he hurries to take off his suit to show the teacher that they are white.

OTHER CHILDREN

With language equipment and a better developed sense of the other person as expressed in his use of "we," the 3 year old can solve his own problems more adequately, and needs less adult guidance than does the 2½ year old. It is sometimes advisable to let children settle their own disputes by fighting it out if they are fairly evenly matched and the aggressive child does not always win. The adult should sense the point beyond which her "ignoring" the conflict would be detrimental to the children involved.

The 3 year old is apt to respond more to the other children than to the adult as he did at two. Therefore the adult may often use a child to help another. "John, you may go in to rest with Bobby." Group squabbles are often best settled by the leader, as when a boy and girl in a group of three were fighting over an armchair. The teacher's stock techniques of, "Who had it first?" or "You could take turns" made no impression upon them. Then the teacher turned to the third child who was the "hostess" and asked her what she was going to do about it. Whereupon she replied immediately, "Only daddies sit in chairs with arms. You sit over there, Nancy." And Nancy complied at once.

The 2 year old's use of substitutions in a dispute can still be used at three. However the 3 year old can wait better, can understand that "Bill is using it now" and may often take the cue from the teacher. "Ask Bill when he is going to be through with it." Bill may answer, "In two minutes" which may mean almost at once.

Since 3 year olds are much more social than formerly, other children can be used successfully to take charge of a difficult child or to help make new adjustments. A 7 or 8 year old child visiting for a day may raise the level of behavior considerably and have a carry-over for some length of time.

42 months: If you treat the annoying commands of 3½ lightly they will often run their course more quickly. The frequent frustrating refrain of "You can't come in" with which children exclude others from their activities may be treated as follows:

a) With a light tone of the positive, "She can come in" sung on a minor third.
b) With a choice, as "Do you want her to bring you some bread or some butter?"
c) With a widening of their horizon by a new word or new concept, as "You could invite her to be your *guest*," or "Show her where she can ring the doorbell before she comes in."
d) With use of the specific, "But this is the postman bringing you some mail."

GROUP ACTIVITY

Three is capable of continuing group play more smoothly and longer than two-and-a-half, and there is more spontaneous group play. The teacher can often keep play from deteriorating by elaborating it with suggestions such as, "Is supper ready?" or "Who's going to be the conductor on your train?"

Rising tension at this age may be relieved, as at 2½, by the adult's setting up parallel group play with clay, etc., which satisfies the "Me, too" characteristic of the 3 year old.

There should be a balance or alternation of quiet and active group play.

The group may need to be subdivided to separate conflicting personalities. This will help to prolong and support group play.

42 months: A group of 3 year old children will generally be calm and quite self-reliant in comparison with the stormy 2½ year old group. However, by the time they reach 3½ they begin forming strong friendships and discriminating against the rest of the group, demanding and commanding each other and resorting to hitting and pushing. This is related to their increased tension, which makes them stumble, fall and become over-excited. As at 2½, their group behavior is quite unpredictable, some days being very stormy and others showing remarkable glimmers of 4 year old cooperation and imagination.

During a difficult period a group of 3½ year olds is frequently better organized if they start the morning with some planned activity such as scrubbing woodwork, blowing soap bubbles, etc., rather than free play.

A Footnote concerning three and a half year old maturity.

Readers of this volume scarcely need to be told that the contrasts which we draw between adjacent ages do not actually appear with sharp suddenness in the growth of the child. He is always in a state of transition. The stretch between three years and four years is a long one; and it is not surprising that there should be some unevenness along the way. This is the reason our text makes frequent reference to the 3½ year old. For a brief period he may be in a stage of developmental awkwardness, manifested in a tendency to stumble or fall, in increased tensional outlets (like nail biting, eye blinking, or tremulous hands), in fear of heights, in a shift of handedness, in temporary stuttering, in repeated seeking of assurance: "Do you love me?" Generally such "disequilibrium" traits are not severe or prolonged; and show a tendency toward resolution as the child grows older.

[223]

19

FOUR YEARS OLD

§1. BEHAVIOR PROFILE

THREE has a conforming mind. FOUR has a lively mind. THREE is assentive; FOUR, assertive. Indeed, FOUR tends to go out of bounds both with muscles and mind. And why should he not? If he remained a delightful, docile THREE, he would not grow up. So he surges ahead with bursts of movement and of imagination. His activity curve again takes on the hither and thither pattern typical of TWO YEARS. But this is not a regression; for he functions at a higher level in all departments of his behavior; motor, adaptive, language, and personal-social. He covers more ground, not only in his running, hopping, jumping, skipping, climbing; but in the lively constructions and antics of his mental imagery.

If at times he seems somewhat voluble, dogmatic, boastful and bossy, it is because he is a blithe amateur swinging into fresh fields of self expression. For a while he scarcely can be too concerned about the feelings of

[224]

others. He is not quite as sensitive to praise as he was at THREE and as he will be again at FIVE. Instead he praises himself through bragging. Besides he is much less experienced than his brave verbal assertiveness might suggest. He has meager appreciation of disappointment and the personal emotions of others. He is inquisitively interested in death, but has scant comprehension of its meaning. He is plausible because his words often outrun his knowledge.

His motor drive is high. He races up and down stairs; he dashes on his velocipede. He trapezes on the jungle gym, with flying commentary while he performs: "I bet you can't do this, I hope!" He can also combine talking and eating. At an earlier age he either talked or ate; now he does both more or less simultaneously. This is a new ability (THREE had to stop undressing when he was speaking).

FOUR's motor equipment including his voice is under finer control. He can throw overhand; he can cut on the line with scissors; saw with a hand saw; lace his shoes; stand on one foot. Although he enjoys gross bodily activity, he is able to sit for a long period at interesting manual tasks. Hands, arms, legs, and feet are becoming emancipated from total postural set. If his general postural development has been fortunate to date, his dancing and his hand movements now assume a natural, untutored gracefulness.

FOUR is a great talker. He is his own self-appointed commentator and often his own audience. He likes to use words, to try them out, to play with them. He likes new, different words (indeed *different* is itself a favorite word for him). He also likes to perpetrate silly words like, "marty-warty," "batty-watty," and "ooshy-wooshy" to describe the soft clay. Questioning comes to a peak. The endless "Why" and "How" questions are not for pure pursuit of knowledge, but are devices for practicing both speech and listening. Therefore, a bright, articulate FOUR YEAR OLD tends to run his topics to the ground, exhausting every verbal possibility. Just as he tries to climb high on the gym, so he climbs high with his vocabulary and grammar. Naturally his syntax often topples.

The key to FOUR's psychology is his high drive combined with a fluid

[225]

mental organization. His imagery is almost mercurial. It moves from one form to another with careless ease. He starts to draw a turtle, before he is through it is an elephant or a truck. This same fluidity makes him a fabricator and a fertile producer of alibis. It also makes it possible for him to dramatize any experience which comes within his ken. A hospital bed scene is readily reenacted with very simple materials serving as properties. A block becomes a bottle of medicine; and in another instant a stethoscope. Such dramatic play with ever running comments and dialogue is a staple form of nursery behavior.

FOUR is voluble, because his imagery is mercurial; and also because he wishes to express his experiences in more flexible and more mature phraseology. He cannot be content with the simple seriated sentences of the THREE YEAR OLD; he wants command of conjunctions, adverbs and expletives. So he uses them with creditable (and incidentally amusing) bravery:—*You see, You know what, I guess, maybe, really, not even, enormous, only, suppose that, still, now see, and everything.* He is adept at picking up phrases from his linguistic culture, such as "You'll never guess in a hundred years." His use of numbers is experimental rather than critical: "There were 77 people there." He "exaggerates" because he is practicing words. But sometimes (parents beware) he reports quite faithfully what happened at home, not sparing family disagreements:— "Mother is careless with money."

Really (!), the FOUR YEAR OLD is very versatile. What can he not do? He can be quiet, noisy, calm, assertive, cozy, imperious, suggestible, independent, social, athletic, artistic, literal, fanciful, cooperative, indifferent, inquisitive, forthright, prolix, humorous, dogmatic, silly, competitive.

He is in a "growthsome" stage, particularly with respect to interpersonal relations and social communication. This is a period of acquisition, of rapid acculturation. At THREE YEARS the child had consolidated earlier gains and was in relatively stable focus; at FOUR he is moving on to another consolidation; for he comes into focus again at FIVE YEARS. It is not strange, therefore, that the FOUR YEAR OLD tends to go out of bounds, notably in the field of speech; but fundamentally he is striving (through his growth impulses) to identify himself with his culture, and to comprehend its intricacies. He is more firmly based than appears on the surface.

Sometimes almost consciously he is trying to grow up. He is interested in becoming FIVE YEARS OLD; he talks about it. He does not, of course, have a concrete comprehension of a year as a unit of time; he is only beginning to understand that Wednesday comes after Tuesday. But he is unmistakably interested in the march of birthdays. Birthday parties are a favorite topic of conversation. To be invited by a FOUR YEAR OLD even months in advance, is a sign of social approval; to be expressly excluded denotes at least temporary disapprobation. Fragments and hints of tribal sociology appear in the group life of the FOUR YEAR OLDS when they foregather in the nursery. They organize themselves into groups of three or four; often with segregation of boys and girls. Commands are given, taboos set up. Lines are drawn sharply and intruders barred. This negative behavior, from a developmental standpoint has a decidedly positive significance. The in-group feeling is a step toward understanding the nature of a social group. There is no old man of the tribe. Mommy is the court of last resort and her authority is frequently cited:—"My Mommy told me to do that."

Social patterns are offset and in part defined by anti-social conduct. The FOUR YEAR OLD takes to calling people names: "You're a rat," "Naughty Lady." He becomes defiant: "I'm mad!" "I'll sock you!" Refusals previously expressed by "No!" are now stated with a vigorous "I won't!" His boastfulness reaches towering ego-centric heights. But all this bravado is not as drastic as appears on the surface. FOUR is feeling his powers and is trying them out. His inconsistencies are similar to the contrarinesses which he displayed as a younger child. Contrary extremes meet in the paradoxical logic of development. The cultural restraints of home and nursery help to keep the extremes within normal bounds.

Basically, the FOUR YEAR OLD is more interested in socialization than in resistance. He shows this in his great fondness for dressing up and acting like grown-ups. That is one more efficacious method of maturing. He does not only don an adult hat; but he indulges in long telephone conversations, which echo the exact inflections of the adult voice. The incessant *WHY?* is directed toward social as well as natural phenomena. The FOUR YEAR OLD takes a significant pleasure in listening to explanations. He also likes to make faces. This is still another method of identification with adults and of perfecting his skill in reading their facial expressions. He is reading into, talking into and acting into the complexities of his culture.

§2. BEHAVIOR DAY

THE FOUR YEAR OLD usually wakes up in a happy mood at about 7 o'clock or a little later. He likes to get up and to go to his parents' bedroom for greeting and conversation. He has lost the romping abandon of a year ago.

With due deference to the household proprieties, he dresses himself while his parents are dressing. He is able to do this without much assistance if his clothes have been laid out for him in advance on the floor or chair. He can complete the dressing with the exception of tying bows and buttoning back buttons.

He can amuse himself if necessary looking at books; back numbers of the Geographic Magazine are favorites. He may help set the breakfast table, but he usually takes his breakfast alone. Once or twice a week, the family may make a special occasion by having him join them at breakfast time.

If he is registered at a nursery school, he usually spends five or six mornings a week away from home. He likes to attend regularly but is not unduly worried if he arrives at school somewhat late.

At home, he plays by himself contentedly indoors for an hour or two at a time. He favors a dramatic combining type of play. He is fond of building blocks and imaginatively converts them into multifarious animate and inanimate objects to suit his dramatic fancies. If he is a boy he likes to play with string, tying the chairs and furniture in intricate but to him meaningful mazes.

After indoor play he enjoys going out into the near neighborhood for a visit or an errand. He responds best if he has occasional supervision at critical points at the beginning and at the termination of an experience. He asks permission to go; he comes back to report. Although he now has a degree of self-reliance, the household does well to keep tabs on him!

He lunches at noon alone or with a younger sibling if he is fortunate enough to have one. His appetite is on the rise. He eats neatly and adeptly, but again he needs an occasional cultural prod and incentive.

He toilets himself after luncheon. His regular bowel movement may come at this time. He attends to himself.

At about 1 o'clock he is ready for a play nap of an hour or two. He relaxes more readily than hitherto, reclines on the bed, looks at books, plays quietly. He may or he may not go to sleep, but he has acquired a rather accurate sense of time. He seems to know when the official nap period is over, and reports to that effect with clock-like regularity.

Even if he has attended nursery school in the morning, he craves company during the afternoon hours from 3 to 5 o'clock. He wishes either to visit at a friend's house or to have a friend come to his house. He generally prefers children of his own maturity with whom he engages in gross motor and dramatic play. Two make good company, three a crowd which releases a tendency to vocal quarrelsomeness.

At about half past five he is ready for supper. He feels proud to have graduated to the kitchen where he eats his supper contentedly alone. He is able to amuse himself until it is time for a session of play with his father. He likes to be read to; he likes to build block structures with his father. He prefers the gramophone to the radio. (For interesting maturity reasons, the radio does not come strongly into the sphere of the child's interest until the age of 5 years.)

The evening bath comes at about 7 o'clock. He may be able to take it alone with the usual incidental cues, though he still needs a minimum of direction.

Although he is relatively self-sufficient, he may want to take his teddy bear to bed with him for dramatized conversation. He likes to have the light on for a short period, but when his parents return for a good-night greeting, he goes off to sleep without protest.

SLEEP

Night

Going to bed is now relatively easy and by 4½ years of age the child may even ask to go to bed. He enjoys hearing stories before he starts for bed. He knows that the hour of 7 o'clock is time for bed, and he can read that particular time on the clock. He responds better to the fact that the clock says it is time to go to bed than that his mother or father says it is bedtime. He may even respond more promptly if an alarm clock is set to go off at bedtime.

A few children not only need a going to bed time, but also a putting out the light time. Without this extra fifteen to thirty minutes to settle down in their beds with the light on, they may be very demanding. The child likes to look at books or to color at this time. His teddy bear, or a whole family of teddy bears (mother, father and baby), are often his favorite bedtime companions. He wants to undress and dress them and treat them like real persons. He often wants to put them under the covers and puts the covers very carefully under their chins. A goodnight kiss for the parent and a long strong hug means that the child is ready for sleep. He now falls asleep rather quickly.

The 4 year old usually awakens by himself if he needs to be toileted during the night. A few children are able to go to the bathroom by themselves, but they usually tell the mother first. They may need only verbal help, and the most difficult part of this procedure is usually getting back into bed. Sometimes verbal suggestion is not quite enough and the mother may need to get up and help the child back into bed. By 5 years he is ready to carry through the entire process without the parent's help.

There is much less wakefulness caused by dreaming at four than there was at 3½ years; but by 4½, the child may again have a period of dreaming about animals, especially about wolves. He may be especially sensitive to any light stimuli coming into the room and therefore may need to have his bed in a dark corner. If the child is afraid of the dark, a light on in the hall is often sufficient to allay his fears.

The 4 year old wakes around 7 to 7:30 A.M. He is now able to put on his bathrobe and slippers if they have been laid out for him, to close the window, to go to the bathroom, and to play in his room until it is time to go to his parents' room. When he goes into his parents' room he often likes to be read to or to look at books until it is time to get dressed. He finds it especially easy to make these shifts if there are whistles which blow, or church bells which punctuate these hours.

[Children who wake up at night and have difficulty getting back to sleep may respond to stories about other children who used to wake up at night but who no longer do so.

The 4 year old is now ready to sleep in a big bed. This change from his crib to a big bed can be helpfully utilized in planning for needed improvements in sleeping patterns.]

Nap

A very small proportion of children nap at this age. They will occasionally take a nap preparatory to staying up late in the evening. This is in marked contrast to the 2 to 3 year old child who if he is told what is going to happen after his nap will become so excited that he will be unable to sleep.

The 4 year old enjoys a play nap from 1 to 3 P.M. He may spend the first half hour or hour on his bed looking at books, and then spend the second hour out of bed. He may no longer need his door tied, goes to the bathroom if necessary, and frankly enjoys this time alone in his room.

Often these hours are very creative ones as long as the child has the proper media to work with. He needs to be alone, to have the pressure of other influences removed, that he may utilize his past stores of knowledge and ability. His inner time clock now seems to be more in tune with the time of the clock on the wall for he senses when it is 3 o'clock and asks if it is time to come out.

EATING

Appetite—The 4 year old appetite is still only fair, but by 4½ it is good to very good, with no special meal leading another. The child drinks his milk well and rapidly.
Refusals and Preferences—There is some tendency to demand repetition. The 4 year old either goes on food jags or food strikes,

which usually drop out by 4½ years, when the appetite is keener.
Self-Help—The 4 year old is beginning to help plan his meal and also to help prepare it. He enjoys helping to set the family table even though he may not come to it for more than two or three breakfasts a week, which is all that many children can handle. A few children, however, show marked improvement in their eating if they come to the family table at this age. Most 4 year olds have difficulty in not letting their talking interfere with their eating; they do not sit well through a meal, and may need to interrupt the meal (especially an evening meal) by going to the bathroom.

When they eat alone they are apt to dawdle but do not usually need to be fed. They often enjoy graduating from their own room to the kitchen at this age. Also such incentives as eating to get big, racing with the baby, finishing within a certain time allotment or working toward a dessert goal, may help. Planning ahead to ring a bell which announces the completion of one course and a desire for the next may be all the incentive the child needs. By 4½ years of age, he is picking up speed, is handling more meals with the family, can listen as well as talk, and is beginning to be sensitive to outside influences, such as those coming over the radio.

ELIMINATION

Bowel—One movement a day, either after breakfast or lunch, is a common 4 year old bowel pattern. Some children have more than one movement, and an irregular time of occurrence. Though some children still tell before they go, the majority tell only after they have gone because they need help in being wiped. A fair proportion take care of themselves completely. Though many are quite matter of fact about having a movement, others consider it a private matter which demands a closed bathroom door, and even a locked door at 4½ years of age.

Bladder—Children of this age are as a rule able to take full responsibility themselves and have only occasional accidents toward the latter part of the morning or afternoon when they have put off going to the toilet too long. In these periods of relapse they again need helpful suggestions and planning from the adult. They show less feeling for privacy than they do when they have a bowel movement, but are very much interested in watching other people in the bathroom, and show a marked interest in strange bathrooms. They are more apt to tell their mothers before they have to go to the bathroom in a strange house. This demand for the bathroom occurs not only because of real curiosity to see new bathrooms but also because the social situation creates tensions which seek outlet.

Very few children wet at night, at this age, or need to be picked up at 10 to 12 P.M. Some still awake to be toileted during the night and, as discussed under *Sleep,* they still need help, especially in getting back to bed.

BATH AND DRESSING

Bath—The bath is now an easy routine. The child is often capable of washing himself fairly well as long as the mother suggests part by part what he is to wash. He is apt to get marooned on one part of his body and keep washing it over and over again. He also lets out the water and washes out the tub on suggestion. He can now dry himself after a fashion. He is better able to make the necessary wrist and hand adjust-

ments to do a creditable job of brushing his teeth.

The bath may well be shifted to before supper, at 4½ years. The child takes his bath more quickly when he is less fatigued and may be looking forward to having his supper in bed. This shift in time is especially helpful in the winter months.

Dressing—The child of this age usually dresses and undresses himself with very little assistance, though he may need his clothes laid down on the floor, each garment separately oriented so that he can slip into it. He now can distinguish the front from the back, can lace his shoes, and some children can even button buttons. The child may for a while continue to dress parallel with the adult. When the novelty of this wears off he often dresses best in a room alone. A few children become angry if things go wrong, and refuse any adult help at this point. Planning ahead with them as to how to put on a garment successfully usually controls their temper outbursts. Almost all children, even though they dress themselves poorly, enjoy dressing up in adult clothes, especially in hats, gloves, shoes, belts and pocketbooks.

SELF-ACTIVITY

The 4 year old is ready for nursery school every day. He prefers to play with children rather than playing alone. Therefore his play alone is restricted to his play nap, and an evening play period. He now combines his toys into a dramatic setting. People are added to his block structures, cars are placed in front of houses. Girls and even boys may indulge in considerable household activity including the dressing and undressing of their dolls or teddies. Because of the speed of the 4 year old he is a rapid utilizer of material, especially of paper and crayons and paste. He more often prefers to draw free hand than to color picture books. He is quite happy as long as he is amply supplied, and each new bit of material seems to stimulate him to new abilities.

He is now beginning to admire his products and wants others to admire them, too. He likes to have his pictures put up on a bulletin board (the back of his door is often the place he chooses, with scotch tape taking the place of thumb tacks). He wants his block structures left up, and enjoys explaining their intricacies of building and of meaning. But his admiration is not prolonged. When he returns to his room he will not add to his block structure. He wants to do something "different." If his mother has warned him ahead of time he does not mind if she re-orders his room. He is more likely to resist if he is present during this re-ordering, though he at times accomplishes it by himself.

He now resists confinement in either his room or his yard unless it is self-imposed. He does not want his door to be tied. If he can understand the "rules" he may now be ready to stay in his room the allotted time, and to go back and forth to the bathroom as needed. Some children may have practiced being 4 years old when they were still only three, by having their door untied now and then when they asked for it. Although the majority of children need this type of restraint (having their door tied), there are some who do not need to have any more restraint than a closed door, and others who become resistant over a closed door which they themselves have not closed, and even panicky if their door is tied.

The 4 year old will manage to open his gate or climb over the fence if the gate is not left open. He now needs more scope, more rope, but he also needs the control of rules for he is apt to go out of bounds

so quickly. When he leaves his backyard and goes to the front, he will willingly announce this shift to his mother by ringing the door bell. He is now allowed to ride his tricycle alone on the sidewalk. He willingly accepts boundaries in both directions as long as they are enlarged at intervals.

The 4 year old enjoys this slow receiving of new privileges, the response to "rules." He becomes surfeited all too quickly if allowed complete freedom, or he becomes resentful if he is held too tightly. With the latter type of handling he is more apt to go too far out of bounds. It is the 4 year old who runs away from home.

SOCIALITY

The 4 year old is a truly social being. He not only wants to join a play group every morning, but he wants to be with playmates every afternoon. He now so definitely prefers children that he may even refuse to go to places where there are no children. He is in fact so busy with his play life, that his former interests in helping around the house have been largely given up. He will, however, run short errands outside of the home, which do not require the crossing of streets.

He is actually developing a strong sense of family and home. His mother or father are often quoted as authorities. Things that he sees away from home are compared with things at home, usually to the home's advantage. In fact, he is given to boasting. Methods of management previously used by the various members of his family is now enacted in his social dramatic play. Some families may well be startled by this re-enactment.

Though the 4 year old tends to be bossy and rather domineering, he does well either alone with one other child or in a supervised group. His play is smoother than that observed at 3 years because of the actual nature of the social dramatic play of house, doctor, etc., and because of his ability to shift rapidly. Although he plays well with one other child without supervision, he may find it difficult to adjust to a third child. The 4 year old still needs very watchful supervision. It is often at this age that too much is put upon the child. He may now be able to fight his own battles, and acquires more self control because he can handle a situation alone. But many of the battles need never have been fought if proper supervision had been given in the first place. This also applies to the years after four.

Excursions and times with father are highly prized by the 4 year old. Saturday and Sunday take on new meaning because father is home and special things are planned with him. The father realizes that these excursions are still best taken alone with the child, who can adjust to a larger group especially on a picnic, but who is most relaxed and happy when alone with one adult.

Because of the fuller social play of the 4 year old, his imaginary playmates do not figure as importantly in his daily life as they did earlier. He may still use his imaginary playmate as an excuse for doing things he wants to do or for not doing things he dislikes to do. Some children continue to pretend they are animals, but imaginative play is usually closer to the realm of likelihood with the child pretending to be a doctor, grocer, or engineer. Imaginative play is now more related to group than to solitary play.

[During periods of stress, music, books or cooking may prove to be helpful in organizing the child's behavior.

In planning ahead with the child it is as important to prepare him for a meeting with another child as for a meeting with an adult.]

§3. CULTURAL AND CREATIVE ACTIVITIES

BOOKS

1. Much more control in listening to stories in larger groups over longer periods.
2. High interest in words, creating stories with silly language and play on words.
3. Enjoyment of nonsense rhymes, as in Edward Lear's, "Nonsense ABC."
4. High interest in poetry, especially rhyming.
5. Delight in the humorous in stories, as in "Junket is Nice."
6. Enjoys exaggeration, as in "Millions of Cats."
7. Interest in alphabet books as "The Jingling ABC's."
8. Interest in stories telling the function and growth of things, as "Mike Mulligan and his Steam Shovel" and "Tim Tadpole and the Great Bullfrog."

9. Particularly enjoys information books answering his "Why?" about everything in the environment.

10. Awakening interest in religious books as "The Christ Child."

MUSIC

1. Increase in voice control with more approximation to correct pitch and rhythm.

2. A few can sing entire songs correctly.

3. More responsive in group singing.

4. Enjoys taking turns at singing alone.

5. Can play simple singing games.

6. High interest in dramatizing songs.

7. Creates songs during play—often teases others on a variation of the minor third.

8. Likes to experiment with instruments, especially combinations of notes on piano.

9. Enjoys identifying melodies.

10. Increased spontaneity in rhythms—likes to demonstrate different ways of interpreting music.

PAINTING

1. Holds brush in adult manner.

2. May work with precision for a long time on one painting.

3. Active imagination with shifting of ideas as he paints.

4. Increase in verbal accompaniment explaining pictures.

5. Makes designs and crude letters.

6. Draws objects with few details.

7. Little size or space relationship—details most important to child are drawn largest.

8. Letters, people, etc. may be drawn horizontally, lying down.

9. Enjoys filling in outlines of objects he has drawn, frequently making them lose any representative character as interpreted by the adult.

10. Beginning of self-criticism.

11. Products have personal value to the child—he wants to take them home.

FINGER PAINTING

1. Continued experimentation with fingers, hands and arms in rhythmical manner.

2. Some representation and naming.

CLAY

1. Large masses of clay used.
2. Increase in representation and imagination.
3. Enjoys painting products.
4. Wants products saved.

BLOCKS

1. Cooperation in building in small groups.
2. Extensive complicated structures combining many shapes of blocks in symmetrical manner.
3. Combines furniture and other equipment with structures, for dramatic play.
4. Enjoyment of finished product and frequently objects to demolishing it.
5. Little carry-over of interest to following day if structure is left standing.

POSSESSIONS

1. Beginning to possess his special contemporaries.
2. Showing off and bragging about possessions to others is common. "Mine's bigger than yours."
3. Is more apt to share possessions with special friends than with others.
4. Shows off new clothes.
5. Strong feeling for teddy-bear. Treats him as a real person, talking to him as a companion and confidant.
6. Proud of big possessions, such as a large bed, about which he can boast.
7. Strong personal feeling for own products made in school; wants to take them home.
8. This is an age of barter and swapping of possessions.
9. May know what a penny will buy and may save pennies to buy more expensive objects. Objects to parting with money.
10. Will help feed and care for pets under parents' direction but not at all dependable about this.

HOLIDAYS AND FESTIVALS

1. Birthdays—Presents are important and he may have asked for special ones beforehand. "Holds birthdays over" others and talks about next birthday party and whom he will invite and whom he will exclude, all during the year.
2. Christmas—There is a real interest in the story of Jesus, which is talked

about and dramatized. Child asks for specific toys for Christmas and talks about them long after Christmas, bragging about size and amount of presents.

3. Valentine's Day—Likes making Valentines to send to others. Has some idea that they are a token of friendship. Great interest in the number received.

4. Easter—Still believes in the Easter Bunny and talks about things Easter Bunny brought him. Still no conception of the meaning of Easter.

5. Hallowe'en—Enjoys Jack O'Lantern and likes to help make his own and take it out in the evening.

6. Thanksgiving—Beginning to have some feeling for the meaning of this holiday. Interested in the story of the Pilgrims.

7. Religion—May sit through a small part of the church service, especially music, but should not be expected to remain through the entire service. Enjoys Sunday School and may say prayers, which he may elaborate from the original. Marked interest in death, heaven, etc. Begins questioning as to the source of things: who made the sun, moon, world. The common answer, "God," either settles the topic without his finding out what he wanted to know, or may lead to the asking of ludicrous questions about God.

EXCURSIONS

1. Excursions are now a good outlet for out-of-bounds behavior. The child enjoys running ahead of the adult but will wait at crossings.

2. Interested in all kinds of transportation and enjoys talking about trips on a train. Not only likes to look at things but is interested in how they work.

3. Can go on a short excursion by himself if it doesn't involve crossing the street.

4. Enjoys nature trips.

5. Interested in planning and carrying out picnics and trips to the beach.

6. Continuing interest in the excursions enjoyed at three.

§4. NURSERY BEHAVIOR

THE FOUR YEAR OLD enters school with less exuberance than the three year old, and is more interested in his companions and older children along the way. He may greet the teacher with "good morning" at her initiation, but his conversation is soon directed to his companions. He joins a small group and proceeds to undress while he entertains his friends with a long recital of experiences, often introduced with "You know what?" This ability to combine dressing and talking is a marked developmental advance over three years of age when he either talked or worked, and is typical of all routines. In fact FOUR is such a conversationalist that he would accomplish little if he had not acquired the ability to combine talking and acting. His tempo has increased considerably since he was three years of age, and he is capable of undressing quite speedily. He generally waits until his particular friend has undressed, then races into the nursery to play with him.

The guidance teacher has materials such as crayons, clay, and wood ready for the children as they enter. FOUR is quite capable of following his own devices and improvising his own activities when he enters the nursery. But the experience of the guidance teacher has taught her that it is well for her to have materials placed suggestively at the outset of the morning. The child often enjoys taking over some activity that the teacher has started, and he continues in an organized manner.

If several members of the group color with crayons they soon begin to chatter, with more or less social reference. After an interval the group spontaneously dissolves. The children may go off in pairs seeking a new activity, or the boys and girls may segregate in separate groups. This sequence of coherent activity followed by dissemination is illustrated in the following stenotype record of conversation and activity:

9:22   Tim goes to large blocks and begins building an extensive house. Sally approaches and watches him. Tim says, "This is my house. You can't come in."

9:23   Sally, unperturbed, gets two chairs and places them in the middle of the house. Tim again says, "You can't come in!" Sally smiles and says, "Could I be the mother?" Tim says, "I'll be the grandmother." Sally: "No, Tims have to be daddies." Sally continues to carry furniture into the house.

9:25   Karl approaches and looks over the domestic scene. Tim to Karl:

[238]

"You can't come in!" Sally to Karl: "Would you like to be the other daddy? Sometimes daddies have rocking chairs."

9:26 Karl: "I brought something to you," handing Sally a block. Sally accepting the block, "All right, but we don't need something in our house." Karl: "This is for when you're ready."

9:27 Karl bringing in more blocks and stacking them in the corner, says to Tim and Sally, "It's time for your breakfast. Hey, you have to have your breakfast. Some sandwiches, some milk and some more milk," handing blocks to them. Karl pretends to eat and says, "This is my soup." Tim and Sally chant with him, "This is my soup." Then, "This is my milk," "This is my paint."

9:28 Elizabeth approaches and is greeted by, "You can't come in," from all three, chanting. Teacher suggests that Elizabeth might be the cook, and the others agree. Elizabeth, however, gets a chair and says, "Hey, we need two chairs for two mummies, don't we?"

9:29 Penny and Marjorie take their crayon pictures to their cubbies. Penny, "I'm going to take my picture home." Marjorie: "I'm going to take mine home too and show it to my mummy."

9:30 Marjorie and Penny run up to the doll corner and start playing with the dolls, carriage, gloves and pocketbook, while Bill, Don and Tony begin building a bridge with large hollow blocks and boards.

9:31 Penny: "Let's play you're sick and I'm the nurse." Marjorie gets in the doll's bed and is covered up by Penny. She takes Marjorie's mouth temperature with a clothes pin and says, "Your temperature is six, eight, you'd better stay in bed."

9:32 Marjorie tries to get up and Penny pushes her down saying, "No, you can't get up. It isn't time to get up." Penny calls to Karl, "Hey, Doctor, we have a sick baby. Me and you." Karl runs up to the doll corner saying, "It's awful cold out today, isn't it? She better have her supper, she'll be shrivelling up in bed. Tell her what I said."

9:33 Penny: "She doesn't want her supper." Karl attempts to feed Marjorie, who resists. She then says, "Go way. I won't invite you to my party." Penny: "But you'll invite me, won't you?" Marjorie: "Penny and Sally and me are coming to my party."

9:34 Karl, undisturbed, changes the subject, picking up blocks. "Let's play these are our skates." All three begin skating, and others join them. Bill, Don and Tony have made a large bridge structure and are adding smaller blocks on top for chimney, coal and decoration. These blocks are brought by Dick and Jimmy, riding on large trains. Each rides under the bridge chanting, "Coal car," then deposits his load.

9:36   Bill: "No more coal," trying to take train away from Dick. Dick: "I'm going to be finished in ten minutes." He rides away and bumps into Jimmy's train, saying, "A wreck!"

9:37   Bill laughs hilariously then rides noisily across the room saying, "Bang, bang, bang, bing-a-bing. Bing-a-bang-a-bang." Dicks falls off and says, "I had another wreck for my engine, Mr. Engineer."

The chanting and in-group activity illustrates the tendency to tribal social behavior referred to in the age level characterization. Incidentally, the foregoing account also illustrates the harmless, transient developmental nature of this taboo behavior.

In order to forestall still another wreck, the guidance teacher of a lively 4 year old group would at once seize the opportunity to divert this liveliness into related, defined channels. She casually suggests that the engineers might like to deliver mail and gives them some postcards. This stimulates the idea of a post office for the reception of the mail and the bridge is soon turned into a post office, with a window, chute, and loading platform. The smaller blocks are readily dramatized into bags of mail. Postcards are put into action and soon slide down the chute. Presently the whole corner becomes a hive of activity, delivering mail, scribbling messages, loading the mail cars, selling stamps, licking stamps. Soon some of the mail is delivered to the group of girls who are occupying the domestic doll corner. This will lead them by way of response, to send replies to the mail received and they will be making journeys to the post office window. In this way two separate groups come into interaction in the course of the morning.

The 4 year olds are very responsive to verbal direction and it takes only a word from the guidance teacher to remind them that toileting time has come. They go to the bathroom in small groups and waiting turns manage the toileting with speed and with practically no help. Then they are ready for the mid-morning lunch.

For the 4 year old the mid-morning lunch begins to take on a social quality. He assists in setting the table and each seeks out a companion at whose side he would prefer to sit. The guidance teacher starts the topic of conversation which the children continue readily on their own impetus. If the teacher fails to set the flow of conversation, it is likely to start and continue along silly lines which the 4 year old is prone to affect for his own amusement and that of others.

Rest follows. The rest behavior is not much different from that of the 3 year old. The teacher reads a story to them or they listen to a quiet piece of music.

When it is time to go out of doors, they are able to dress themselves quite quickly. The patterns of outdoor activity are comparable to those under the nursery roof. There is somewhat less necessity for the initial direction of this activity. It may take the form of romping or gross motor climbing on the jungle gym, but the 4 year old is such an inveterate dramatizer that even the gym may be converted into a hospital, the leaves and the sands being put to therapeutic uses.

The 4 year old is likely to go out of bounds and a conducted excursion is a controlled way of satisfying this tendency. He enjoys going on these excursions in a group. He is amenable if his tendency to go out of bounds is given some rein. The guidance teacher, for example, may suggest that the group may run unattended to a distant tree, but she will ask them to wait for her at that tree. The typical 4 year old conforms to such a limitation. The tendency to dramatization is irrepressible and while he is on the excursion he may don a dress-up hat and carry a shopping bag.

On his return to the nursery he is apt to seek out the colored drawings which engaged his attention in the morning and take them home. His mother is greeted with a "Guess what, Mommie" and a flow of conversation which tells about the day's happenings.

§5. NURSERY TECHNIQUES

PHYSICAL ENVIRONMENT

Environmental restrictions such as doors or gates being closed do not hold the child of four years. He responds better to verbal restrictions. The boundaries of a playground can be set verbally, "as far as the tree," "as far as the gate"; or he can be told to run ahead to the corner and then wait. A feeling of responsibility can be built up in the child. He seems to enjoy knowing what the "rules" are, and will even enforce a rule such as that only four children may go into the playhouse. *Four* may forget rules when led on by gang spirit.

At this age particularly it is desirable to provide nature experiences, such as an opportunity to plant a garden or to care for (caged) animals.

For this age, a large room can be effectively divided by means of rugs or some similar device which set up boundaries without creating actual barriers. This holds the children informally to a sphere of interest.

ADJUSTMENT

When adjustment difficulties occur at this age they do not result from difficulty at leaving the mother, but rather from the child's preferring other interests outside of school and not wanting to come to school. Preferred activities may be playing at home with older children or indulging in some particular passion of the moment.

ROUTINES

Routines such as washing, toileting, dressing and undressing, mid-morning lunch and rest go even more smoothly and independently at *Four* than at *Three*. Toileting needs more supervision at this age than formerly because of the extremes of curiosity and reticence displayed by certain children. Some need teacher help in maintaining their privacy from others who are displaying extreme curiosity and silliness in regard to these functions. Mid-morning rest is readily accepted and for the first ten to fifteen minutes may not need to be accompanied by music or reading. The final few minutes are held up better by such accompaniments.

TRANSITIONS

At the earlier ages transitions from one activity to another are best accomplished by shifting the group to another room. At this age, however, the same type of transition may be accomplished within the room by adding new materials.

[242]

Since this is an age of "tricks," new acquirements such as hopping or skipping can be utilized as activators. For example, "Let's skip to the bathroom."

Their awakening interest in numbers can also be used as an activating technique, as "One for the money, two for the show." "Can you get your suit off before I count ten?" The clock can also be used in connection with their recognition of numbers, as "When the big hand gets on twelve you may get up."

TEACHER

The need for adult techniques is dropping out considerably at *Four*. What previously was in the realm of adult techniques is now being used spontaneously by the children and is under voluntary control rather than being superimposed.

It is easier to think preventively with the four year old by planning situations in advance with him so that he can work them out himself. Since he is characterized by extremes of activity and inhibition, handling him should be a mixture of holding to the dotted line and yet giving him the freedom he needs.

The teacher needs to have ready several different constructive materials such as wood that can be hammered and sawed, blocks, clay, paint, from which the child may choose. Often the appearance of free choice can be given if the teacher is working on a material, thereby arousing the child's interest. Sometimes the same material can be utilized in different ways on succeeding days and plans for this may be made in advance. However, *Four* thrives on variety, and the teacher should provide for this in her planning. With this planning, activities are kept on a higher level than if the morning starts with free play.

The activity of four year olds will often deteriorate through silliness if not controlled. The adult can anticipate when play is about to deteriorate and can bring in interesting new ideas or can elaborate the play. A teacher of four year olds needs a wealth of information at her finger-tips.

Isolation is an even more effective measure at four than at three because of the stronger social drive. The child accepts isolation best if he is given something to do and is made to feel that he is being isolated because he is tired or not getting on well with the other children rather than because he is being bad. Since this technique is resorted to when the child's behavior is already very low, any suggestion of a punishing attitude would only lower his behavior. Being isolated from the group or having a privilege removed is serious enough without further punishment. The child organizes his behavior if told that he may look at a book and that the teacher will be back in a few minutes.

VERBAL

Key words used by the adult at 3½ such as "different," "surprise," "guess," etc., are now in the verbal equipment of the child and are used spontaneously, but he still responds to adult use of them. His use of language is so adequate that he does not respond as markedly to key words as earlier. The general *manner* of handling is more important, i.e., he responds to a man-to-man attitude in conversation and management.

The 4 year old demands reasons with "Why?" and "How?" and frequently can be answered by turning a question back to him.

Whispering is still as effective as at 3½.

Children of this age enjoy new, different, and big words. They use and like exaggeration: "As high as the sky," "In a hundred years." This exaggeration often leads to the telling of "tall stories" which should be enjoyed momentarily by adult and child and then should be brought into perspective by pointing out the difference between real and imaginary.

HUMOR

Their silly language such as "mitsy, witsy, bitsy" can be enjoyed by both adults and children through reading such nursery rhymes as Edward Lear's "Nonsense ABC." If it becomes excessive it can often be controlled by writing down and reading back to the child what he has said.

OTHER CHILDREN

The tendency (so marked at 42 months) of two children to exclude any third from their activity, persists and can be handled by the techniques already suggested.

Tattling and disputes are fairly frequent and should be handled according to the demands of the situation or of the specific child involved. For instance, the teacher may ask, "What do you want me to do about it?", or, "You can take care of that yourself." More serious reports should be commended with some such remark as, "I'm glad you told me that the glass is broken. We can pick up the pieces so that no one will get hurt."

Four year olds enjoy taking on a teacher or mother role in helping to initiate a shy child into group activities. They may do this spontaneously, whereas at three the suggestion usually came from the teacher.

[244]

GROUP ACTIVITY

Four is cooperative and imaginative. He can work for a goal such as making a building for dramatic play, instead of merely getting enjoyment from construction as the three-year-old does.

Four year olds are more apt to choose group play and to play better in groups than do younger children. Their activities need more careful planning. As discussed under teacher techniques, the teacher can advantageously give children an initial start by doing something that they can take over and elaborate, or by giving verbal suggestions for play. If they do not have this initial start, their own spontaneous play often begins at a much lower level with racing around and pushing each other. Usually both indoor and outdoor play need this initial start which carries the play through in a constructive manner even though they shift from their original occupation.

20

FIVE AND THE YEARS
AFTER FIVE

§1. FIVE YEAR OLDNESS

FIVE IS IN FOCUS; FOUR is fluid. Ask FOUR "What scratches?" He will tell you promptly enough "A cat"; but then he will go on to relate about his dog and the dog will chase the cat, and one mental association will chase another. FIVE, on the other hand, with business-like preciseness will say, "A cat," and let it go at that. Comparatively FIVE is curt, clear, and complete. This typifies the maturity difference between the two ages, subject, of course, to individuality differences which come to increased definition at the focal age of FIVE.

This typical maturity difference is, also, revealed in spontaneous drawings. FOUR draws fortuitously and opportunistically; his crude representations metamorphose from turtle to truck to elephant. FIVE has a defined idea in mind *before* and not after he executes his drawing. His outlines recognizably represent his intent. He is capable of self-criticism.

[246]

"I want to draw a horse, but I don't know how." Blithe FOUR would never be fazed by a horse!

Similarly, FIVE likes to finish what he has started, whether in play or in an assigned task. FOUR is much less sensitive to incompleteness and inconclusiveness. FOUR rambles. FIVE knows how to stop.

The greater decisiveness of FIVE shows itself in a marked diminution of dawdling. His motor coordinations, his images, his sentences, even his personal-social relations,—his concept of himself, his adjustments to home, school, and community are better defined. Accordingly he gives us an impression of self-containedness. He is not in conflict with himself or with his environment. In emergencies he is capable of calmness, because of the smooth operation of his action system. He does not get lost; he knows his address. If his parents cannot find him, *they* must be lost! This imperturbability accounts for the remarkable stamina which the FIVE YEAR OLD so often shows under privation and hardship.

For the time being he is something of a finished product; he has climbed the developmental ladder and reached a gently sloping plateau. Many thousands of years ago, the race in the evolution of its nervous system reached a level of culture which required a similar degree of maturity. FIVE seems reminiscent of that ancient by-gone stage. He is "a little man" ready to enter the kindergarten vestibule of a culture which today is so vastly complex that it will take him twenty years more to become a true adult. Meanwhile he is too advanced for the "babyish" three and four year olds of the ordinary nursery school. No wonder he is called a forgotten man when he has graduated from nursery school and has no place to go.

He is ripe for enlarged community experience. Home is not quite enough. He is already well domesticated; indeed almost self-dependent in the every-day personal duties of washing, dressing, eating, toilet, sleep, errands, and simple household tasks. He wants to go to school; he is anxious to be on time when he does go; he glows with pride when he brings home his drawings and handicraft for admiration. He is proud of his possessions, proud of his clothes. He has a vivid sense of his own identity. He likes to come back to home-base, but he displays a pleasing seriousness of purpose and interest in the wide-wide-world. He is beginning to distinguish between truth and falsehood. All told, he presents a remarkable equilibrium of qualities and patterns,—of self-sufficiency and sociality; of self-reliance and cultural conformance; of serenity and seriousness; of carefulness and conclusiveness; of politeness and insouciance; of friendliness and self-containedness. If not a super-man he is at least a super-infant! He is an advanced version of delightful three year oldness.

Now that we have done him full justice, something should be said of his limitations. Despite his excellent general postural control, he lacks many refinements in manual coordination. He has difficulty in making oblique strokes. He is not ready for penmanship. Also for sensory-motor reasons he is not ready for the mechanics of reading. He speaks without infantile articulation, but his conversation reveals great unsophistication.

Here is a transcript of the back and forth talk of a group of bright FIVE YEAR OLDS seated about a table, contentedly drawing birds and bird houses. The theme had been suggested by one of the children and was promptly taken up by all the others. Nora was filling in the sky with bold blue:

Nora: "Pretty soon it will be as long as the whole sky."

Michael: "Pretty soon it will be as long as the whole world." "The cars would come along and get the pictures all dirtied up." "And all the boats would be rubbish boats."

Lester (Talking about his picture): "He's got some mail on his wing—this is the birdie's pole so he can climb down if he wants to."

Ned: "He could fly."

Lester: "But he wants to climb down. He's a different kind."

Michael: "Maybe he's a baby one."

Lester: "Yes, he's a baby one."

All still at table drawing birds and bird houses.

Lester: "My little baby bird flew out the attic window."

Michael: "Maybe he had a flying lesson." "This is going to be a purple one—I always think of everything and I never have time to finish it. This tree is so baby that it only has one branch and no leaves at all. A little baby one."

Lester: "Mine hasn't got no leaves on it."

Nora: "We've got some blue birds in our back yard."

Lester: "I know it."

Michael: "We've got a lot of tulips—they've got buds and they're about to burst. This morning, when I was in bed, I heard them burst."

Ned: "You can't hear buds burst."

Michael: "But I heard them burst, because I have sharp ears."

Ned: "Sharp beer-bottles, you mean."

Michael: "No,—sharp ears."

The foregoing dialogue which occupied about ten minutes, justifies a little semantic analysis, for the clues it affords to the FIVE YEAR mind. The thinking is very concrete; it never gets away from the solid realities of birds, bird houses, buds, audible bursts and sharp beer bottles. There are short upward flights of imagination, but they come back speedily to perch. Abstraction is very meager; it is almost limited to metaphor. A tree is a baby because both are small. There is a vague sense of smallness; but the tree is almost literally visualized as a baby. The bigness of the sky, the longness of the world are faintly conceived, but they are identified with the strokes of the crayon. Perhaps the most conceptual notion of all was contained in the word *lesson.*

In spite of all the naivetes there is a vein of serious auto-criticism in the conversations of the FIVE YEAR OLD. He is somewhat conscious of his ignorance and intellectual fallibilities. Yet he sets his own flying-lessons and makes frequent forays into the unknown. He naturally has great difficulties with problems of crime and war, but this does not deter him from tackling them:

Lester: "Will you play burglars with me? Who's going to steal from you, red-headed woodpecker?"

Michael: "Hey, Ned, when you said you were a red-headed woodpecker to a policeman, you have to be a red-headed woodpecker because you can't change your mind." "Lester, we'll put the policeman and the birds in our jail, won't we?"

Patricia: "We're going to arrest them too."

Michael: "We'll get our swords—we'll catch the other people O.K.? But it will be a tough job to get those, too."

Lester: "No, it's very easy to get those."

Ned: "We'll tie them all up."

Nora: "You say, 'They can kill you'."

Michael: "My daddy's got a real gun at home."

Lester: "Michael, I have a little plan to tell you. Let's all be soldiers."

Nora: "I'm a soldier and they can't catch me."

Ned: "I'm a bat."

Nora: "No, bats are bad."

Ned: "What do they do?"

Nora: "I don't know, but they're bad."

Ned: "Well, I'll be an eagle then."

When a group of Five Year Old kindergarten children recently came back to the familiar haunts of a nursery school which they had attended a year before, they took over, initiated their own enterprises, called each other by name, and managed their social groupings without conflict or confusion. No intervention or assistance from the guidance teachers was necessary,—another indication of the well balanced organization of the FIVE YEAR OLD action system.

One of our nursery alumni was once asked what college he expected to attend when grown. "Are you going to Yale?" Answer: "No, I have already gone there."

If the period of second dentition did not lie just ahead, we might consider the FIVE YEAR OLD a somewhat finished product. He presents in his person a rather complete diagram of his constitutional make-up. The dynamic traits of his durable individuality are evident. He is the father of the man he is to be.

§2. CHILDHOOD AND ADOLESCENCE

FIVE IS A NODAL AGE because it marks a transition from milk teeth to permanent molars. Physically and psychologically there are many suggestions that the child is reaching a stage of maturity which in a transfigured way corresponds to a very remote stage of life in the history of the race.

Even today under primitive conditions an American Indian child at five or six years of age may show an advanced degree of maturity in relation to his culture. The recent autobiography of a Hopi Indian carries a revealing paragraph as follows:

"By the time I was six, therefore, I had learned to find my way about the mesa and to avoid graves, shrines, and harmful plants, to size up people, and to watch out for witches. . . . My hair was clipped just above my eyes, but left long in back and tied in a knot at the nape of my neck. . . . I wore silver earrings, a missionary shirt or one made of a flour sack, and was always bare-legged, except for a blanket in cold weather. When no Whites were present, I went naked. I slept out on the housetop in summer and sometimes in the kiva with other boys in winter. I could help plant and weed, went out herding with my father, and was a kiva trader. I owned a dog and a cat, a small bow made by my father, and a few good arrows. Sometimes I carried stolen matches tucked in the hem of my shirt collar. I could ride a tame burro, kill a kangaroo rat, and catch small birds, but I could not make fire with a drill and I was not a good runner like the other fellows. . . . But I had made a name for myself by healing people; and I had almost stopped running after my mother for her milk." (By permission from *Sun Chief,* Edited by Leo W. Simmons, Yale University Press, New Haven, 1942, pp. 460.)

G. Stanley Hall, with a mixture of poetry and science, detected at the age of five years "the ripple marks of an ancient pubic beach now lifted high above the tides of a receding shore-line as human infancy has been prolonged." Such interpretations must not be dismissed too lightly; because the child and the race are in sober fact keys to each other, in the same sense that embryology and evolution are reciprocal keys. The human mind as an action system is a structure. In the individual it grows: in the race it evolved. Against an evolutionary background of hundreds of thousands of years we gain a better appreciation of the task of acculturation which confronts the modern child and youth in the long journey from the nursery school through college. There are three laps to this journey: The Primary School Years; Preadolescence; and, Adolescence.

Primary School Years: The five year old goes to kindergarten. The six year old (with his sixth year molar) is ready for the primary school. Years six, seven, and eight correspond to the first, second, and third "grades" during which society somewhat formally introduces the American child to the tools and elements of its culture,—reading, writing, and arithmetic, and the rudiments of literature, art, and science.

These are years of increasing sophistication. The child has "a world" to learn. We have noted that the five year old is amazingly ignorant of many simple facts of life; amazingly so because we take them too much for granted. The young child has to acquire these facts by the gradual process of growth. He must assimilate the meanings of countless words and phrases. Otherwise he would remain too unsophisticated in a world which makes almost excessive use of words. At age Five, a ball is something to play with. It is envisaged in terms of use. By age Eight, the child can describe a ball in terms of shape, size, texture, and color. Skill, and pride in skill, come at 8. Thus he enriches his old words with elaborating associations; his vocabulary expands to some 3,000 words. Many of these words are adjectives and adverbs, because he is learning not only the names of things and of actions; but also the names of qualities, of differences, and likenesses.

The child perceives opposites and analogies. He detects differences before he recognizes similarities. At six, he can tell us the difference between *wood* and *glass*; at eight he may be able to tell us in what way they are alike. His judgments are rather concrete, but they lay the foundation for abstractions and generalizations. At twelve, he is capable of defining abstract terms like *courage* and *charity*. There is no way of short-circuiting this concrete thinking of the primary school years. Growth proceeds by gradations. Creeping comes before walking; banging before poking; vertical strokes before oblique; concrete before abstract. The five year old can copy a triangle; yet it takes two years more before he can copy a diamond, even though a diamond geometrically is nothing more than two triangles with a common base.

The geometry of development takes time. The environment of the child and the corresponding organization of his nervous system are infinitely more detailed and complex than we are wont to suppose. The child does not absorb his culture through mere exposure to it; he has to achieve it through the slow but sure mechanisms of growth.

The primary school child therefore is essentially interested in the "here and now." To be sure he likes to dress up; he is fond of dramatics; he converts himself readily into a taxi-driver, a doctor, an Eskimo, a witch, or even the wind on which the witch rides or the clouds which obscure the moon. Nevertheless his mind is bound to the familiar. There is nothing miraculous about these flights of dramatic imagination. It is impossible to create an Eskimo out of the stuff that dreams are made of. The growing primary child is simply reorganizing and readapting his familiar mental materials (behavior patterns) to penetrate further into his immediate environment and into foreign territory. Like a coral he grows by accretion, like a tree he grows by branching out. Rich experience with things, with handicrafts and group activities, is necessary for the sound development of words, ideas and attitudes.

Preadolescent Years: The years between eight and the teens constitute a somewhat distinctive period in the cycle of human development. Once again, but at a higher and more sophisticated level the child appears to be virtually a finished product. He certainly assumes that he is one and he organizes a life of his own outside of home and school, displaying a significant independence of adult influence. Instead of imitating his elders in naive kindergarten style, he becomes a pre-adult in his own right and takes on adult prerogatives. In the primary years he amassed enough information and stock in trade to make this new self-reliant role possible. Sometimes he evinces a positive lack of interest in chronological adults.

He becomes a small business man. He sets up a lemonade stand. He organizes clubs and gangs; he competes with his fellows, not infrequently resorting to combat, to derision and to feuds and the formation of secret plots. Often the antagonism is inter-sexual. Boys and girls segregate, form separate groups and launch separate enterprises. The leadership arrangements and hierarchies, the jealous defense of possessions and preempted rights, all are reminiscent of primitive tribal modes of behavior, greatly altered, of course, by the folkways of modern culture. Viewed in the deep perspective of the pre-history of the race, such behavior patterns are suggestive of a culminating stage of human evolution when perhaps in a warm climate, "the young of our species once shifted for themselves independently of further parental aid."

These genetic analogies must not be carried too far. There have been transformations in the cycle of child development since the time of Neanderthal man who lived 500,000 years ago. Life is not as tame as it used to be in those ancient days. The modern pre-adolescent thrills with a much larger number and wider range of adventures through movies, radio, talkies, printed page and funnies. Technological gadgets galore, electricity, the ether and engines implement his imagination.

He is beginning to think in terms of physical cause and effect. As a school beginner he scarcely comprehended how a bicycle operates, could not explain the functions of the sprockets, the pedals and the chain. As a pre-adolescent he acquires a deepening insight into mechanisms and machines. He soars out of the here and now. He also has a more self-detached interest in foreign peoples and distant lands. He gains an intellectual grasp of the more fundamental human relationships. He understands the moral philosophy of most of Aesop's fables.

Nevertheless he is far from a finished product. He has not yet come into the organic inheritance of the most recent acquisitions of the racial nervous system. These await the teens.

The Adolescent Years: Although the brain had achieved almost its adult weight by the age of eight, adolescence brings profound changes in the finer organization of the central nervous system and in the biochemical controls of the organism. With these changes come equally profound alterations of behavior patterns and of emotional attitudes. The basic individuality of the child remains constant enough even during the transitions of youth, but his outlook upon himself and upon his culture undergoes far-reaching reorientations. The higher human traits now make their appearance. They were acquired late in the history of the race; they naturally arrive late in the developmental cycle of the individual. Sometimes they appear with the same sudden spurt which marks his physical growth.

[255]

Only a short time ago he was indifferent to adults. Now he becomes sensitive to their opinions, to the proprieties of their behavior; he seeks out among them models to imitate; heroes to worship. He also seeks out heroes of history and of biography. He is now extremely sensitized to cultural influences; the old self-containedness gives way to a search for ideals. Literature, art, religion take on new meanings and may create new confusions in his thinking. He has a strangely novel interest in abstract ideas. He pursues them in order to find himself.

In this pursuit he goes back and forth from one idea to another, in the hither and thither manner of the two and a half year old. The preschool child has similar difficulties in getting his bearings, making distinctions, balancing opposites. It is well to recall that the preschool difficulties represented a temporary developmental stage. In the adolescent we witness comparable growth problems and growth mechanisms.

He is subject to the limitations of immaturity, even though he is now peculiarly susceptible to the influence of other personalities and is striving as never before to come into rapport with the culture of his day. Environmental forces perhaps operate with increased power; but neither he nor his parents in their zeal can transcend the basic laws of development. He continues to grow essentially in the same manner in which he grew as he advanced from the toddling stage of two years, through the paradoxical stage of two and a half, and the consolidating stage of three. When he was a nursery school child we ventured to compare him with an adolescent. Now that he is an adolescent we compare him retrospectively with what he was as a preschool child.

The comparison is just, because the most basic laws of development are universal and uniform. Every individual has at once a unique pattern of growth, and a generic pattern which is characteristic of the species to which he belongs. To understand him both as an individual and as a representative of the species, we need more insight into the biological mechanisms of development. Society has not taken sufficient account of these mechanisms, and has concentrated too exclusively on superimposed acculturation. Too little is scientifically established as to the developmental morphology of the child's mind in the important years after five. We need new knowledge to define the sequences and the content of guidance and educational measures. The developmental interpretations which have proved to be so necessary in the psychological care of the first five years of life apply with equal force to later childhood and youth. For such reasons there are far reaching psychological and cultural implications in the nursery school as a guidance center.

21

THE NURSERY SCHOOL AS A GUIDANCE CENTER

§1. CULTURAL ORIGINS OF THE NURSERY SCHOOL

COMPLEX SOCIAL FORCES brought the nursery school into being; yet more complex forces are shaping its organization today. The industrial revolution, economic poverty, war, urbanization, the decline of the birth rate, the progressive education movement, and the growth of the life sciences have all played a role in the establishment of day nurseries, kindergartens, preschools and child care centers.

The nursery school is therefore both a symptom and a product of cultural forces. Pestalozzi feared the portent of these forces, and addressed an appeal to the British public in 1818, to inaugurate a system whereby mankind might receive its preschool education from mothers at home. Exactly a century later, however, the British Parliament passed an act authorizing the establishment of nursery schools for children over two and under five years of age, "whose attendance at such a school is necessary for their healthy physical and mental development." The early British nursery schools were protective social measures to overcome the dire effects of economic poverty. They are historically continuous with the present day preschool nurseries and shelters which have had their inception in the yet more tragic circumstances of the second world war.

The nursery school in America had its beginnings in 1914 as an educational movement. Some of the initial impulse came from Britain. By 1930 about 300 nursery schools had been established, a few of them as integral parts of the public school system. The motivation behind all these schools was primarily educational. But with the onset of the world depression, economic forces began to operate; 3,000 nursery school units serving 65,000 needy children were organized in the thirties, under the Federal Emergency Education Program. Some 1,500 of these nursery schools were continued under the Works Projects Administration, with 150,000 families enrolled in a Family Life Education Program.

The industrial employment of women in the second world war is creating acute conditions reminiscent of the beginnings of the industrial revolution, when Robert Owen established infant schools in New Lanark, Scotland and also in New Harmony, Indiana. Once more the welfare of the preschool child is jeopardized. Once more emergency nursery schools and child care centers are being hastily formed to meet another exigency. All of which suggests that the nursery school is a byproduct of economic conditions as well as a device for cultural control.

This brief glimpse into historical backgrounds emphasizes the potential significance of the nursery school as a guidance center. In its most characteristic form, the nursery school in the United States of America is not a corrective reaction to faulty economic conditions, but is a cultural instrument for strengthening the normal functions of a normal home. In many instances nursery schools in America are associated with research centers devoted to the scientific study of child development and of educational psychology. Such schools, frequently, are attended by children

[259]

from prosperous homes. They are part of a broad, diversified movement which is at once sociological, scientific and educational in its inceptions.

The day nursery has come under similar social influences. Although it may still provide day-time care for children from less favored homes, it considers itself responsible for the mental as well as physical welfare of its charges. Its program is becoming educational, with guidance services added. A democratic culture strives for freedom from educational want as well as freedom from material want.

The American nursery school may also be interpreted as a reaction to the psychological needs of the urban child, beset by the restrictions of modern life. In his fundamental constitution this child is not much different from the rural child of Pestalozzi's day; but the cultural complex in which he lives has both shrunken and expanded to an almost fantastic degree,—shrunken by the confines of an apartment without brother or sister, at one extreme; expanded by the space defying technologies of radio, motion picture, telephone, automobile and airplane. These paradoxical extremes have complicated the whole process by which infant and child are inducted into the culture of today.

In more olden times, the world of nature and of human relations expanded in a rather orderly manner, keeping pace with the maturity of the child. The home was large, the membership of the family numerous, and usually there was yet another child to be born. Some one was always near to look after the preschool child and to take him by graduated stages into his widening world, step by step, as his demands gradually increased. There was free space around his home,—a field, a meadow, an orchard. There were animals in barn, pen, coop and pasture. Some of these fellow creatures were young like himself. He could feast his eyes on them, touch them, sometimes even embrace them.

Time has played a transforming trick with this environment. The apartment child, and to some extent even the suburban child of today, has been greatly deprived of his former companions, human and infrahuman. Domestic living space has contracted to the dimensions of a few rooms, a porch, a yard; perhaps to a single room, with one or two windows.

To be sure there are compensating elaborations of his surroundings,—sidewalk, street, traffic lights, automobile, filling station, etc., etc. But the et cetera does not usually include ample intimate contact with growing life, with other children, with a variety of adults.

The preschool child cannot articulate this sense of deprivation. Yet he has an irrepressible interest in human beings, and even at 18 months he will exclaim, "Baby!" with ecstatic delight when he sees another child. He was not meant to live alone!

When a perceptive mother witnesses such spontaneous interest in other children, she begins to wonder how she can restore some of the human relations which were a natural part of family life in a simpler culture. She wonders whether her young child should not be playing with other children similarly circumstanced. Should she plan for more frequent visits with the neighbor; should she organize a play group? Besides, she has some concrete questions about what is the best thing to do for her child, questions she would like to ask of someone who knows. Even though she represents a "well-to-do" family, she has a feeling that in some way her child is under-privileged, so far as his full psychological development is concerned.

This is the cultural setting of the nursery school problem. And even when a nursery school is available there is the further question, "Should I, after all, send my child to a nursery school?" Life refuses to be simple in our modern culture.

§2. SHOULD MY CHILD GO TO NURSERY SCHOOL?

THE QUESTION IS CATEGORICAL. For the sake of brevity and pointea-ness we shall reply by a categorical *Yes* or *No*. But it is also an "if" ques-tion. Therefore we list below some of the qualifications which determine the answer. Most of the *No* qualifications are remediable; but it is well to realize that the whole question of nursery school attendance hinges not on an absolute antithesis, but on a complex set of factors which are largely cultural and which differ with particular homes and particular communities. The practices of different nursery schools vary tremendously with the personalities of the directing guidance teachers and their insight into child development. Finally, of course, the decision will be rested on the welfare of the child, his total welfare including his home-life. Different possibilities must be considered on their relative merits; and an affirmative decision to enter the child should be made in a tentative way if there are serious doubts.

Many parents have adopted the informal (and sometimes too casual) device of a neighborhood preschool play group. Under the direction of a competent leader such a group may function very successfully. It may increase the amount of outdoor life for the children. The proximity to home, the avoidance of transportation difficulties, the similarity to home conditions may all work advantageously. If mothers alone and in rotation are utilized to conduct the group, the arrangement, however, may produce difficulties. Some of the distinctive advantages of a nursery unit with its change of scene and "strange" personnel are lost. Safeguards against infection are overlooked or neglected. Individualized guidance advice as to individual children is not available. Poorly supervised nursery groups conducted by persons with inadequate training must naturally be looked upon with suspicion.

A guidance type of nursery is in a position to render individualized counsel, and to take heed of the special needs of individual children. Such a nursery supplements the home-life of the child and at the same time strengthens it, without attempting to instill "habits" for the purpose of a specific carry-over into the home. The parents are regarded as the fundamental guidance agents for the child. In a democracy it is for them to make the decision which will determine whether *their* child shall attend a nursery unit, and to determine also what kind of unit it will be. Intelligent parent opinion, in the long run, will also determine what kind of guidance nurseries will be evolved in the culture of tomorrow.

With this introduction we return to our categorical question, and to the conditional answers which follow. Some of the qualifying considerations will receive special discussion in later sections of this chapter.

Should my child go to nursery school?

YES, IF,—

The child is an only child and has few companions.

The child lives in an apartment and lacks adequate space, materials and opportunity for play, especially gross motor play.

He is three years or more of age. Or, if he is younger, if the school makes special provision for the understanding handling of younger children.

The child's initial adjustment difficulties can be readily overcome by good techniques.

The child's individuality can be respected so that he does not have to conform to standards which are alien to him at the time (such as sociability).

The school is willing to make special arrangements (reduced attendance, vacations, etc.) to prevent overstimulation.

Health safeguards and practices are carefully set up to reduce infections, including common colds.

The mother needs help with her child or if she feels that she does not really understand him.

The mother wishes to supplement the ordinary home-life with a social situation which will expand the child's experience and increase his social adaptivity.

The mother realizes that she really needs brief but regular vacations from constant care of her child.

NO, IF,—

He is under three years of age and the school is not organized to give discriminating, special attention to the younger ages.

His adjustment difficulties prove too great, or if his general health is not adequate.

He turns out to be over-stimulated or too fatigued by the group and attendance seems to be harming him rather than benefiting him. (Thus even a child who seems to be adjusting well may not be benefiting by the experience as shown by a radical change for the worse in his home behavior.)

[263]

The school is not willing to acknowledge and respect individual differences. If it is going to insist on uniform and similar participation from all children. If it places excess emphasis on "cooperation."

The strain of transportation is going to be too fatiguing for the child.

§3. INDIVIDUALIZED ATTENDANCE

IDEALLY, attendance in the nursery school should depend upon the maturity of the child, the disposition and interest of the child, and the motives of the parents. The amount and times of attendance should so far as practicable be adjusted to the optimal needs of the individual child. Just as in the field of feeding the best practice is now based to some degree on self-demand and self-regulation, so attendance in the nursery school should when possible be determined by similar considerations. By self-demand we here mean the capacity of the child to enjoy and to benefit by attendance. Experience has shown that with increasing age the amount of advantageous attendance tends to increase, both with respect to the length of the session and the number of times per week. The following gradient is suggestive of the age differences which have shown themselves in our guidance nursery, attended chiefly by children from homes of favorable socio-economic status.

18 months .... 1 hour once a week
21 months .... 2 hours twice a week
24 months .... 2 to 2½ hours three times a week
30 and 36 months .... 2½ hours three times a week

42 months .... 2½ hours five times a week
4 to 5 years .... Single session kindergarten
6 years .... Primary school, preferably single session

Such a sliding scale leads away from the traditional policy of daily, full-time attendance to graduated and spaced attendance. Sessions are adjusted both with regard to their length and to the number per week. Just as an individual child may need a gradual induction into the nursery school, so the demands of attendance over a period of years are tempered to his maturity.

The maturity differences are reflected in the time sense of the child at different ages. The 18 month old child naturally has very little sense of time. He does not differentiate the days of the week, but associates attendance at school with some ritual at home. The 2 year old may ask, "School today?" The 3 year old may remember the specific days that he attends school and may ask, "What day is today?" The 4 year old child, if he is in attendance daily, reserves his questions for Saturdays and Sundays.

It is acknowledged that adjusted attendance is not suitable for all conditions, but on the basis of the Yale experience with homes of favorable socio-economic status we can report that parents and children alike approve the arrangement. Both father and mother feel less pushed, because of the free days when the preparations for the nursery school give way to contact with the child at home. The mother can reserve certain experiences like taking the child to market for the home days. The child on his part enjoys the days at home, which gain in their status because of the contrasted school experience. Children are unquestionably less fatigued by part-time attendance and this may be related to our findings that colds and exposure to infectious diseases are reduced as a result. School is considered more of a treat and parents are more apt to have time to stay and observe.

Spaced attendance is in harmony with the needs of the developmental processes in the preschool child. Development during the preschool years proceeds rapidly, and the child uses the non-attendance days unconsciously for assimilating and consolidating experiences which he has previously enjoyed. The argument that there is no carry-over from day to day falls short of the facts of growth, because the mental life of the child is not advanced by habit conditioning so much as by growth organization. According to old doctrines of habituation, training depends upon regularity and frequency of experience. The growth process, however, is such that brief and occasional experiences may have considerable transforming effect upon the individual. For this reason even a restricted nursery school attendance exerts a potent influence upon certain children.

Flexible and part-time arrangements also make it possible for the 18 month old child and the 21 month old child to attend, whereas more rigid practice would postpone the nursery school experience, since it would be unwise to send a child less than 2 years old to a nursery school which made heavier demands. (All good rules are subject to exceptions. There is a type of child who at certain ages, especially at 3 to 4 years, clings to nursery school and perseverates in his behavior. He demands daily attendance for a period and in certain cases his welfare is favored for a time by making such attendance possible.)

It would be easy to point out how a rigid, unvarying schedule of attendance inflicts hardships on certain homes and certain children. Flexible attendance avoids these hardships. It takes account of seasonal variations in the child and of many variations that are a natural accompaniment of the irregularities of growth. Some children of limited stamina benefit from nursery school attendance in the spring and fall when their morale is higher than in the winter months. Difficulties of transportation also introduce complications. Such variations are entitled to respect in the pre-school years. The argument that rigid daily attendance has disciplinary values for the young child is scarcely defensible.

The policy of individualized attendance has a pervasive effect upon the attitude of the parents toward the nursery school, and of the guidance teacher toward the children. It makes the teacher alert to symptoms of poor adjustment to the group to which the child belongs. She will recognize symptoms which suggest the necessity of a vacation period for the child who is not adjusting satisfactorily. The failure to adjust to the group is indicated by aggressiveness and other maladjusted behavior. The teacher and parents can then take counsel together and recognize the advisability of interrupting the regular attendance for a week or more.

If the child shows evidence of over-stimulation in his home behavior the parents feel free to so report to the nursery.

From this summary it is clear that the policy of regulated attendance is designed to protect all concerned, particularly the child. Even the tuition arrangements are kept flexible so that no one feels undue pressure. Tuition charges may be based on the entire term or on actual days of attendance. The latter arrangement favors better cooperation on the part of the mother. She is less likely to send her child to school when he is fatigued or below par.

One of the chief virtues of the method of regulated attendance is that it enables the parents to take a more rational view of the assets and liabilities of their child. The nursery school is a social test for the parents as well as the child and it foreshadows similar tests which will come when the child is confronted with entrance requirements and adjustment to elementary school, high school, and college. The principle of regulated attendance is solely designed to offer the utmost protection for the child. If he is unequal to the social test of constant attendance, this fact should be frankly and cheerfully faced.

§4. INITIAL ADJUSTMENT OF CHILD TO NURSERY SCHOOL

THE INDUCTION of a child into a nursery group is comparable to a weaning process. The mother must surrender her child and the child must surrender, at least temporarily, his mother. How shall it be done?

The manner in which the initiation is accomplished is an index of the quality of the nursery school concerned, although some allowance must be made for circumstances which under given conditions are insuperable. A busy and understaffed day nursery can scarcely undertake all the gentle adjustments which are necessary to overcome the resistance of an intransigent newcomer. So he is left to cry it out. A formal goodbye to mother may even be insisted on, which only makes matters worse. Sometimes, it is said that he may as well cry it out. "He has to learn someday: he might just as well cry it out now!" the argument runs.

A guidance nursery would consider such a drastic initiation as possibly traumatic and certainly undesirable. Primitive cultures which inflict severe endurance tests as part of the initiation rites at puberty have more justification for their procedures. But the nursery school candidate is no stripling; he is more comparable to a shorn lamb, who in a modern culture is entitled to a treatment tempered to his immaturity. A guidance nursery never entirely overlooks the principle of self-demand, even when an overinsistent parent is *determined* that her child *shall* join the nursery group,—before he is ready!

In actual practice most of the difficulties which may arise at the beginning of the nursery school experience are preventable and so manageable as to be relatively benign. Here as so often happens in the field of child care the problem does not exist until it is created,—by an overzealous mother, an overdetermined father or a misguided teacher. So we would begin with this simple proposition: If your child shows an unmistakable and genuine resistance to joining a nursery group, do not force the issue.

The great majority of children adjust readily to nursery school life after the age of 2 years and almost all do so after the age of 3 years. Our experience in the guidance nursery at Yale has shown that the initial adjustments are greatly facilitated if the induction includes the following steps:

a) A preliminary conference with the parent to talk "the whole thing" over, with candid questions by both parties. b) An introductory report which outlines the developmental history of the child and informally summarizes his present behavior day. c) A developmental examination of the child designed chiefly to determine personality characteristics and his maturity in various fields of behavior. d) An observation of the child's first reactions to the nursery with the mother present or nearby. e) An interview which supplements the developmental examination and which explores the child's previous career and behavior characteristics, with more emphasis on the positive traits than on behavior problems and difficulties. f) Graduated detachment from the mother and progressive introduction into the group.

On the entrance day the child again meets the guidance teacher, whose name the mother has already taken pains to communicate to him. He therefore, has already had an opportunity to practice her name. This is an important feature of the transition because we expect the child to transfer some of his home attitudes to the new person. He is re-introduced to his teacher, whom he first met on the day of the developmental examination. She takes him over and makes him feel at home in the nursery, graduating the new experience to his shyness or his courage, as the case may be. (Introduction to the rest or nap period may be deferred a week or a month in certain cases, in the interests of optimal adjustment.) Then the mother absents herself with or without a goodbye, again depending upon the child's hardihood.

Following conservative procedure, the child is next introduced to a small group of children of similar age, and is protected from any undue aggressors in this group. The first day is of some importance to a child of nursery school age. It warrants the utmost skill and consideration, because much ground is gained if the child's confidence is secured on this first day. Part of this skill may consist in a partial withdrawal of the teacher, who sees the advantage of letting the child make his own adjustment or of having another child assist in the adjustment. A child who is already familiar with the nursery environment becomes a very valuable liaison officer, but such a child must be carefully chosen.

The stages in induction vary not only with the individual temperaments of the children, but with their maturity, somewhat as follows:

18 months: The child adjusts through things.

24 months: Adjusts through an adult (teacher). Teacher must be with him all the time. It is generally better at this age for the mother to go out quietly without saying goodbye.

30 months: The child may need a formal goodbye from his mother.

36 months: Acceptance is the rule at this age. Minor resistances are readily overcome indirectly through simple ruses.

These precautions and gradients show that the objective uppermost in the mind of the guidance teacher is not a smoothly running nursery for its own sake but optimal protection and guidance of each individual child.

If in spite of these precautions the child shows some difficulty in achieving easy adjustment, some simple measures such as the following may be used:

a) Mother may be permitted to stay in the nursery for part or all of the session.

b) The child may be verbally assured that his mother will wait in the next room for him.

c) He may be told that she has gone out but will come back.

d) Mother may leave her scarf or some personal belonging which will be a tangible token of her certain return and will, because of its tangibility, give him an anchorage.

e) Separation from mother is made at home instead of at the nursery and the child is brought to the nursery by a relative or neighbor, coming, perhaps, also under the herd influence of fellow travellers.

(These expedients are not recommended as clever devices. They are to be regarded as legitimate techniques which are designed to meet and to support the child's psychology.)

Usually the developmental examination, the interview and incidental observation on the day of the examination will suffice to determine whether the child is ready for the nursery school socialization. He may not seem ready to the examiner and to the nursery teacher, but the parent hopes that he will adjust. If the contra-indication is not too strong, the question can be put to a test on two or three occasions. If on these trials he does not show a definite trend toward accepting the nursery group, the parent should be frankly told that it is desirable to postpone the nursery experience. These failures in initial adjustment may be due to temporary causes including a high degree of emotional dependence upon the mother or home surroundings. These difficulties are most likely to occur around 2 years of age, and they usually disappear by 3 years even in the emotionally dependent child. The 3 year old typically has the hardihood to accept the nursery school.

Amusingly enough the problem sometimes goes into reverse: the child resists leaving the nursery school, even when he is called for by his mother! It is the transition which troubles the child and not his mother. He is torn between two alternatives, both of which have values for him. The reader will not be surprised to learn that this paradoxical two-way response occurs most frequently at about 30 months, suggesting that maturity factors are responsible. Individual peculiarities, however, may also make the child reluctant to go.

Other things equal, the most promising type of initial adjustment is one which proceeds by easy and progressive stages. Children who accept the first day unreservedly and uncritically are the very children who later may lapse into resistance and withdrawal. The more stably organized child adjusts by slow degrees. A little initial shyness, some wariness in his attitudes are to be welcomed, because they suggest that the child is exercising his intelligence and is sizing up the situation in order to become thoroughly acquainted with it.

The concepts of guidance and of growth alone can solve confusions or perplexities which may arise in the initial adjustment of the child in his first formal induction into a cultural institution.

§5. CHARACTERISTICS OF A SKILLED GUIDANCE-TEACHER

WE USE the hyphenated term guidance-teacher to emphasize the fact that the workers in the field of early child development should think of the child in terms of guidance rather than of instruction or training. The most fundamental qualification of a guidance-teacher is her philosophy, her point of view. If the motives which have led her to select work with preschool children are sentimental, she is likely to be too undiscriminating. If she is actuated by a desire to reform, she will attempt too much and again too undiscriminatingly. Work with preschool children demands a combination of wholesome warm interest in children, and a professional realism with respect to their psychology. This combination heightens both the interest and the social significance of the work of the guidance-teacher. A developmental point of view is the most important feature of her vocational equipment.

At the risk of delineating a paragon we shall outline below the various personal qualifications and skills which make up the professional equipment of a capable guidance-teacher. The human problems with which she works are so diversified and demanding that she needs above all to be alert, adjustable and well-balanced. A sense of humor naturally helps, because it is very easy to magnify the seriousness of numerous problems which prove to be transitory, because they yield to the benevolent correctives of sheer growth. On the other hand she has to have an expert eye for inconspicuous behavior signs and symptoms which superficially lack seriousness but which are very important in the welfare of the child. This expert perceptiveness for the small but significant does not depend upon sporadic intuition, but rather on experience fortified by some theoretical knowledge. With the increase of scientific information it is becoming more and more clear that the guidance-teacher needs an intellectual insight into development as a process. She can get that insight only through study. She needs to study the infant as well as the nursery school child, because through the infant she may get a more transparent view of the meaning of maturation and maturity.

The following personnel specifications and comments are tabulated under three headings: Physical Traits and Demeanor; Mental Traits; Emotional Traits and Attitudes.

Desirable Physical Traits and Demeanor.
Good health, especially freedom from colds.
Good functional vision; peripheral vision particularly useful. Overchannelized focal vision, disadvantageous.
Acute hearing which helps the teacher to identify and pick up the

language cues of a child. With practice and aptitude the teacher is able to echo back these cues,—a very useful accomplishment.

A pleasing voice capable of inflections, modulations and intonations. Excessive inflections startle and confuse the child. An overly calm and matter of fact voice fails to activate him. An effective, flexible voice registers in between.

Nimbleness and manual facility are an asset. A guidance-teacher may have to steady a child on the jungle gym with one arm and keep her attention and the other arm poised for marginal emergencies.

Calm motor demeanor with moderate tempo of movements. A hyperactive person experiences real difficulty in suiting her tempo to the children. Leisureliness of tempo combined with quickness of reaction and alertness of attention constitute the ideal combination.

Desirable Mental Traits.

A fundamental knowledge of the theory and principles of child development. A familiarity with the individual characteristics of each child, interpreted so far as possible in terms of growth rather than in terms of success and failure. (Nor should the teacher credit herself too much personally for improvements in child behavior which may well have a developmental basis.)

A realistic interpretation of the child in terms of himself and his past behavior rather than in terms of other children in the group. A discriminating recognition of individual differences, suiting activities and guidance to these individual differences.

General sensory alertness to environmental conditions: temperature, drafts, doors open or shut, toys under foot, potential physical hazards, marginal awareness of room conditions. (For example, home toys that need to be returned with the child when he leaves, etc.)

Desirable Emotional Traits and Attitudes.

General flexibility which avoids excessive fixation on any adopted schedule or program. Capacity to revise plans on short notice on the basis of cues detected in the children. A knack for capitalizing such cues and incorporating them into the children's play.

A sensitivity for the psychological moment. This implies emotional flexibility and the absence of a disciplinary or dominating attitude. A skillful teacher exercises patience and refrains from unnecessarily touching children, waits for the right moment and then steps in with opportune, directive guidance. This perceptiveness for opportuneness demands a knowledge of maturity levels as well as individual personalities.

An ability to anticipate and prevent difficulties. Being able to foresee what a child is going to do next.

A warm, outgoing interest in young children; a respect for them as individuals. This fundamental quality is most significantly expressed not in the feelings but in the response of the children to her. By this criterion some teachers are better qualified to work with the older age groups, some with the younger age groups.

A lack of self-consciousness and ability to lose herself in the group. Also a good balance of give and take. An ability to accept criticism and suggestions from parents and to take cues from children.

An ability to take responsibility and yet to get children to take responsibility, at the same time not expecting too much of a child.

A double sense of humor,—it must be double because the guidance-teacher should have an appreciation of the sense of humor of the children themselves as well as a personal sense of humor which enables her to preserve a sense of proportion in the field of social values. There are amusing age differences in the humor sense at various preschool maturity levels. It is a saving sense for the guidance-teacher because it increases the pliancy of her own mental life under the varied conditions of a guidance nursery.

Although no one person is likely to embody in full measure all of the foregoing desirable traits, the listing of the traits may serve a purpose in estimating the aptitudes of nursery school workers at different levels of responsibility. The temperamental characteristics are of supreme importance. The most elaborate academic training cannot compensate for the absence of fundamental aptitudes which depend upon personality attitudes and emotional and motor demeanors. Underlying motives also count heavily. Society should place a premium upon the recognition and conserving of these temperamental qualities for the benefit of infants and young children.

High school girls should not be sought as caretakers simply for utilitarian reasons. A personnel effort should be made to select girls (and perhaps boys) on the basis of natural aptitude, who can contribute important services in the daytime care of infants and young children. Our home economics courses have already indicated that there are rich human resources of this kind only poorly conserved.

It is also well known that among the colored race there are many women who are supremely endowed with an almost unique emotional equipment which makes their services ideal for infants and young children. There can be little doubt that in the period of post-war reconstruction our culture will place a heavier premium upon the human qualities which are so significantly typified in the devoted and skilled guidance-teacher of preschool children.

§6. GUIDANCE ADAPTATIONS TO INDIVIDUAL AND GROUP DIFFERENCES

THE SKILL of the guidance-teacher depends not only upon her knowledge of child development and of methodology. With experience, reinforced by a background of theory, she becomes familiar with the basic maturity differences of various age groups. She comes to understand what the 2 year old is like and she interprets the individual differences in relation to maturity traits. She realizes that there is no precise science of personality types; but she recognizes a certain characteristicness which distinguishes from each other: the watcher, the dependent child, the

[275]

sensitive child, the perseverators and shifters, the dominator, the submissive, the imaginative, the realistic. Furthermore, groups as well as individuals have behavioral individuality.

There is, first of all, the *watcher* who enters all new situations slowly and only after a long period of sitting unobtrusively on the sidelines absorbing every detail of play. He enters into the group much faster if his personality is respected and if he is allowed to wait until he is ready. He will frequently enter the group sooner if approached through a socially gracious child rather than through an adult, for this child is seldom dependent upon adults. He frequently will begin to play by himself on the periphery of the room with an ever watchful eye on the rest of the group. He may report the events of the day in elaborate detail at home, and may re-enact much of the school's proceedings when alone in his own familiar surroundings. This child usually does not enjoy being the center of attention; he is a follower rather than a leader.

The *dependent* child is more difficult to manage. The watcher merely needs a friendly smile or occasional word, or a proffer of play materials placed near him. One soon knows when he is ready to join other children. The dependent child, however, is a persistent appendage to the teacher, trailing her every step, holding her hand, or making demands upon her by crying and whining. To give the over-dependent child the attention that he needs and still supervise the rest of the group adequately is a difficult problem for the guidance-teacher. An assistant may be needed. It is important that the teacher to whom the dependent child is attached should remain with him throughout the day.

Such dependence may last for days or months, but when it is finally broken, beware! The pendulum may swing full opposite. The hitherto clinging, quiet child becomes surprisingly aggressive, hitting and attacking other children whom he seemed to fear only a few days before. Even though he is no longer attached to the teacher, he demands considerable attention, for his social approaches are frequently annoying to other children. After swinging one or more times from dependence to aggression this kind of child generally strikes a mean and becomes an industrious, enjoyable member of the group.

The dependent child may be in the assertive phase when he enters school. He is aggressive in his first approaches, but in a few days subsides into dependency and tears.

The guidance-teacher needs to keep in mind that the dependent child is sensitive and incomplete and that he needs more protecting than do other children, even when he is on an even keel. Isolation, which may be an organizing experience for some children, is frequently a traumatic experience for the dependent child and may bring about deterioration of behavior. Putting him temporarily into a simpler situation (a group of younger children), or excluding him from his own age group, with an adult, not as a punishment but as a relief from group pressure, will often improve his behavior. Criticism is difficult for him to accept and should be given tactfully at an opportune moment.

There is also the *sensitive* child who adjusts slowly but steadily, and who forms the firm, reliable basis of the group. He demands little of the teacher's attention if he is made to feel comfortable in the group during the first few days of school. He soon loses his self-consciousness and be-comes engrossed in other children and in play materials. He has little difficulty in making transitions or performing routines. Frequently he proves helpful in adjusting other children to difficult situations. The guidance-teacher needs to protect this child from fatigue and overstimu-lation, for he appears more hardy than he actually is and does not protect himself as do the watcher and the dependent child. He fatigues rapidly at the end of the morning, but may not display the usual evidences of fatigue until his mother arrives. Irritability brought on by fatigue may increase after he reaches home and may even aggravate a cold.

Within each of these behavior types we find diverse characteristics. There are, for instance, the *high verbal,* and the *high action* children. In the high verbal child not only is language equipment advanced but also interest in language is keen, and the child responds readily to reasoning; while the high action child is gross-motor minded and is motivated by action images. The verbal child responds to a comment such as, "You need your sweater on because it is cold out in the yard," while the action child responds to, "After you put on your sweater, you may skip outdoors."

There are also the *perseverators* and the *shifters*. The perseverators may be either watchers or dependents. The watchers may play for as long as an hour with material placed near them, while the dependent children are apt to channelize their activity and play day after day with one kind of material such as trains; or they fix upon one special child. On the other hand, the children who are sensitive to the variety in their environment approach it gradually and often shift rapidly, sampling the entire gamut of materials in the room. If a toy is taken from such a child he finds something equally alluring, and waits his turn for a desired object, whereas the dependent child is often extremely impatient.

The guidance-teacher knows that during an adjustment period the play materials of the perseverator should be protected from the rest of the group until he has gained some social security. Marauders are redirected to other materials with the comment that, "Johnny *needs* that train"; and he actually does need it. When he acquires more self-confidence, he can begin to learn techniques of sharing, and he acquires these techniques faster because he is ready for them. The gradual approach used in so many other connections in nursery school has yet another use here.

Children may also be classified as *dominating* or *submissive*. In general, the watchers are apt to be the submissive children, the aggressive-dependent ones are frequently dominating, while the keenly aware, gradual-approach child may be a combination of both. In this last group are the children who have both the ability to direct group play and to take suggestions from others. They may be dominating with some children and submissive with others. The guidance-teacher needs to be aware of the relationship of one child to another, and to see that one child does not dominate another to the detriment of the submissive child. By skillful planning of activity, and arrangement of groups, all children can be given some chances to lead as well as to follow. The function of the guidance-teacher is to build up the submissive child and to temper the domineering into tolerance.

If the majority of children in the group are of the dominating type there will be many centers of interest and high activity, while a more submissive group will follow a leader and will constitute larger groups playing together with relative control.

Imaginative and *realistic* children may be distinguished. The most imaginative children are found in the aggressive-dependent group. It is they who have imaginary companions, elaborate fears, extensive play with little equipment (though they may demand much more equipment than other children). If they ask for materials that are not available they are generally satisfied when handed imaginary substitutes. The realist, on the other hand, is annoyed by any such play, has to have the real object, and calls each toy by its correct name. A cream-colored engine which an imaginative child calls "The Milkman" is always just an engine to the realist. One varies techniques with these two types of children, knowing that an imaginative suggestion will generally fall unheeded or be resisted by the realist.

The experienced guidance-teacher realizes that there is considerable variation not only from child to child, but also within a single child from day to day. The child who returns to school after an illness needs much more adult protection from fatigue than the same child when he is in excellent health, and his amount of school attendance should be adjusted accordingly. Knowing the individual characteristics of the children, the alert nursery school teacher detects behavior deviations which are indicative of incipient illnesses. Infection of others may be prevented by immediate isolation.

The teacher should also be aware of individual physiological rhythms in children. One child may have to urinate more frequently, rest longer, or eat more often than his companions.

This analysis could be extended further to types of children with nervous habits, children of special abilities, distinctive temperaments, etc. The experienced nursery teacher will empirically define her own classifications and methods of approach. She comes to know, for example, the techniques that work best with the watcher, the signs which indicate that he is ready for group contact, and the length of time that it will probably take before he is assimilated into the group play. This knowledge lends poise to her teaching. She does not feel uneasiness simply because he is unoccupied. On the other hand she is not content with mere classifications, leaving the child completely to his own resources. She uses her skill in approaching him indirectly through his major interests, sits beside him engaging him in casual conversation, and gives him some special attention to make him feel that he is a member of the group. Such subtle, casual approaches distinguish the skillful teacher.

Her skill, however, must not be expended upon the individual at the expense of the group. The group also needs finesse in management.

Groups vary in somewhat the same manner that individual children vary. Some groups are easily guided, others are consistently difficult. A group, not unlike an individual, may be relatively unsocial, tangled or disorganized for days on end, and then burst forth with a spurt of integration at a higher level. A three year group may begin the year in the fall with mildly social, constructive play which makes few demands upon the adult. However, by February this same group may become demanding, irritable, tense. A combination of causes may be operating such as growth factors, weather, lowered vitality. But the turbulence is temporary. In another month the group shows glimmers of four year old dramatic play, and even adopts some adult modes of interpersonal control.

The behavior of a group varies with its environment as well as its own personnel. The effects of constructive surroundings and limited materials soon show themselves. The conduct of a group also varies with changes of the adults in charge. One teacher may promote calm, creative behavior in the group while another may stimulate to excess activity. (However, the self-same teacher who is unsuccessful with two year olds, may show real ability with an older group.)

The behavior of the group is much influenced by the amount and kind

[280]

of preliminary planning by the teacher. A laissez-faire atmosphere does not foster integrated group behavior. The experienced teacher realizes that different kinds of plans are necessary not only for different age groups, but also for different groups of the same age, and for the same group on different days. She makes a provisional plan of procedure for each day but adapts it to the tempo and interests of the day. She sees that routines, such as toileting and mid-morning lunch, are carried out in the middle of the morning and that there is a proportionate balance of active and quiet play. She senses the point at which group play is beginning to deteriorate, and whether she should divert the activity. She tries to know when to intervene and when to remain an interested observer.

The truly clever guidance-teacher is skilled in watchful waiting. She herself is a watcher rather than a governor. She watches for behavior signs. She waits for her cues. She "steps in" not so much for the purpose of carrying out a preconceived plan of her own, but in order to give constructive and preventive direction to a tide of activity, in the child or in the group. Sensitive to individual differences, she is exercising a high order of skill when she is watching alertly; she is not relaxing, she is waiting for the optimal moment when a quiet well-timed stroke of guidance will yield the maximum developmental result.

§7. THE GUIDANCE FUNCTIONS OF A NURSERY UNIT

A NURSERY UNIT may aim at three related but distinguishable objectives. It may concern itself mainly with semi-custodial care of the children ("minding care," as it is called in England). It may conduct its work on a pre-kindergarten basis, for the avowed purpose of "training the children in good habits." Or, finally it may conceive its work in terms of guidance,—developmental guidance for the children, educational guidance for the parents. These two forms of guidance are inseparably interrelated and they are typical of the progressive nursery in the culture of today.

A sincere and systematic espousal of the concept of guidance inevitably affects the spirit and the very organization of a nursery unit. When guidance is made the central, controlling objective, the every-day work and methods of the nursery become individualized,—and humanized. The child is envisaged as a member of a family group,—his own true family and not the metaphorical family of the nursery group. The guidance-teacher does not set herself up as a substitute mother. She thinks of the nursery as a supplement to the child's home, designed to enrich his experience rather than to remake his household behavior. So conceived, the nursery becomes a cultural tool which is deliberately utilized to increase the developmental opportunities of the child on one hand; and to assist his parents to understand the nature and needs of his development.

But even these utilitarian functions should not be overemphasized. Why not also think of the nursery as a cultural boon which simply adds to the sum of human happiness? When society learns to use its vast wealth for the conservation of the most promising human traits, it will create conditions and contrivances for early child development, such as hitherto we have been too faint-hearted to invent.

Child guidance and parent guidance are inseparable concepts. In application they overlap to a significant degree. This volume has formulated in considerable detail the various "techniques" by means of which the guidance-teachers in a nursery assist and direct the growing behavior of preschool children. This may be called guidance by direct action.

The guidance-teacher, however, also reaches the developmental complex of a child indirectly through counsel and contacts with the parents. Then her "techniques" operate by direct action on the parent, but indirectly on the child. The term "techniques" is permissible if it is understood that some of the most valuable guidance is unpremeditated, incidental, informal and even accidental:—a suggestive question, a brief hint in connection with the morning greeting, even a facial expression in reaction to the behavior of the child or a fleeting conversation with the parent as she is about to make her departure. All such interchanges mount up in the course of a year and produce a cumulative and important quota of guidance. Indeed some of the most potent guidance is that which comes most naturally and spontaneously in the course of natural events.

However, there is a distinct place for scheduled guidance. This is formal in the sense that it is based upon fixed appointment and is directed to a survey of the assets and liabilities of both parents and child. A skilled guidance-teacher can undertake a responsible interview which is directed toward what might be called the normal problems of child development and parental care. In this sense all children are normal problem children because no child escapes the continuous problem of growing up. Even parents are still in the process of growth and surely in the process of attempting to understand the meaning of growth. Two or even more interviews a year, which explore the child's behavior and to a reasonable degree the parent-child relationship are an essential part of the program of a well-rounded guidance nursery.* These interviews are not undertaken in the presence of the child. They may include the father as well as the mother and sometimes a grandparent comes appropriately into the picture. Such interviews take into account the child's home behavior as well as the behavior at the nursery.

The guidance-teacher in this type of service functions as a liaison person between the child and the parent. She fully understands that the child's behavior at home may be at either a higher or a lower level than that at the nursery. There is no real equivalence between a nursery group and the family group. In fact the teacher-child relationship is simpler

---

* Some nursery schools make it a practice to render periodic reports of their young charges, dealing with such matters as attendance; motor coordination; moods; emotional security; crying; language; memory; cooperation; initiative; responsibility; music and art. When these reports are rendered in terms of the child's maturity they serve a descriptive purpose and may to some extent define guidance measures.

Even so, the reports may invite misunderstanding and misuse or may be filed away without any dynamic projection into the actual management of the child. The limitations of the reports accentuate the significance and the vitality of all guidance contacts which emerge in the life situations and are related immediately and concretely to these situations.

than the parent-child relationship. Furthermore the teacher approaches the child with a clean slate without the long association of turbulent periods and old patterns of behavior, and can induce new methods of responding with greater ease than can the mother. Also the teacher has a strong motivation factor in the social pressure of the child's contemporaries, which is usually lacking at home. Conversely, it should be kept in mind that some children do better at home with their mother than at school with the teacher. (The teacher makes only difficulties for herself if she allows herself to come into the role of a mother substitute.)

It is desirable for the parent and guidance-teacher to see eye to eye. One task of the guidance nursery is to strengthen the home situation. The initial parental interview is of special importance because it can take into account the significant events in the prior developmental history of the child. This type of guidance should not be dispensed on a prescription basis. It is fundamentally concerned with interpretation. The parent should not be encouraged to develop undue reliance upon the staff of the nursery. However, parents should be encouraged to report signs of illness or unusual behavior and particularly unusual trends of behavior which cause a legitimate doubt or worry. It may appear to the teacher that a child is adjusting adequately in school but in reality home behavior may show that he is being overstimulated to the extent that eating and sleeping are completely upset.

Many of these problems can be adequately met by telephone conversations after a solid background of mutual understanding has been built up between the parent and guidance-teacher. A fixed period set aside for telephone consultation helps to control this type of guidance and to make it more effective. Needless to say, the guidance-teacher should never attempt to go beyond her depth. She cannot be considered professionally skilled until she recognizes the limitations of her scope and is able to detect premonitory signs of difficulties which demand medical or clinical attention. She does not assume the role of a practitioner. She regards herself as an educational adviser.

There is another form of parent "guidance" which might be called

[284]

self-guidance. It is a kind of illumination which comes to parents as a result of their own thinking and their own observations of their own children and of other children. We have found that this type of observation is greatly reinforced by one-way-vision screen facilities such as are described in the Appendix.

This screen although transparent (in one direction) has the peculiar psychological effect of increasing the detachment of the observer from the thing observed. The simple intervention of the diaphanous barrier of the screen creates a new perspective, a wholesome shift toward psychological detachment and objectivity. Seeing is believing. The parent begins to see in a new light. This is an efficacious form of visual education and self-guidance. It reduces the necessity of verbal explanation and exhortation. We have talked less to parents since one-way screens were installed. One-way-vision increases the intimacy, the piquancy, and the objectivity of observation.

The one-way-vision screen has also proved useful in connection with the developmental examination of nursery school children at advancing ages. As already suggested, there are occasional developmental difficulties and behavior disorders which are serious enough to demand expert diagnosis and interpretation. The nursery unit may still render some service with these cases when they are not disturbing to the normal group. When such disturbance is produced the problem should be handled on a more restricted and individualized basis.

This will require a diagnostic examination in which developmental behavior tests are used to ascertain the maturity of the child's behavior and the shape of his behavior patterns. The formal, channelized character of such a diagnostic examination helps to expose the child's behavior equipment to the examiner. Now if the parent can take a station behind a one-way-vision screen and observe the whole course of the examination with its revealing release of behavior patterns,—the orientation of the parent to the problem may be definitely improved. Similar behavior examinations may be conducted at an educational level in the study of the characteristics of non-problem children. These examinations can also be observed by the parents to advantage through the one-way-vision screen. (Up to the age of 4 years we have found it advantageous to have the parent in the examination room with the child.)

Our modern culture is developing new attitudes with respect to mental examinations, child guidance and parent guidance. Parents are overcoming undue sensitiveness with regard to the behavior characteristics of their children. Modern mothers and fathers appreciate that a realistic attitude with respect to the mechanisms of psychological growth promotes a wholesome parent-child relationship. The nursery school as a guidance center thus serves a far reaching social function.

PART THREE

THE GUIDANCE OF GROWTH

22

A DEVELOPMENTAL PHILOSOPHY

EVERY CULTURE breeds its distinctive philosophies which reflect the spirit of the age. And potent philosophies in turn reshape the culture which gave them birth. Thomas Aquinas, Jonathan Edwards, John Wesley, Rousseau, Pestalozzi, Froebel, Emerson, G. Stanley Hall,—to mention a miscellaneous few, were marked by their times, and in turn left a mark on concepts of child development. These thinkers were not professional philosophers, but they had ideas. Some of the ideas retain a vitality to this day; others are vanishing, among them Jonathan Edwards' concept of infant damnation and child depravity. In his view of original sin, children were "young vipers and (to God) infinitely more hateful than vipers." Ideas which have dogmatically insisted on fixity, fate, and rigorous absolutes have shown the least permanence; and have, by their harshness, tended to do the most harm to man's progress. More modern concepts of Christianity, of democracy, and of organic evolution

[287]

on the other hand have had an ameliorating effect on the interpretation of child life and child care.

Democracies do not have an official ideology to impose. Every parent, every teacher, every child welfare worker must arrive at a philosophy of his own concerning the nature and meaning of infancy and childhood. The philosophy may never be formulated in words; but it will always be implicit in attitudes assumed and procedures applied. In this sense every adult already has some more or less articulate philosophy or group of ideas concerning the relationship of infant and child to the culture of today.

§1. ABSOLUTE VERSUS RELATIVE CONCEPTS

THERE ARE three major brands of philosophy which deal with the principles and practices of child care: 1) authoritarian; 2) laissez-faire; 3) developmental.

The authoritarian approach takes its point of departure from the culture. It assumes that the adult culture knows what the rising generation needs to know. The culture proceeds accordingly to impose its imprint. In its extreme form this philosophy holds that children are habit forming creatures, who can be moulded to the patterns of the culture through the processes of learning and of the conditioned-reflex. Behaviorism as a social theory concedes little to the child's heredity, and has great confidence in the power and the authority invested in the environment. It is not inconsistent with totalitarian trends of thought.

Laissez-faire doctrine applies to the child as it does to economic forces. The underlying theory is that "the world goes of itself." Constrain neither child nor culture. Things will work out for the best. For the child will know and select what is best for him if you do not confuse and restrict him. It is the policy of non-interference. It encourages almost complete freedom of action for the child, and requires little effort at intelligent guidance on the part of the adult.

[288]

A *developmental philosophy* in temper and in principle lies inter-mediate between the two foregoing extremes. In matters of child care this outlook is suspicious of absolutes and does not favor license. It is sensitive to the relativities of growth and maturity. It takes its point of departure from the child's nature and needs. It acknowledges the pro-found forces of racial and familial inheritance which determine the growth sequences and the distinctive growth pattern of each individual child. It envisages the problem of acculturation in terms of growth; but this increases rather than relaxes the responsibility of cultural guidance. Developmental guidance at a conscious level demands an active use of intelligence to understand the laws and the mechanisms of the growth process.

It is easy to see how these three contrasted points of view affect all human relations, including those between adult and child. Discipline under authoritarian auspices tends to be severe, even cruel. The flogging of sailors, corporal punishment, and regimentation are autocratic in temper. Indulgence, excessive freedom, and egocentric self-direction re-place severity at the other lackadaisical extreme. The developmental ap-proach does not admit such self-direction. It holds for cultural guidance controls; but it believes in self-regulation and self-adjustment within these controls. It has such confidence in the wisdom of Nature (as opposed to authoritarian cultural goals) that it takes its cues from the child. It aims to conserve all the best potentialities of the child in the broad framework but not in the narrow and rigid compartments of culture.

This requires an intimate knowledge of the growth process; the same kind of knowledge which the present day mechanic has with respect to the operations of an internal combustion engine. Our culture has arrived at that stage of sophistication and discernment that it can no longer carry on satisfactorily in the field of child care without the aids of modern science. There is a type of native intelligence which appreciates the im-port of growth factors, without formal instruction. But we can scarcely rely on intuition and improvisation in the rearing of children. We must make it our business to better comprehend how their minds grow, how

[289]

their personalities are formed. Their psychological care needs an informed developmental philosophy, based upon a sympathetic familiarity with the detailed operations of growth.

In other words we must learn to think of growth as a living reality, rather than merely the label of an intricate process. Growth (or development) is not an empty abstraction; it is a series of events governed by laws and forces just as real as those which apply to an internal combustion engine. The psychological growth of the child is a marvellous series of patterned events, outwardly manifested in behavior. The nervous system is the vital part of the machinery which makes the events possible. It weaves within itself a complicated continuous fabric as it matures, a fabric which comes to light in the actions, the attitudes, the personality of the child. Growth ceases to be merely an abstract or rather useless label, if we think of development as a weaving process which gives shape and structure to the mind.

§2. THE DYNAMICS OF THE GROWTH COMPLEX

THE PURPOSE of this volume has been to give substance and form to this concept of the mind. We do not think that the child mind can be explained in terms of forces and faculties operating from behind the scenes or from the depths of the unconscious. To be understood, the mind must be regarded as a living, growing "organism." In the next chapter we shall summarize the sequences of organization and reorganization which characterize this living *growth complex* from birth through the first five years. These lawful sequences are the foundation of a developmental philosophy of child care. By concentrating our summary in a single chapter we can get an overview of the total unitary action-system in dynamic flow.

What are the outstanding features of this dynamic growth complex? There are three: 1. The Day Cycle, 2. Self-Regulatory Fluctuations,

3. Constitutional Individuality. Each of these has already been discussed separately and at some length. Now we shall see that these characteristics are interrelated, and that they determine the principles and precepts of a developmental philosophy of child care.

1. *The Day Cycle.* Growth is at once a self-renewing, a self-perpetuating, and a self-expanding process. It occurs every day. In a sense it follows a daily calendar; because the earth itself has been taking a daily spin since time immemorial. And so the baby accomplishes a bit of growth each and every day. To no small extent these diurnal increments are patterned. They are patterned by the natural metabolic characteristics of the organism as a storer and expender of energy. They are also inevitably patterned by the culture which conducts its affairs on a day by day basis. The baby likewise transacts his growth business on a diurnal basis. He grows up each day. A developmental philosophy recognizes the growth trends within a single day and over a series of days. The trends will not always be perceptible, but they will be assumed; for a developmental theorem affirms that there is a basic tendency toward an optimum in all normal growth. With this outlook a mother's margin of tolerance is widened. She will not be too disappointed with apparent lapses: and she may even detect a positive value in certain variations which on the surface do not look progressive.

The *Behavior Day,* therefore, has received detailed consideration in Part Two because it bears so significantly upon the economy of psychological development. Each day is sufficient unto itself: but from a philosophical standpoint it takes on new meaning and new interest as part and parcel of a larger cycle of development.

2. *Self-regulatory Fluctuations.* When a larger sector of the growth cycle is viewed in perspective, we find that the course of development does not pursue a straight and narrow path. It deviates now right, now left, now up, now down, although the general trend is toward a goal,

[291]

for these deviations are constructive gropings which lay down a pathway. A flowing stream must find its bed.

The living growth complex during the period of infancy and childhood is in a state of formative instability combined with a progressive movement toward stability. The interaction between two apparently opposing tendencies results in see-saw fluctuations. The growing organism does not advance in an undeviating line, but oscillates along a spiral course toward maturity.

In previous chapters we have shown how these fluctuations appear in the organization of the baby's feeding and sleep behavior. When the fluctuations are charted they seem, on first glance, to be irregular and whimsical. But looked at in perspective they prove to be expressions of a basic mechanism of self adjustment. The infant is constantly working toward and working out a schedule which is most suitable for his stage of maturity. From a developmental standpoint this is not an aimless variability.

Similar fluctuations operate all along the course of early development. Strangely enough they often take on the guise of resistance and of an "obstinate" clinging to routines expressed in ritualisms. These ritualisms have been repeatedly referred to: they will be mentioned again in the next succeeding chapter. Precisely because they seem so unreasonable, they need a philosophical interpretation. Through the ritual the child is holding on to that which he has found good. He is not quite ready to take the next step which the parent thinks he ought to take. But he is going to use the ritual as a foothold for a variation which will lead him safely into new territory. Once more from a developmental viewpoint the ritualism has a rationale. It is a growth mechanism; and having a meaning it can be more intelligently guided.

An authoritarian ideology exalts absolutes and professes perfectionism; it places a premium upon undeviated straight line progressions. It tries to whip the organism into line. Fluctuations are frowned upon. A developmental philosophy sees a manifestation of natural law in these fluctuations. A ship cannot always sail on even keel. It must dip with the waves. The organism of the growing child has comparable ups and downs. It cannot remain in stable balance indefinitely; it may come to relative rest, but then it must again forge ahead. More or less rhythmically it comes into relative equilibrium, passes into disequilibrium, and then returns again to relative equilibrium. This is a dynamic method of development which is of great value in interpreting the child's behavior. We may call it *the mechanism of recurrent equilibrium*. Its operation in shaping the growth complex will be considered in the next chapter, §6. There are discernible periods of relative equilibrium which coincide approximately with the following nodal or key ages: 4, 16, 28, and 40 weeks; one year, 18 months, 2, 3, 4 and 5 years.

Conceived as a growth mechanism, disequilibrium (so often associated with "naughty" behavior) takes on a less moralistic aspect. This form of disequilibrium is a transitional phase, during which the organism is creating a new ability or achieving a reorientation of some kind. It is a phase of *innovation*. The child withdraws from his former self, and also somewhat from his environment, as though to gather strength for a forward thrust, which may be so vigorous that it has the appearance of aggression. But even during the aggressive thrust new patterns are being incorporated into the old. A working balance is achieved between the new and the old and presently the organism settles down into a period of relative equilibrium, of assimilation, and consolidation. This period again is temporary; but it is also recurrent, for time and again and again, the child forges forward by the three step method of innovation—integration—equilibrium. Here is a mechanism and a concept which the developmentally minded parent can use to good advantage in interpreting the child and in shaping suitable guidance procedures. Many of his "strange" and passing fears, for example, are associated with a phase of innovation which leads to introversion. If the fear is wisely handled by the culture, during its nascent phase, it tends to resolve in the equilibrium phase which follows.

3. *Constitutional Individuality.* Now these various fluctuation phenomena are not equally marked in all children, nor do they conform to a uniform pattern. Every child has a distinct mode of growth which is unique, and which is also highly characteristic, for it is grounded in his psychic constitution. Observant parents will begin to detect even in a child's infancy how he meets a new situation, how he travels from one stage of maturity to another. As he grows older they will see this method of maturing repeating itself over and over again. This characteristicness expresses the child's constitutional individuality. Every child, therefore, has a growth career which represents his biological make-up,—his potentialities and his style of growth.

Once more, developmental concepts prove their usefulness. They enable the parent and the student to see the longer stretches of the growth career in perspective. To no small degree during the first year, and certainly by the end of the third year it is possible to ascertain the most characteristic features of the growth plan which the child is likely to evidence throughout the whole growth span, including the period of adolescence. Incidentally, an informed developmental philosophy is nothing less than a boon in interpreting adolescent behavior. Absolute concepts, unrelieved by the relativities of growth concepts, prove to be sterile and misleading as explanatory devices.

A perceptiveness for growth career is most indispensable for accurate guidance in the earliest years. The parent must acquire a sense of timing; must learn to detect the emergence and the recession of a period of disequilibrium; must learn when to disregard, when to step in with a timely aid or prod, and when to withdraw again. These developmental phases run a natural course. They cannot be overcome by duress: they can be assisted by finesse. But finesse is quite impossible without a developmental philosophy based upon a knowledge of the ways of growth.

§3. BEHAVIOR DEVIATIONS

A DEVELOPMENTAL APPROACH is of supreme importance in the management of those variations of conduct which are sufficiently atypical or pronounced to deserve the designation of behavior deviations. In infancy and early childhood it is especially difficult to draw a sharp line between normal and abnormal behavior. In a sense all children are problem children, because none can escape the universal problem of development which always presents some difficulties. On the other hand, there are few forms of malbehavior which are not in history and essence a variation or deflection of normal mechanisms. Both benign and serious behavior deviations demand interpretation and treatment in terms of the mechanics of development.

Many behavior deviations have their inception at a specific age when a mild degree of manifestation is well nigh universal. The deviation is in the nature of an exaggeration, or an "over-individuation." Over-individuation means that in a period of normal disequilibrium, the behavior did not become duly subordinated to the total action system: it grew out of proportion. Nevertheless, it may not reach permanent and pathological dimensions. It may run its course; for even deviations may have a normal course determined by the normal sequences of the growth career. The seriousness of various forms of thumb sucking can be adjudged by this criterion, as will be shown in the next chapter. Transient speech defects such as stuttering often make their appearance at about $2\frac{1}{2}$ and $4\frac{1}{2}$ years during periods of relative disequilibrium. A child of somewhat unstable constitution tends to show his instabilities in a manner characteristic of type as suggested in Chapter 4 in the section on the individuality of growth patterns. Or a relatively stable child, say at the age of 21 months, may show an extraordinary upset of accustomed behavior, simply because his father happens on an exceptional day to come home at noon rather than at five in the afternoon! A knowledge of the

[295]

maturity characteristics of this age would help to set matters straight. In dealing with "difficult" children from one to three years of age, simplifications of environment often work wonders.

It is the mother who is attuned to the developmental tempo and tune of the child who best knows how to time and to apportion her guidance. Absolute concepts, rules of thumb, and management devices have very limited uses. Children are constantly changing. What is true today is not true tomorrow. As the old Greek philosopher said, "Nothing is, everything is becoming." The logic of development lies in its sequences. These sequences we shall attempt to summarize in the next chapter, with incidental reference to the behavior deviations which always have a context in normal patterns and normal successions. A genetic philosophy enables us to see this context. It widens the areas of patience and of understanding.

The developmental outlook also tempers the almost irresistible desire to do something about everything and to do it immediately. In child care we fall prone to a certain kind of meddlesomeness,—a tendency to set matters right with dispatch. Now development is a little like the weather. It should be accepted at least within reason. Good judgment will tell us when to put a garment on or off, and which garment to wear. But we should not attempt to substitute the garment for the weather. In over-meddlesome child care there is a vicious temptation to substitute the garments of our own devices for the deeper devices of development.

*   *   *   *

A developmental philosophy has one further and far-reaching virtue: it enables you to enjoy your children. A broad knowledge of the sequences and trends of development, its ins and outs and ups and downs, gives one a general sense of direction. This is not a blind faith but a confidence in the constructive essence of growth. Guidance is given; but the child is in league with Nature and he does his own growing. There is ancient wisdom in the natural mechanisms of growth. An appreciation of the ingenuity and inevitability of the growth mechanisms reduces tensions and relieves many an illfounded anxiety. One does not have to be so soberly solicitous and grimly determined after all. Of all natural phenomena none is more variegated and marvellous than the cycle of child development. No spectacle offers a more intriguing mixture of the unpredictable and the predictable. Why not enjoy it?

23

THE GROWTH COMPLEX

§1. SLEEP

LIFE almost begins with sleep. Sleep is one of the most primitive functions of which the organism is capable, so primitive that sometimes it may even simulate death. But human sleep does not remain on a primitive, vegetative level. It becomes extensively integrated with the total economy of man's activities. It has undergone great changes in the course of evolution. It undergoes great changes in the development of the child. Our survey of the growth complex may well start with an examination of this paradoxical reaction for producing inaction.

Sleep is behavior. One is accustomed to think of sleep as a cessation of behavior. It is, however, a positive function. It is not a mere stoppage of machinery; it is a readjustment of the whole machinery of the organism, including the central nervous system, to protect the total and remote welfare of this organism.

Perfect sleep is a total response. In this sense sleep differs from other forms of behavior. All other behavior represents an adjustment or an adaptation to more or less specific situations. Sleep, on the contrary, is a totalitarian response which is as inclusive and fundamental as nutrition. Indeed, it can be envisaged as an expression of nutritional economy.

When we undertake to study the characteristics of sleep in infant and child, we find that sleep behavior is genetically inseparable from nutrition. Sleep is not a simple function in spite of its apparent simplicity. It is so complex that physiology has not yet succeeded in establishing a satisfactory theory of sleep. The very abundance of theories indicates that we really do not know very much about its actual mechanism.

Many of the misconceptions concerning sleep arise from the fact that it has been over-simplified. In the care of infants and children it must be recognized that sleep is not a well-defined, uniform response, but that it varies enormously with the individuality of the child and still more with his maturity. The biological function of sleep is to preserve the integrity of the total organism and its entire life cycle. Sleep, therefore, undergoes significant changes with age. The sleep of the fetus, if indeed the fetus does sleep, is quite different from the sleep of the adult: sleep of infancy is different from the sleep of youth. In later maturity and senectitude sleep assumes new forms, some of which are reminiscent of childhood and infancy. These grosser changes in the rhythms, nature, and depth of sleep should at once remind us that in child care we must be prepared to find variations in sleep behavior from time to time; sometimes from day to day. Such variations betray the complexity of sleep as behavior.

The child has to learn to sleep in the same manner that he learns to grasp a spoon or learns to creep and stand and walk. Just as prehension and locomotion undergo palpable developmental changes as they mature, so do the patterns of sleep change with maturity. Perfect sleep must, then, be defined as a form of positive inhibition which embraces the entire organism and which serves best to protect its developmental needs.

Such perfection is ideal. Sleep may be more or less partial. It is quite conceivable that in defects and deviations of development, certain organ systems do not get an adequate quota of sleep. Sleep may be disintegrated, incomplete, just as the positive behavior of the waking child may be disintegrated and incomplete. Indeed a normal balance must be achieved between waking behavior and sleep behavior. The organism must acquire adequate methods of going to sleep and emerging from sleep. From this broad point of view, sleep behavior is closely related to attention. Certain forms of attention, idling, dawdling, periods of abstraction, naps, "play-naps," to say nothing of lethargy and mild forms of hibernation are all in some manner related to the function of sleep, if we recall our definition that sleep is a biological device for inducing inactivity in order to protect the organism's capacity for later activity.

And what is meant by the fighting of sleep, an interesting form of behavior sometimes found to an intense degree in vital, perhaps generously endowed children? What is the philosophical rationalization of such a contest against an adjustment which nature apparently designed for our best interests?

Sleep has often been compared to death. Shelley speaks of Death and his brother Sleep. Even Shakespeare called sleep "the death of each day's life," but in the very next breath he also called it "great nature's second course, chief nourisher in life's feast." This last characterization is scientifically acceptable, for sleep is more than a sweet restorer. It is a nourisher. It is allied to nutrition.

The early association between feeding and sleep is extremely close. The baby eats to sleep and he wakes to eat which promptly puts him again to sleep, so that the two functions almost overlap. A young premature infant may not stop sleeping at all: he may not even be arousable. His whole muscle tone is limp. Indeed, his "sleep" is very shallow as though it had no structure. He may fluctuate in a thin twilight zone, without definitively sleeping or waking, as though he did not know how to do either, which is true. As he grows older his muscle tone becomes firmer and lasts longer. He is less fragile in every way. His sleep becomes more defined, more clear cut. He falls off to sleep more decisively, he wakes up more decisively. All of this means that sleep is a complex function which requires developmental organization from the moment of birth (and before). It will never cease to need such organization, for, as we have said, it is articulated with the total economy and make-up of the human action system.

The newborn infant, accordingly, has a few elementary differentiations to make between eating-sleeping-waking. He knows how to nurse. Having "learned" how to sleep, he must learn how to wake and to keep awake. At first he wakes up from sheer necessity (need of food). This requires no special mechanism, as Kleitman has shown, other than a subcortical wakefulness center. He wakes with a demanding hunger cry. Is it pain or is it rage?

As he grows older, he is no longer so purely subcortical. His cry may be delayed a little after he opens his eyes: it takes on a more cultivated fussing quality. In time it becomes intermittent. It intersperses short periods of wakefulness. He is "learning" to stay awake and to enjoy it. His cortex (the higher nerve centers of the brain) is growing rapidly: millions of cortical nerve cells make connection with his eyes, ears, and the twelve oculo-motor muscles that he uses in his staring and looking. This keeps his cortex wide awake. He is developing nerve centers for a "wakefulness of choice."

There are, accordingly, three distinguishable phases to the sleep cycle: a) going to sleep b) staying asleep c) awakening. It is not always easy to distinguish between the first and the third phases. The first depends upon a higher cortical control which enables the child *to release into sleep*; the third upon an active wakefulness nerve center. Is failure to go to sleep due to faulty release or to excessive activity of the wake-up center? Between release *into* and release *out* of sleep lies an intermediate stage: the consolidation of sleep. The task of development is to bring about a proportionate balance between these three phases. As the child grows up the first or release-into-sleep phase seems to give him the most trouble; the third the least. We shall consider each phase in turn, beginning with

[301]

the third phase, which appears to be the first to which the baby gives his developmental attention.

1. *The Awakening Phase.* As we have seen, the young baby does not wake up smoothly or expertly. He often wakes with a sharp cry. His waking seems to depend upon an internal prod, a nudge from the gastrointestinal tract or some other incitement from inside. Significantly enough, he does not respond readily to a prod from the outside. He does not arouse easily to a pat or a shake, which confirms the suggestion that waking depends upon an internal mechanism operated by his own private nervous system.

As the weeks go by, he occasionally wakes up more smoothly: he does not always cry, or his cry is briefer and softer. He also wakes up oftener. He becomes more facile. By 16 weeks his waking mechanism is working with comparative efficiency. Thereafter, it does not, as such, make much trouble for the culture. At $2\frac{1}{2}$ years, however, he not only has difficulty in going to sleep; but he has difficulty in getting out of sleep. The two difficulties seem to be related to each other at this highly unsettled stage of maturity. He temporarily loses the knack of waking up. He regains it; but at adolescence he may again show a similar developmental clinging to sleep. Further aspects of waking behavior are considered in connection with the other two phases of the sleep cycle.

2. *The Consolidation Phase.* It does not pay to be too clever at waking. That would, as we say, interfere with sleep. The child must "learn" to stay soundly asleep in sizable stretches. This is the consolidation phase, and it is subject to growth processes. We have, in our research files, a behavior day chart which is several feet tall, for it plots the progressive organization of sleeping and waking periods over a long stretch of time beginning with birth. The dark strands represent sleep: the white waking, as already illustrated by Figure 2 in the chapter on self-regulation. Viewed in perspective, these strands are comparable to narrow streams which at first flow separately, merge, and part for distances, and finally become confluent in wider streams. The night sleep becomes less broken,

the day naps coalesce. At first they are short and irregular; but by 12 weeks, two or three adjacent naps have consolidated into one. The long process of achieving a mono-phasic sleep-waking cycle is under way. At 12 weeks the infant may have 4 to 5 sleep periods in 24 hours: at 12 months, 2 to 3; at 4 years, only one. As an adult, he can remain awake from choice eighteen hours or more. This process is not merely one of quantitative reduction of sleep: it involves complicated pattern transformations, adjustments to the schedule of the entire behavior day, and readjustments to the ever-changing interests and abilities of the growing child.

All sleep is, so to speak, vulnerable; how vulnerable depends upon two factors: the constitution of the child and the maturity of the child. He is especially likely to show disturbances of sleep behavior during transitional periods of disequilibrium, when growth changes are most actively taking place. It is as though the organism had to assist in making readjustments even during sleep. Some of the apparent disturbances may actually have a positive usefulness in the economy of development. (The reader may be reminded that in this chapter we are attempting to interpret all behavior in its relation to an everchanging growth complex.)

Up to the age of 16 weeks, the variabilities of the gastro-intestinal tract tend to discompose his slumbers. Later it may be wetness, or some bodily discomfort, or noises. Still later it may be emotional experiences,—change of scene, undue excitement, new fears. At 15 months, and at 21 months, the child often wakes during the night, and, in an almost whimsical manner, remains awake for an hour or two. The 3 year old is apparently a little less settled during the night than during the day. He may get up out of his bed. He is disquieted if his mother goes out of an evening. Dreams become more frequent at $3\frac{1}{2}$ and $4\frac{1}{2}$ years, a reminder that sleep varies greatly in depth, in scope, and in integratedness; though we must be mindful of Freud's suggestion that dreams are the guardians of sleep. The organism does the best it can even through dreams. Indeed, it works while you sleep. In the recurrent periods of equilibrium, the organism is under the least stress and strain.

The sleep disturbances just outlined are the common lot of humanity. No man, no child, escapes from himself merely by going to sleep. But some individuals have a much firmer grasp on the sleep which they possess.

"Poor sleepers" are comparable to the "poor eaters" who will be discussed in the following section. They do not hold fast to the sleep which they acquire, and they do not consolidate their gains readily. All the foregoing disturbances are intensified in degree and protracted in time. Poor sleepers do not shift readily from one maturity stage to another. They do not tolerate changes in accustomed routines and orientations. Even at the age of 16 weeks a shift from bassinet to crib may not be accomplished with ease. The infant may accept the crib for a day-time nap; but rebels at night. It may take two weeks to wean him to this apparently simple change. At 36 weeks or later, the same child suffers derangement of sleep if his crib is moved from its accustomed position, or if a favorite blanket or pad is removed. Throughout the preschool years, he may be unusually dependent upon an adult, sometimes a particular adult, in his sleep adjustments. He persists longer than normally in a given stage of adjustment, and does not adjust by slow degrees, but in a somewhat abrupt manner. His symptoms tend to exacerbate during periods of disequilibrium. Although his behavior is atypical, it follows normal sequences. It is best understood as a deviation from the normal rather than a perversity. It requires unusual patience and even compliances; for the simple reason that deviations of this type are grounded in the growth complex, and do not respond to rigorous, disciplinary measures. An appreciation of the developmental trend of the deviations makes for sympathetic and wise management.

3. *Release into Sleep.* The new born infant, as previously noted, apparently has no difficulty in going to sleep. He is already there, and his sleep is so intimately bound up with his eating that transitions are easy. Moreover, his sleeping, like his waking, is at a subcortical level. He has neither inhibitory mechanisms nor inhibitory problems so far as sleeping is concerned. But as he acquires wakefulness of choice, these very

problems,—and also mechanisms begin to take shape. His cortex appears on the scene, and once it becomes active, he must learn to inhibit its activity. This is the task of release-into-sleep.

As the child grows older this task becomes more and more complex, for the cortex is both the agent and the storer of his ever increasing experiences. And our high-geared culture keeps urging the cortex to cumulative rather than rhythmic activity. Not even the cosmic rhythm of night and day can compete with that relentless stress. Therefore, instead of being a simple, vegetative function, which ought to take care of itself, sleep creates, in our modern culture, a host of vexatious putting-to-bed problems. Under more primitive conditions of living, fatigue and ennui play a more prominent role in the regulation of sleep. Under modern conditions, the tyranny of the clock, and the tensions of life complicate the reconciliation of sleep and waking. Some of the difficulties, however, it must be emphasized, are definitely based on maturity factors. The organism, in its nervous system, lacks the equipment for complete voluntary control. Recall how long it takes the child to acquire the simple ability to let go of an object at will. By trying, he can, at 15 months, place one block on another, and relax his hold of it; but even then he tends to release awkwardly, with too much intensity and with poor timing. This is physiological awkwardness. The same kind of awkwardness complicates his sleep mechanisms, particularly during periods of tension and disequilibrium. Going to sleep from choice is a release act, a voluntary inhibition of the wakefulness center. It is like prehensory release.

The ability to release into sleep tends to be at its best during the recurrent periods of equilibrium when the muscles of flexion and extension, and other opposing functions are in check and balance. Accordingly, the 16 weeks old child releases smoothly into sleep. Even during his waking hours, as he lies in supine symmetry, he gives a picture of composure. He has come through a period at 8-12 weeks when the growth tendency toward wakefulness was pronounced. He did not release so well: he may have needed some judicious soothing,—through rocking, singing, or a light to gaze upon. (Of course, the soothing will not work unless it is so

[305]

nicely adjusted that he himself contributes just the right amount of self-hypnosis, which is but another name for the function of release-into-sleep.)

DIFFICULTIES AND DEVIATIONS

It is this same period from 8 to 12 weeks, that *thumb sucking* has its onset. This sucking, as we shall see, is related to the control of feeding behavior as well as of sleep. When the linkage to feeding is primary, the sucking may run a short course. If, however, for personality or other reasons, it establishes its main linkage with sleep, it is likely to continue longer and the tie-up with sleep will become more rather than less tenacious. Being well grounded in the growth complex, it runs a longer course. It may have its onset at variable times throughout the first year. It tends to recede somewhat during periods of equilibrium. At 28 weeks, for example, mouthing of objects may take its place. Sometimes it may come to a sharp termination, as though a developmental hurdle had been passed. This again suggests that a combination of personality and growth factors is at work. When the sucking is still strong after the first birthday, it tends to run a long but resolving course, vanishing any time between 2 and 5 years. This type of pattern is related not only to sleep and hunger, but becomes a generalized tension outlet, utilized for escape and relaxation in situations of fatigue, embarrassment, frustration, fear, and also excitement.

Thumb sucking reaches its highest peak between 18 and 21 months, when some children will spend hours, busy with thumb in mouth, either alone or watching other children, but not partaking in their activities. Between the ages of 2 and 3 years, the pattern begins to break. It is less absorbing. However, it is most tenaciously associated with sleep: it not only induces, but it accompanies sleep. There is an exacerbation of intensity at $2\frac{1}{2}$ years, but by 3 years it definitely begins to fade out during the day, and returns to its older linkage with hunger and sleepiness. The 3 year old tolerates removal of thumb after he has fallen to sleep (not so the 2 year old), but he sucks again when he wakes. At 4 years, the suck-ing occurs only prior to sleep: it does not invade the domain of sleep at all. A mere minute or two with the thumb suffices. The 5 year old is able to verbalize the situation and cooperates with his parents in any plan of action. If the "habit" is associated with some accessory article like a blan-ket or a teddy bear, weaning is easily effected by a well-timed removal of the article in whose context the sucking is enmeshed, that is, if the child himself carries through the weaning.

Thumb sucking functions as a real component of the growth complex. Its harmfulness varies greatly with the type of child and associated be-havior. The fact that in complicated cases it pursues a characteristic de-velopmental course and undergoes spontaneous extinction, suggests that artificial curbs and restraints have doubtful value. There is no conclusive evidence that thumb sucking, if discontinued by the age of 5 or 6 years, has a permanent deforming effect upon denture and occlusion.

This brief recital illustrates that behavior deviations, as well as normal behavior traits, are subject to developmental sequences. A behavior devi-ation should always be considered and approached in terms of the total growth complex. This gives rationale to any corrective measures which are used. It overcomes the temptation to unwise "discipline." Even when guidance is ineffective, the developmental interpretation tends to keep the problem in hopeful suspension and in proper perspective.

Whether the thumb is sucked or not, the release-into-sleep presents ever changing problems as the child matures. It is not a specific, press-the-button mechanism, which simply needs training and regularity. It is a complex communication system, which must be hooked up with a network of ever changing higher controls. The hook-up which served for 12 months does not serve for 21 months nor even for 15 months, because the whole city of man-soul (as Bunyan might have called it) has changed: new forms of posture, locomotion, language, and personal rela-tions have come into recent developments. The sleep-release mechanism is not a thing apart; it is enmeshed in this total growth complex.

On the whole, sleep-release during the first year is relatively simple.

The child is almost able to ask for sleep as he goes along. The mother knows exactly what he means by a certain querulous cry and wriggling at the age of 40 weeks. He readily admits being placed on his back in his welcome crib. Indeed, until about the age of 21 months, he tends to accept the whole bedtime situation as a matter of course. He contrives various pre-sleep devices he may need to put himself to sleep. He takes one or two toys with him: he talks and sings to himself: he brandishes his hands before his eyes: he may even indulge in a brief work-out wrestle with his bed clothes. These seem to be relaxational expedients. Some children apparently need them more than others, for constitutional reasons. If the culture is too rigid, and arbitrary, the pre-sleep patterns may become more distorted. Or culture may combine with constitution to set up more or less serious behavior deviations.

Rocking on hands and knees, and bed shaking are common forms of deviation. Head banging and head rolling also have their origin in this period from 40 weeks to 21 months. They may run a transient course; they may be superseded or elaborated in the next growth period. However annoying they may be, it is apparent that they are but variants and exaggerations of normal methods of sleep release,—in our present culture. Removal of the physical restraint of a sleeping bag, postponement of bedtime to increase fatigue, are helpful measures. If the deviation persists beyond the second year, a shift from the accustomed crib to a new bed may bring about a dramatic termination.

As the child approaches his second birthday, a new and important factor comes into the picture. It may exaggerate already deviant behavior. It is bound to complicate normal and ordinary behavior; for it is a growth phenomenon: the child is becoming more dependent upon an adult.

Hitherto, he has managed the sleep situation largely through his own resources. Now he relates himself to someone else at bedtime (and subconsciously during sleep-time). We should, in fact, be grateful for this new manifestation; because it represents an increment of maturity. He is yet too young to go to bed "like a little man" and forget everyone else, including his mother. So, he does not fall to sleep so readily. He calls her back. He asks to go to the toilet. Sometimes the culture regards this as a clever ruse, a perverse form of filibustering; or as "stalling" which it thinks must be severely and arbitrarily handled. (Strict discipline has a way of becoming very arbitrary with young children.) Actually his pre-sleep behavior is probably accompanied by a transitional instability in the control of the sphincters of the urinary system. Sphincter control, like sleep control, involves inhibitory and release mechanisms.

At the age of 2½ years, going-to-bed and going-to-sleep *rituals* are strong and elaborate. The young baby simply falls off to sleep; the young child walks a winding path along the precipice of wakefulness before *he* falls off to sleep. It is as though he had to pick his way, before he finds just the right spot for the plunge. Rituals must have some such rationale. They cannot be senseless, even though they become grotesquely extended in the deviating child who inveterately finds difficulty in making transitions. He may be over-conscious of his mother in his ritualistic demands. It is often better for him as well as for her to have someone else put him to bed. He then has to modify his ritual, and in the process he can contract it. That is the guidance precept for rituals. Respect them, but by wise manoeuvers, well-timed and nicely modulated, restrict the area of the ritual. In time, it contracts to a vanishing point: it loses its vitality in the growth complex. Unwise combative measures, on the contrary, may lead to a deeper ramification of the ritual into the growth complex.

In ordinary and normal course, rituals are shed by processes of growth. They have a lighter hold after the age of three years. The 4 year old is usually ready for a change from crib to bed. The change is regarded as a social promotion. It is made the subject of advance planning and conversation. It connotes so much cultural prestige that the change may bring about a sharp termination of persistent bed-wetting. As usual, the 5 year old has his sleep-behavior better in hand; although new developmental changes may be expected prior to and during adolescence.

It is probable that many sleep difficulties are man-made rather than child-made, and arise from over-rigid methods of management. Primitive peoples have experimented with various methods of binding and cradling their infants to restrict mobility and to induce that distinctive immobility which goes by the familiar name of sleep. Modern cultures are engaged in similar experimentation, employing such gadgets as sleep harnesses, slumber bags, and snuggle-duckies. Sometimes, the gadget works deceptively like a charm. The child becomes completely conditioned to the device. Another untamable youngster will rend it with the ferocity of a feral child. Yet another child becomes so conditioned that he cannot endure a single omission: he must have this man-made envelope, night in, night out, without exception, summer as well as winter. Such minor complications in very reasonable children show how complex and personalized sleep behavior has become in our culture.

Knowing so little about the mechanisms of sleep, we ought to pay more respect to the physiological self-demands for sleep, not only in infancy, but in early childhood. Half, and over half, of every behavior day is expended in sleep during the early years. It is important that science should further our insight into the determinations and modifiability of this engrossing, powerful function, which is so pervasively identified with the growth complex, with the organization of personality, and the conventions of culture. The mounting tensions of civilization make this a fertile field for cultural control, because sleep is by nature an inhibitory adjustment,—a beneficent terminator of tensions. With increased insight, daytime, as well as night sleep, will be brought under greater personal control and this will be accomplished during infancy and the preschoo'
years.

§2. FEEDING

IN THE BEGINNING of the baby's life, there is much sleep; but also there is hunger. When sleep is deepest, respiration is regular, tonus relaxed, the body motionless. But on the least diminution of oxygen intake, breathing hastens, tonus tightens, muscles stir; for air hunger is the most fundamental of all hungers,—and there are many hungers.

Food hunger comes next. This is so imperative that the total body posture alters: mouth opens, eyes open. Crying and seeking movements ensue. The baby wakes to eat, and he eats to sleep. But as we have already shown, in due season he wakes for other reasons; he also eats for other reasons. At first food satiety alone suffices. His alimentary tract, invested with a mucous membrane over 2000 square cm. in extent, affords him some inward glow to which he pays blissful attention. Somewhat before the age of 8 weeks, his smile becomes less introverted. His sensorium is less completely alimentary: it includes vision and sound. His smile accordingly migrates from his alimentary tract to his mother's face; he may even vocalize with a quasi-gastric chuckle on her social approach. Thus horizons widen and the feeding situation proves to be a growth matrix out of which other forms of adaptive, language, and social behavior emerge as though they were so many branchings from a main stem. In truth, feeding behavior with its manifold ramifications constitutes a major network in the organization of mind and personality, throughout infancy and childhood. It lies at the core of the growth complex.

This network, in the early periods of development, is closely related to that of sleep behavior. The developmental factors which organize feeding behavior are not unlike those of sleep. The feeding pattern may be considered in three aspects as follows: 1) appetite 2) retention 3) self-help and acculturation. Appetite is the first phase: the child must seek food and want it. Secondly, he must hold fast to it. This is the phase of retention. At first, he is entirely dependent upon others for the satisfaction of his hungers, but he desires increasingly to become self-dependent, and the culture encourages him in this desire.

1. *Appetite*. Appetite lies at the basis of self-regulation. In Chapter 5, we have dwelt at length on the significance of self-regulation combined with cultural guidance. In Chapter 8, we have shown concretely how these simple principles can be put into application in the first four months to

initiate a good start for mother and child. The same principles apply throughout the period of childhood.

At first, the physiological impulsion behind growth is so intense that virtually all children, whether reared on the breast or on the bottle, after an initial adjustment, can make their hunger known. With time, sheer craving gives way to variations in appetite. Appetite varies in intensity within a behavior day. It also varies from age to age. It differentiates in manifold changes of food preferences. There is an almost inextricable mixture of maturity factors and individual equations.

Appetite is especially strong in the period from 8 to 12 weeks,—so strong that problems of retention, as we shall see later, begin to manifest themselves. Ordinarily, the infant's feeding behavior is well organized at 16 weeks. He eats with moderate vigor: he retains well what he eats. His sucking ability is competent. His sucking propensity is so strong that it tends to interfere with the acceptance of solids at this time.

In the period from 20 to 28 weeks, his appetite curve again shows irregularity. He demands an extra feeding, often in the early hours of the morning, but there is a decrease in the sucking demands, and he is able to adjust to solids before he takes the bottle. At 36 weeks, there is a noticeable increase of eagerness for food. His appetite is reinforced by the mere sight of the food in process of preparation. At 40 weeks, his appetite again comes to a high peak. He eats what is given to him, and he cleans his bowl. Between 1 and 2 years, there is a decrease in vividness of appetite and in the amount of food taken at each meal.

After 18 months, appetite becomes more sophisticated. The 2 year old child begins to name foods; preferences define themselves; he indulges in special runs on foods that he fastens on; he is intrigued by certain colors, he shows bits of fastidiousness as to service; he likes to have his dishes match! By all these tokens, we can see that the food complex within the total growth complex is expanding, differentiating, and taking on environmental specifications. Brute appetite is being civilized through the culture. One hardly knows where appetite stops and acculturation begins. But from time to time, the child initiates food behavior which is so self-assertive that it seems to spring from the organism rather than the cultural milieu. He indulges in whims: he goes on food jags (Dr. Clara Davis reports a child who, on a self-selection regime, sometimes ate several eggs at one sitting, and went on an egg spree twice a year in spring and in fall!). He tries one food and then another; he adopts favorites, and normally he steadily widens his range of choice. He goes from milk and cereal to fruit and meat, to vegetables, to combinations and salads. The 5 year old has acquired a catholic appetite.

Such, in brief, is the course of a normally developing appetite. There is a sizable and diversified group of children who do not conform to this developmental pattern. Many of them have appeared in child guidance literature as the horrible consequences of poor management. Pop-eye has done his best to set matters right! It is barely possible that parents, in some instances, have been overcriticized. There is evidence that some children are constitutionally *poor feeders* by usual cultural standards. They are also underweight, but their muscular tone is good: motor activity, motor coordination, and intelligence may be superior. They are often good sleepers as well.

The poor eater may manifest himself as early as 12 weeks. His intake is low per meal, and he rarely goes above a low limit; he does not show the ordinary fluctuations, but holds close to his low optimum. He may be a vomiter; he may or may not be a thumb sucker. But his margin of tolerance is narrow. He insists rather orthodoxically on being fed the same food, the same way, in the same place, by the same person. He is slow in making a shift from food *a* to food *b*, and having accepted *b*, he may for a while reject *a*: he does not combine foods progressively in the ordinary manner. He clings long to purée (he distinguishes like a connoisseur between brand G and brand H). He is a poor chewer. He may not be allergic by clinical tests at the age of two or three, but proves to be so on tests made at a later age. This vaguely suggests a generalized pre-allergic status.

In any event, his behavior from year to year indicates a sluggish gastro-intestinal equipment, or an equipment which has not been fully incorporated into the total action system. It is somewhat as though the latter and the former were developing in slightly separated streams. The dissociation, however, is not complete; and by one device or another, including some very dramatic accessories, the child is fed and grows up. At 5 or 6 years of age he may have outgrown much of his indifference. He is able to throw himself more fully into the task of feeding.

Before that fortunate issue, he eats abstractedly, almost unconsciously, while his caretaker may be amusing him with toys, books, pictures, and reading. Up to the age of 2 years, he eats best with his mother; thereafter, he does better with someone else. The socialized lunch of the nursery school may improve his eating. More often a group is too much for him. He does not like to see others eat; he gags on slight provocation; he cannot abide the sight of slimy foods, etc.

To what extent these peculiarities of behavior are due to faulty management is by no means clear. When the difficulties are chiefly the result of constitutional factors, parents are well advised to respect the child's weakness in this particular field. They should not be too disturbed by periods of stationary weight. It is a mistake to overstimulate the child. It is better to go along with him in his conservatisms, and to wait for an opportune moment to introduce a variation and to widen his diet. He should be handled through things and externals rather than through emotional appeals and dramatic diversions. If complicating personality factors are present they should be reached by indirection and flank approach, but not through the feeding situation. One should be interested in the total growth complex rather than the specific behavior deviation. Although this deviation may cause enough household annoyance, it should be treated without excessive anxiety. Somewhat like thumb sucking, it runs a developmental course, which is based on maturational, constitutional factors.

It is significant that appetite should be subject to so many developmental changes. If we knew all the factors which determine these changes we would have a deepened insight, because they are related, not only to caloric and dietary needs, but also to psychological traits. For that matter, the subtleties of body chemistry and child behavior are one.

2. *Retention.* Food must not only be sought and taken. It must be retained. Even this is not a simple matter. The gastro-intestinal tract is more than a passive receptacle. Its walls are muscular and active. They move in rhythms and waves which must be coordinated, seriated in the right direction, and brought under partial voluntary control. These are retention problems which can be solved only through progressive developmental changes within the central and vegetative nervous systems.

There is a steady rise in intake up to the age of from 8 to 12 weeks, which may reach a maximum of nearly 45 ounces in one day. It seems that the organism has to stoke up for the exacting growth changes which are in progress. There is a tendency to overload. The alimentary tract does not handle its increased task smoothly. There is more gastric distress and passage of gas in both directions. Premature solids and cod liver oil fed to the infant at this time may exacerbate his difficulties. He regurgitates; he may even vomit, the vomiting, if due to neuro-motor instability, being in the nature of an excessive deviation of regurgitating.

Intake and retention have to be balanced. Peristalsis has to be kept going in the right direction throughout the entire alimentary tract. The organism must also acquire the protective ability to reject and to regurgitate. This poses a definite developmental problem, which brings into prominence a group of infants who have a more or less inherently defective peristalsis control. These infants must be differentiated from those who vomit from birth because of partial closure of the pyloric end of the stomach,—cases of pyloric stenosis and pylorospasm which need medical treatment.

Some of the thumb sucking at about the age of 8 to 12 weeks seems to be more closely related to feeding than to sleep behavior. It is induced by hunger; it continues after the feeding, as though the child, for reasons of his developmental economy, needed additional sucking activity. Or the supplementary sucking may be a physiological adjuvant which keeps peristalsis moving in the right direction. It serves as an anti-vomit stimulus. He may continue to suck when hungry up to the age of about 3 years. Thereafter, the sucking is mainly linked to sleep.

In most infants, the early instability is limited to regurgitation and proves to be relatively transient. They usually settle into equilibrium at 16 weeks, and are then even able to expel gastric gas without help. This new ability is evidence of stability. It means that the excessive expulsion tendency is coming under control. A favorable growth change has taken place.

In less favored cases, the vomiting recurs and may not terminate until 6 months or even until 2 years of age. In these cases, the principle of self-demand again shows its importance. Taking cues from the child, it becomes evident that he does better with a reduction in the number of feedings. He benefits from longer rest periods which he uses to build up his retention. If young, he needs careful bubbling. He retains better if he is put in a semi-propped position for an hour after his feeding. For similar reasons at 24 weeks or later, he may prefer to take his bottle in two stages. There is a physiological sanction for the split bottle: he is building up retention.

The tendency to vomiting may be based on a specific neuro-motor susceptibility or on more generalized personality factors. In the latter case, vomiting, at the age of 4 or 5 years, may be used as a threat or as an act to dominate the environment. This is an infantile type of hunger strike, a kind of neurotic utilization. There are many grades and forms. Some individuals have a very effective and discriminating equipment for rejecting adverse food intake. They use their ability when it is really needed. They may be very stable persons.

Gastric instability tends to show itself also at about the age of 3½ years, often in connection with school situations. The first signs are those of abdominal pain which, at 4 years, may develop into frank vomiting. The child is unequal to the stress of transition to school. He reacts by a rejection or distaste response: he vomits. The reaction is not limited to the gastro-intestinal tract, for step by step it invades the domain of personality: he vomits not only in the schoolroom; he vomits on the way to school; later he may even vomit at home on the mere mention of school. This type of vomiting seems to be rooted (if vomiting is ever rooted!) in a sense of insecurity. It often disappears very readily with a little moral support. The mother or a friend accompanies the child to the school-room door, or a neighborhood playmate is allowed to join the strange school group. Then all is suddenly well. The vomiting vanishes. Abdominal pain or vomiting, however, should always be regarded as a significant symptom, which demands and repays careful investigation, particularly of associated personality factors.

3. *Self-help and Acculturation.* Although the alimentary tract is racially the oldest part of man's anatomy, it has always preserved a connection with his highest and most recent brain organization. The whole process of feeding is inseparably linked with his manners and customs. Feeding customs and meal time mores constitute an important chapter in cultural anthropology.

It will be interesting to trace in outline how the infant writes himself into that chapter. We have already noted how his earliest smiles emerge out of satiety and lead to a lengthening of the waking period in a sequence as follows: sleeping-eating-satiety-smiling-sociality-wakefulness-drowsi-ness-sleep. Thus from the beginning, the egocentric act of eating has, nevertheless, a socializing aspect. The socialization of the child is in large measure built around meals. Which, incidentally, makes one wonder whether it is culturally wise to shake a baby out of deep slumber in order to have him eat. It seems to violate the more amiable pattern of nature. One of the tasks of development is to dissociate sleeping and eating with an intervening smile.

The development of feeding behavior in the human infant is a story of progressive self-dependence combined with cultural conformance. The course of this development is not a smooth one. Eating utensils are complex; dining room decorums are exacting; and modern parents are often extraordinarily insistent on tidiness in table manners. Every household works out its own compromise in this task of accommodating the culture to the neurological and psychological limitations of the child. Needless to say, our practices would improve if we recognized these limitations in advance. Even weaning problems are greatly simplified if our procedures are not imposed arbitrarily, but are adapted to the child's immaturity. Under favorable conditions, he weans himself into ever increasing self-dependence. He does so in primitive tribes; he can do it in more complex cultures.

If bottle-fed, he begins to pat the bottle while he is sucking as early as 20 weeks. Transitions to solids are readily made now because the maturity of the nervous system so permits. At 36 weeks he can usually maintain a sustained hold of the bottle. In another month he may sit up and hold and tilt it with the skill of a cornetist. He can feed himself a cracker. At 40 weeks, he also begins to finger feed, plucking small morsels. At 1 year, his strong drive to stand interferes with the further refinement of sedentary eating habits. Wise mothers learn to accept these postural drives when they make their unmistakable appearance in the growth complex. Upright posture, for the moment, is more than meat; and there is no difficulty in feeding him while he is in the standing position.

At this time, an independent child may, of his own initiative, refuse a bottle. He weans himself with dramatic suddenness. He does not shuffle off a coil, he casts it off. By simple and graduated devices weaning from bottle to cup can be achieved without traumatic damage. A few children who show unusual attachment to the bottle continue with it as long as 18 months to 2 years; in some cultures still longer.

By 15 months, he has "learned" to inhibit his former instinctive grasping of dish and tray. One of the first steps in the fine art of table manners is to resist grabbing the bowl that holds your porridge. This new inhibition is based not so much on practice as on a maturational change in the neuro-motor connections of hand and brain. There is a pretty cultural corollary of this pattern of independence: the child insists that his mother should *not* put *her* hand on the tray. He also handles his spoon manfully and begins to feed himself in part, though not without spilling; for the spoon is a complex tool and he has not acquired the postural orientations and pre-perceptions necessary for dexterity.

This surge of independence is a growth phenomenon. It is, of course, counterbalanced by other trends. Indeed, a child who is assertive at 15 months and feeds himself well for a year or two, may then ask for help from his mother, and accept spoonfeeding. At 2 years, he inhibits the turning of the spoon as it enters the mouth, and feeds himself very acceptably. However, the new ability is complex and only delicately supported by his nervous system. Therefore, he feeds himself best when he handles only part of the meal and the food which he particularly likes. Given too much range, he messes and mixes.

It is well to recognize how really difficult these complex acts of motor skill are in their early stages. The child's command of time, space, form, and order are correspondingly immature. If we had a clearer view of the growth complex at the moment, we would pay more attention to details of placement and service, we would see the value of simple arrangements and single courses. It is a mistake to further complicate the child's tasks of coordination and adjustment by trying to assimilate him too soon into the mealtime family circle. He should eat in relative seclusion, unless he is the exceptional type of child who might benefit from the extra stimulation of the full gathering.

When he is a little older he will give cues that lead to occasional admission to the family board. At 3½ years he enjoys a Sunday breakfast with the family. He also likes to eat at his own small table in a corner of the dining room while the family is eating. At 4 years he can join the group a few times oftener; but his talking and restlessness tend to interfere with his eating. He has, however, graduated from meals in his room to meals in the kitchen. At 5 years he manages breakfast nicely with the family and is soon invited to other meals. He is susceptible to the food promotions that come over the radio. He likes to eat away from home, especially at a restaurant. He is more of a man of the world!

Thus we see that when arbitrary procedures are avoided, the child normally tends to induct himself into the culture which surrounds him. His lapses and resistances arise mainly out of his immaturities; and spring from over-rigid schedules which ignore his self-demands.

There are, however, two more or less clearly defined types of children who do not acquire self-help by the ordinary progressions. They are the *poor feeders* already discussed, and the *perfectionists*. The poor feeder does not have a lusty gastro-intestinal tract which is closely integrated with his personality. He therefore lacks the drive toward self-help, which normally comes from this source. The source is somewhat separated from his motivations. He therefore fails to show an interest in self-help.

The perfectionist also remains dependent. His self-help is retarded and awkward. Apparently, he suffers from a diffuse or generalized motor insufficiency which gives him an excessive amount of caution and disinclination. He will not blunder; he will not undertake an act before he is quite sure of himself. He has an extraordinary sense of form, and sensitiveness to incompleteness of form. He cannot abide untidiness. A spilled drop must be wiped up before he proceeds. He does not even finger feed. He does not like sticky fingers! But he likes ice cream and at the age of 4 or 5 years he can be inveigled into feeding himself this delicacy. By slow stages the self-feeding spreads to other foods; and his onlookers heave a sigh of relief.

Because the deepest and the most vital cravings of the infant and child have to do with food and sleep, his daily schedules of feeding and sleeping assume great psychological significance. We are too accustomed to think of these schedules from the narrow standpoint of physical regimen and to underrate their effects on mental welfare. Only by individualizing the regimen on the basis of growth needs can we meet his organic needs promptly and fully. By meeting them with certainty, we multiply those experiences of satisfied expectations which create an increasing sense of security, the first essential of mental health.

§3. BOWEL CONTROL

THE EXCRETORY FUNCTIONS are controlled by a complex combination of voluntary and involuntary mechanisms,—and by cultural proprieties. These proprieties are expressed in customs, in strict taboos and in repugnances colored by more or less intense emotion. Anthropological literature is replete with details, showing how different peoples react to these natural functions. Present day social groups in our culture have tended to place excessive emphasis on early toilet training, euphemistically called "habit training."

Such habit training is based on the naive theory that practice makes perfect, and that by beginning in time the desired cleanliness can be established early. In its zeal the household often goes to extremes in this particular field of acculturaticn. Punishment, bribes, shaming, scolding, and relentless instruction are resorted to, and yet the child does not learn. Is there some fault in the child? Or some weakness in the theory of habit formation?

Bowel control is in fact an extremely complicated function. The involuntary act of evacuation consists in peristaltic contractions of the colon, governed by the vegetative nervous system; but the voluntary delay and initiation of the act under variable conditions requires a marked degree of inhibition by the higher centers of the brain. This inhibition cannot be acquired by steady straight line progression, by mere habit training, because the control of the bowel involves not only the sphincter muscles but the entire child as a total organism. Voluntary defecation is not a simple localized reaction, but a total response; and the entire child changes from age to age. Therefore the total response is different from age to age, in its neurology, in its psychology.

This is the reason that cultural control is so difficult; cultural intervention so often misguided. Far from being a simple physiological reflex, bowel control is a complicated behavior pattern profoundly influenced by maturity factors.

[321]

The growth of patterns of bowel behavior, therefore, is marked by irregularities, by ups and downs, by self-regulatory fluctuations, comparable to those which characterize the early patterning of sleep and feeding. As the child matures there are changes in the frequency of bowel movements, in the times of occurrence, in promptness of release; in postural attitudes, in self and social reference, in perceptual interest, in anticipatory adjustments, and in the accompanying verbalizations. These changes, to say nothing of personality differences, are developmental in nature. To a significant extent they are beyond cultural prescription; yet they determine the difficulties, the failures, and the successes of so-called toilet training.

The acquisition of bowel control, therefore, must be interpreted in terms of growth and maturity, rather than from the narrow standpoint of habit and learning. The parent's (and the physician's) guidance should be shaped with reference to the developmental factors. The short-comings of the young child cannot be regarded as perversities; often they are paradoxical but positive steps toward ultimate control. It is the discrepancy between the cultural pattern and the maturing behavior pattern which is at the root of maladjustment. The maladjustments are greatly reduced if the lawful developmental factors are recognized in advance. It is the purpose of the following summary to present these factors concretely in their time sequence and in dynamic perspective.

In the first few weeks bowel movements are extraordinarily numerous. They occur somewhat sporadically; but by *4 weeks* they are more closely associated with the act of waking, as though they were emerging out of sheer vegetativeness and entering into the conscious life of the infant. They tend to occur in the daytime and their number falls to three or four daily. By *8 weeks* there may be only two movements and they come not only on waking but also at the close of a feeding and occasionally during a feeding. The infant gives visible evidence of attention, which suggests still more clearly that at least the sensory aspect of this behavior is coming within the scope of adaptive attention. In other words, even now the act is not purely automatic.

By *16 weeks* there may be a definite interval of delay between the feeding and the evacuation, as though Nature were intent on making a more clearcut distinction between eating and elimination. Culture in the form of a vigilant mother notes this delay; seizes upon it, by placing the baby on a receptacle, and for a dozen days, perhaps, the baby is already toilet trained!

But alas, this is the very transitional time when the baby is undergoing an almost revolutionary change in his postural-perceptual makeup. He is beginning to sit up, with support. The neat little "habit" of regularity, which he has just acquired, was suitable to a supine infant and no longer fits neatly into his new behavior equipment. So he "has to learn all over again." And that is precisely what he is constantly doing throughout the whole period of his rapid growth. Changes in his postural, prehensory, adaptive and emotional behavior are reflected in changes in his bowel behavior. If he had remained on a 12 to 16 week level of maturity he would remain "trained."

At *28 weeks* his movements show temporary irregularity. They are no longer closely associated with waking or eating. One may occur early during the morning in the play period, another late in the afternoon. A few infants, chiefly girls, fuss when soiled; but most infants are indifferent and usually are resistant to "training."

By *40 weeks* the capacity to sit has been well mastered, and for a period of several weeks the infant responds to training; that is he reacts adaptively to toilet placement. He grunts and looks up at the mother's face during the act; all of which means that the behavior pattern is undergoing progressive elaboration, and becoming more completely incorporated into the child's action system.

But by *1 year* postural developments again introduce complications. "Successes" are less frequent; resistance again appears; the relation of looking at the mother also is lost. Some of these irregularities and apparent losses may be ascribed to the assumption of the upright posture. The irregularities occur because the nervous system is undergoing a reorganization which simultaneously has to take care of the several sphincter

[323]

controls, the mastery of standing up, and obedience to cultural directions. If the various developments proceeded on an even front there would be no fluctuations, no necessity for interweaving with its alternating rhythms and accents.

By *15 months,* standing upright is already well achieved and the irregularities and resistances lessen. The child now likes to go to the toilet. Some children of this age instinctively assume a squat position, as though they had just come by inheritance into an ancient pattern. On the toilet they often show prolonged sphincter contraction; they release this contraction on removal, as though waiting for the stimulus of the diaper. This again is a temporary phase, which reveals that the developmental task is to achieve a working balance between contraction and relaxation. Each at first comes under voluntary control separately. Coordination of the two comes later. First a then b; then a:b::b:a.

By *18 months* contraction is sometimes too strong, at other times release is explosive. Words, also, are coming into the total behavior situation, and they play no mean part in personal and cultural control. The articulate child who is able to say "Toidy" and to relate it to the bowel movement thereby increases his voluntary control. This is the type of child who thenceforth may have few accidents. He is trained, because he has matured all the requisite components for a pattern which is at once personal and cultural.

A second type of child with the same amount of "training" is slow in "learning." He does not use words as aptly. He is more interested in sounds and non-essentials. He does not fasten on the salient features of process and product. He has to progress by more intimate and direct experience. He may even dabble with the feces. Innocent forms of "stool smearing" have their inception in this circumstance. He does not relate the act to a social setting; he does not relate it to his mother. He relates it to his own taking care of himself. He is likely to have his movement in mid-morning while he is alone, standing in his crib or pen. Occasionally he may cry out in distress as though he did not know what it is all about.

There may be a simple guilt sense, but we are inclined to ascribe such symptoms to a combination of physiological and personal awkwardness.

At *21 months* there may be a transient period of physiological lability manifested in a form of diarrhea which is not traceable to mucoid irritation. During the same period there may be a marked increase in the frequency of urination. This suggests another transitional stage during which higher nervous controls are being incorporated.

The *2 year old* is quite trainable if he is permitted to take over himself. The parent removes the child's pants and then leaves him to his own devices. Some children manage best when divested of all clothes. This freedom apparently favors a more totalized response.

At the paradoxical age of *2½ years,* the child naturally shows a tendency to extremes and exaggeration. At this period he may not have a bowel movement for a whole day or a succession of two days. The organism is acquiring an increased span of retention, but in so doing it temporarily exaggerates a constructive growth trend. Fruit laxatives are a legitimate cultural aid.

By the *age of 3* there is an increased ability to withhold and to postpone. The daily bowel movement tends to occur in late afternoon or even after supper. The child accepts and even asks for cultural help.

By the *age of 4* this function has become a private affair. The child manages almost completely for himself. He insists on a closed bathroom door, but is inquisitive to ascertain how this function occurs in others. He has curiosity about animal behavior and is somewhat perplexed by their indifference to the conventions of human culture. He has a child-like interest in volume, color, consistency and conformation. This interest is wholesome and intelligent, not immodest. In all his aspects, the 4 year old is a frank, forthright individual. In spite of his independent competence, he may occasionally have an accident, by way of tension outlet under excitement or strain.

Slight incontinence occurs at *6 years* of age under the stress of school life. By this time he has become a member of the social group ready to cast hot aspersion on any member who shows lapses in the field of elimination behavior.

Culture has put opprobrium on any weakness of this kind, and yet in the phrase "intestinal fortitude" it makes half humorous acknowledgment of a human frailty. The fact that under excessive strain even the adult shows such frailty should make us more sympathetic to the developmental difficulties of the young child.

The foregoing developmental survey, however, is not intended to overstate these difficulties. On the contrary, many of the disappointments and the emotional tensions and perturbations which parents encounter in toilet training are self afflicted. If the complexity of the growth mechanisms is recognized, and if the organization of bowel control is understood in terms of growth, the tensions subside and the child is spared unnecessary confusions.

Although the developmental sequences which have been outlined are typical, they will naturally be modified by individual differences in psychic constitution. Benign and transient stool exploitation (stool smearing) has already been mentioned as one deviation. It may occur at any age from 1 to 2½ years. It may occur once or twice, intermittently, or in some instances two or three times a day. It usually originates in a clumsy effort at self care; it may have the novelty of self discovery and the stool is naively exploited as though it were so much plasticene; it may even be neatly disposed on the door trimmings with some respect for design.

When the propensity is unduly prolonged and does not yield to common sense measures, it may be regarded as a symptom of poor personality organization. The child is functioning in a fragmentary way and is not assimilating his toilet behavior into an integrating action system. He does not have a sufficiently vigorous sense of self when he is alone to subordinate this, to him, interesting and half autonomous behavior. Significantly enough when he is with another person he does not indulge in the behavior at all.

The more frequent and milder manifestations of this malbehavior are readily overcome by providing plasticene for exploitation, by dressing

the child in impervious coveralls, and by encouraging self-management
by slow degrees. Needless to say, marked emotions and severe disciplinary
measures harm rather than help.

In the whole task of toilet acculturation parents are in danger of ex-
pending too much emotion and too little wise tolerance. When we take
a long range view of the underlying developmental mechanisms, we immediately see the child's growth problems in a more rational light. That
is the basis of intelligent guidance.

§4. BLADDER CONTROL

THE MECHANISMS which govern the bladder are comparable to those
which govern the bowel. In both instances we are dealing with an involuntary mechanism, into which voluntary control is incorporated
through the slow and devious processes of development. The vegetative
nervous system and the higher brain centers are coordinated to bring
about this control. An extremely elaborate network of nerve cell connections must be built up during the first five years of life. And even
then the controls are not perfected; growth continues through adolescence, and the bladder walls and sphincter always remain very sensitive
to the psychical activities of the individual, whether in infancy, childhood or adult years. The bladder is a component of the genito-urinary
system and inseparable from the total organism. Voluntary urination is
not a simple local reaction, but a total response of a total organism
which is subject to the manifold changes of growth and maturity. These
changes are reflected in times and modes of elimination, in postural attitudes, in motor and verbal adjustments and in psychological orientations.

The acquisition of bladder control, therefore, is marked by the same
variabilities, the same ups and downs and regulatory fluctuations which
we have noted in tracing the development of bowel control. Indeed our
studies have demonstrated a significant correspondence in the growth
of these two functions from age to age. There is almost a parallelism which

is based upon common, coinciding maturity factors. Naturally the guidance and "training" procedures will also have much in common.

At about *4 weeks* of age the infant may burst into a brief cry during sleep on the occurrence of micturition. It is as though the passage of the urine and the consequent wetness punctured the unconsciousness of sleep with a glimmer of wakefulness. The infant must learn to wake, and these early experiences in bladder and bowel response may represent faint acts of attention. Indeed the whole development of voluntary bladder control consists in the formation of increasingly specific and elaborate patterns of attention.

By *16 weeks* the number of daily micturitions has decreased and the volume of certain micturitions has definitely increased. Nature is channelizing the output by the same developmental methods whereby she channelizes and consolidates the baby's naps.

At *28 weeks* this is evidenced by soaking wet diapers. Intervals of dryness from one to two hours in length now occur.

At *40 weeks* it may be noted that the baby is dry for a whole hour, after a given nap, or after an hour's ride in his carriage. Capitalizing the import of these dry periods, the mother toilet-places him immediately after the nap and the ride. A few children can be "trained" in this way as early as 28 weeks. But the control is limited to one or two episodes during the day, and is subject to lapses. The results are not permanent or deepseated and they do more credit to the mother's vigilance than the baby's self-control. They are not permanent, because the new postural abilities create new complications, which require further reorganization of his total behavior equipment. It must always be remembered that a single function like bladder control, feeding, or sleep is always part of an ever changing growth complex; and that any individual function or "habit" is inevitably modified by ever changing contexts. Habits do not grow. The child grows.

As he grows he acquires experiences which direct his further growth. At 40 weeks and later, it will be recalled, his index finger becomes a prying instrument for exploring his environment and for penetrating

[328]

into the third dimension. Accordingly he probes on occasion into urine which he has produced. Although he does this only a few times it helps him toward an understanding of what is actually a complex situation.

At *1 year* dryness after nap may persist. He may show intolerance of wetness at certain times of the day. Often he responds to toilet placement, and would appear to be a good candidate for training; but the development of standing and walking apparently introduces difficulties and resistances. Past learnings prove ephemeral.

At *15 months* postural difficulties have lessened. He likes to sit on the toilet, and responds at optimal times. But at other times he resists. This is because he is in a transitional stage in which contraction of the sphincters of the bladder eclipses relaxation. His retention span has lengthened to two or three hours. Placement on the toilet may stimulate him to withhold urine. He exercises this capacity while he sits. The moment he is removed, he promptly releases urine. This is a common household phenomenon. The mother, unaware of the growth factors at work, interprets the whole performance as wilfulness. If exasperated she may resort to unwise discipline. It should be recalled that the same type of behavior shows itself in bowel situations. This also is the time when the child has not yet gained modulated control of manual release. Having seized an object he may hold it in his hand and "let go" with exaggerated release. It takes time for the nervous system to attain smoothly working balances in its inner machinery.

But all the time he is widening the basis for ultimate control. He is just learning to talk and he promptly brings speech into the expanding behavior pattern. He points, not without pride, at a puddle and says, "uh, uh," or "See!" He uses the same word (uh) indifferently for the product of bowel or bladder. Not until some months later will he make a distinction. By way of further verification he sometimes pats the puddle. Patting is characteristic of this age of maturity; he pats his picture book in the same manner. There is nothing portentous in this passing exploitation.

Language assumes an increased role at *18 months*. If he is asked whether he needs to go to the toilet he can respond with a discriminating nod of his head or a "No." Using his recently acquired word "uh" he can even occasionally ask in advance. Words which are rooted in the child's own experience are instruments of control. He is becoming susceptible to "shaming." He understands when he is asked to get a cloth to wipe up a puddle. He goes on the errand with alacrity. At this age, in contrast to his 15 months response of over-contraction, he now may respond with explosive over-release to toilet placement. He may also report any "accidents."

At *21 months*, likewise, his natural tendency is to report, unless he has been unwisely spanked. Such reporting is part of the learning-growing process. He reports or announces not only after but occasionally before. He tells. He is greatly pleased with his successes.

The developmental pendulum is swinging from the contraction phase (withholding) to a relaxation phase. The number of urinations greatly increases. Lapses multiply; and the child calls his mother back frequently after he has been put to bed. To the head of the family it all looks like sheer backsliding. This is the time when father steps in and applies stern punishment. And of all times, this is the worst; for the child is in the midst of a constructive growth transition when he is bringing the opposing functions of sphincter contraction and relaxation into more stable balance (a:b::b:a).

By the age of 2 years these functions are in better equilibrium. The *2 year old* therefore shows a definite advance in control. He offers no resistance to routine toilet placements. He definitely tells in advance. He may go to the bathroom by himself and pull his pants down. He expresses pride in achievement, saying, "Good Boy." He is beginning to differentiate between products of bowel and bladder by whatever omnipoetic or other slang the household has adopted. But he is not over-precise,—he may call a puddle "Bad Boy!"

In spite of the definite gains in voluntary control, night fluctuations persist. If the developmental pattern is one of quick shifting he may be dry for two nights, then wet, then dry again for two nights. Or if he is a "slow shifter" the fluctuating intervals may be two weeks long. These fluctuations themselves are part of a yet further consolidation of gains.

The retention span is lengthening. It may stretch to five or more hours by the age of $2\frac{1}{2}$ years. This is the period when the contraction both of the bowel and the bladder sphincters is in the ascendancy. Girls, who in general are ahead of boys in sphincter control, may wake up dry even after relatively long naps. The child is now learning to stop and to resume in the midst of a micturition. This is a new elaboration. However he still has difficulty in initiating release, he is dependent on the conditioning circumstances of his own bathroom and cannot command his emerging abilities in strange surroundings. He may need verbal props from his mother. But he is consistently advancing; he is more sophisticated, he watches with great interest the elimination behavior of others, including animals.

The *3 year old* as we have so often observed is in focus. Accordingly he is well routinized in his bladder functions. He accepts assistance. Accidents are infrequent. He demands to be changed if they occur. Some 3 year olds sleep dry throughout the night; some even wake up by themselves and ask to be taken to the toilet. Others can be taken up for toileting without being roused out of sleep.

The *4 year old* likewise remains routinized, but he more or less insists on taking over the routine himself. He makes it a private affair, behind closed doors; although he is frankly inquisitive about the same affair in others. He also displays an almost amusing degree of interest in strange bathrooms. He seems to be intrigued by them when he goes abroad. This, after all, is a natural growth symptom. At 2 years he was resistant to or even fearful of strange bathrooms and unaccustomed plumbing.

Although the 4 year old is blithely self-reliant, he makes errors of judgment, due to his immature time sense, and the low threshold of his voluntary control. The result is that he is often caught in predicaments which produce panicky dismay. The culture might well spare him some of these unpleasant experiences by more thoughtful planning.

The *5 year old* again shows more aplomb. He does not feel the same childish interest in novel bathrooms; he takes them as a matter of course. He is not so subject to surprise and tension outlets. He sleeps dry; and if he rises at night he can take care of himself. His thresholds are higher; he is not as likely as the 4 year old to suffer lapses with the onset of a cold, or the beginning of cold weather.

Ordinary individual differences and deviations in the acquisition of bladder control are correlated with constitutional differences in thresholds and in modes of growth. The developmental sequences, outlined above, are grounded in the architectonics of the nervous system and therefore should prove useful in interpreting individual deviations. Maturation of the nervous structures does not always advance at an even pace, or one component lags while another goes forward. Some children seem discouragingly slow in training, but on some fine day, perhaps under the stroke of a stimulating personal event, a missing connection is shunted in, and control is achieved with dramatic suddenness. Something has been added; maturation had taken place after all. Having "clicked" these children usually stay controlled.

In other children, control is not so durable. The physiological threshold of their urinary system is low and the tensions of even slight vicissitudes find their outlet through this system. The wriggling and susceptibility which is normal enough in a 4 year old when he is excited, persists into the later school years. These children develop various forms of wetting, which should be distinguished from the serious degrees of clinical enuresis. Simple physiological awkwardness should be considered, before ascribing the weakness to more profound personality disorders.

A small group of boys show related inadequacies in postural and manual control which make it difficult for them to shift from a seated to a standing posture during urination. Hand to mouth reactions likewise were slow, meager, and clumsy. And yet these children may be so fastidious and perfectionistic that their failures prevent them from taking the usual next developmental step forward.

There is another group of cases in which the "slowness in training" is due to specific retardation. These children are intelligent and well constituted emotionally yet they are backward and inept in sphincter control. It is almost as though they were handicapped by a specific disability (like constitutional poor spelling). They may not begin to sleep dry all night until the age of 4 or 5 years. Even after they reach school age their records are chequered. They have a dry period for several weeks in spring followed by lapses in autumn and winter. They organize slowly; but with a tendency toward improvement. They do better at 7 years than at 6 years; and sometimes a fortunate change of scene during holidays brings about a reorientation that may lead to permanent control. Such cases need strategic planning rather than detailed therapeusis. The difficulties so transparently have a developmental origin that they should be guided on that basis.

Indeed the whole problem of bladder control is so charged with developmental factors in normal as well as deviated children, that they should have primary consideration both in interpretation and in treatment. All things considered, it seems that our modern culture still has much to learn from the child himself in this delicate sphere of personal-social behavior. The culture is inclined to be too meddlesome and too emotional. We would not advocate more neglect, although this would often be less harmful; because it would give the wisdom of nature a fuller scope. What we need, instead of neglect, is timely help with a light rather than heavy hand; and above all with a discerning hand. But how can the hand be deft or discerning without a knowledge of the ways of development?

§5. PERSONAL AND SEX INTERESTS

UNDER THIS HEADING we consider a group of problems which concern a very personal aspect of the development of the individual. The problems are complex and are charged with cultural inhibitions. Moreover, certain theories and popular misconceptions of early personality development have invested the whole subject with such portentous implications

[333]

that it is difficult to see the issues in proportion. A simple factual statement of the sequences of development as observed in actual children should help to put the problems of guidance in their true light. They are not as portentous as they have been made to seem.

The problems of personal and sex interests in infant and young child are, after all, not essentially different from those which have already been discussed. The principles of development and guidance which apply to sleep, feeding, and elimination apply in precisely the same manner to the patterning of personal-sex behavior. As indicated in Chapter 3, there are no special or unique laws for the organization of emotions. Indeed, so integrated and unified are the processes of psychological growth that an intelligent management of feeding, sleep, and elimination behavior, in itself, almost insures a favorable organization of other fields of behavior. The problems of so-called sex-hygiene may be approached with confidence, and without an undue sense of mystery.

The newborn infant has no personality problems. He is so deeply immersed in the cosmos and the culture which has accepted him, that in his nonage he neither needs nor craves a clear sense of self-identity. But as he grows up he must disengage himself from this universality, and become a well-defined individual. By the time he is five or six years old he must see himself for what he is. There are many stepping stones along the way,—articulate and inarticulate. Here are some of them:

Johnny,—that's me. * I am I. * That is my mother. * That is my father. * He is a man. * I am a boy. * Susan is a girl. * She has a father and mother too. * I was a baby. * I grew. * I came from my mother. * I am going to get bigger. * I am going to go to school.

These thirteen propositions cumulatively create the outlook of a school beginner. They make a logical sequence, but they are by no means automatic axioms. They are complicated judgments which the young child has to achieve through the slow and steady processes of growth, aided by experience which sometimes is bitter. Each successive proposition represents one more step in a progressive differentiation which disengages him more fully from the culture in which he is so deeply involved. Paradoxically this very disengagement also identifies him more fully with his culture; he transforms from a mere ward to a working member.

The process of disengagement entails a continuous reorganization of his emotions. He is "attached" to his mother, to his father, to the household. He feels this attachment vividly when fatigue or helplessness causes him to seek comfort and refuge. Affection has its root in such dependency and protectiveness. But he also feels detachment, particularly when he exercises some new power which gives him a sense of independence. He is driven, as it were, toward two opposite poles: to cling to safety and to emancipate himself from its restrictions. He must at least have enough defiance to grow. Normal emotional growth requires a proper balance of affection and of self-reliance.

But, as already suggested, his developmental task is not simply emotional; he must achieve judgments as to his place in the social scheme, he must identify himself as one kind of person, his mother as another kind, his father as still another kind. He must distinguish between parent and child, between male and female, between senior and junior, between conformance and defiance. *These judgments, although strongly tinged with personal emotions, are essentially intellectual. They require perception, discrimination, and intelligence.* It is this part of the story which needs emphasis, for here lies the key to understanding and successful guidance.

At *4 weeks* of age, the baby's face is generally impassive. By *8 weeks* it breaks into a spontaneous social smile at the sight of another person's face. Whether at that moment he is more conscious of his interior smile or of the external face, might be debated. In any event, this double reference is at the basis of the child's socialization and personalization. At *16 weeks* the social smile is spontaneous or self-induced.

By *28 weeks* he already reacts differently to a stranger's face. This discrimination shows that the development of complex personal perceptions is already under way. He has already made an elementary distinction,—a personal-social judgment.

[335]

By *40 weeks* or a year he has made significant advances in self-discovery. Whether sitting up or lying down, his arms and hands now have more freedom of movement, and he uses them to explore his own physical self. At 16 weeks they were at his mouth; at 20 weeks they engaged above his chest. Following the head to foot trend which is characteristic of development, the hands at 40 weeks (and later) come down to the thighs. Just as he used to indulge in mutual fingering, he now makes contact with his genitals when not clothed. Ordinarily his exploitive manipulation is a more or less transient event in the course of his physical self-discovery.

In the period from *1 to 2 years* there is an increasing amount of social reference. Although the infant-child is capable of long stretches of self-absorbed activity, he is also given to numerous social advances which are the charm of this age period. He extends a toy to a person; he holds out his arm for the sleeve; he says "ta-ta"; he hands the empty cereal dish to his mother; he tugs at her skirt to bring her to an object of interest; he asks for food, drink, and toilet; he echoes back the last two words of conversation. By all these tokens and devices, he builds up a vast body of specific perceptual experience which ultimately enables him to draw the momentous conclusion that there are other persons in the world more or less like himself. The urge to discover these persons is a growth phenomenon. It shows itself in various personal and sex interests which follow in natural sequence.

This discovery of other persons is of such great magnitude that it must come piecemeal, and gradually, otherwise he might be overwhelmed. Even so he seeks increased refuge in giving and receiving affection. He is willing to be called darling; he will spurn it later. He is willing to be held by the hand; he will refuse it later. He likes to nestle on occasion in his mother's lap. (She may remember this period as the time when he used to be so much more affectionate than he is now!) The stern fact is that affection is related to the varying balances of security and insecurity. For example, at 18 months, he seeks and shows affection when he suffers from the physical (and mental?) discomfort of having wet himself. At about 21 months he grows more tender toward the end of the day. He expresses affection by kissing, particularly at bedtime. Children are affectionate by nature, but the amount, the times, and the depths of their affection vary with the necessities of development. Affection is not a diffuse, general trait, but it is a structured network of attitudes, shaped within a total growth complex. We must be prepared to see changes in its structure as the child matures.

Two years is a transitional period when the child both clings to moorings and cuts from them. *Johnny* is his name, and in his inarticulate psychology, the spoken word Johnny which he hears is nothing more or less than he himself! His name is Johnny as a person.—He will soon use the pronouns *you*, *me*, and *I*,—a further indication of a fundamental change in the psychology of his self. But he still refers to himself by name (Johnny) rather than pronoun, and if one wishes to secure his *personal* attention it is advisable to address him by *Johnny* rather than *You*. All of which proves our thesis that we are dealing with a complicated growth process,—the growth of intricate perceptions.

The *2 year old* thinks that all the world is peopled with "mommies" and "daddies" and that all the children are "babies." This flight of generalization does him no little credit but he has much more to learn. He has to differentiate between *the* mommie and *a* mommie. He also has to make a sharper distinction between his mother and his father. In the natural course of household events he has observed differences in their clothing and their methods of toileting. His early distinctions of sex are based on dress, hair style, and possibly voice.

At about the age of *2½ years*, having acquired more comprehension of his own urinary functions, he is interested in the difference between boys and girls, in their mode of micturition. This might be called a genito-urinary interest, because that is the point of departure, and it leads to a new awareness of genitalia in self and others.

Now the keenness and suddenness of that awareness will depend upon several factors: the age and sex of the child; the child's temperament; the presence or absence of brothers and sisters; the bathroom and beach folkways of the household in which he is reared. These folkways vary tremendously in our American culture from extreme modesty and deception to undiscriminating lack of reserve. The latter can scarcely be recommended from the standpoint of the guidance of growth. If the parents note undue interest and extreme awareness at this age, it is wise to graduate the experiences of the child to his capacity to assimilate them. It is not a question of concealment, but of commonsense adjustment, particularly to the needs of over-sensitive or over-susceptible children.

The *2½ year old* child has a more vigorous sense of self. He says *I* want. *I* need. He is negative as well as positive. He says, "I don't like." He can state his own sex by negation: "No, I'm not a girl."

Inasmuch as this is a nodal age, the organism is in sensitive equilibrium. Nature must check and countercheck. If his sense of *I* and his will to power waxed too strong he would go off on a developmental tangent. Besides, his sense of *I* needs content. A full sense of I-ness demands an appreciation of the biographic *I* in which the present 2½ year old *I* had its origin. Accordingly he becomes spontaneously interested in his own infancy. Nature provides for his instruction in a charming way. She has this budding child relive his babyhood. Through question and answer, pictures and stories, he is enabled to relive in short scenes and acts the infantile parts which once he played. For even he has a past. The revival of that past consolidates his sense of self, gives it substance, and even flatters it with a feeling of superiority; for he is no longer a baby like that!

Such reliving seems to us not a backwash of regression, but a method of growth. It takes on ominous import only in the over-sensitized child who lingers too long in the retrospect, and whose constitutional style of growth is so deviated that he shows similarly faulty mechanisms along the whole course of maturing. It is not abnormal for a child, say 33 months old, to wish to be carried as though he were a baby. It is a passing phase, part of the dramatic recapture of the infancy now being superseded.

Even by the age of *3 years*, the child has attained a well-balanced sense of self. He has no marked preference for either sex, although earlier he may have shown a fixation upon one sex in a manner suggestive of a possible temperamental trend. He knows his own sex with assurance. His interest in human anatomy remains strong; he talks freely and naturally about differences which he has observed. He has a rather catholic although fragmented interest in the structure of family life. He wants a baby in somewhat the same way in which he wants a tricycle.

By the age of *3½ years* questions about marriage begin. Both boys and girls show an intellectual interest in brides! (Bridegrooms and fathers scarcely figure at all in the marital interests of the next few years!) Weddings are vaguely explored in questions and dramatic play. Children, more or less regardless of sex, propose marriage to their fathers and mothers.

An articulate child of three or so may ask where he was before he was born. He may ask other questions which seem to bear very profoundly on the origin of babies. In reality the questions are usually not deep. Extremely simple answers satisfy his rather fragmentary curiosity. His mind has just thrown out a pseudopod: he is not absorbed in the eternal verities. He wants an answer that makes sense for *him* and not for you. To find out what makes sense for him, counter with a few naive questions of your own. His naive answers will indicate how you may shape your replies. You are guiding his growth. This is not the time to get out a picture book on Life and its Origin, which "explains" the whole story from Genesis to Exodus.—We shudder to think that even at the age of five he may be called to sit in a circle at the feet of the Kindergarten teacher who, book in hand, will make it all plain!

Even the blithe and boisterous *4 year old* is none too ready for complete information. On occasion, with bravado, he would like to be a man of the world; but he really is still closely bound to his mother. He cites her as authority in cases of dispute. MY mommie says so! He will, therefore, believe her if she tells him how babies are born; but for the time being he would almost prefer to compromise on the fiction that the baby was bought at the hospital, and that it cost money (which lessens the fiction!). One reason why he is intellectually satisfied with such a fiction is that his imagination and comprehension do not include the selling side of transac-

[339]

tions. He is not interested in selling as such. Temporarily, on account of his immaturity, he understands buying, but not selling.

We do not cite this fact in order to recommend a fiction, but rather to suggest how precisely the maturation of the child determines the effectiveness of instruction and guidance. A child whose comprehension is so neatly delimited that he understands only the buying part of a two-way market transaction, may well not be ready for the whole story of reproduction. He has, nevertheless, some interest in growth, including the period of prenatal growth. He likes to weigh and measure himself and by dramatic gesticulation to boast how he is getting bigger and bigger.

Indeed, the mental organization of the 4 year old is somewhat fluid. He is quite likely to worry about how the baby "gets out." He may spontaneously decide it is through the navel. The navel is an enigma to him, and may become the focus of his modesty and secretiveness. If he is given to exposure, it is the navel, as well as genitals which he exposes. His urinary function, it will be recalled, tends to show some instability. Under the excitement of being in a strange house, he asks to go to the toilet. Under stress he tends to grasp his genitals. The urogenital-system is a frequent tension outlet at this age.

Between *5 and 6 years* the child again comes into developmental equilibrium and focus as he did at 3 years. He does so at a more sophisticated level. He has lost some of the sophomoric traits of 4 year oldness, and has more sense of status and propriety. He has a better appreciation of the folkways of culture. He shows the conservatism of youth in deferring to them, and citing them to his parents for their consideration. He does not want to be different from humanity. Boys and girls alike at this age talk freely about having babies of their own (without making any reference to marriage or the father's role). They also ask their parents directly for a brother or a sister.

*   *   *   *

And so the spiral once more comes to a full turn. By slow and not altogether painless stages the 5 year old has achieved the thirteen sequential judgments which register his cultural maturity. He has even foreshadowed a fourteenth judgment which vaguely prophesies that when he grows up he will be a parent as once he was a baby.

But this is no time to say "Presto, we shall now tell him all the facts of life!" Children learn these facts in terms of circumstances, contexts, and contingencies, many of which cannot be foreseen. The child needs a background and a frame of reference for acquiring more knowledge. There is some point in the warning of "too little and too late." But there is also danger in "too much and too early." Specific guidance should be adjusted to the child's ability to assimilate.

Now it happens that from some apparently instinctive logic, children have a sense of hierarchy. Almost always the older child behaves as such toward a junior. Nearly all children are interested in babies. This is the matrix of their personal and sex curiosities. But this interest should not be imposed upon. A 2 year old may look on entranced while he sees a baby nurse at the breast: but he may project himself too tensely into this situation, and over-react. Such over-reaction may be avoided if his immaturity is not imposed upon. This holds true of all of the "crises" which we have recounted for the first five years of life. These crises are handled successfully by the great mass of normal children. There are a few children who show a strange lack of interest in life origins and in sex, even at the age of seven or eight years. Wise parents may plan simple circumstances which will bring the interest into focus; but the interest cannot be imparted. The impulse must come from within the child.

The greatest source of serious deviations in this field of personal-social behavior is the oversensitive child in combination with an overzealous parent. This leads to overawareness on both sides. The patience and moderation of a normal developmental tempo are sacrificed for the purpose of outwitting development. The policy of excessive, ill-timed frankness creates difficulties instead of solving them.

Perhaps there is something to be said, after all, in favor of certain reserves between parent and child,—to say nothing about the cultural reserves which amateur anthropologists too glibly designate as taboos.

[341]

Intelligent reserve has its place in our relations with children. It lies at the basis of courtesy and deference. It demands an acknowledgment of the sequences and the logic of development.

*   *   *   *

A *Tabular Summary* of the sequences of development which have just been considered is presented on the following three pages. The sequences are listed in two parallel columns to emphasize the close correspondences between the growth of the *personal-social self* and the growth of the *differentiations of the self and other selves*. This is primarily a process of perceptual organization. It is a process of self-discovery in which the child relates what he perceives in others to what he knows concerning his own self. The identification proceeds reciprocally from these others to self and self to others. At first the identification is limited to hands and face, later it takes its departure in the organs and functions of elimination, and then goes into the historical part of the self, namely, the child's own babyhood. All this perceptual and emotional organization is part of a total unitary growth complex. There is no evidence that the specific sex factors are all determining. To appreciate the full implication of the tabular summary it should be read both vertically and transversely from column to column.

The table also has practical uses. It suggests how much a child is likely to understand at a given stage of development. This may help the parent to determine how much needs to be told to the inquiring child.

COMPARATIVE GROWTH SEQUENCES

Personal-Social Self (Individual and Inter-Personal Status)	*Differentiation of Self & Others* (Elimination—Sex—Babies)
8 weeks	
Social smile at sight of another person's face	

Personal-Social Self
(Individual and Inter-Personal Status)

Differentiation of Self & Others
(Elimination—Sex—Babies)

12 weeks

Regards own hand
Vocal social response
Knows mother and recognizes her
Enjoys evening play with father

16 weeks

Fingers his own fingers
Spontaneous social smile

20 weeks

Smiles at mirror image
Cries when someone leaves him

24 weeks

Smiles and vocalizes at mirror image
Discriminates strangers

28 weeks

Grasps his feet
Pats mirror image

32 weeks

Withdraws from strangers

36 weeks

Responds to his own name

40 weeks

Waves bye-bye and pat-a-cakes

44 weeks

Extends object to person without release
Again withdraws from strangers

52 weeks

Gives object to another on request

18 months

Hugs and shows affection toward doll or
teddy bear

40-52 weeks

When clothes are off, handles genitals.
This may be the onset of masturbation
in a few girls but this is rare
When urinating, girls look at their moth-
ers and smile
Fusses to be changed when wet or soiled

18 months

Affectionate toward mother when tired,
in trouble or if pants are wet
No verbal distinction between boys and
girls

Personal-Social Self
(Individual and Inter-Personal Status)

Differentiation of Self & Others
(Elimination—Sex—Babies)

21 months

Calls all other children "Baby"

24 months

Can call himself by his own name
Calls all men and women "Mommies" and
"Daddies"

24 months

Kisses at bedtime
Unable to function in strange bathrooms
Distinguishes boys from girls by clothes
and style of haircut

27 months

Says: "I want"

30 months

Calls self "I" and has an increasing sense
of "I" especially in relation to immediate abilities
Defines his sense of "I" by his very imperiousness
Calls other people "You"
A few, who have a slowly developing
awareness of self, confuse "I" and "You"
Calls women "Lady" and men "Man" as
distinguished from mommy and daddy
Calls other children "Boys" and "Girls"
Knows he is a boy, like father and that he
is different from girls and mothers (and
vice versa)
Says: "I need," "I don't like"

30 months

Conscious of own sex organs and may
handle them when clothes are off
Interested in watching others in bathroom
or when they are undressed
Distinguishes boys from girls by different
postures when urinating. Notices these
differences but does not verbalize them
Beginning of interest in physiological differences between the sexes
Inquires about mother's breasts
Non-verbalized generalization that boys
and fathers have a distinctive genital
and stand when they urinate; girls and
mothers do not

33 months

Relives his babyhood verbally. May even
want to be a baby

36 months

Sense of "I" increasing
Combines self with another in use of "We"
Can tell difference between boys and girls
but makes no distinction in his play
Says: "I like"

36 months

Verbally expressed interest in physiological differences between the sexes and in
different postures for urinating
Girls make one or two experimental attempts to urinate standing up
Desire to look at or touch adults, especially mother's breasts
Expresses a general interest in babies and
wants the family to have one

42 months

Beginning of temporary attachments to
some one playmate often of the opposite

Personal-Social Self
(Individual and Inter-Personal Status)

sex. Girls are more often the initiators of these attachments

Interest in marriage and marrying. Proposes to parents and others

Says "I love"

Interchange of parent-child role

Imaginary playmates

Child plays the role of animals

48 months

Expanding sense of self indicated by bragging, boasting and out of bounds behavior

Tendency in play groups for a division along sex lines, boys playing with boys and girls with girls

Beginning of strong feeling for family and home

Exhibits some self criticism

60 months

More secure in sense of self. No longer brags

Differentiation of Self & Others
(Elimination—Sex—Babies)

Asks questions about babies: what can the baby do when it comes; where does it come from; where is it before it was born

May not understand answers mother gives that babies grow inside the mother

Asks where he was himself before he was born

48 months

Under social stress grasps genitals and may have to urinate

Extremely conscious of the navel

May play the game of "show," either exposing genitals or urinating before another child out of doors

Verbal play about elimination and calling names such as, "You old bowel movement"

Interest in other people's bathrooms; demand for privacy himself but extreme interest in the bathroom activities of others

May believe mother's answers as to where babies come from but may cling to the notion that they are purchased

Questions about how babies get out of the mother's "stomach." May spontaneously think that the baby is born through the navel

60 months

Marked interest in anatomical difference between sexes is often dropping out

Questions as to how babies got in as well as how they will get out of their mother's "stomachs"

Interest in parents' babyhood; in having a baby brother or sister; and in having a baby himself when he grows up (boys as well as girls)

[345]

Personal-Social Self	*Differentiation of Self & Others*
(Individual and Inter-Personal Status)	(Elimination—Sex—Babies)
72 months	72 months
Beginning of value judgments about his own behavior; setting up standards for himself	Boys may ask factual questions about their testicles Factual questions about having a baby: does it hurt? May be the beginning of slight interest in the part the father plays in reproduction

§6. SELF-ACTIVITY, SOCIALITY, SELF-CONTAINMENT

THE GROWTH complex never stands still. It is comparable to an ever-moving stream,—a very intricate stream full of currents and cross currents, eddies and pools, and yet a stream which manages to carve itself a channel and to reach a destination. Should the stream congeal, life itself would stop. The currents within the stream have their checks and counterchecks. At times the flow may slow down as though to gather force for an onrush, which in turn slows down.

Or the growth complex is comparable to a complicated melody, of varying tempo, with crescendos, diminuendos, legato, staccato, turns and inverted turns. In spite of momentary disharmonies, the melody has structured form and moves forward with more or less rhythmic pauses.

In the previous chapter (page 293) we described the phenomenon of *recurrent equilibrium* which is characteristic of the psychological growth of infant and child. The organism makes a forward thrust at its growing margin, producing new patterns of behavior. These innovations are then integrated into the total action system; there follows a period of relative equilibrium, followed in turn by another forward thrust: *Innovation—integration—equilibrium—innovation—integration—equilibrium—innovation . . . .* Such seems to be the formula of growth, for separate areas of behavior and also for the entire organism over a period of time.

The culture somewhat heedlessly (not to say ignorantly) tends to insist on a continuous state of equilibrium in the child. This leads to aggravations of all kinds, because it is contrary to an insuperable mechanism of development, whose laws are written in three part rather than one part time.

It is helpful, therefore, to think of the growth complex in terms of opposite trends which counteract each other, but which are so skewed that they are progressively resolved in recurring phases of relative equilibrium. The developmental stream keeps flowing onward, seeks an optimal channel and finds it. A discerning culture can ease the tensions and ebullitions along the way.

To some extent *self-activity* and *sociality* are opposing tendencies. Nature through maturation, and Culture through guidance brings these tendencies into balance and proportion. Excessive self-activity would make the child an isolationist. Excessive sociality would lead to extreme conformance. There is an intermediate state of equipoise and equanimity in which the child realizes a maximum of equilibrium. This is the state of self-containment. It is a relative state and it is transient; but it is also recurrent. Each recurrence marks a higher stage of maturity and a wider base for the expanding pyramid of personality.

Since we are nearing the summit of our climb through this volume, let us look back on the panoramic scene and locate, if we can, the areas of recurrent equilibrium. Conveniently they tend to coincide with ages which have been delineated in the behavior profiles: 4, 16, 28, 40 weeks; 1 year, 18 months, 2, 3, 4, 5 years. These are key ages for the interpretation of the growing child. The intermediate ages give many evidences of developmental innovation and disequilibrium. The 2½ year old level is peculiarly instructive for this reason.

In the panoramic survey which follows, it must be understood that all normal children do not show with equal definition the recurrent phases of self-containment and of readjustment. Constitutional differences reflect themselves in this very respect. Some temperaments show considerable imperturbability throughout. Others seem never to be in prolonged states of tranquilized equilibrium. However, the broad trends which we shall now trace are characteristic of human growth. The sequences are significant. The age designations are naturally approximate. Having made ample qualifications, we shall stress the periodicity of disequilibrium and self-containment as a function of the patterning of behavior in infant and child.

Compared with the irregularities of the early neonatal period, the behavior status of the *4 week* old infant is stable and coordinated. He shows less stress and struggle in his brief waking hours. But at 6 or 8 weeks he displays a new kind of discontent in his evening crying, as though he were making a groping thrust for some new experience. He is less self-satisfied. He apparently wants some social contact. His responsive smile on sight of a face will prove to be a partial fulfillment of this vague striving. The culture does not always know just what to do for the baby in his obscure fretting innovations. But even so he incorporates new experience into his action system, and some fine day at about *16 weeks* of age he basks for a while in self-containment.

Gone are the indistinct strivings and frettings. He smiles spontaneously. His postures are symmetric. Tremors and startles are rare. He brings his hands competently and comfortably to his mouth. Confusions are gone. His oculo-motor muscles are under improved control. He can look and hold at the same time. He is content with the self-activity of mutual fingering. He enjoys his caretakers; beams alike on father or mother, laughs aloud for personal as well as social reasons. All things considered, this is a period of self-containment. For the time being the culture has less perplexity. In his self-activity and sociality he seems to know what he wants and he is getting it.

But naturally, this is a passing phase. In another month there are evidences of transitional disequilibrium. He begins to discriminate strangers. He is sensitive to brusque changes. He cries when someone at whom he has been looking suddenly disappears. The householders can no longer drift in and out of his room as they used to in the good old days of 16 weeks! The baby now has tiny timidities associated with his new powers of perception. He would like to sit up and be sociable but he is not quite equal to combining his self-activity with sociality. Even on his stomach he may not be content. He would like to get into a low creep position, but he has (to us) amusing difficulties in coordinating his fore and hind quarters. Such faulty coordination is a symptom of developmental disequilibrium.

But in accordance with Nature's blueprints all these difficulties will be resolved in the fullness of time,—indeed at about the age of *28 weeks*. The 28 week old infant presents a classic picture of self-containment, whether supine, prone, or seated. He can combine his perceptual and prehensory abilities with the posture at his disposal. He can look, manipulate and smile all at one time. Anything satisfies him as a toy. He makes friends easily. He can be handed from one lap to another with impunity and without warning. (What equanimity!) He can play contentedly by himself. Or he can alternate between solitary and interpersonal play, between self-activity and sociality, with the ease of a virtuoso. He is so harmoniously and amiably constituted that culture has a breathing spell which coincides with his developmental equilibrium.

At about 32 weeks the smooth waters begin to ruffle again. He loses his postural aplomb. He strives to sit without the support he formerly accepted; he strives to go from the sitting position to prone. He gets caught in awkward positions and entangled with himself in his crib. (Culture has to intervene to disentangle him.) He has a fear of strangers. He gets too excited by social contacts and cannot readily shift from sociality to self-amusement. In the prone position he is more likely to go backwards than forwards. Life is not as simple and straightforward as it used to be.

But at *40 weeks* sailing is again smoother. In prone he can now creep forward and secure the object which formerly only baffled him. He can sit alone. He can pull himself to the thrilling heights of standing. He can play alone, combining objects ad libitum and exploiting them with fine motor coordination. For the first time in his eventful life he can correlate gross

[349]

postures, fine motor control, and social behavior. He is contented in his pen. He enjoys a rich though temporary measure of self-containment.

In another month or two he displays new fears which so often accompany new powers. He becomes frightened at some of his own self-activities; he may be terrified of his new loud sounds. He is frightened by strangers, particularly if they touch him. He has a fear of the doctor's office. Such timidities remind us of the difficulties previously detailed (§5) which the child encounters in making valid differentiations between himself and other selves.

When he is in equilibrium these difficulties do not trouble him. This is the case at *1 year* of age, when he maintains a delightful rapport and easy give and take commerce with the household. His action system is in such nice balance that he is ready for almost any two-way nursery game. He likes to-and-fro play, in which there is a reciprocating social and self-reference. He likes it over and over again, for when a top is in fine balance why should it not spin round and round and round again?

At *15 months* this circularity gives way to tangential and propulsive behavior. He has become a biped. He likes to dart and dash. He has a great propensity to cast objects, heedless of their destination. (At 1 year he liked to have the objects stay in an orbit so that they would return to him.) This is a dynamo stage, a uni-directional stage. As yet this active baby is capable of starting but not of stopping. From a cultural standpoint he is not in equipoise. He needs constant shifts and assistances, unless he is confined by chair, crib or pen. Outdoors he takes free rein. He is at extremes rather than in even balance. Culture has to anticipate and plan for his dogmatic one way tendencies.

At *18 months* he is still very active; but he has himself in better hand. He has become more of a person, who can be easily trafficked with on his level. To be sure, he can wear out his mother with the exactions of the daily routines, but otherwise he accepts almost any stranger as companion on his excursions. He is so self-sufficient that he will play by himself for two consecutive hours. He manipulates things with competence and assurance. Persons do not give him undue concern. Consequently he shows a high degree of self-containment, in spite of his mercurial bumbling demeanors.

At *21 months,* with his increase of maturity, he comes into a new awareness of persons again, and with it a fear of strangers. He clings closer to the familiar adults of the home circle, his adjustment to nursery school weakens and wavers. He has a new sense of ownership of things which complicates life for him, because the culture is rather blind to the patterns by which he manifests his rudimentary possessiveness. He has poor command of words, but he has much to say so he "bawls" in what is said to be a most unreasonable manner. He may also speak with temper tantrums. In some ways his behavior is reminiscent of an older deaf child who likewise is so often misunderstood, and in a similar manner. He lacks, moreover, a flexible command of time and space relationships which makes him cleave to routines. He is not equal to reorientations. No wonder he lacks equipoise.

Now the *2 year old* is in better equilibrium, with a less precarious orientation in time and space. He adjusts more completely to familiar places, including a nursery school. He is more at home with himself, content to play quietly in smaller spaces and with smaller objects. He is capable of parallel as well as independent play. Indeed he enjoys it and is content not to disrupt the play of other children. He is not excessively dependent on his mother, but he likes to have her around and greets her from time to time with an approving smile. He is emotionally attached to her but not over-dependent on her. He is self-contained.

But in another semester this composure all but vanishes; for he is then *2½ years* old. And this age is distinguished for its dramatic manifestations of unsettled equilibrium. If 28 weeks affords the classic example of self-containedness, 30 months is the classic example of its polar opposite. It is almost as though the pyramid of personality were trying to rest on its peak rather than on its base, and therefore wobbled on the slightest provocation or no provocation at all. In our behavior profile of this age we listed some of the numerous and diametric opposites which struggle for mastery within the child's complex action system. If like the fabled don key and the haystacks, he were precisely at the middle point between all these opposites he would be the essence of neutrality; but he is just enough off center to be the epitome of double contrariness and disequilibrium. What he wills to do he can't; what he can do he won't. Yes and No, Affection and Resistance, Running-away and Clinging, Holding-on-too-hard and Giving-up-too-easily, Whispering and Shouting, these and a host of other opposites alternate with such poor timing that the child is neither at home with himself nor with his environment. And the culture is often out of gear with him as well.

He is not sure of himself. His salvation lies in his routines. These are his old and established self. These he has mastered. Accordingly he insists on them with spirit and with repetitiveness. He converts them into life-preserver rituals. Being in the midstream of a growth transition he has a very small margin of tolerance; *but he has a little*. It is a wise culture which recognizes how little and concedes the rationale of the ritualism. However by utilizing the small margin of tolerance the ritual is varied gradually. It loses its vitality (to the parents' relief) when it has lost its necessity.

Lo and behold, this same child in another semester, at the age of *3 years*, may become a paragon of self-containment. He has recaptured the power of choice through his winning battles with the warring opposites. He is sure of himself. He is emotionally less turned in on himself. With his widened margin of tolerance he has a fund of good will for mankind. The culture can bargain with him on even terms. He is at home in the domestic circle, at nursery school, on the playground, at a picnic down the river. He has flexible personal relations with his father, as well as mother, as well as with other children. Self-activity and sociality are well apportioned. He takes his routines sensibly. He uses his behavior equipment in culturally acceptable ways. Or more precisely, he has an effective behavior equipment because, for the time, he is in good working equilibrium. The rest follows.

But it does not endure. For in yet another semester, at the age of *3½ years*, there are new growth signs of unsettledness. Even his general motor control, which one might well think would be by this time stabilized, betrays signs of weakening. His penciled strokes waver; his voice quavers; he is prone to stutter. He overcomes the tendency to vocal tremor by speaking in loud high pitch. He gives vent to his motor tensions in endless scrubbing and rubbing activities. His inner life of phantasy betrays stresses and insecurities. He has many fears. He may dread deformities and darkness. Dreams multiply and intensify. He spends hours and days with imaginary playmates. In dramatic fancy he exchanges the roles of parent and child. He becomes the parent. He may trot about all day in the privately impersonated role of a horse or dog. He takes this role seriously. He wishes the culture to take it seriously too; he will extend his paw but not his hand. And when he shouts, "Don't laugh," some heed should be paid, for these are developmental devices whereby he, almost, without the aid of culture, initiates himself into the complexities of culture with its manifold human relationships. Imaginary roles like more infantile rituals are scaffoldings for emerging patterns of social behavior.

The *4 year old* is already a more patterned person with increased savoir faire. He has, as once before noted, a fluid organization, but he is in relatively stable equilibrium. This fluid organization spreads in all directions and includes with almost equal force all fields of his behavior. The expanding periphery pushes across frontiers and thus his horizons are widened. His fine and gross motor control has greatly improved. He is no longer fearful of the high rungs of the gym as he was a half year ago. He is well oriented to his family. He likes nursery school and wants to attend every day. He is capable of sustained cooperative play. He is sensitive to the hints, the commissions and the commands which come from his culture.

But once more six months of added maturity bring about a difference. The *4 ½ year old* child tends to go out of bounds. He is as it were pushed out of bounds from the unregulated momentum of his expansion into widening horizons. He tells tall tales. He boasts. He shows off. He stands on his head. Inwardly, however, he is not so brave or composed. He has his fears, symptomatic of another transitional stage of disequilibrium which inevitably produces insecurity. He dreams of wolves. He is afraid of jails. He is afraid of the red traffic light, which means danger to him. He is afraid of the policeman who is perceived as a threat rather than as a patron of protection.

The *5 year old,* on the other hand, has so matured that he sees the policeman in his truer light, both as a mentor and as a guardian. This added mite of maturity brings with it a more catholic outlook, an ability to see two sides and to weigh them proportionately. The 5 year old has a much more balanced awareness of himself in relation to other persons. He is conscious of differences in hierarchy and prestige. He accepts the social scheme. He goes to and from kindergarten like an embryo citizen, as indeed he is. We need not celebrate his virtues again. He has completed the first long lap on the pathway to maturity.

* * * *

It has indeed been a long journey marked as we have now seen by a succession of phases of recurrent equilibrium with intermediate stages of relative disequilibrium and readjustment. The whole purpose of this chapter has been to bring these almost rhythmic alternations of readjustment and self-containment into sequential perspective. The interludes and the transitions are all but meaningless if they are regarded as separate episodes or fortuitous variations. They have a profound logic when viewed in the continuity of the single, biographic growth career. They show that everything which the infant or child does has a functional or symptomatic significance in the economy of development. Nothing is sheer nonsense, sheer deviltry, or sheer obstinacy. Every patterned action must have a rationale in the physiology of development. Growth as a process is as lawful as metabolism, digestion, respiration, secretion, or any living process. It is in fact the sum of all the living processes of the organism. And when we are concerned with nothing less than the growth of a human personality, this all-inclusive process is the greatest challenge to culture. The culture did not create this process, but it determines its products,—within the limitations of the law of recurrent equilibrium, and all other laws of development. That there is an element of recurrence in this equilibrium should give all parents and all philosophies a modicum of optimism.

* * * *

One more glance at the panorama. Let us look not on the developmental stream but on the cultural landscape. We then see that during these first five years the child has steadily penetrated into the cultural milieu and thereby has widened his physical horizons as well as his psychological orientations. With each expansion he has formed a new niche. His first translation was from uterus to bassinet, and then in quick succession from bassinet to crib, to high chair, to pen. The pen itself has its gradients. At first it is in the living room with mother nearby. Stage by stage it migrates into the playroom, onto the porch, and into the vast space of the yard. As the child draws closer to the civic community the pen is moved to the front yard. Further excursions are made by perambulator and stroller and velocipede. More formally the excursions may take him across the threshold of the nursery school, at first on one or two days during the week, later thrice, later daily. At 5 years he is able to attend the kindergarten, usually without escort. He has almost graduated into member status in the community. These gradations reveal the stage by stage progression of the complicated process of acculturation. Each stage is dependent upon an increment of maturity in the behavior equipment of infant and child.

24

CHILD DEVELOPMENT AND THE CULTURE OF TOMORROW

PARTLY BY WAY of epilogue, we venture in this concluding chapter upon a very spacious theme,—the changing status of the child in a culture which is destined to undergo profound reorientations with the termination of the war. It is a war of peoples, and there is every prospect that the protection of child development will be increased and enriched during the period of reconstruction. Something will be learned from the aftermath,—from the uncounted children whose physical and mental development was impoverished and maimed. But ultimately more will be learned through a rededication of science to a fuller study of the normal sources of life and human growth.

It is being said that one aim of the peace must be to so reorder the world that another apocalypse of violence will not be necessary. How can this be done except by a profound, socialized reaffirmation of the dignity of life as it is embodied in infancy and childhood?

Perhaps the most ameliorative social force that can be released in the years of reconstruction which lie ahead is an intensified conservation of the development of infants and young children. They are the carriers and sources of life. This must be a socialized conservation which will be felt and effected by the masses as well as by the medical world and by political leaders and educators. A heightened solicitude for the early years of human growth will not only have a therapeutic benefit for the adult inheritors of the aftermath; it must be the basis for all prophylaxis of war. For how can we ever overcome systematic destruction of life, if life and growth are not cherished at their source?

§1. A SCIENCE OF CHILD DEVELOPMENT AS A CULTURAL FORCE

SOCIALIZED CONSERVATION will need all the resources of the life sciences, as well as new visions of cultural welfare. It will be the task of science to define more clearly the limitations of culture as a determinant of human behavior. The anthropologist sees in living cultures, in spite of their apparent diversity, a pervading sameness, arising out of common traits of human nature. This quality of sameness denotes underlying psychological laws which should enable us better to understand ourselves and our cultures, including religion, morals, mores, child care, and government. Thus also we may arrive at more insight into the diseases of culture as manifested in poverty, economic crises, crime and war. It is not strange that cultural anthropology claims to be the very basis of social science. But scientific anthropology, no less than psychology, is inextricably bound up with physics, chemistry, physiology and biology. Culture began with a very primitive man whose descendants have not lost all his primitiveness.

The culture of tomorrow will begin and always rebegin with the development of individual infants and children; for, as Malinowski aptly said, culture is nothing but the organized behavior of man,—"a large-scale

[357]

molding matrix, a gigantic conditioning apparatus. In each generation it produces its type of individual. In each generation it is in turn reshaped by its carriers."

Now, however, more than ever before, it is necessary to understand realistically the limiting factors in this conditioning mechanism. They are growth factors. They are the laws of child development. Indeed, it might be well to reserve the term matrix for the maturational mechanisms which literally establish the basic patterns of behavior and of growth career. A matrix is that which gives form and foundation to something which is incorporated, in this instance, through growth. By growth we do not mean a mystical essence, but a physiological process of organization which is registered in the structural and functional unity of the individual. In this sense the maturational matrix is the primary determinant of child behavior.

This process of organization, as a life process, is infinitely older than human culture. It is so ancient that man shares it with plants and animals. Darwin grasped the unity of a world web of life. His passionate genius reduced the vast reaches of the evolution of the human race to a comprehensible order; but he left unsolved the great problem of man's capacity to carry the cultures which he creates.

This brings us back to the basic problem of environmental conditioning,—the relationships between maturation and acculturation. In the heyday of behaviorism it was seriously suggested that "almost nothing is given in heredity" and that practically the whole psychology of the child is built in by the mechanisms of habit formation and the conditioned reflex. Such an extreme theory of human development explains too much. It explains, of course, how totalitarian systems of education and government can mold their subjects to a pre-conceived model. But it does not sufficiently explain how this molding process also fails, and why an inexorable spirit of liberty defies it. Surely it has now been demonstrated that any culture which has an overweening confidence in its own authority over the individual endangers the collective sanity. Even the most highly technological civilization cannot survive unless it is compatible with laws of human behavior and organic growth.

For these reasons, the culture of tomorrow will be dependent in no small measure upon adequate sciences of child development and of human behavior. There will also be profounder spiritual insights, but even these must reckon with the laws and limitations of human nature, as embodied in infants and children. Symbolic concepts which oversimplify the intricate problems of good and evil can, alone, no longer suffice as goals and guides. We need a much more penetrating knowledge of the mechanisms of mental development and motivation. Our present-day knowledge of the personality of infant and child is extremely meager and fragmentary. Science can and will in time supply a fuller understanding. And this understanding will have a refining and humanizing effect upon the culture itself. Or shall we say that such science generously expended is an expression of an improving culture?

§2. DEVELOPMENTAL SUPERVISION AND GUIDANCE

ASSUMING then that an abundance for peacetime life has been restored and that the four freedoms prevail, how may a technological civilization foster the fuller development of its infants and children? Without attempting precise prophecy a few possibilities can be suggested.

First and foremost, there will be a remobilization of medical and biological science directed toward the measurement and elucidation of individual development from infancy through adolescence. The already brilliant achievements of chemotherapy and immunology indicate yet greater applications in the universal field of nutrition. The diagnosis of biochemical and bioelectrical conditions in infant and child will lead to dietary controls which will augment strength, stamina, and emotional well-being. In many ways this area of control may prove to be the most influential. But it cannot displace the mechanisms of growth and generation embodied in the laws of heredity. Nor can it supersede the inborn sequences of behavior development.

Behavior as well as physique will be brought under more systematic supervision through a developmental type of pediatrics. A complete system of developmental supervision will begin with an anticipatory mental hygiene of the expectant parents, and with the birth of the infant. Using improved and to some extent socialized methods of diagnosis, it will follow the child's development at significant intervals to ascertain the assets and liabilities of his growth makeup. For social reasons it will have regard for positive potentialities as well as for deficits and abnormalities. For the social welfare it will be directed toward detecting and conserving what is distinctive and superior in the individual infant and preschool child. A rigorous recognition of the factor of individuality would save even a partially socialized system of developmental supervision from the dangers of regimentation. Parents even today want to know all that it is possible to know about *their* child. Culture will some day see to it that the parents will be told.

The inequalities of our present-day social provisions for the preschool child are glaring. At one extreme we have the infant born without record and without medical supervision in the squalor of a rural or city slum. At the other extreme is the infant born in a hospital and surrounded with continuous safeguards and periodic protections. *Only through a democratically conceived system of developmental supervision can we attain a more just and universal distribution of developmental opportunity for infants and preschool children.*

This ideal is no more utopian than the principle of universal elementary education. Indeed it represents the next logical extension of this principle in the culture of tomorrow.

Freedom from want in a socio-economic sense remains a first essential for freedom from psychological want. Underprivileged preschool children suffer not only in a physical sense. They suffer psychologically. They feel mental insecurity. In crowded and shiftless homes, they develop anxieties and perplexities. They see sights and experience shocks from which more fortunate children are, in decency, spared. Some of the most elementary reserves which lie at the basis of respect for the individual are made impossible.

Overcrowding takes a terrible psychological toll. The newborn infant is entitled to a bassinet. As he grows older, he is entitled to a crib, a pen, and a bed of his own, and a room or a section of a room which he can claim as his own. He deserves this degree of privacy and possession that he may develop a normal sense of individuality. Lacking such a normal sense, he will not respect the individuality of others. Much of the crime which even political democracies have not controlled has its roots in disordered homes which impoverish and distort the early mental development of future citizens. Here is a tangible task in preventive mental hygiene. How can society enter upon this vast task, which if left undone weakens the foundations of democracy? By better housing and increased economic security. Freedom from want is in many ways the first of the four freedoms.

The crippling influence of cramped apartments and squalid tenements cannot be fully overcome by public parks, playgrounds, and school buildings. It is the intimate architecture of the home which ceaselessly impinges on the growing child. The postwar period is bound to bring about far-reaching alterations in domestic housing. There will be need of a new technology which will create more than shelter and physical comfort. It will plan for psychological and educational values, particularly in behalf of the infant and young child. Such planning must be undertaken by architects who work in close cooperation with hygienists and scientists who understand the needs of child development. Socio-economic security thus reaches down into the most fundamental determinants of mental health.

Better housing means better homes,—but only when parents are guided and educated into proper methods of child care. There are countless homes in America in which mothers, fathers, and other elders in the household use harsh modes of punishment even toward young children: scolding, slapping, cuffing, shaming, and beating. These primitive, undemocratic methods of discipline have no place in the culture of tomor-

[361]

row. They are grossly inconsistent with the spirit of democracy, and as such they must be reached and overcome by public health and education measures.

§3. PARENTAL AND PREPARENTAL EDUCATION

A WELL-KNOWN BEHAVIORIST, interested in the welfare of children, said, some years ago: "It is a serious question in my mind whether there should be individual homes for children—or even whether children should know their own parents." This thought-provoking remark brings into sharp focus the significance of parent education and parent guidance.

There is no evidence in the biology of the species or in the structure of society that the family and the home will cease to be the most fundamental component of the culture of tomorrow. The inadequacies of the home will be steadily reduced by direct approach through adult education, and by specific guidance. Such personalized guidance can be effected through the nursery school as a guidance center, supplemented by periodic examinations of the growing child under a system of developmental supervision.

In addition to specific, individualized parent guidance, there are vast areas of general education. Much of this must continue on an adult level, contemporaneously with the development of the child. But a great deal more can be accomplished at a preadult level, in the secondary school and junior college years.

From the standpoint of public policy, preparental education is in many ways more basic than parental education. The culture of yesterday has been a bit squeamish about attacking this great educational problem which concerns particularly the preadult years, ignoring the certain prospect that most maturing adolescents will in time become mothers and fathers. If, in a constructive way, we can reach the attitudes of these adolescents in their latent strength we shall be performing double educational service. We shall be shaping the careers of the adolescents as individuals and at the same stroke shall be erecting safeguards for the healthier development of the oncoming generation.

How can these adolescents, these preadults, be reached? By a more frank presentation of the elementary facts concerning the cycle of human growth. Biology, in spite of its concreteness, has been studied too much in the abstract as far as human life is concerned. We need a humanized biology, or rather we need an adequate course of instruction in human biology dealing candidly with the origin, physical growth, and mental growth of the human child. In this way we can bring into the curriculum a practical type of psychology concerned with the laws of human nature and with the development of the child mind. Such a psychology, far from being overintrospective, would tend to take the adolescent out of himself and enable him ultimately to assume more objective views of the problems of parenthood. Education frankly addressed to the problems of early human development and child behavior would bear fruit in a decade, because in a few years these youths, whether in shop or college, will be fathers and mothers with a more intelligent outlook upon the life cycle of a newborn infant of their own.

And outlook is more basic than technique; for the wise application of technique requires an appreciation of principles, a *philosophy* of *individual development*. A developmental philosophy is part of the democratic ideology. It is a motivating cultural force in determining methods of child care in the home and in the nursery school.

* * * *

The culture of tomorrow will be increasingly child-centered. There is no more powerful corrective for the aberrations of culture than folkways which pay respect to the individual. That respect must be based upon refinement of understanding. Every generation rediscovers and re-evaluates the meaning of infancy and childhood.

APPENDIX A

THE ACCOMPANYING FIGURES 16 and 17 illustrate the method of scheduling the self-regulation behavior days. The blank record form, Figure 16, provides for a lunar month period of 4 weeks or 28 days. It also provides for notations of the date, age, and weight, and for a brief daily comment in the vertical marginal columns.

The events of the day are recorded on the thin horizontal line which traverses the whole day from midnight to midnight on an hourly basis.

The heavy vertical lines locate 6:00 A.M., 12:00 noon, and 6:00 P.M.

Figure 17 pictures excerpts from an actual chart showing how the recordings were made for the 4th week, 16th week, and 28th week of Infant S.

In actual use, cross hatching or solid color indicates sleep. Clear stretches indicate wakefulness. Feeding is indicated by the short horizontal bars under which the amount of the feeding is recorded in ounces. X indicates crying; V, vomiting; BM, bowel movement; OJ, orange juice; B, bath; AW, awakened; WA, water; CG, carriage.

By this method of charting, the trends from day to day can be read down the course of the chart.*

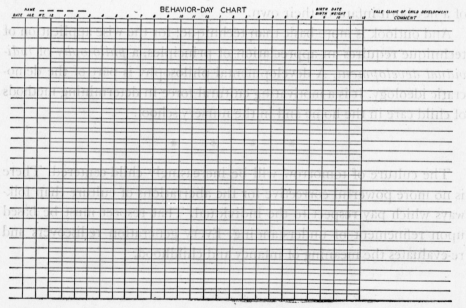

* Blank forms (11 x 17) for these Behavior Day Charts are available at cost price. Address: The Psychological Corp., 522 Fifth Avenue, New York City, New York.

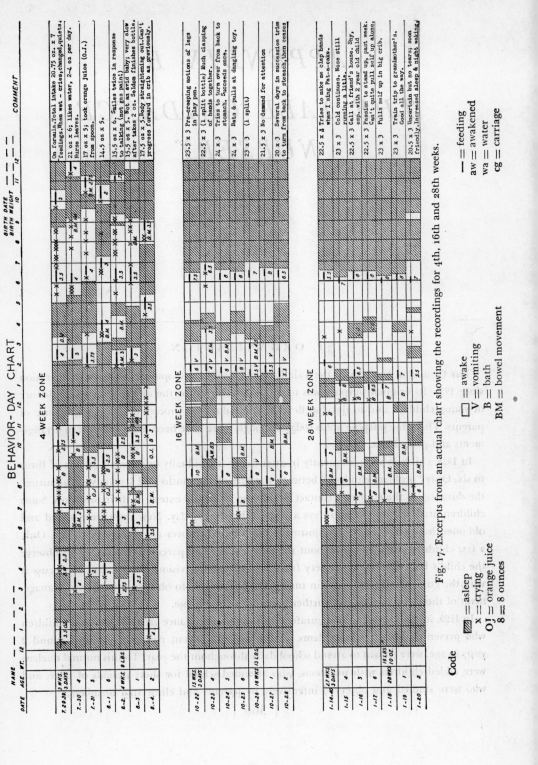

Fig. 17. Excerpts from an actual chart showing the recordings for 4th, 16th and 28th weeks.

APPENDIX B
THE YALE GUIDANCE NURSERY

§1. ORGANIZATION

THE GUIDANCE NURSERY of the Yale Clinic of Child Development has been in operation since 1926. Its original purpose was to provide facilities for the observation and guidance of young children and to develop flexible, individualized procedures for the guidance of parents. This same purpose holds today although there have been many changes in arrangements and procedures.

In 1926, children were frequently in attendance individually or in small groups of three to six. Only "problem children" between the ages of 18 months and 5 years were admitted, the duration of their nursery contact depending upon the extent of their problems. Some children attended one or two days a week, others every day. New cases were added and old ones dropped when their adjustment could be taken over entirely by the home. Only a few children attended throughout the entire year. The parent was expected to observe the child's behavior in the nursery from behind one-way-vision screens, and to discuss it with the guidance teacher, who in turn made home visits to observe the parents' management of the child, and to give further guidance in the home.

In 1929, it was decided to inaugurate a continuous attendance group made up of children who presented no special problems. Five stable, intelligent children, varying around 2 years in age, were chosen to attend school daily throughout the year. To this normal nucleus were added children with problems, who attended school for short periods of time, and who were studied and observed intensively by parents and clinic staff members.

In 1935, the nursery school was expanded so that two groups of children from 2 to 3, and from 3 to 5 years of age attended simultaneously. In this way more children could be followed, with a greater number of contemporaries for comparison. This service was on a non-tuition basis until 1936, when a small fee was charged.

The present system was inaugurated in 1939, when the normal-problem basis for accepting children was abandoned, since the "normal" children frequently had difficulties comparable to the "problem" children. The emphasis at this time also changed from studying problems, as such, to analyzing behavior in relation to various types of personality and different levels of development. To obtain a cross section of development at succeeding age levels the nursery was again reorganized into five groups with the following age ranges when the children enter in September:

Age in months	Days attending	Hours	Maximum no. in group
A. 18-21	Wednesday	9:30-11:00	8
B. 21-24	Monday, Friday	9:00-11:00	10
C. 24-30	Tues., Thurs., Sat.	9:00-11:30	12
D. 30-36	Mon., Wed., Fri.	9:00-11:30	15
E. 36-42	Tues., Thurs., Sat.	9:00-11:30	18

These children not only attend school throughout the academic year, but also may continue in the nursery for two or three years. Occasionally a child has been followed at the Clinic from infancy. Most of the children are in the high average or superior range of developmental status and home environment. In general, the children are chosen in order of application, exceptions being made when the need for nursery school is urgent.

A tuition of seventy-five cents a morning is now charged, but there is a sliding scale for parents who are unable to afford this fee. Occasionally scholarships are given to children who would otherwise be unable to attend school. Tuition charges are based, not upon the entire term, but on the actual days of attendance.

Each group is started in September with a small number of children and is gradually increased to the maximum that can be handled efficiently. Since the older children can absorb more stimulation from contemporaries and need less adult supervision, their groups are somewhat larger than those for younger children. There is a waiting list for each age group "on call"; whenever a regular member of the group is absent, children are invited from this reserve list.

Lunch and afternoon naps were discontinued when the alternate day system was introduced, as it was felt that eating and sleeping problems could be handled better at home where the situation is simpler for the child. Each individual problem is discussed in detail with the parent and techniques of guidance in relation to home behavior are given.

§2. PERSONNEL AND EDUCATIONAL ACTIVITIES

THE NURSERY is under the supervision of a pediatrician who makes developmental examinations of the children prior to admission, and conducts repeated interviews with the parents by way of guidance. The children are re-examined at 6-month intervals. In selected cases, examinations are also made during the period of infancy and continued up to the age of six and beyond. Extended conferences are held with the parents after each examination.

The staff includes, also, a principal and an associate guidance teacher, two assistants, and two home externs. The two head teachers render specific assistance, both in connection with the examinations and the guidance work. The home externs divide their time between the guidance nursery and the homes of children who are in attendance at the nursery. Each extern resides in a home, which arrangement provides a 24-hour association with the child under observation. This arrangement has served to define the problems of home guidance in relation to the nursery guidance. These, and other problems, are discussed in weekly conferences of the staff under the direction of the pediatrician.

The Guidance Nursery is housed in the Yale Clinic of Child Development which is a subdivision of the School of Medicine of Yale University. The nursery functions as an adjunct of the diagnostic and advisory service of the Clinic.

The nursery occupies seven rooms of various sizes which accommodate two age groups simultaneously. A play court and a grassy play yard are immediately accessible.

The nursery in its university setting serves three distinguishable but closely related functions: (1) guidance and educational service for children and parents (2) scientific observation of child behavior and guidance methods (3) instruction for graduate students, medical students, and students of the School of Nursing. To carry out all of these functions with a minimum of disturbance to the children presented a ubiquitous problem which has been solved by the installation of one-way-vision facilities.

The accompanying illustration (Figure 18) pictures the arrangements of The Yale Guidance Nursery and shows the various provisions for one-way-vision observation. Figure 19 pictures a corner of the large observation station (1a) which can accommodate as many as twenty-five observers.

Figures 20 and 21 picture a combination-convertible play house, climbing gym, and post-office, etc. The post-office section is removable and when shifted to other parts of the nursery it becomes a very effective prop for many different uses.—Almost any manual training department can build a similar unit adapted to some available corner.

[368]

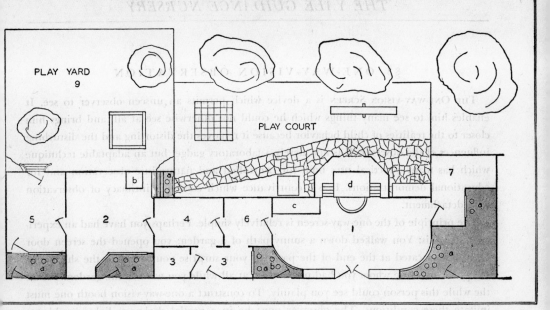

18. Arrangements of The Yale Guidance Nursery. 1. Main Room: Older Age Groups 1c. Convertible Playhouse Gym 1d. Housekeeping Unit (on elevated platform) 2. Room for Junior Age Group 2b. Housekeeping Unit and 3. Toilet and Wash Rooms 4. Cloak Room: Older Age Groups 5. Cloak Room: Junior Age Groups 6. Music Room Kitchenette and Studio 8. Play Court: Older Groups 9. Play Yard: Younger Groups

One-Way-Vision Facilities *

b, 2a, 3b = Observation Stations 3a. Observation Station (with one-way mirror) 5a, 7a, 8a = Observation Stations

Screen indicated by =

il of interior of one way vision
vation station. Screen affords view
of Guidance Nursery (Fig. 19).

Detail of Convertible Play House
Equipment (Fig. 20).

Fig. 21. House converted into gym by
detachment of the "post office section." The post office section is a movable feature, which can be used for a
diversity of dramatic purposes (post
office, ticket office, store, etc.)

§3. ONE-WAY-VISION OBSERVATION

THE ONE-WAY-VISION SCREEN is a device which permits an unseen observer to see. It enables him to see many things which he could not otherwise see at all, and brings him closer to the realities of child behavior because it removes the distorting and the disturbing influences of the observer. It is not merely a laboratory gadget but an adaptable technique which has many practical uses both for controlled and naturalistic observation and for educational demonstrations. It is a contrivance which combines intimacy of observation with detachment.

The principle of the one-way-screen is relatively simple. Perhaps you have had an experience like this: You walked down a sunny path of a garden; you opened the screen door of a porch located at the end of the path; to your surprise you found in the shadow of the porch someone whom you had not noticed at all while you were in the garden. Yet all the while this person could see you plainly. To construct a one-way-vision booth one must imitate these conditions. The observer must be in a partial darkness; light should not stream directly through the screen. The observer's station should also be carpeted to absorb sound and light. The surface of the screen which faces the field of observation is painted white, or painted scenically in bright-colored enamel, to produce a diffuse dazzle which makes the screen appear opaque. Thus the screen is transparent in one direction only.

In the guidance nursery at Yale an expansive screen of this nature serves for a commodious room which accommodates thirty stools of graduated heights, so that a group of students may assemble amphitheatre-wise for observation of activities and demonstrations in the main nursery. An offset provides close-up observation of the children in the kitchen unit. A second nursery play-room is also provided with a screen the wainscote of which is decorated with murals.

It should be emphasized that concealment is a subsidiary or negative value of one-way-vision. The screen was not designed for spying, but for positive educational and scientific controls of observation. One would emphasize that one-way-vision protects the privacy of the children and, on occasions, the privacy of their attendants and their parents. The invisibility of the observers serves to make the observation more serious and purposeful.

The nursery is abundantly equipped with large and small observation stations effectively concealed by one-way-vision screening. (Observation of the bathroom is accomplished through a one-way-vision mirror.) These observation stations can be readily entered from a hallway and the flexibility of this arrangement facilitates brief and incidental observations as well as prolonged observations and study. Similar arrangements can be incorporated into almost any nursery school unit with a slight expenditure of ingenuity. The preparation of a one-way-vision screen offers no great difficulties. The method of preparation is described below.

The Preparation of a one-way-vision screen. Ordinary 16-mesh-wire screen can be used. Thin white enamel paint may be applied with a painter's brush in the regular manner, if done with care so as not to clog the mesh. The paint should dry between the several coats. No. 30 wire cloth has definite advantages, particularly if casein paint instead of ordinary enamel is used. The casein paint should be thinned down with water to the consistency of thin cream and then applied with an air brush. At intervals the air brush should be used to force air only through the screen in order to blow out any excess paint which may have clogged the mesh. This process is repeated four or five times. Casein paint dries rapidly and the successive coats may be applied in the course of one day.

It is best to apply the paint before the screens are permanently mounted. If the screens are already in position, an absorbent barrier should be placed behind the screen to collect the transmitted paint spray.

The location of the observers' station is of critical importance. The station should be as dark as possible. Enough light for ordinary recording purposes will in any event enter through the screen. Ideally the observation station should be located on the window side of the room. Care should be taken so that direct light from windows or from lamps will not strike directly through the screens. Such direct rays of light tend to reveal the observers' eye-glasses and light colored objects. Invisibility is increased by wearing dark clothes. The efficiency of the one-way-vision screen is also increased if the room upon which the screen gives is illuminated by indirect rather than direct lighting.

The walls of the observation station should be painted black or midnight blue. Dark curtains draped on the walls and thick carpeting on the floor serve to silence sounds inadvertently made by the observers. Placement of plate glass behind the screen excludes sound but interferes with ventilation. Strict silence is an extremely important rule. Our injunction to the observer who enters the station for the first time is, "Be absolutely quiet. The child can hear you even though he cannot see you."

APPENDIX C
TOYS, PLAY MATERIALS,
AND EQUIPMENT

IMPROVISED AND CASUAL MATERIALS such as clothespins, discarded containers, firm cloth, clean short lengths of rope, and similar materials are often superior to more elaborate manufactured toys. The choice of any toys must, of course, be safeguarded. Toys should be clean, and should be of such shape, size, and material that they cannot do harm to eyes, ears, nose, or throat!

Birth-3 months

Bright dangling objects
Bright piece of cloth to hang over crib
Ring rattle—bright colored plastic rings on one larger ring
Small silver dumbbell rattle
Rubber squeaking toy

3-9 months

Cradle Gym
Rubber blocks with bells inside
Teething beads
Water ball—heavy celluloid with floating objects inside

6-12 months

"Babee Tenda"—seat suspended in the middle of a table (In place of high chair—no tipping, convertible into table)

"Tot seat"—can be used in home or car

Nested measuring cups

Spoon and cup

Cradle Bounce

Cradle Spin

9-12 months

Play pen

Hard rubber blocks—good for biting

Square or round block stacks—colorful blocks fitted on large peg

Box or basket with large clothespins

Small ball—encourages locomotion

Water toys

Wrist bells

Bright colored heavy plastic cereal bowls

12-18 months

Taylor Tot—for mother to push child in, and for child to use as Kiddie Kar

Kiddie Kar—low enough so that child has whole foot on ground

Cart—to fill and pull

Pull toy—as Caterpillar of various colors

Push toy—a small cart with long handle

Sweeping sets with broom and mop

Balls

Blocks—small, bright colored

Boxes—simple ones to open and close

Color cone—bright colored rings of graduated size to fit over disk

Water toys

Woolly or cloth soft animals—eyes should be painted or embroidered, not buttons attached with sharp points

Cloth dolls

Books—cloth and heavy cardboard with familiar objects and bright colors

Equipment suitable throughout the Preschool Years

Climbing apparatus—as climbing gyms, ladders and boxes
   Small and large boards in combination with climbing apparatus increase its usefulness
Packing boxes—large and sturdy enough for child to climb on
Slide
Boards for balancing and sliding—with cleat on each end to hold securely
Bouncing board—suggested proportions 1 in. $\times$ 15 in. $\times$ 13 ft. ash board
Boards and saw horse—for see-saw, inclines, etc.
Small boards—for building, hauling, etc., suggested size $\frac{3}{4}$ in. $\times$ 6 in. $\times$ 36 in.
Hollow blocks—suggested size 6 in. $\times$ 12 in. $\times$ 12 in., and 6 in. $\times$ 12 in. $\times$ 24 in.
   Building possibilities increased when combined with small boards
Logs
Kegs
Sand box
Sand toys: spoon, sugar scoop, pail, cans, sifter
Swing—better home than school equipment
Wheelbarrow
Wagon
Train, dump truck, steam shovel, etc.—large enough for child to ride on
Small airplanes, automobiles, trucks, boats, and trains
Baskets and boxes
Nests of boxes or cans
Boxes of spools, small blocks, etc.
Rope and string
Animals—domestic or Noah's ark sets
Dolls—rubber preferable for bathing purposes
Doll clothing—with large buttons and buttonholes
Doll carriage
Doll bed—sturdy and large enough for child to get in
Covers, mattress, pillow
Chest of drawers, cupboard
Suitcases, chest
Table and chair—child's size
Stove
Dishes and cooking utensils
Telephone
Broom, dustpan, mop, dustcloth

Laundry tub, ironing board, iron, adult size clothespins

Bright colored squares of cloth—for doll covers, table covers, laundry, costumes, etc.

Costume box—pocketbooks, hats, gloves, scarf, jewelry, curtains, various lengths of cloth, etc.

Clay

Crayons—large size

Easel

Easel paper—unprinted newspaper satisfactory

Brushes—long handle with brush at least ½ in. wide for paint. Wider brush with short handle better for "painting" with water

Paint—powder paint mixed with water. Ingredients should be harmless and non-staining

Musical instruments—as wrist bells, drum, dinner gong, xylophone, music box

Nature specimens—as fish, turtles, salamanders, snails, birds, plants, animals

Equipment especially suitable for:

18 months

Stairs

Swing

Rocking horse

Push cart

Pull toy—peg wagon, small cart, animal

Chest of drawers—child's size, easily manipulated

Large ball

Bingo Bed—hammer and peg toy

Blocks—colored and small (about 2" cubes)

Color cone—graduated wooden rings on peg

Pots and pans with covers

Pocketbook

Soft cloth or woolly animals

Wrist bells

Music box

Pylox blocks

24 months

Boards—for walking up inclines, bouncing, etc. (with cleats on end)

Climbing apparatus with platform easily accessible

Slide—attached to climbing apparatus or steps

Rocking boat

Kiddie Kar
Cars and trucks
Interlocking trains
Light hollow blocks
Small colored blocks—cylinders, cubes, etc.
Peg boards with large pegs in a variety of colors
Jars with screwing tops
Baskets
Doll—soft and washable
Doll carriage
Doll bed—large and sturdy enough for child to get in
Dishes—non-breakable
Iron
Cloth squares of bright colors—for doll covers, table cloths, etc.
Telephone
Crayons—large size
House that Jack Built

30 months

Large packing boxes
Logs
Boards for building, carrying, hauling, and walking
Large hollow blocks
Tricycle
Wheelbarrow
Fire truck, train, steam shovel, dump truck large enough for child to sit on
Large wooden beads and string with long metal tip
Screwing toys
Advanced pegboard—pegs of varying sizes fitting holes on cover of box
Rotogear
Clay
Finger paint
Soap bubble pipes
Large paint brushes for painting with water

36 months

Climbing apparatus with boards for different platform levels
Saw horses and boards—for see-saw, bridges, etc.

Large hollow blocks with boards
Kegs
Tricycle
Transportation toys—wagon, train, dump truck, etc.
Solid blocks with unit and multiples of unit, cylinders, quarter circles, triangles, etc.
Toys with large nuts, bolts, wrench, etc., such as Tot's tool box
Simple wooden puzzles with few pieces
Object lotto—matching game
Soap bubble pipes
Dolls
Doll equipment—bed, carriage, covers
Housekeeping equipment—stove, dishes, broom, clothesline, clothespins, iron
Costume box—with hats, gloves, cloth, pocketbooks, etc.
Blunt scissors
Colored paper
Easel, easel paper, water color paint, brushes, at least ½″ wide
Finger paint
Clay
Postcard collection
Mounted pictures of nature, transportation, etc.

48 months

Climbing equipment
Trapeze and rings
See-Saw
Garden tools
Work bench with adult size hammer, saw, nails
Blocks—large hollow and small multi-shaped
Wooden picture puzzles
Lotto matching games
Tinker toys
Families of dolls and teddy bears
Doll clothes with large buttons and buttonholes
Housekeeping equipment
Store material
Nurses' and doctors' kits
Costume box
Blackboard and chalk

Whiteboard with crayons
Blunt scissors—sturdy and fairly large
Paste and colored paper
Paint
Clay
Finger paint
Wide variety of nature specimens

APPENDIX D
BOOKS FOR PRESCHOOL CHILDREN

The books are classified by age under five headings: 1. Story Collections 2. Picture and Story Books 3. Collections of Poetry 4. Information Books 5. Song Books. The books are approximately graded by ages.

§1. STORY COLLECTIONS

AGE	AUTHOR OR ILLUSTRATOR	TITLE	PUBLISHER
2–4 yrs.	Brown, Eleanor	The Little Story Book	Oxford
2–6 yrs.	Assoc. for Childhood Education	Told Under the Blue Umbrella	Macmillan
2–6 yrs.	Mitchell, Lucy S.	The Here and Now Story Book	Dutton
2–6 yrs.	Mitchell, Lucy S.	Another Here and Now Story Book	Dutton
4–6 yrs.	Bacmeister, Rhoda	Stories to Begin On	Dutton
4–6 yrs.	Gay, Romney	Book of Nursery Tales	Grosset & Dunlap
4–6+ yrs.	Assoc. for Childhood Education	Told Under the Green Umbrella	Macmillan

AGE	AUTHOR OR ILLUSTRATOR	TITLE	PUBLISHER
4–6+ yrs.	Huber, Miriam	Story and Verse for Children	Macmillan
4–6+ yrs.	Richardson, Frederick	Old, Old Tales Retold	Donohue
4–6+ yrs.	Rojankovsky, Feodor	Tall Book of Nursery Tales	Harper

§2. PICTURE AND STORY BOOKS

AGE	AUTHOR OR ILLUSTRATOR	TITLE	PUBLISHER
15 mo.–2 yrs.	Cloth or heavy cardboard books of familiar objects.*		
15 mo.–2 yrs.	Cloth or heavy cardboard books of domestic animals.*		
15 mo.–2 yrs.	Kunhardt, Dorothy	Pat the Bunny	Simon & Schuster
15 mo.–2 yrs.	Palmer, Robbin	Timothy's Shoes	Whitman
15 mo.–2 yrs.	Smith, Bob	My First Book	Simon & Schuster
2–3 yrs.	Bertail, Inez	Time for Bed	Doubleday
2–3 yrs.	Beyer, Evelyn	Just Like You	Wm. Scott
2–3 yrs.	Flack, Marjorie	Angus and the Cat	Doubleday
2–3 yrs.	Flack, Marjorie	Angus and the Ducks	Doubleday
2–3 yrs.	Flack, Marjorie	Ask Mr. Bear	Macmillan
2–3 yrs.	Gay, Romney	Cinder	Grosset & Dunlap
2–3 yrs.	Gay, Romney	Corally Crothers' Birthday	Grosset & Dunlap
2–3 yrs.	Green, Mary McB.	Everybody Eats	Wm. Scott
2–3 yrs.	Hurd, Clement	Bumble Bugs & Elephants	Wm. Scott
2–3 yrs.	Lenski, Lois	Davy's Day	Oxford
2–3 yrs.	Lenski, Lois	The Little Family	Doubleday
2–3 yrs.	Little, Irene	A Rainy Day Story on the Farm	Whitman
2–3 yrs.	Maloy, Lois	Toby Can Fly	Grosset & Dunlap
2–3 yrs.	Masha	Three Little Kittens	Simon & Schuster
2–3 yrs.	Mathews, Virginia	Stop-Look-Listen	Hampton
2–3 yrs.	Wright, Ethel	Saturday Walk	Wm. Scott
2–4 yrs.	Becker, Charlotte	The Unlike Twins in Nursery School	Scribners
2–4 yrs.	Brown, Margaret W.	A Child's Goodnight Book	Wm. Scott
2–4 yrs.	Brown, Margaret W.	The Little Fireman	Wm. Scott

* Since this particular type of book goes out of print very quickly, we are not suggesting specific titles.

AGE	AUTHOR OR ILLUSTRATOR	TITLE	PUBLISHER
2–4 yrs.	Brown, M. W. & Hurd, C.	Goodnight Moon	Harper
2–4 yrs.	Francoise	The Gay ABC	Scribners
2–4 yrs.	Freund, Rudolph	The Animals of Farmer Jones	Simon & Schuster
2–4 yrs.	Hader, Berta & Elmer	Whiffy McMann	Oxford
2–4 yrs.	Lenski, Lois	The Little Auto	Oxford
2–4 yrs.	Lenski, Lois	The Little Sailboat	Oxford
2–4 yrs.	McDonald, Golden	Big Dog, Little Dog	Doubleday
2–4 yrs.	McDonald, Golden	Red Light, Green Light	Doubleday
2–4 yrs.	Moore, Clement C.	The Night Before Christmas	Simon & Schuster
2–4 yrs.	Rey, H. A.	Where's My Baby?	Houghton Mifflin
3–4 yrs.	Bertail, Inez	Summer & Winter	Veritas
3–4 yrs.	Brann, Esther	Bobbie & Donnie Were Twins	Macmillan
3–4 yrs.	Ets, Marie Hall	In the Forest	Viking
3–4 yrs.	Evers, Helen & Alf	Copy Kitten	Rand McNally
3–4 yrs.	Martin, Dahris	Little Lamb	Harper
3–4 yrs.	Tudor, Tasha	Pumpkin Moonshine	Oxford
3–4 yrs.	Williams, Gweneira	Timid Timothy	Wm. Scott
3–5 yrs.	Brown, Margaret W.	Baby Animals	Random House
3–5 yrs.	Brown, Margaret W.	The Noisy Book	Wm. Scott
3–5 yrs.	Brown, Margaret W.	Shhhhhh.....Bang	Harper
3–5 yrs.	Coe, Lloyd	Charcoal	Crowell
3–5 yrs.	Donaldson, Lois	Karl's Wooden Horse	Albert Whitman
3–5 yrs.	Hogan, Inez	Twin Kids	Dutton
3–5 yrs.	Lowrey, Janette	The Poky Little Puppy	Simon & Schuster
3–5 yrs.	Morris, Dudley	The Truck that Flew	Putnam
3–5 yrs.	Wiese, Kurt	The Story about Ping	Viking
3–6 yrs.	Bannerman, Helen	Little Black Sambo	Lippincott
3–6 yrs.	Beskow, Elsa	Pelle's New Suit	Harper
3–6 yrs.	Brooke, L. Leslie	Johnny Crow's Garden	Warne
3–6 yrs.	Brown, Margaret W.	The Little Fisherman	Wm. Scott
3–6 yrs.	Burton, Virginia L.	Choo-choo	Houghton Mifflin
3–6 yrs.	Burton, Virginia L.	Mike Mulligan and his Steam Shovel	Houghton Mifflin

AGE	AUTHOR OR ILLUSTRATOR	TITLE	PUBLISHER
3–6 yrs.	DeAngeli, Margaret	Ted and Nina Go to the Grocery Store	Doubleday
3–6 yrs.	deBrunhoff, Jean	The Story of Babar	Random House
3–6 yrs.	Flack, Marjorie	The Boats on the River	Viking
3–6 yrs.	Flack, Marjorie	The New Pet	Doubleday
3–6 yrs.	Flack, Marjorie	Tim Tadpole and the Great Bullfrog	Doubleday
3–6 yrs.	Hartell, J. A.	Over in the Meadow	Harper
3–6 yrs.	Hartwell, Marjorie	Into the Ark	Franklin Watts
3–6 yrs.	King, Dorothy N.	Find the Animals	Harcourt Brace
3–6 yrs.	Lenski, Lois	The Little Airplane	Oxford
3–6 yrs.	Lenski, Lois	The Little Farm	Oxford
3–6 yrs.	Lenski, Lois	The Little Fire Engine	Oxford
3–6 yrs.	Lenski, Lois	The Little Train	Oxford
3–6 yrs.	Lindman, Maj	Snipp, Snapp, Snurr and the Gingerbread	Albert Whitman
3–6 yrs.	Lindman, Maj	Snipp, Snapp, Snurr and the Red Shoes	Albert Whitman
3–6 yrs.	Petersham, Maud & Miska	The Christ Child	Doubleday
3–6 yrs.	Scott, William	The Milk that Jack Drank	Wm. Scott
3–6 yrs.	Slobodkina, Esphyr	Caps for Sale	Wm. Scott
4–6 yrs.	Austin, Margot	Peter Churchmouse	Dutton
4–6 yrs.	Black, Irma S.	This is the Bread that Betsy Ate	Wm. Scott
4–6 yrs.	Bragg, Mabel	The Little Engine that Could	Platt & Munk
4–6 yrs.	Brown, Margaret W.	The Runaway Bunny	Harper
4–6 yrs.	Gag, Wanda	Millions of Cats	Coward McCann
4–6 yrs.	Hall, William	Tell Time the Rabbit	Crowell
4–6 yrs.	Hurd, Edith T.	The Annie Moran	Lothrop, Lee & Shephard
4–6 yrs.	Hurd, Edith T.	Hurry, Hurry	Wm. Scott
4–6 yrs.	Heyward, DuBose	The Country Bunny	Houghton Mifflin
4–6 yrs.	Johnson, Laura & Jack	The Leaky Whale	Houghton Mifflin

AGE	AUTHOR OR ILLUSTRATOR	TITLE	PUBLISHER
4–6 yrs.	Leaf, Munro	The Story of Ferdinand	Viking
4–6 yrs.	McDonald, Golden	The Little Island	Doubleday
4–6 yrs.	Mitchell, Lucy S.	The New House in the Forest	Simon & Schuster
4–6 yrs.	Sage, Juniper	The Man in the Manhole	Wm. Scott
4–6 yrs.	Schneider, Herman & Nina	How Big is Big?	Wm. Scott
4–6 yrs.	Spiegel, Doris	Danny and Company 92	Coward McCann
4–6 yrs.	Turner, N. & Gergely, T.	When it Rained Cats and Dogs	Lippincott
5–6 yrs.	d'Aulaire, I. & E. P.	Children of the Northlights	Viking
5–6 yrs.	Milne, A. A.	Winnie the Pooh	Dutton
5–6 yrs.	Suess, Dr.	And to Think that I Saw it on Mulberry St.	Vanguard

§3. COLLECTIONS OF POETRY

AGE	AUTHOR OR ILLUSTRATOR	TITLE	PUBLISHER
2–4 yrs.	Doane, Pelagie	Mother Goose	Random House
2–4 yrs.	Elliot, Miss	Round the Mulberry Bush	Harper
2–4 yrs.	Gay, Romney	Picture Book	Grosset & Dunlap
2–4 yrs.	Gay, Romney	Mother Goose	Grosset & Dunlap
2–4 yrs.	Rojankovsky, Feodor	The Tall Book of Mother Goose	Harper
2–4 yrs.	Tenggren	The Tenggren Mother Goose	Little Brown
2–4 yrs.	Wright, Blanche F.	The Real Mother Goose	Rand McNally
2–6 yrs.	Assoc. for Childhood Education	Sung Under the Silver Umbrella	Macmillan
2–6 yrs.	Geismer, B. P. & Suter, A. B.	Very Young Verses	Houghton Mifflin
3–6 yrs.	Hubbard, A. and Babbitt, A.	The Golden Flute	John Day
3–6 yrs.	Petersham, Maud & Miska	The Rooster Crows	Macmillan

AGE	AUTHOR OR ILLUSTRATOR	TITLE	PUBLISHER
3–6 yrs.	Rossetti, Christine	Sing Song	Macmillan
3–6 yrs.	Stevenson, Robert L.	A Child's Garden of Verses	U. S. Camera
3–6 yrs.	Thompson, Blanche	Silver Pennies	Macmillan
3–6 yrs.	Tippett, James	I Go A-Travelling	Harper
3–6 yrs.	Tippett, James	I Live in a City	Harper
4–6 yrs.	Milne, A. A.	Now We Are Six	Dutton
4–6 yrs.	Milne, A. A.	When We Were Very Young	Dutton
4–6 yrs.	Rhys, Ernest	Book of Nonsense	Dutton

§4. INFORMATION BOOKS

The text of many of these books is above the preschool level, but the illustrations and the information simplified will appeal to many preschool children of all ages, according to their interests.

AUTHOR OR ILLUSTRATOR	TITLE	PUBLISHER
Audubon, John J.	Birds of America	Macmillan
Basic Science Education Series	(63 titles)	Row Peterson
	Animals of the Seashore	
	Birds	
	Doing Work	
	Fish	
	Insects and their Ways	
	The Pet Show	
	Useful Plants and Animals (etc.)	
Elting, Mary	Trucks at Work	Garden City
Humphreys, Dena	The Zoo Book	Henry Holt
Huntington, Harriet	Let's Go Outdoors	Doubleday
Huntington, Harriet	Let's Go to the Seashore	Doubleday
Huntington, Harriet	Tune Up	Doubleday
Lent, Henry	Clear Track Ahead	Macmillan
Lent, Henry	Diggers and Builders	Macmillan

AUTHOR OR ILLUSTRATOR	TITLE	PUBLISHER
Little Wonder Book Series	(90 titles)	Chas. Merrill
	Policemen	
	The Circus	
	Our Houses	
	The Grocery Store (etc.)	
Petersham, Maud & Miska	Story Book Series (18 titles)	Winston
	The Story Book of Clothes	
	The Story Book of Coal	
	The Story Book of Food	
	The Story Book of Trains (etc.)	
Peterson, Roger	Junior Book of Birds	Houghton Mifflin
Picture Scripts Series		Grosset & Dunlap
	Fire! Fire!	
	The Fireboat	
	The Tugboat	
Pratt, Gladys L.	American Garden Flowers	Random
Pratt, Gladys L.	Butterflies and Moths	Random
Pryor, William	The Streamline Train Book	Harcourt Brace
Walpole, Ellen W.	Golden Dictionary	Simon & Schuster

§5. SONG BOOKS

Songs in all of the following books range so widely in difficulty that each book, with the exception of "Little Singing Time," is suitable for children throughout the preschool period. The books are listed in order of difficulty, the simplest ones being first on the list.

COMPOSER OR COLLECTOR	TITLE	PUBLISHER
Coleman, S. & Thorn, A.	The Little Singing Time	John Day
Coleman, S. & Thorn, A.	Singing Time	John Day
Coleman, S. & Thorn, A.	Another Singing Time	John Day
Gale, Leah	Nursery Songs	Simon & Schuster
Doane, Pelagie	Favorite Nursery Songs	Random House
MacCarteney, Laura P.	Songs for the Nursery School	Willis
VanLoon, Wilhelm	The Songs We Sing	Simon & Schuster

COMPOSER OR COLLECTOR	TITLE	PUBLISHER
Wessells, Katherine T.	Golden Song Book	Simon & Schuster
Baker and Kohlsaat, L.	Songs for the Little Child	Abingdon
Bradford, M. and Woodruff, B.	Keep Singing, Keep Humming	Wm. Scott
Surrette, T. W.	Songs from Many Lands	Houghton Mifflin
Davidson and Surrette, T. W.	140 Folk Songs	Schirmer Music Co.
Carter, Jessie	Fifty Favorite Lullabies	Whitman
Gordon, Dorothy	Sing it Yourself	Dutton
Graham, M. N.	Christmas Carols	Whitman
Wyckoff, Marjorie	Christmas Carols	Simon & Schuster
Wyckoff, Marjorie	A Child's Book of Hymns	Random House
Seigmeister, Elie	Work and Sing	Wm. Scott

APPENDIX E
MUSICAL RECORDS
FOR INFANTS
AND YOUNG CHILDREN

It is impossible to arrange phonograph records according to age levels, because of the great range in ability and interest of young children in music. The list includes the various kinds of music which children enjoy. However, all of these recordings will not appeal to all children. Therefore, the list should be used with discrimination. Albums not infrequently combine unsuitable with suitable records. It is regrettable that excellent records so often go quickly out of press.

A useful guide to recorded music for children "from 6 months to 16 years" is published by Oliver Durrell, Inc., N. Y., 1947 (Barbour and Freeman: *The Children's Record Book*.)

Capitol Number	Title	Composer	Artist
Album BD 27	Chisholm Trail (and others)		Tex Ritter
Album BD 52	Here Comes the Band		Louis Castellucci Band

[387]

Columbia

Number	Title	Composer	Artist
Album C-94	Christmas Carols		Lyn Murray—Singers
Album M-481	Music of Johann Strauss	Strauss	Kostelanetz Orchestra
Album M-440	Patter Songs from Gilbert & Sullivan	Gilbert & Sullivan	Nelson Eddy
Album C-79	Yale Glee Club		Marshall Bartholomew, Director

Decca

Number			
Albums 4 and 24	French Folk Songs for Children		Louis Chartier
C.V. 100	Mother Goose		Frank Luther
C.V. 100	Nursery Rhymes		Frank Luther
C.S. 5	Nursery Rhymes		Frank Luther
Albums 113 and 302	Songs of the South African Veld		Joseph Marais

Disc

Number			
Album 607	America's Favorite Songs		Bess Lomax, Pete Seeger, Tom Glazer, Butch Hawes
Album 604	Songs to Grow On (School Days)		Charity Bailey Pete Seeger, Lead Belly Cisco Huston

Victor

Number			
Album MS-478	American Spirituals		Kenneth Spencer
7252	Bolero (part 3)	Ravel	Koussevitsky-Boston Symphony Orchestra
Album M-354	De Camptown Races (in Stephen Foster Album)	Foster	Richard Crooks
Album M-785	Carnival of the Animals	Saint-Saens	Stokowski-Philadelphia Orchestra

Victor Number	Title	Composer	Artist
Album M-639	The Children's Hour	Debussy	Barrere, Salzedo, Britt (Flute, Harp, Cello)
Y-315	El Capitan March	Sousa	Stokowski-Philadelphia Orchestra
4375	Espana Rapsodie	Chabrier	Fiedler-Boston "Pops" Orchestra
1645	The Flight of the Bumble Bee	Rimsky-Korsakow	Jascha Heifetz
Album M-1086	Folk Songs and Ballads		Susan Reed
2122	The Frog Went Courting		John Jacob Niles
11825	Hallelujah Chorus	Handel	Royal Choral Society
10-1273	Home on the Range		Robert Merrill
35792	A Hunt in the Black Forest	Voelker	Victor Orchestra
11880	I Got Plenty O' Nuttin'	Gershwin	Lawrence Tibbett
35792	In a Clock Store	Orth	Victor Concert
10-1089	1) Jazz Legato 2) Jazz Pizzicato	Anderson	Fiedler-Boston "Pops" Orchestra
Y-9	Jingle Bells Fantasy		Victor Salon Orchestra
10-1273	The Last Round Up		Robert Merrill
4314	Marche Militaire	Schubert	Fiedler-Boston "Pops" Orchestra
4390	Music Box	Liadow	Fiedler-Boston "Pops" Orchestra
Y-9	The Night Before Christmas (Recitation)	Moore	Milton Cross
Album M-265	Nutcracker Suite	Tschaikowsky	Stokowski-Philadelphia Orchestra
Album M-354	Oh, Susanna (in Stephen Foster Album)	Foster	Richard Crooks
2122	The Old Woman and the Pig		John Jacob Niles
11986	Poet and Peasant Overture	Von Suppe	Fiedler-Boston "Pops" Orchestra
4397	Pop Goes the Weasel		Fiedler-Boston "Pops" Orchestra

Victor Number	Title	Composer	Artist
Y-315	Stars and Stripes Forever	Sousa	Stokowski-Philadelphia Orchestra
2168	Swing Low, Sweet Chariot		John Thomas
1896	Trampin'		Marian Anderson
10-1271	Traumerei	Schumann	Mischa Elman
4390	Turkey in the Straw		Fiedler-Boston "Pops" Orchestra
14726	Valse Triste	Sibelius	Stokowski-Philadelphia Orchestra
15800	Die Walküre (Magic Fire Music)	Wagner	Stokowski-Philadelphia Orchestra

Young Peoples Record Club

Number			
403	Let's All Join In		Peter Seeger

APPENDIX F
SUGGESTIVE READINGS

1. Aldrich, C. Anderson and Aldrich, Mary M. Babies are human beings. New York: Macmillan, 1938, ix + 128.

2. Bacmeister, Rhoda W. Caring for the run-about. New York: Dutton, 1937, pp. 263.

3. Bakwin, Ruth M. and Bakwin, Harry. Psychological care during infancy and childhood. New York: D. Appleton, 1942, xv + 317.

4. Bradbury, Dorothy E. and Skeels, Esther L. A Bibliography of nursery school education, 1935–1939. Nat'l. Assoc. for Nursery Education, 71 East Ferry Ave., Detroit, Michigan.

5. Breckenridge, Marian E. and Vincent, E. Lee. Child development: Physical and psychological growth through the school years. Philadelphia and London: W. B. Saunders Co., 1943, ix + 592.

6. Child Study. A Quarterly Journal of Parent Education. New York: The Child Study Association, 221 West 57th Street.

7. Ets, Marie Hall. The Story of a baby. New York: Viking Press, 1939, pp. 63.

8. Foster, Josephine and Mattson, Marion L. Nursery School Education. New York: D. Appleton-Century, 1939, xii + 361.

9. Gilbert, Margaret Shea. Biography of the unborn. Baltimore: Williams & Wilkins, 1938, x + 132.

10. Hattwick, LaBerta A. and Sanders, Mollie Krom. Age differences in behavior at the nursery school level. Child Development, 1938, 9, 1, 27–47.

11. Jersild, Arthur T. Child Psychology. New York: Prentice-Hall, Inc., 1940, xiii + 592.

12. Johnson, Harriet M. Children in the nursery school. New York: John Day, 1934, xx + 325.

13. Kawin, Ethel. The wise choice of toys. Chicago: Univ. Chicago Press, 1940, x + 154.

14. Lerrigo, Marion Olive. Children can help themselves. New York: Macmillan, 1943, ix + 219.

15. Lowenberg, Miriam E. Your child's food. New York: McGraw-Hill, 1939, xviii + 299.

16. Manwell, Elizabeth M. and Sophia L. Fahs. Consider the children—how they grow. Boston: The Beacon Press, 1941, x + 261.

17. Reynolds, Martha May. Children from seed to saplings. New York: McGraw-Hill, 1939, x + 337.

18. Sheldon, William H. The varieties of human physique. New York: Harper, 1940, pp. 347.

19. Sheldon, William H. The varieties of temperament. New York: Harper, 1942, pp. 532.

20. Sherbon, Florence B. The child: his origin, development and care. New York: McGraw-Hill, 1934, xix + 707.

21. Spock, Benjamin. The Common Sense Book of Baby and Child Care. New York: Duell, Sloan and Pearce, 1945.

22. Updegraff, Ruth. Practice in preschool education. New York: McGraw-Hill, 1938, xvi + 408.

23. Woodcock, Louise P. Life and ways of the two year old. New York: Dutton, 1941, pp. 267.

24. U. S. Department of Labor, Children's Bureau, Selected list of publications, 1940, iv + 23; and U. S. Department of the Interior, Office of Education, Govt. Printing Office, Bibliography no. 45, 1936, 10 pp.

Associated Publications from the Yale Clinic of Child Development

25. Gesell, Arnold and Ames, Louise B. Guide to the Yale films of child development, 16 mm. silent series. Encyclopedia Britannica Films, Inc., Chicago, Illinois, pp. 40.

26. Gesell, Arnold and Ilg, Frances L. The feeding behavior of infants. A pediatric approach to the mental hygiene of early life. Philadelphia: Lippincott, 1937, ix + 201.

27. Gesell, Arnold and others. The first five years of life. A guide to the study of the preschool child. New York: Harper, 1940, xiii + 393. (A comprehensive summary of the development of behavior from 4 weeks through 5 years with specific treatment of Motor, Adaptive, Language and Personal-Social behavior. Methods for the developmental examination, with special reference to children of preschool ages.)

28. Gesell, Arnold and Thompson, Helen. Twins T and C from infancy to adolescence.

A biogenetic study of individual differences by the method of co-twin control. Genet. Psychol. Monogr., 1941, 24, 3–121.

29. Gesell, Arnold. Wolf child and human child. A narrative interpretation of the life history of Kamala, the wolf girl. New York: Harper, xvi + 107.

30. Gesell, Arnold. How a baby grows. A story in pictures. New York: Harper, 1945, pp. 78.

31. Gesell, Arnold and Ilg, Frances L. In collaboration with Louise B. Ames and Glenna Bullis. The child from five to ten. New York: Harper, 1946, xii + 475.

32. Gesell, Arnold. The Yale films of child development. Encyclopedia Britannica Films, Inc., 20 N. Wacker Drive, Chicago 6, Illinois.

Sound Films—16 mm.

The growth of infant behavior: early stages—one reel.

The growth of infant behavior: later stages—one reel.

Posture and locomotion—one reel.

From creeping to walking—one reel.

A baby's day at twelve weeks—one reel.

A thirty-six weeks behavior day—one reel.

A baby's day at forty-eight weeks—one reel.

Behavior patterns at one year—one reel.

Learning and growth—one reel.

Early social behavior—one reel.

Life begins—six reels.

Silent Films—8 and 16 mm.

How behavior grows (The patterning of prone progression) —one reel.

The growth of motor behavior (In the first five years) —¾ reel.

The growth of adaptive behavior (In the first five years) —one reel.

Infants are individuals (The beginnings of personality) —one reel.

Twins are individuals (From infancy to adolescence) —one reel.

The baby's bath—¾ reel.

Bottle and cup feeding—one reel.

The conquest of the spoon—one reel.

Self-discovery in a mirror—one reel.

Early play—one reel.

33. The March of Time recently made a documentary film recording the work of the Yale Clinic of Child Development. The film is sound scored and is now available in 16 mm. size in the Forum Edition of The March of Time, 369 Lexington Avenue, New York 17, New York.

[393]

INDEX

For convenience of reference the age levels are printed in bold face type and arranged in chronological order.

Thin.
16 Dec. 1950.